Enlightenment and Poli

The easy accessibility of political fiction in the long eighteenth century made it possible for any reader or listener to enter into the intellectual debates of the time, as much of the core of modern political and economic theory was to be found first in the fiction, not the theory, of this age. Amusingly, many of these abstract ideas were presented for the first time in stories featuring less-than-gifted central characters. The five particular works of fiction examined here, which this book takes as embodying the core of the Enlightenment, focus more on the individual than on social groups. Nevertheless, in these same works of fiction, this individual has responsibilities as well as rights—and these responsibilities and rights apply to every individual, across the board, regardless of social class, financial status, race, age, or gender. Unlike studies of the Enlightenment which focus only on theory and nonfiction, this study of fiction makes evident that there was a vibrant concern for the constructive as well as the destructive aspects of emotion during the Enlightenment, rather than an exclusive concern for rationality.

Cecilia Miller is Associate Professor of History and Tutor in the College of Social Studies at Wesleyan University.

Routledge Studies in Cultural History

For a full list of titles in this series, please visit www.routledge.com

Enlightenment and Political Fiction

The Everyday Intellectual

Cecilia Miller

Routledge
Taylor & Francis Group

LONDON AND NEW YORK

First published 2016
by Routledge

2 Park Square, Milton Park, Abingdon, Oxfordshire OX14 4RN
711 Third Avenue, New York, NY 10017

Routledge is an imprint of the Taylor & Francis Group, an informa business

First issued in paperback 2018

Library of Congress Cataloging-in-Publication Data
Names: Miller, Cecilia, author.
Title: Enlightenment and political fiction : the everyday intellectual / Cecilia Miller.
Description: New York ; London : Routledge, 2016. | Series: Routledge studies
  in cultural history | Includes bibliographical references and index.
Identifiers: LCCN 2015041769 (print) | LCCN 2015050237 (ebook) |
  ISBN 9781138954175 (alk. paper) | ISBN 9781315667072 (ebook)
Subjects: LCSH: Fiction—18th century—History and criticism. | Politics and
  literature—Europe—History—17th century. | Politics and literature—Europe—
  History—18th century. | Literature and society—Europe—History—17th century. |
  Literature and society—Europe—History—18th century. | Reason in literature. |
  Emotions in literature. | Enlightenment—Europe.
Classification: LCC PN3495 .49 2016 (print) | LCC PN3495 (ebook) |
  DDC 809.3/033—dc23
LC record available at http://lccn.loc.gov/2015041769

ISBN: 978-1-138-95417-5 (hbk)
ISBN: 978-0-8153-8143-3 (pbk)

Typeset in Sabon
by Apex CoVantage, LLC

For my students

Contents

Preface

This book was written as a tribute to E.P. Thompson's *The Making of the English Working Class* (1963), by telling the story of the making of the everyday intellectual. I realized my connection to Thompson's book in an unexpected way. Some years ago, on a bus ride from Mexico City to Querétaro, I was talking with a Mexican engineer about our respective jobs, and he asked me what my favorite history book was. I immediately answered the E.P. Thompson book, but I was almost as quickly annoyed by my response. As a professor in a very small academic field—somewhat ironically, the history of ideas—I should have automatically mentioned a book strictly in my own field. Yet this brief encounter was good for me. In time, it helped me realize not just why I am drawn to Thompson, but also how much I have been influenced by other books, books even further beyond my field, and then how these interactions might make me stronger at my own work.

Another intellectual surprise followed, changing the course of my research. At that stage, my research was wholly on eighteenth-century theory, not literature. I had written a book on the philosophy of history and I was ensconced in new research on political economy. Yet it was in my pleasure reading—admittedly, eighteenth-century novels—that I began to find abstract ideas that were not yet present in the theory of the same time. After some resistance on my part (initially not wanting to blend my reading for work and my reading for myself), this intersection of theory and fiction became the focus of my research. The result of these marked mental transitions is this book, which—following the model of the long eighteenth century—deliberately blends political economy and fiction.

In the twenty-first century, European literature tends to be discussed in a national context, with the focus on books from only one language. *Gulliver's Travels*, for example, is still most often considered in terms of other works of literature written in English, and not so often in terms of other contemporary works of fiction written in Spanish, German, French, and Italian. Even when theory is introduced into the mix, it is usually theory from the same language as that work of fiction—for example, the influence of John Locke on Jonathan Swift, author of *Gulliver's Travels*. However, in the eighteenth century, European readers and writers were immersed in the best-selling fiction and theory from across Europe, demanding rapid translations of works already well regarded elsewhere. All five of the works of fiction to be examined here were translated very quickly after their first publication.

Somewhat peculiarly, this book will thus argue that it was specifically this strong desire for up-to-date fiction in the eighteenth century that led to the Enlightenment, and that that Enlightenment is still recognizable, but somewhat rearranged—perhaps akin to seeing, for the first time, family members of someone you know well. This rearrangement will proceed through the presentation of detailed textual analysis of some of the major abstract ideas put forward in these celebrated works of fiction.

The works of fiction chosen for this study are the following:

Cervantes, *Don Quixote* (1605, 1615, in Spanish),
Grimmelshausen, *Simplicissimus* (1668, 1699, in German),
Swift, *Gulliver's Travels* (1726, 1735 in English),
Voltaire, *Candide* (1759, in French), and
Manzoni, *I promessi sposi* (*The Betrothed*, 1825–1827, 1840–1842, in Italian).

Somewhat oddly, few secondary works examine even two of these works, and none attempts to contend with all five of these major works, selected from five different languages and cultures, and taken from across a broad geographical and chronological range. These books also cross a range of modern academic fields including history, political science, the history of economic thought, philosophy, theology, and law, as well as literature. The hope is that this book will encourage other such studies.

This book goes beyond these five chosen works of fiction not so much by concentrating on immediate context, but rather by identifying how these particular books fit into the ever-changing canon of books that comprise the history of European ideas. This study is grounded in primary sources drawn from both literature and theory in its attempt to create a picture of European thought by studying these particular works. Nevertheless, this study aims to educate readers about not only politics and economics, but also about literature. It is studded with short references to related books, some dating from antiquity, many of which are now relatively unknown. This book could thus also be regarded as an annotated reading list, both for the theory and fiction. Yet, once again, these numerous references— from history, philosophy, and political and economic theory, in addition to literature—are deemed an essential part of the book's multidisciplinary approach, as one of its key goals is to demonstrate the development of theory in a number of diverse genres.

In analytical terms, this book takes as its task the reexamination of the stereotypical tenets of the Enlightenment: the emphasis on rationality; the rejection of religion; the allegiance to the modern sciences; the stress on the individual: children, women, and men; and the belief in the perfectibility of the human mind.

Overall this book makes three main claims. (1) The easy accessibility of political fiction in the long eighteenth century made it possible for any reader or listener to enter into the intellectual debates of the time, as much of the core of modern political and economic theory was to be found first in the fiction, not the theory, of this age. Amusingly, many of these abstract ideas were presented for the first time in stories featuring less-than-gifted central characters. (2) The five particular works of fiction examined, which this book takes as embodying the core of the Enlightenment, focus more on the individual than on social groups. Nevertheless, in these same works of fiction, this individual has responsibilities as well as rights—and these responsibilities and rights apply to every individual, across the board, regardless of social class, financial status, race, age, or gender. Following Thompson, this book attempts to locate unexpected sources of theorizing about politics and economics that led to the empowerment of previously marginalized individuals. (3) Unlike studies of the Enlightenment that focus only on theory and nonfiction, this study of fiction makes evident that there was a vibrant concern for the constructive as well as the destructive aspects of emotion during the Enlightenment, rather than an exclusive concern for rationality.

Building on the substantial secondary literature on the Enlightenment, as well as on primary texts, all three of these arguments lead to qualifications of the stereotypes of the Enlightenment—qualifications that highlight the ongoing utility of the Enlightenment and that have implications for our understanding of the shift to the modern age.

Acknowledgments

Over the years, I have had substantial support for my research on the philosophy of history, political economy, the Enlightenment, political fiction, and, more recently, for all these subjects together in the form of this book. An Alexander von Humboldt Research Fellowship in Berlin and Munich was fundamental to my early work on the Enlightenment. Thank you to Axel Honneth, Wilhelm Schmidt-Biggemann, and Hans Walter Gabler for their support during my time as a Humboldt Fellow. My thanks to many other scholars—especially my colleagues in Spain, Germany, Britain, France, and Italy, who were so supportive during 13 years I lived in Europe—are noted throughout this book.

Librarians at the New York Public Library, the Beinecke Rare Book & Manuscript Library at Yale, the Vatican Library in Rome, the Staatsbibliothek Berlin, the Bayerische Staatsbibliothek in Munich, the Bibliothèque nationale in Paris, the Biblioteca Nacional in Madrid, the Bodleian Library and the Taylor Institution Library in Oxford, and especially the British Library in London, have shown astonishing enthusiasm for this large enterprise.

I am grateful to have had a number of specialists help me with this project. Thank you to Giuseppe Mazzotta, Michael Armstrong-Roche, Rüdiger Campe, Claude Rawson, Catherine Labio, and Mary Ann Carolan for responding in detail to particular chapters of this manuscript. Thank you to Geoffrey Parker for his comments on a series of crucial topics cutting across this book. Jonathan Clark, the series editor for my first book, provided encouragement and apt suggestions for this later book project as well. Especially given such a distinguished set of advisers, I wish to assert that any remaining mistakes in this book are manifestly my own.

I have had the opportunity to present almost all of this book manuscript as lectures at numerous universities and conferences in Europe and North America. I have noted these occasions in the relevant sections of this book. Thank you to both my hosts and audiences at these events for their lively comments and questions.

At Olin Library, at Wesleyan University in Connecticut, many people have worked very hard for me. To begin, I wish to thank Alan Nathanson, who was a marvelous help to me both in Connecticut and in London. Steve Lebergott, Elizabeth Swaim, Dianne Kelly, Suzy Taraba, EunJoo Lee, Barbara Jones, Pat Tully, Diane Klare, Erhard Konerding, Kendall Hobbs, Kate Wolfe, Kathy Stefanowicz, Lisa Pinette, and Jennifer Hadley made this project possible.

In the Department of History at Wesleyan University, I wish to thank Stew Gillmor, Dick Buel, Phil Pomper, Nat Greene, Ollie Holmes, Rick Elphick, Vera Schwarcz, Ron Schatz, Ann Wightman, Bill Johnston, and Demetrius Eudell. And I am happy to recognize the support of Donna Martin, Laverne Roberts, Kay Poursine, Lori Flannigan, and Ann Tanasi.

Thank you to my colleagues in the College of Social Studies (CSS) at Wesleyan. I have benefited from comments on my manuscript from Peter Kilby, Richie Adelstein, Peter Rutland, Nancy Schwartz, Don Moon, and Giulio Gallarotti. Thank you to Joyce Jacobsen for her suggestions following my CSS Monday Lunch Talk that was given from this manuscript. I am honored by Bill Barber's ongoing encouragement of my research in the history of economic thought. Thank you to Fran Warren, Madeleine Howenstine, and Mickie Dame. And I still miss David Titus.

I have been particularly fortunate to have had so many strong research assistants for this project: Peter Hagan, James Steiner, Eliza Handayani, Tristan Chirico, Andrew Carr, Mark Kelley, Frances Jones, Ari Edmundson, Adam Tinkle, Melissa Tuckman, Ernesto Rodriguez, Emily Iversen, and Dominick DeJoy. I look forward to reading their books in the near future.

Many other individuals and institutions have provided aid at decisive moments. Thank you to Suzanna Tamminen for her enthusiasm for the idea of this book, well before there was a book. I appreciate Julia Perkins's assistance. Max Yurkofsky, Benedict Bernstein, and Howie Lempel helped with the title of this book. Anne Greene is for me the model of a gracious critic. I am indebted to David Pesci, Gina Ulysse, and Typhaine Leservot for crucial bits of advice. Thank you to Jill Morawski, the former Director of the Center for Humanities (CHUM) at Wesleyan, for a marvelous semester at CHUM. I would like to recognize my highly intelligent ITS support staff: John Hammond, Jim Kamm, Kevin Wiliarty, Heric Flores-Ruedes, and Steve Machuga. I am happy to acknowledge the support I have received from The Colonel Return Jonathan Meigs First (1740–1823) Fund; St. Deniol's Library, in Hawarden, Wales; and the British School at Rome. Thank you to Balliol College, Oxford, for providing me with housing during my repeated trips back to Oxford to use the libraries. Thank you to Lorraine and Tom Pangle, the Co-Directors of the Thomas Jefferson Center for the Study of Core Texts and Ideas, and Jacqueline Jones, Chair of History, for making me welcome during my time at the University of Texas at Austin.

I have received help from many quarters in the final stages of this project. I am grateful to Rick Elphick and to James Steiner for their detailed comments on the manuscript. I have been blessed to have Max Novick, at Routledge, as my editor.

Teachers, colleagues, friends, and family, on both sides of the Atlantic, have sustained me: Milka Velázquez Rossiki Diamond, Anne Hunt, Paul and Mary Kubricht, Walt and Rachel Olsen, Chris Smout, Izzy Guy and Duffy White, Gordon DesBrisay, Mario and Sonia Pines, Bill Fike, Isaiah Berlin, Julia Hore, Dan Terkla, Ursula and Hugh Sampath, Niels, Rohini, and Ahren Sampath, Ayse Turkseven and Boyd Johnson, Karen O'Brien and Peter McDonald, Lorán Chollete, Jim McGuire, Janice Cavanaugh, Mary Baltayan, Mary Glynn, Leroy and Geraldine Daniels, Marianne Kilby, Emily Meyer Pomper, Sandy Adelstein, David Monaco, Khazret Nirov, Ed Hagan and Denise Lepicier, Tanya Rosenblat, Markus Möbius, Jane Kalim, Laura Southard, Vicki Perkins, Mikail McIntosh-Doty and Philip Doty, Mike Heffley, Mary-Hannah Jones, Fred Curtis, Burgel Schmitt, Ellen (Puffin) D'Oench, Hollie Rose, Mavis Haut, Asia Haut, Rachel Weightman, Catherine Wacker, Cecilia Ruhnke, John Anderson, Alice and Jim Hadler, Barbara and Darrel Jantz, Ray Chen, Gloria Chen, Stony Lo, Lucia Zapata Mirabel, Chris Parks, Pauline Jones, Paul Miller, Don Miller, Charlene True, Delmar Mayo, Don Howard, and Maida Kimes.

As always, my best supporters were my parents and my siblings, J. Melvin Miller and Wanda (Howard) Miller, Kyle Miller, and Celesta Ulle. My father was at the center of our impassioned family discussion—often about politics, and from diverse perspectives—hours that taught me how to ask questions, to debate, and most of all to appreciate good conversation.

This project emerged out of my reading, and then from my teaching. I am delighted by my students' curiosity and enthusiasm. This book is dedicated to my students.

Austin
October 5, 2015

Introduction

1 READING FICTION FOR POLITICAL AND ECONOMIC THEORY

Advanced, theoretical ideas can be found in the most unlikely books. A handful of books—sometimes surprising ones—not only entertain the reader, but also contribute to new ways of seeing the world. Indeed, some theorists explicitly cite literature. Adam Smith makes repeated references to Voltaire, and Marx later refers to numerous literary sources, including *Don Quixote*. Why, though, should a historian of ideas direct sustained scholarly attention to literature? And what exactly, beyond high entertainment, should anyone not in literary studies expect when reading great fiction?

To address these questions, I examine the particular textures and peculiarities of thought in five celebrated works of fiction, written from 1600 to 1850. I have found a web of text-based, interrelated ideas that are attributed to the Enlightenment, and yet that existed well before the early-modern period, and in many cases, that lasted into our own time.[1] Ideas about the sphere of influence of children, women, and men in society, and ideas ascribed to later thinkers—John Locke on private property in the very late seventeenth century, to give just one example—can be found in much earlier works of fiction. In that case, however, Locke himself directly acknowledges his debt to Cervantes, but this connection has been forgotten because few modern readers read both the theory and the fiction of the past. The works of fiction examined here, therefore, not only reflect European Enlightenment thinking, but in some cases, they helped create the Enlightenment.

I present this analysis through close textual examination of five famous works of European fiction; each represents a distinct culture, intellectual *milieu*, and literary tradition:

Cervantes, *Don Quixote* (1605, 1615, in Spanish),
Grimmelshausen, *Simplicissimus* (1668, 1699, in German),
Swift, *Gulliver's Travels* (1726, 1735 in English),
Voltaire, *Candide* (1759, in French), and
Manzoni, *I promessi sposi* (*The Betrothed*, 1825–1827, 1840–1842, in Italian).

Some of these books have been reckoned to be the best works of fiction of their national literature, and three of them—*Don Quixote, Gulliver's Travels,* and *Candide*—achieved both immediate and long-lasting, international fame, thus becoming not only best sellers, but also steady sellers. By contrast, however, most educated Germans today have not read *Simplicissimus* in its entirety, and the same is now the case for *I promessi sposi* (*The Betrothed*) for educated Italians. I thus deliberately chose a combination of very well-known and relatively obscure books as a means first of drawing readers into the subject, and then of introducing them to at least a couple works of fiction that would probably be new to them. I would be very pleased if this book leads to a new popular interest in *Simplicissimus* and *The Betrothed,* both of which I consider to be as substantial as the other three books in both literary and intellectual terms. In addition, the inclusion of works that today are rarely read, but that were extremely popular when first published (the German and Italian novels above), also gives a sharper picture of the political and intellectual concerns of the time, 1605–1840, the first and last publication dates of these books, than is generally represented in studies of the long eighteenth century.[2]

Overall I argue that access to political and economic theory by way of fiction made it possible for any person, even someone beyond traditional scholarly circles, to become part of an ongoing, vital academic debate. *Enlightenment and Political Fiction: The Everyday Intellectual* is designed as an homage to E. P. Thompson's *The Making of the English Working Class* (1963) by telling the story of the making of the everyday intellectual.[3] The stress here is on the abstract theory to be found in a few famous works of fiction, ideas presented in a format highly attractive to contemporary (and, in many cases, later) readers, ideas exhibited in a manner that showed respect for the intelligence of the average reader. Extrapolating from Thompson, I maintain that it was not passive reception, but the active participation of readers—which, by extension, includes those who listened to books, read out loud—that initiated the Enlightenment from below. The decision to engage in this intellectual debate, grounded in ideas often first found in fiction, and much of it featuring less-than-gifted central characters, allowed everyday people—the vast majority of whom were removed from both salons and universities—to participate in the questioning, and eventually the decision making, of their own states. This led to greater political participation, which is often cited as one of the indicators of the shift to the modern age.

Rather than concentrating wholly on either the history of the book (including the publishing history of these novels) or on how these books were received in their own time, this work primarily examines the presentation, the process, of theorizing in literature. Looking at fiction alongside philosophy, political theory, and economic analysis enriches our notion of theorizing, and shifts our understanding about which texts should be addressed. Authors, in the midst of developing theories, take their source materials from ideas in their own cultures and then systematize particular concepts. In some cases, nascent political and economic ideas appear first in literature, as in Cervantes's *Don Quixote*, and in other cases, theorists deliberately used literature to propound their theories to a much wider audience, as in Voltaire's *Candide*, which might be regarded as a novelization of moral theory. It is not that the former case—abstract ideas breaking through first in fiction—is the rule in this period, and the latter—theorists manipulating fiction for their own purposes—the exception, but rather that there is a dialectical relationship between fiction and theory in the long eighteenth century.[4] Not incidentally, the time of the rise of the novel was also a time of rising literacy and of growing European influence around the world.

This work, therefore, makes arguments about the range of Enlightenment thought through an examination of these five particular works, written in five different languages. This book analyzes the Enlightenment, the supposed break from medieval to modern ways of thinking, as a category, not just as a time and a place. This is done in two ways. First, this book identifies three stereotypical characteristics of the Enlightenment—an emphasis on rationality and science, a rejection of the political and theological power of the Church, and a growing concern for the individual—and then locates these characteristics in texts that supposedly fall outside of the Enlightenment. Second, this book then locates concepts generally considered post-Enlightenment—especially Romantic concerns for emotion, the arts, and humanities; conservative political thought; private religion; social relations versus the abstract individual; and the theoretical outline of a market economy—which are then demonstrated to have existed in sophisticated forms within the traditional place and time commonly called the Enlightenment. This calls for a reconsideration of the dating, geographical spread, and ideological content of the Enlightenment. Many of these arguments have been presented before; I hope here to ground some of these arguments in literature. This book aims to be suggestive, at times provocative, in the hope that other scholars might take up some of these threads. Thus, the overall approach is to examine a number of distinct, even contradictory, ways in which abstract ideas are developed (not always from above, or always from below), all the while keeping the attention on abstract ideas in literature, ideas that were asserted in a manner that allows the general reading public to engage with them directly.[5]

There are therefore multiple goals for this work. One overarching purpose of it is to contribute in a small way to an ongoing appreciation for even the stereotypical Enlightenment concepts by examining this intellectual movement in a distinctive way. The complicated, long-eighteenth-century debate—which took place at the same time that Europe was consolidating political control around the world, and during the more general move toward a world society—stressed three other Enlightenment values: the need to examine one's own beliefs with care; the gradual acceptance of the validity of a variety of different opinions; and the creative, effective influence of the individual on society. It might be argued that the problem today with the Enlightenment is not its limitations, but rather that the Enlightenment was never realized in the form its long-eighteenth-century advocates anticipated.

I argue that these five works of fiction are still worth reading today not just because they are so well written, but even more so because their inclusion of abstract political and economic ideas continues to enable readers outside the academy to debate these issues. These works of fiction draw readers not just because of the astonishing humor, the hapless characters, and the absurd plots, but more fundamentally because they function as mental puzzles, with dazzling permutations, on the range of options for individuals and their societies. This is an argument grounded in an Enlightenment assumption that the average person has great intellectual curiosity, a sign of high mental capacity.

2 THE LONG EIGHTEENTH CENTURY

The long eighteenth century, sometimes defined as the period from the Glorious Revolution (in England in 1688) to the Revolutions of 1848 (across continental Europe), is often characterized as a time marked by the growth of towns, the demand for political, social, and humanitarian reform, and the establishment of parliamentary government.[6] The five works being examined here, for all their greatness, are neither wholly unrepresentative of their times and places nor altogether superior to all other contemporary works of fiction. Other such works of fiction, including Daniel Defoe's *Robinson Crusoe* (1719–1722), Charles-Louis de Secondat Montesquieu's *Les Lettres persanes* (*Persian Letters*, 1721), Jean-Jacques Rousseau's *Julie, ou La nouvelle Héloïse* (*Julie, or the New Héloïse*, 1761), Johann Wolfgang von Goethe's *Die Leiden des jungen Werthers* (*Sorrows of Young Werther*, 1774), and Mary Shelley's *Frankenstein* (1818), would also serve well as textual examples of the preoccupations of the long Enlightenment that are the subject of this book. The emphasis on the long eighteenth century is an effort to identify the actual, extended time period that shared these features and intellectual concerns, thus putting aside the obviously arbitrary division of epochs into hundred-year-long periods—albeit still retaining the word "century."

Enlightenment Studies have gone through numerous phases. It was dominated for decades by the excellent work of Daniel Mornet, Peter Gay, and Franco Venturi. Mornet uses the Enlightenment as a means of finding the roots of the French Revolution. Gay stresses rationality and science in an Enlightenment that is specifically Parisian.[7] Venturi emphasizes the regional nature of the Enlightenment in the Italian states, and the active participation of Enlightenment thinkers in economics, especially in Milan and Naples.[8] Roy Porter and Mikulás Teich's *The Enlightenment in National Context* follows Venturi's model of a regional Enlightenment, and their work sets the standard for a broader interpretation of a pan-European Enlightenment.[9]

Recent studies have queried the dating, geographical spread, and political orientation of the Enlightenment. Jonathan Israel, for example, is particularly concerned with the seventeenth-century roots of the Enlightenment and also in defending the Enlightenment against its many detractors.[10] Countless other studies continue to deepen our knowledge of the Enlightenment period, to give just four examples, the work of Karen O'Brien on the role of women, Robert Darnton on the book trade, Dena Goodman on salons, and John Pocock on commerce and economic theory.[11]

In a different mode, twentieth-century German studies of the Enlightenment stress ongoing modern and personal connections to the Enlightenment. Even the idealist philosopher Ernst Cassirer writes in his *Die Philosophie der Aufklärung* (*The Philosophy of the Enlightenment*, 1932) of self-realization, as outlined by Immanuel Kant, as a means bringing individual freedom to modern readers.[12] More recent Enlightenment theory strongly stresses the potential use of Enlightenment thought for analyzing, hopefully changing, first, the lives of individuals and, then, modern society itself. Much of this German work has been written by members of the Frankfurt School, a neo-Marxist group of thinkers rethinking the possibilities of modern society.[13]

Some of the German work on the Enlightenment was actually written in opposition to the Enlightenment, and some of it in opposition to the Frankfurt School. The starting point of this tradition is Max Horkheimer and Theodor Adorno's *Dialektik der Aufklärung* (*Dialectic of Enlightenment*, 1947), generally taken as an attack on the Enlightenment. Horkheimer and Adorno blame the Enlightenment for not implementing a fairer society, and more bluntly, for leaving the way open for totalitarianism, from both Adolf Hitler and Henry Ford, in their view.[14] Jürgen Habermas, one of the most famous thinkers of the twentieth century, broke from his professors in the Frankfurt School. Habermas's notion of the public sphere includes all spaces for free discussion and draws directly from the German Enlightenment, particularly from Kant. Later, Reinhart Koselleck uses Habermas's notion of the public sphere, to devise the notion of private spaces of influence in a time of public oppression. Habermas employs the concept of the public sphere in order to analyze the present, whereas Koselleck turns it around and uses it as a means to analyze, and often condemn, the Enlightenment.[15]

Nevertheless, both studies of alternative Enlightenments and even attacks on the Enlightenment have typically been focused on the traditional works of theory written at that time, to the exclusion of theoretical notions to be found in other genres. For example, in the history of the book, studies of the publishing trade often concentrate on the relative popularity of Enlightenment works of theory when they were first published—for example, the contemporary popularity of books published by Voltaire. Although this approach goes beyond the texts, into context of those texts, it still pays attention to the same texts.[16] The goal of *Enlightenment and Political Fiction* is to build on this substantial body of secondary literature in order to identify Enlightenment ways of thinking in a genre—fiction—rarely considered, even in later centuries, to be a source of advanced theoretical ideas. The lack of attention to even the possibility of the development of theory within fiction tends to remains relatively constant even among scholars who, following Adam Smith, recognize fiction as fundamental in encouraging sympathy for the poor and the powerless.[17]

Given the range of texts that demonstrate these tendencies, and building on the considerable scholarship on the Enlightenment in recent years, I argue for a definition of the Enlightenment that shifts, indeed expands, its dates, geographical spread, and political orientation. I propose that Enlightenment occurred in at least five countries (not just in Paris), from 1605 to 1840 (not only during the middle decades of the eighteenth century), and that it encompassed writing across the political spectrum (thus refuting what I take to be the false dilemma of an Enlightenment and anti-Enlightenment). Following in the path of a number of distinguished scholars, I seek, for example, to incorporate the study of Spain into the story of the European Enlightenment.[18] No longer do scholars regularly exclude Spain from this story. This book seeks to demonstrate that the Enlightenment's core emphasis on the abstract individual and on the rights of that individual is to be found in deliberate, not simply unconscious, form in works of fiction from across Europe in the long eighteenth century. I also stress the ancient, medieval, and early-modern theoretical texts that served as the intellectual basis for these five selected works of fiction, and for the Enlightenment itself.

I suggest that it is necessary to read the fiction as well as the theory of this age in order to discover the quintessential Enlightenment arguments; indeed, that the theory often lagged behind the fiction in the development of the same political and economic ideas, not just that the fiction mirrored the theory. This work also moves away from the identification of the Enlightenment wholly with rationality. In other words, because there is no doubt about Enlightenment commitment to rationality and science, I seek to trace other concerns of that same intellectual movement. My overall emphasis here is on the evolving notion of the abstract individual, in terms of both rights and responsibilities, particularly in regard to the parallel development of fiction in the transition from the early-modern to modern period, and especially on the origins of the novel.

Following the path set by Michael Valdez Moses in *The Novel and the Globalization of Culture*; John B. Bender in *Ends of Enlightenment*; David Armitage in "What's the Big Idea? Intellectual History and the *Longue Durée*; Jo Guldi and David Armitage in *The History Manifesto*; and Larry Siedentop in *Inventing the Individual: The Origins of Western Liberalism*, this present book seeks to identify abstract ideas that have occurred and repeatedly reoccurred in varied places and across time, often in categories that seem at first unfamiliar.[19] Valdez Moses argues for the need to recognize that abstract ideas can be found in both popular culture and in high culture, and throughout world culture. Bender views Enlightenment fiction as a distinct category, and he analyzes it in multidisciplinary terms, particularly in regard to the scientific theories gaining currency at that same time. Armitage focuses attention once again on the *longue durée*, an approach that, in intellectual history, attempts to trace how ideas ebb and flow across hundreds or thousands of years. Guldi and Armitage wish to bring together the strengths of big history (a relatively new historical field that begins in prehistory, and stresses how late human beings became part of world history and likewise the ongoing interaction of nature and human society today) and of microhistory (the intense study of one place and time) with a broader sweep throughout time in intellectual history. Siedentop identifies the ancient and medieval and roots of the notion of the abstract individual, rejecting the story that this individual somehow emerges spontaneously in the eighteenth century. Together Valdez Moses, Armitage, Guldi, and Siedentop set out an agenda that allows for the identification of both specific cultural and temporal preferences and also of shared preoccupations that extend well beyond standard expectations regarding place and time.

In terms of the structure of this current book, there are four distinct models: the work of Michel Foucault and Edward Said, and of Bertrand Russell and Erich Auerbach. Following Foucault, especially from *L'Archéologie du savoir* (*The Archaeology of Knowledge*, 1969), and also Said, this book seeks to trace the history of modernity by identifying commonalities and differences in thought over time.[20] In a not altogether different spirit, Bertrand Russell, in *A History of Western Philosophy* (1945), attempts to distill the essence of a series of philosophers across time. The final model is Erich Auerbach's *Mimesis* (1946).[21]

Following the particular example of Auerbach's *Mimesis*, the second half of each of the five chapters of this book is composed of arguments that connect a particular passage from the set fictional text with an abstract idea from another work, often a work of philosophy or political or economic theory, sometimes from a different time period. This approach was chosen as a way to demonstrate the presence of ideas generally categorized as eighteenth century to be, at times, present in very different centuries, sometimes earlier, sometimes later. In the *Don Quixote* chapter, for example, there is a section titled "*Don Quixote* Reconsidered: Sancho Panza on Good Government, John Locke, and the Origins of Market Capitalism." Thus I also follow the example of close textual readings in Auerbach's *Mimesis* that has served a model for so many thinkers, certainly including Said.[22] I was not surprised when I realized I also share Auerbach and Said's fascination with the eighteenth-century Neapolitan philosopher of history, Giambattista Vico. Auerbach and Said are both concerned with Vichian notions: early society as barbarous and yet creative in ways we can no longer reproduce. Vico's emphasis on the "modifications of our own human mind," implies both change in the individual mind and the evolution of social groups over time, and this is linked to his notion that because "the world of civil society has certainly been made by men," we are particularly well suited to grasp human history.[23] The five works of fiction addressed in this book are also emblematic of these same inclinations: curiosity about how human beings would behave without society; questioning of the limits of the perfectibility of the human mind; and the desire to present theoretical concepts in an accessible and pleasing form. Following Foucault and Said, and Russell and Auerbach, each of whom tried to mark continuity and change in thought over time, it remains necessary to find ways to make the past—in this case, Enlightenment thought—attractive to modern readers; this book is such an attempt.

With these goals in mind, the book is organized such that each chapter contends with core aspects of the Enlightenment. The *Don Quixote* chapter addresses rationality and forms of government, in terms of economic systems. The *Simplicissimus* chapter reflects on religious toleration and friendship. The *Gulliver's Travels* chapter examines the topics of science and social class. The *Candide* chapter takes up multiple aspects of the theme of sexuality and the modern individual. Finally, the chapter on *The Betrothed* reflects on the interconnection between political revolution and a revolution in a way of thinking, that is revolution and the perfectibility of the human mind. In an eighteenth-century gesture, each section ends with a Link, a brief discussion of another book, sometimes a much-earlier earlier work or even one from our own time. There are final Links, to give two examples, on François Rabelais and on Michel Tournier. These short references to other books are produced as a means of discussing similar themes, ones generally associated with the Enlightenment, from often markedly different perspectives and time periods. I have attempted at all stages to cite other works that are worth reading in their own right, rather than simply citing sources for isolated references. In particular, the books discussed in the Links are to be treated as bonus primary texts, worthy of debate in their own right, and they are a pleasure to read. In these diverse ways, the five chapters attempt to assess the problems and concepts that, taken together, are generally acknowledged to demarcate the Enlightenment.

These repeated gestures toward a wide variety of other texts are not extraneous to the central purpose of this book; rather, the many, brief discussions of works of fiction and theory from different times and places are deemed to be highly relevant, part of the fabric of this work in the history of ideas. (A model for this approach is Paul Fussell's *The Great War and Modern Memory*, 1975, which presents the World War I experience of trench warfare by means of constant commentary on World War II and Vietnam literature.) These additional books are certainly mentioned in passing as recommendations for future reading; more crucially, for the purposes of this study, they are also examples of how the Enlightenment concepts in this book can be discovered throughout the range of European thought from antiquity to the present. The design of this repeated blending of sources is to stress the interconnectedness of theory and fiction and to demonstrate that these interests, although showcased in the long eighteenth century, were not bound even to the adjacent centuries, but can be identified, to some degree, from antiquity to the present, throughout European thought.

3 SETTING THIS BOOK IN CONTEXT

Overall, this book, *Enlightenment and Political Fiction: The Everyday Intellectual* is a history of ideas. The primary emphasis here is neither on the historical context of the books being investigated nor on the intellectual currents in the times when these books were written. After the Background sections of each chapter, the book does not, for the most part, overtly stress other writers or political events of the time. The need for contextual studies of famous authors and their writings has been rightly recognized for some time, and most intellectual historians and literary scholars, and numerous other scholars, are at present involved in some aspect of this project.[24] What is now often ignored is the relationship of books to one another over time. The emphasis here is on debating the political and economic ideas in a small number of works of fiction in terms of similar concepts located in sometimes much earlier, and often much later, works. In this process, interdisciplinary comparisons and contrasts are made as far back as antiquity to Herodotus, Livy, and Marcus Aurelius, and at times, moving forward, to modern authors, several with strong links beyond Europe, to Michel Tournier, Carlos Fuentes, Mario Vargas Llosa, and Hanif Kureishi. This is not only a history of ideas, it is in some respects a cultural history of how and why ideas develop over time.[25] Fundamentally, it is an examination of the complicated, sometimes counterintuitive ways in which abstract ideas are created.

This book is largely in agreement with two recent works: Nancy Armstrong's *How Novels Think: The Limits of Individualism from 1719 to 1900*, and Lynn Hunt's *Inventing Human Rights: A History*.[26] Armstrong links the eighteenth-century development of the novel and its distinctive lead characters, with the rise of the theory of the abstract individual, culminating in the work of classical liberals, especially that of John Stuart Mill. Both Armstrong and Hunt identify novels as a source of the shift in thinking of the modern age. Hunt does so by stressing how identification with genuinely pitiful central characters led the reading public in the eighteenth century to support programs that would better the life of the unfortunate. In addition, a study of much more recent writers, Christopher Hitchens's *Unacknowledged Legislation: Writers in the Public Sphere* (2000) shows the continuation of this eighteenth-century dynamic.[27] The *Everyday Individual* draws on all three of these books in an attempt to identify novels as the source of, not just the motivation for, a broad range of Enlightenment theories designed to change European society.

Hunt considers romances, especially the epistolary novels—novels written exclusively in the forms of letters—of the eighteenth century as the critical factor that enabled the expanding reading public to identify with those having no legal rights, no financial means, and no recourse in grim times.[28] Hunt follows Benedict Anderson's emphasis on newspapers and novels as means of solidifying a community.[29] Epistolary novels were almost ludicrously popular in Europe in the 1760s–1780s. In contrast with Anderson, however,

Hunt argues that this "imagined empathy" of mid-eighteenth-century readers provided "the foundation of human rights rather than nationalism."[30]

Implicitly, at least, *The Everyday Intellectual* argues that both Anderson and Hunt are correct. For some time, scholars have linked eighteenth-century novels to the rise of capitalism (citing such contemporary literary examples such as Defoe's *Robinson Crusoe*, 1719–1722, on extreme self-sufficiency, and Defoe's *Moll Flanders*, 1722, which deliberately links the financial success of a charming, highly intelligent prostitute as analogous to the rise of the British Empire), yet Hunt makes the connection not between fiction and the growth of the *laissez-faire* economy, but between fiction and the development of the notion of human rights.[31] She contends that reading accounts of torture in novels (many of which included torture scenes, and this was not just in novels by Sade, but also in the form of extreme domestic neglect, for example, in Samuel Richardson's *Clarissa*) made the reading public regard social and political life altogether differently than they had before.[32] Hunt rightly notes the move away from the ancient, medieval, and even early-modern emphasis in fiction on aristocratic, or would-be-aristocratic, heroines and heroes, such as Quixote, and toward the working-class or at least middle-class hero and heroine of the eighteenth century.[33] All these shifts were occurring in a time of increased literacy in Europe and the rest of the world and in a time when more women were reading and writing. Hunt's emphasis is on three prominent novels written by men but with female title characters—Jean-Jacques Rousseau's *Julie, ou la nouvelle Héloïse* (1761), Richardson's *Pamela* (1740, which gained even more attention when parodied by Henry Fielding in *Shamela*, 1741), and Richardson's *Clarissa* (1747–1748).[34] Although it is now sometimes assumed that Voltaire's *Candide* was the most influential fictional work of the eighteenth century, in the eighteenth century the question was whether Rousseau's *Julie* or Richardson's *Clarissa* dominated. Hunt argues that the three novels she chose, in particular, created in readers a sense of equality and empathy with distraught, sometimes even working-class, heroines. Eighteenth-century readers, both male and female, recognized their own inner selves in the plight of these feckless heroines. She further argues that the success of the novels demonstrated the need for interiority in order to withstand the difficulties in life that everyone suffers.[35] She backs up her assessment with quotations from some of the great thinkers, not only creative writers, of this age: Thomas Jefferson, for example, began his list of recommended books with poetry, plays, and novels because such works of literature would, according to Jefferson, give readers the "strong desire in ourselves of doing charitable and grateful acts."[36] Hunt claims this impetus toward the public good, supposedly gained in the eighteenth century from reading fiction, should also be viewed as the creation of a secular, social life that embraced social reform in an organized fashion. She argues that it was through these three highly popular novels—Rousseau's *Julie* and Richardson's *Pamela and Clarissa*, all written in the form of letters—that the lack of rights of women, children, and all those not from the privileged classes were brought to center stage of public consciousness. The epistolary format, a story told in a series of letters, seems to allow closer contact between the central character and the reader. The popularity of romances, and the political implications thereof, existed, of course, at a time when women had very few legal rights separate from their fathers and husbands, and divorce was virtually impossible. As William Blackstone, author of the highly influential *Commentaries on the Laws of England* (1765–1769), is commonly believed to have succinctly phrased it: "husband and wife are one, and the husband is that one."[37] Long-eighteenth-century readers confronted new ideas about the individual and society—ideas that confronted established figures, such as Blackstone himself—in fiction, law, and theory. In some cases fiction was the spearhead.

This book, *Enlightenment and Political Fiction*, also underscores the emerging concept of rights, it differs, however, from Hunt's work in that its emphasis is textual, not contextual. In this work, I emphasize the text-based debates in famous long-eighteenth-century works of fiction and nonfiction (often the ones that have retained their classic status and thus have had more impact on later generations), rather than primarily emphasizing the impact of these books at the time they were published. Hunt's work is a social and cultural history, whereas this book is a history of ideas. Nevertheless, even though Hunt's work is largely contextual, and this book is largely textual, the approaches are complementary, and both essential, in order to grasp the arguments of this crucial age.

In sum, Hunt's book, *Inventing Human Rights: A History*, focuses on the role of fiction in developing a culture of rights, and does so as an historical study, not as a textual study of the major works of fiction and theory in Europe during the long eighteenth century. This book argues that Enlightenment fiction not only inspired sympathy for victims—which is Hunt's argument—but that it already contained the core of Enlightenment theory, highlighting the responsibilities as well as the rights of individuals, thus setting up the full range of individual participation in modern political society.

To return to this book, I have written *Enlightenment and Political Fiction* to be comprehensible to educated general readers who do not have in-depth knowledge of the original languages of these five works, much less a background in the scholarship on these works. The Background sections to the chapters are relatively neutral in terms of debate and are designed primarily for those unfamiliar with the specific work under discussion. This book's real work takes place in the second section of each chapter. Some readers, already familiar with the particular work of fiction, may thus wish to skip the Background sections and go directly to the second section. In addition, two easy entry points into this book, especially for those not familiar with this overall subject, would be Chapter 4 on *Candide*, or part way into Chapter 5, on *The Betrothed*, in II, 6, "Renzo as a Reluctant Revolutionary." Reading the chapters in reverse order, thus starting with Chapter 5: *The Betrothed*, and working backward to Chapter 1: *Don Quixote*, might also, in some respects, help those less familiar with older European history. In sum, the arguments about Enlightenment are to be found throughout this book, and hence the various chapters and parts of the book can be read in almost any order, following the model of so many eighteenth-century works.

I maintain that these same multidisciplinary arguments spilled across the seventeenth, eighteenth, and nineteenth centuries, and that this collection of ideas—which we know as the Enlightenment—might now perhaps be best viewed as a category, not bound to particular times and places. This is in line with what we already do with other major categories of ideas, such as Stoicism and Romanticism. Ideas across time are mixed together throughout the book, and this is representative of what is to be found in the history of ideas since antiquity and up to our own time. The intent is to look at novels and narration as possible, if implicit, political theory, ideas that can be found beyond the boundaries of genre and the typical historical categories.

Thus the understanding of the process and scope of theorizing is examined here in terms of particular overarching themes, the very shifts that make up Enlightenment thinking. These changes in attitude—the shift to the modern age—include recognition of the inadequacies of periodization, the rise of analytic philosophy of history (the study of the study of history, based on reason and scientific principles, without attributing a set pattern to history, which is the major characteristic of speculative philosophy of history), a high degree of interest in emotion as well as in rationality (confronting the accepted view that the Enlightenment was wholly anti-emotion), and the emergence of the concept of the abstract individual.[38] This crucial notion assumes that the individual is situated in a state in which there is rule of law, equality of law, and restraints on the ruler, all of which are essential in order for the autonomous individual to have both adequate protection and freedom of movement.[39] Thus, as many of the critical shifts of the modern age are to be discovered not only first, sometimes even in extended form, in the fiction of the long eighteenth century, there is a need to examine how theories are developed in fiction.

In sum, the goal of this book is to make both fiction and theory accessible to readers no matter what subject they may have studied in the past or how long ago that might have been. One of the arguments here is that these five works are still worth debating, in contrast to many other well-written books of the long eighteenth century, precisely because these particular books give readers of all backgrounds an opportunity to reflect on ongoing social, political, and economic themes of modernity, which include, for example, religion in addition to rights, and science as distinct from the rise of capitalism. The development of individual rights can be located in long-eighteenth-century European works of fiction that criticize an existing society, and in those that present an alternative, and sometimes fantastic, reality. The emerging view of the individual in these works helps to elucidate ongoing questions, of which the following two are merely a choice sample: Is it possible to find a view of the individual in the long eighteenth century that is not abstract, and not passive? Did family structure help or hinder the shaping of the notion of the modern individual? The Enlightenment mission of making education, and the great books of the past, accessible to everyone, not just to an elite group, is predicated on a committed belief in the intelligence of the average person. It was this shared belief that led directly to the Enlightenment emphasis on both individual rights and responsibilities.

NOTES

1 See Clifford Geertz, *Interpretation of Culture*, ch. 1.
2 See Jonathan Clark, *English Society, 1688–1832*, on the notion of the long eighteenth century. Clark cites an earlier work on this theme as one of his models: Betty Kemp, *King and Commons, 1660–1832*.
3 E. P. Thompson, *The Making of the English Working Class*. And see Joan Wallach Scott, "Women in *The Making of the English Working Class*," pt. 2, ch. 4, pp. 68–90, in *Gender and the Politics of History* (1989).
4 Three older works on political fiction are still worth consulting: Morris Edmund Speare, *The Political Novel: Its Development in England and in America* (1924); René Wellek and Austin Warren, *Theory of Literature* (1949); and Irving Howe, *Politics and the Novel* (1957). Ian P. Watt, *The Rise of the Novel* (2007), first published in 1957, is still often regarded as the key text on the development of the English novel in the eighteenth century, and the study of rise of the novel.
5 See Peter Ekegren, *The Reading of Theoretical Texts*.
6 Frank O'Gorman, *The Long Eighteenth Century*, p. xii.
7 Daniel Mornet, *Les Origines intellectuelles de la révolution française, 1715–1787*. Peter Gay, *The Enlightenment: The Rise of Modern Paganism* and *The Enlightenment: The Science of Freedom*, 2 vols.
8 Franco Venturi, *Italy and the Enlightenment: Studies in a Cosmopolitan Century*, and *Utopia and Reform in the Enlightenment*. John Robertson, "Franco Venturi's Enlightenment."
9 Roy Porter and Mikuláš Teich, eds., *The Enlightenment in National Context*. Roy Porter, *The Creation of the Modern World: The Untold Story of the British Enlightenment*. Gabriel Paquette, ed., *Enlightened Reform in Southern Europe and Its Atlantic Colonies, c. 1750–1830*.
10 Jonathan Israel, *Radical Enlightenment: Philosophy and the Making of Modernity, 1650–1750*. Jonathan Israel, *Enlightenment Contested: Philosophy, Modernity, and the Emancipation of Man, 1652–1752*. Also Jonathan Israel, "Enlightenment! Which Enlightenment?" in *Journal of the History of Ideas*, 67 (2006): 523–545.
11 Karen O'Brien, *Women and Enlightenment in Eighteenth-Century Britain*. Robert Darnton, *The Business of Enlightenment: A Publishing History of the Encyclopédie, 1775–1800*. Dena Goodman, *The Republic of Letters: A Cultural History of the French Enlightenment* on French *salon* culture. J. G. A. Pocock, *Virtue, Commerce, and History*.
12 Ernst Cassirer, *Die Philosophie der Aufklärung*. Cassirer, *The Philosophy of the Enlightenment*.
13 Martin Jay, *The Dialectical Imagination: A History of the Frankfurt School and the Institute of Social Research, 1923–1950*.
14 Max Horkheimer and Theodor Adorno, *Dialektik der Aufklärung*. Horkheimer and Adorno, *Dialectic of the Enlightenment*.

15 Reinhart Koselleck, *Critique and Crisis: Enlightenment and Pathogenesis of Modern Society.*

16 Robert Darnton, "What is the History of the Book?" *Daedalus.* Thank you to Elizabeth Swaim.

17 See below, in this Introduction, on Lynn Hunt, *Inventing Human Rights.*

18 On the Salamanca School, see Anthony Pagden, *Lords of All the World: Ideologies of Empire in Spain, Britain and France c. 1500–c. 1800,* and *The Fall of Natural Man: The American Indian and the Origins of Comparative Ethnology.* See also Quentin Skinner on the sixteenth- and seventeenth-century Spanish contribution, which he rates as fundamental in particular to European political philosophy and social contract theory: *The Foundations of Modern Political Thought,* 2 vols. See the following: Jean Sarrailh, *L'Espagne éclairée de la seconde moitié du XVIIIe siècle,* Richard Herr, *The Eighteenth-Century Revolution in Spain,* and *An Historical Essay on Modern Spain*; and Alfonso E. Pérez Sánchez and Eleanor A. Sayre, eds., *Goya and the Spirit of Enlightenment.* More recently, see Paquette, *Enlightenment, Governance, and Reform in Spain and Its Empire, 1759–1808.*

19 Michael Valdez Moses, *The Novel and The Globalization of Culture.* John B. Bender, *Ends of Enlightenment.* David Armitage, "What's the Big Idea? Intellectual History and the *Longue Durée*" in *History of European Ideas.* Jo Guldi and David Armitage, *The History Manifesto.* Larry Siedentop, *Inventing the Individual: The Origins of Western Liberalism.*

20 Michel Foucault, *L'Archéologie du Savoir.* Foucault, *The Archaeology of Knowledge.*

21 Auerbach, *Mimesis: The Representation of Reality in Western Literature.* First published in German in 1946, and in English in 1953.

22 See Edward Said, *Humanism and Democratic Criticism,* esp. the "Introduction to Erich Auerbach's *Mimesis,*" pp. 85–122. Thank you to Ernesto Rodriguez.

23 Giambattista Vico, *The New Science of Giambattista Vico,* Thomas Bergin and Max Fisch, eds., trs.: both quotations are from #331, p. 96. Hereafter as *The New Science.*

24 Perhaps the best theoretical discussion of the contextual approach to intellectual history, which is most closely associated with Quentin Skinner, and sometimes called the Cambridge School, is James Tully, ed., *Meaning and Context: Quentin Skinner and His Critics.*

25 This approach follows that of Peter Burke. See especially Peter Burke, *A Social History of Knowledge: From Gutenberg to Diderot.*

26 Nancy Armstrong, *How Novels Think: The Limits of British Individualism from 1719–1900.* And, again: Hunt, *Inventing Human Rights.*

27 Christopher Hitchens, *Unacknowledged Legislation: Writers in the Public Sphere.*

28 Hunt, *Inventing Human Rights,* p. 32. Also see Carla Hesse, *The Other Enlightenment: How French Women Became Modern* for a very different perspective on women and the Enlightenment.

29 Benedict Anderson, *Imagined Communities: Reflections on the Origin and Spread of Nationalism,* chs. 2–3 in particular.

30 Hunt, *Inventing Human Rights,* p. 32.

31 Hunt, *Inventing Human Rights,* p. 41.

32 Hunt, *Inventing Human Rights,* pp. 35–69.

33 Hunt, *Inventing Human Rights,* p. 41.

34 See my comments on Rousseau's *Julie* in Chapter Four, of this volume, on *Candide.*

35 Hunt, *Inventing Human Rights,* p. 48.

36 *The Papers of Thomas Jefferson,* Julian P. Boyd, ed., vol. 1, pp. 76–81, esp. p. 76. Cited by Hunt, *Inventing Human Rights,* p. 57.

37 This line is generally attributed to William Blackstone. See his *Commentaries on the Laws of England: In Four Books*, vol. 1, book 1, ch. 15, pp. 432–444, for the substance of this idea, although not the exact quotation. This work was first published in 1765–1769.

38 The vexed relationship of rationality and emotion continues to get close attention from many quarters. See, to give two examples, neuroscientist Antonio R. Damasio's *Descartes' Error: Emotion, Reason, and the Human Brain*, and philosopher Martha Nussbaum's *Upheavals of Thought: The Intelligence of Emotions*.

39 Again, a worthwhile recent book on the abstract individual is Siedentop, *Inventing the Individual: The Origins of Western Liberalism*.

REFERENCES

Anderson, Benedict, *Imagined Communities: Reflections on the Origin and Spread of Nationalism* (London: Verso, 1996).

Armitage, David, "What's the Big Idea? Intellectual History and the *Longue Durée*" in *History of European Ideas* 38 (4): 493–507.

Armstrong, Nancy, *How Novels Think: The Limits of British Individualism from 1719–1900* (New York: Columbia University Press, 2006).

Auerbach, Eric, *Mimesis: The Representation of Reality in Western Literature*, Willard R. Trask, tr. (Princeton: Princeton University Press, 2003).

Bender, John B., *The Ends of Enlightenment* (Stanford, CA: Stanford University Press, 2012).

Blackstone, William, *Commentaries on the Laws of England: In Four Books*, 2 vols. (Clark, NJ: Lawbook Exchange, 2003).

Burke, Peter, *A Social History of Knowledge: From Gutenberg to Diderot* (Cambridge, U.K.: Polity Press, 2000).

Cassirer, Ernst, *Die Philosophie der Aufklärung* (Tübinen: Morh., 1932).

———. *The Philosophy of the Enlightenment*, James P. Pettegrove, tr. (Princeton: Princeton University Press, 2009).

Clark, J. C. D., *English Society, 1688–1832: Ideology, Social Structure and Political Practice during the Ancien Regime*, 2nd ed. (Cambridge: Cambridge University Press, 2000).

Damasio, Antonio R., *Descartes' Error: Emotion, Reason, and the Human Brain* (New York: G. P. Putnam's Sons, 1994).

Darnton, Robert, *The Business of Enlightenment: A Publishing History of the Encyclopédie, 1775–1800* (Cambridge, MA: Belknap Press of Harvard University Press, 1979).

———. "What is the History of the Book?" *Daedalus* (Summer 1982: 65–83).

Ekegren, Peter, *The Reading of Theoretical Texts: A Critique of Criticism in the Social Sciences* (London: Taylor & Francis, 2002).

Foucault, Michel, *L'Archéologie du savoir* (Paris: Éditions Gallimard, 1969).

———. *The Archaeology of Knowledge* (London: Routledge Classics, 1989).

Gay, Peter, *The Enlightenment: The Rise of Modern Paganism* and *The Enlightenment: The Science of Freedom*, 2 vols. (New York: Knopf, 1966–1969).

Geertz, Clifford, *Interpretation of Culture* (New York: Basic Books, 1977).

Goodman, Dena, *The Republic of Letters: A Cultural History of the French Enlightenment* (Ithaca, NY: Cornell University Press, 1994).

Guldi, Jo, and David Armitage, *The History Manifesto* (Cambridge: Cambridge University Press, 2014).

Herr, Richard, *The Eighteenth-Century Revolution in Spain* (Princeton: Princeton University Press, 1958).

——. *An Historical Essay on Modern Spain* (Berkeley: University of California Press, 1974).

Hesse, Carla, *The Other Enlightenment: How French Women Became Modern* (Princeton: Princeton University Press, 2003).

Hitchens, Christopher, *Unacknowledged Legislation: Writers in the Public Sphere* (London: Verso, 2000).

Horkheimer, Max, and Theodor Adorno, *Dialectic of the Enlightenment*, Edmund Jephcott, tr. (Stanford, CA: Stanford University Press, 2002).

——. *Dialektik der Aufklärung* (Amsterdam: Querido Verlag, 1947).

Howe, Irving, *Politics and the Novel* (New York: Horizon Press, 1957).

Hunt, Lynn, *Inventing Human Rights: A History* (New York: W.W. Norton, 2007).

Israel, Jonathan, *Enlightenment Contested: Philosophy, Modernity, and the Emancipation of Man, 1652–1752* (Oxford: Oxford University Press, 2006).

——. "Enlightenment! Which Enlightenment?" *Journal of the History of Ideas* 67 (2006): 523–545.

——. *Radical Enlightenment: Philosophy and the Making of Modernity, 1650–1750* (New York: Oxford University Press, 2001).

Jay, Martin, *The Dialectical Imagination: A History of the Frankfurt School and the Institute of Social Research, 1923–1950* (Berkeley: University of California Press, 1996).

Jefferson, Thomas, *The Papers of Thomas Jefferson*, Julian P. Boyd, ed., 35 vols. (Princeton: Princeton University Press, 1950).

Kemp, Betty, *King and Commons, 1660–1832* (London: Macmillan, 1957).

Koselleck, Reinhart, *Critique and Crisis: Enlightenment and Pathogenesis of Modern Society* (Cambridge, MA: The MIT Press, 1988).

Mornet, Daniel, *Les Origines intellectuelles de la révolution française, 1715–1787* (Paris: A. Colin, 1933).

Nussbaum, Martha, *Upheavals of Thought: The Intelligence of Emotions* (Cambridge: Cambridge University Press, 2001).

O'Brien, Karen, *Narratives of Enlightenment: Cosmopolitan History from Voltaire to Gibbon* (Cambridge: Cambridge University Press, 1997).

O'Gorman, Frank, *The Long Eighteenth Century: British Political & Social History, 1688–1832* (London: Arnold, 1997).

Pagden, Anthony, *Lords of All the World: Ideologies of Empire in Spain, Britain and France*
c. 1500–c. 1800 (New Haven: Yale University Press, 1998).

——. *The Fall of Natural Man: The American Indian and the Origins of Comparative Ethnology* (Cambridge: Cambridge University Press, 1987).

Paquette, Gabriel, *Enlightenment, Governance, and Reform in Spain and Its Empire, 1759–1808* (Basingstoke, U.K.: Palgrave Macmillan, 2008).

Paquette, Gabriel, ed., *Enlightened Reform in Southern Europe and Its Atlantic Colonies, c. 1750–1830* (Farnham, Surrey, U.K.: Ashgate, 2009).

Pérez Sánchez, Alfonso E., and Eleanor A. Sayre, eds., *Goya and the Spirit of Enlightenment* (Madrid/Boston/New York: Prado, Boston Museum of Fine Arts, and The Metropolitan Museum of Art, 1989).

Pocock, J. G. A., *Virtue, Commerce, and History: Essays in Political Thought and History, Chiefly in the Eighteenth Century* (Cambridge: Cambridge University Press, 1988).

Porter, Roy, and Mikulás Teich, eds., *The Enlightenment in National Context* (Cambridge: Cambridge University Press, 1981).

———. *The Creation of the Modern World: The Untold Story of the British Enlightenment* (New York: W. W. Norton, 2000).

Robertson, John, "Franco Venturi's Enlightenment." *Past and Present* 137 (1992): 183–206.

Said, Edward W., *Humanism and Democratic Criticism* (Houndsmills, U.K.: Palgrave, 2004).

Sarrailh, Jean, *L'Espagne éclairée de la seconde moitié du XVIIIe siècle* (Paris: Impr. Nationale, 1954).

Scott, Joan Wallach, *Gender and the Politics of History* (New York: Columbia University Press, 1999, revised ed).

Siedentop, Larry, *Inventing the Individual: The Origins of Western Liberalism* (Cambridge, MA: The Belknap Press of Harvard University Press, 2014).

Skinner, Quentin, *The Foundations of Modern Political Thought*, 2 vols. (Cambridge: Cambridge University Press, 1978).

Speare, Morris Edmund, *The Political Novel: Its Development in England and in America* (New York: Oxford University Press, 1924).

Thompson, E. P., *The Making of the English Working Class* (London: Victor Gollancz, 1963).

Tully, James, ed., *Meaning and Context: Quentin Skinner and His Critics* (Princeton: Princeton University Press, 1989).

Valdez Moses, Michael, *The Novel and The Globalization of Culture* (New York: Oxford University Press, 1995).

Venturi, Franco, *Italy and the Enlightenment: Studies in a Cosmopolitan Century*, Susan Corsi, tr., Stuart Woolf, ed. (London: Longman, 1972).

———. *Utopia and Reform in the Enlightenment* (Cambridge: Cambridge University Press, 1971).

Vico, Giambattista, *The New Science of Giambattista Vico*, Thomas Bergin and Max Fisch, trs., eds. (Ithaca, NY: Cornell University Press, 1948).

Watt, Ian P., *The Rise of the Novel: Studies in Defoe, Richardson, and Fielding* (Whitefish, MT: Kessinger Publishing, 2007).

Wellek, René, and Austin Warren, *Theory of Literature* (New York: Harcourt, Brace, and Company, 1949).

1 *Don Quixote* (1605, 1615), Rationality, and Forms of Government

I BACKGROUND

1 Preamble: A New Interpretation of Sancho Panza

A tall, skinny, early-modern Spanish country gentleman, from the lower gentry, steeped in books of medieval chivalry, has, according to those around him, gone mad from too much reading.[1] Repulsed by modern trends, he reinvents himself as a latter-day, medieval knight. This includes, in this order: locating armor "which had belonged to his ancestors, and had lain for ages forgotten in a corner, eaten with rust and covered with mould"; giving his horse a name, Rocinante; taking the name of Don Quixote for himself; choosing a lady love; beginning to travel in order to find adventure—in time wearing a barber's basin as a helmet; being knighted; and finally taking a local working man, Sancho Panza, as his squire (Sancho gets a mule as his steed, and the mule's name does not even remain fixed, unlike that of Quixote's horse).[2] Additionally, Quixote imagines the basin to be a magical helmet.[3] Mystical qualities and the grubbiness of real life are mixed at all stages.

Don Quixote focuses at all stages on madness and liberty. For example, it is relatively easy to discern a relationship between themes Robert Burton raises in *The Anatomy of Melancholy* (1621) and the evolving concept of personal liberty in European thought and the presentation of the magic helmet (drawn from Ludovico Ariosto's *Orlando furioso*, *Mad Orlando*, 1516) in *Don Quixote*. In Part I, Don Quixote and Sancho Panza travel relatively little in terms of distance, but a lot in miles, each time circling around a local inn, where Quixote is treated with little respect. Quixote, however, does not do much to garner respect. His adventures regularly get him roughed up, often left with broken bones and missing teeth, and the people he intends to help almost always suffer much more after his interference. He is, however, not only a buffoon, but he also kills people. Both in genre, and tone, the book changes frequently, alternating between romance, chivalry, poetry, songs, novellas, burlesque, tragedy, epic, pastoral, picaresque, letters, narrative, and political writing, just to name a few.[4] The story of Quixote and Sancho is interspersed with other long tales—one of a tedious love triangle (which is a novella in its own right, in the style of medieval allegory, as perfected earlier by Giovanni Boccaccio in *The Decameron*, 1350–1353), and another of a captive Christian and his Moorish lady friend. These stories are often told by travelers at the inn, and by aristocrats who pass in and out of the story. Impossibly long digressions both show off the virtuosity of the book, demonstrating an astonishing range of literary styles, and offer examples of, exceptions to, and counter-arguments regarding the major themes of the work. The magic helmet—that is, a barber's basin—for example, is used as a device to demonstrate how people can actually claim what they need if only they believe they have the power to do so.

By Part II, Quixote has become relatively famous locally, and many rash men on the local scene—most presumably impoverished, mad, or both—pretend to be Don Quixote in order to share in the success of the main character. They symbolize the many false sequels to Part I of *Don Quixote*, which were published quickly after 1605. In Cervantes's Part II, the real Quixote continues to pursue his quest, still with Sancho, but on a much less frenetic level. There are flamboyant discussions, and prolonged scenes. Many of the adventures take place as highly organized farces, arranged by specific aristocrats, who amuse themselves greatly at the leading pair's expense. For example, this group of aristocrats plays an extended, complicated trick on Sancho in order to lead him to believe that he has finally realized his overarching dream of becoming the governor of an island. Yet in the midst of this particular farce, the book forces us to ponder the surprising possibility that Sancho Panza might be a source on good government. Part II, especially Chapter 51, on Sancho's island, presents proto-Lockean economic and political ideas. The joke is that Sancho, known for his repeated trite sayings, sometimes called *sanchismos*, could devise a new political order. Nevertheless, it is this chapter of *Don Quixote* that indicates a break with the Spanish emphasis on economic and political theory—especially the School of Salamanca on monetary theory, just war, and international relations—toward an emphasis on practical politics and political institutions. Indeed, Part II of *Don Quixote*, from 1615, crisply outlines many ideas credited to Locke in 1690. This debt was acknowledged by Locke, but has not been probed by later scholars.

Throughout the book, Basques, gypsies, Turks, and even people from the less fashionable parts of Spain, as represented by the Asturian maid at the inn, are all briefly put in the spotlight not just as entertainment—thus as a means of mocking the religious and ethnic complexities of the fractured Iberian peninsula—but also as distinct means of telling the multiple stories of the nation of Spain, thus emphasizing that the story would not be complete without each voice.[5] At the end of the book, Quixote is dying, and he repudiates his commitment not only to chivalry, but also to all kinds of stylized, altruistic, and even noble deeds. In this particularly extended, final scene, Quixote goes so far as to change his will to read that his niece would be disinherited if she were to marry a man who believes in chivalry, that is, a man like Quixote himself had been before his deathbed conversion. The implication is clear that Quixote's manner of dying—his preferences regarding the routine of his daily life as much as his ideological preferences—has significance for all Spaniards, regardless of their gender, ethnic background, religious preferences, or even wealth. In economic terms, the deathbed scene and the injunction to his niece do not have to be seen as pitiful acts of desperation, of Quixote giving up his quest. Rather, they could be interpreted as Quixote, in a constructive mode, identifying a new economic system—emerging capitalism, in stark opposition to his previous choices of feudalism and chivalry—as the best way to care for his family in the future.

Yet much of the story is embedded in the past, not the future, for not far below the surface of this tale of two travelers is a parallel story by the Spanish narrator of how he found the account of Don Quixote in the writing of a Muslim historian, and thus, of history being recovered both by accident and then by deliberate effort. The narrator mouths anti-Moorish sentiments throughout the book, and uses the materials written in Arabic by the historian, with relatively little thanks to the earlier scholar. However, these repeated racial slurs by the narrator might well have been intentional, not unthinking, in the text, a secure means to get across a subtle but powerful message about both Quixote's sanity and the richness of Arab learning.

Consider, if the Moorish historian deems Quixote to be mad, and the message is clearly that the Moor is not to be trusted, then perhaps this work should be read as a palimpsest, a manuscript that had been written on, cleaned off, and written on again many times. The message thus becomes the exact opposite: with Arab medieval learning as a background and a clever Moorish historian, Quixote could then be argued to be the only sane person in his time and place, the only one who recognizes the social, political, and economic abuses of his time and who even has some ideas about how to change his society, and it is only through the lens of a different culture and religion that this becomes apparent.

The dominant Spanish narrator's growing obsession with the Quixote story is linked to his concern to analyze history. The narrator has questions about whether there is a pattern to history, and also whether there are specific means by which history might be comprehended. The novel thus delivers, in the midst of grandiose pranks, prolonged references to what would now be referred to as academic subfields, including speculative philosophy of history and analytic philosophy of history, in addition to grandstanding designed to promote political revolt.

In general, most scholars prefer Part II of this book; most children, Part I. Part I is best known for Quixote's jousts with windmills—often taken to symbolize modern industry—which he is convinced are evil enchanters, and also for Quixote's first meeting with his lady love, renamed Dulcinea by Quixote, actually a working girl, Aldonza Lorenzo, who has no interest in him whatsoever. Dulcinea never appears directly in the book, however frequently she is mentioned, and astonishingly, Aldonza only appears once. The difference between the two parts has to do with content as well as style. Part I demands attention to the fundamental question: What choices should a moral person make while living in an immoral society, even under a corrupt government? Part I tells the Quixote/Sancho story as a universal trope, that could be played out in any place and time. Part II delineates the range of choices for scholars, and the problems that writers face in all times and places. This chapter, however, gives substantial attention to the child-friendly Part I; even if the symbolism is starker and less academic, the early part of the book—almost half of the total text—contains more universally accessible themes.

It is through the sympathetic but plodding Sancho Panza that the reader of *Don Quixote* encounters the frantic need to find additional income, which most families experience, and the disrespect that such deliberate financial choices often invoke. One commonplace view of *Don Quixote* is that the supposed servant, Sancho Panza, a peasant motivated by money, food, and alcohol (and not always in that order), increasingly willingly accompanies Quixote on his travel. Certainly at the outset, Sancho is the more passive and witless of the two. Yet Sancho manifests both loyalty to, and trust in, the man who at first he had only hoped would assist him in earning status and wealth. Taking work with Don Quixote indicates Sancho's desperation, not shared by his wife, to raise the growing Panza family's social standing as much as its financial status; his wife Teresa focuses on their urgent need for more money.[6] She symbolizes the power of feudalism, for her choices make sense in the midst of a system lacking any commitment to the people on the bottom of the social scale. Sancho, however, can be read as symbolizing the insecurity of a world shifting from feudalism to capitalism, yet in a time of want, not a time of plenty. Sancho cannot be properly understood without recognizing the power structure in which he is enmeshed.[7]

This novel made new economic contributions on two fronts: by distilling the economic criticisms of the time and by putting forward its own original economic contributions, including proposing alternatives that broke with the Mediterranean economic approaches. *Don Quixote* is the most extreme example, of the five novels examined in this book, of the limitation of using the term "Enlightenment" only for mid-eighteenth-century French thought, a restriction that seems no longer tenable, especially for the history of economic thought. This book suggests that the Enlightenment was to be not so much a time and place, but rather a profitable category of thought, and a pointer toward a method of study. Given this new definition, a book published in 1605 (Part I) and 1615 (Part II) can be considered part of the Enlightenment tradition, and would count as an early example of *pensamiento ilustrado*, Spanish Enlightenment thought.[8]

Although modernity arguably includes cultural elements, economic connections, and political connections, *Don Quixote* is not necessarily modern in all three ways. This has to do primarily with the economic context of the book: during Cervantes's lifetime, Spain was in what would be later called its "Golden Age," a world leader with a far-flung empire, and yet, following the defeat of the Spanish Armada in 1588, and plague in Castile in the late 1500s, by the early 1600s, when this book was first published, Spain was becoming increasingly economically backward. Early-modern Spain suffered from inflation, largely due to the influx of precious metals from the Americas; workers were being thrown off the land; and yet, in the midst of all this financial turmoil, substantial economic theory was developed in Spain, to give one specific example, at the School of Salamanca, notably the development of the Quantity Theory of Money on the velocity of circulation (later worked on by David Hume).[9] The setting of the book in a rural region of an increasingly poor country shakes some of the long-standing assumptions about the development of the modern novel—generally viewed as an urban, bourgeois phenomenon—as it tells the story of the decline of Spain.

Especially given the economic woes of Spain at the time, a case might be made that Sancho, an impoverished family man, a proto-working-class man, should have been the title character of this proto-modern book. Sancho's character is arguably richer than that of Quixote. Both Sancho's personality and his deliberate choices evolve, especially in Part II, in line with what is later taken to be the goal for the everyman, the every woman, or the every child reading the book. Despite Quixote's patronizing attitude toward Sancho, and Quixote's peculiarly annoying means of teaching morals, the surprising result is a new Sancho, one who is able to speak in public in an articulate and persuasive manner that Quixote himself never attains. Thus in terms of the seventeenth-century Quarrel of the Ancients and Moderns, it is not the subjects studied by the ancients that are necessarily unparalleled, but rather the systematic, formulaic approach of ancient learning that breeds a particular inclination and motivation in the student, however reluctant the student might be to begin. Sancho learns not so much from the words, but from the stylized actions—including the remarkable, oft-repeated mistakes—of his teacher. Symbolically, Sancho's development over time indicates the necessity for individuals—children, women, and men—to assert themselves in any given situation, as nothing will ever be given to them in set organized educational settings. This interpretation of Sancho is similar to that of one of the leading character in Daniel Defoe's novels, particularly the fierce entrepreneurial spirit of Robinson Crusoe on his all-but-uninhabited island. Moll Flanders and Roxana, title characters of two other marvelous books by Defoe, also display this inventive, unstoppable spirit, which blatantly symbolizes the birthing of modern capitalism in all its glory and gore.

Yet there is no shortage of other possible readings of *Don Quixote*. One reading is psychological, that of Quixote as a below-average hero—"mad in patches, full of lucid streaks"—who constructs his own eccentric but satisfying philosophy of life in order to escape the life he cannot physically leave until he dies.[10] The emphasis here is on Quixote's quest, rather than on the goal of that quest, a journey taken up in middle-age crisis, for Quixote is in his 50's (*cincuentón*).[11] In this reading, Sancho can be viewed as primarily facilitating Quixote's ideological Holy Crusade, ostensibly to revive chivalry, thus a crusade that has nothing to do with religion, but is rather appropriately centered on love, and perhaps on a not-wholly unrequited love. Sancho is here the full-time caregiver, monitoring, but also moderating, his supposed master's activities.

Another reading stresses the class relationship, specifically the master–servant relationship more fully, a relationship that goes through distinct phases (at times Hegelian or Nietzschean), but evolving (anti-chronologically) into an Aristotelian arrangement of "ruling, and being ruled in turn," by equals.[12] By the end of Part II, according to this reading, the two main characters have surely become friends. Quixote's latent efforts to assert, even to reassert, the lines of authority between himself and Sancho indicate that he eventually realizes that he has become too fond of, and too intimate with, a working man; and predictably, he blames Sancho, not himself, for the transformation of their relationship from primarily a financial arrangement to primarily a personal bond.[13] This all happens so slowly that it is not exactly clear when their relationship stops being primarily financial, and begins to transcend class lines. Granted that Sancho was rarely, if ever, paid for his services, nevertheless the relationship was at first grounded on Quixote's sense that he was in charge and on Sancho's hope of financial gain.[14]

Thus a surprising array of textual evidence indicates either that Sancho's travels with Don Quixote were inspired by greed, or not entirely conversely, that Sancho's desire to be a good family man—not only to provide for his wife and children but also to better their overall situation—took him on the road. These only slightly differing interpretations are not essentially about Sancho's often pitiful actions, but about possible interpretations of his character, and the extent to which his own personality traits were determined by his material circumstances. Thus the question is how to understand Sancho: as a natural servant (similar to Aristotle's "natural slave"); a man working for a fussy, rigid employer in order to earn enough money for a dowry for his beloved daughter, Sanchica (thus, a working man in the tradition of Adam Smith); or a developing individual who is receiving an intensive adult education (hence, a Rousseauian "noble savage," a "Hottentot," to use Rousseau's unflattering example, moving toward actualized life in the city). A fourth option, which is argued in this chapter, is that of Sancho, in a Kantian sense, symbolically breaking from tutelage in order to gain his own personal enlightenment. Sancho's individual development (remembering that this character's first name is both a pig sound, and close to "santa" or "holy," and that the last name means "potbelly") occurs in the midst of the most inauspicious circumstances.

Overall, Quixote and Sancho are not simply devices by which the reader can find larger theoretical notions in the text. Throughout this travel story, both Don Quixote and Sancho Panza play proactive roles, if not always making well-informed choices, even though their characters are generally accepted to have only been players in a set piece and farce. Quixote is not only a tragic figure, but also at times a perceptive, even shrewd, character. He is the only one willing to speak out against the abuses around him. Thus, much of the social action, not just the theoretical discussion, revolves around the character of Quixote himself.

This reading of Quixote supports the argument that the book should be viewed as a constructive study of feudalism (not a repudiation of it), which encompasses the identification of a natural, if at times awkward, and certainly staccato, segue to a commercial and scientific society. In this way, the book embraces Scholasticism, the Western European system of learning from at least 1100 to 1500, which stressed the dialectical method and integrated Greek classical thought with biblical, especially New Testament, teaching. Although it embodied much more than this, some would call it the medieval study of Aristotle as codified by Augustine and Aquinas. In *Don Quixote*, Scholasticism and proto-Smithian thought are used to the same end, both means of improving both the individual's quality of life and standard of living. This approach obviously takes Quixote's favorite books of chivalry and uses them to defend, and indeed to better, the emerging mercantile world that he loathes. This argument is, of course, about the message of the book, not about Quixote's literal pronouncements.

This proto-capitalist argument is, somewhat oddly, supported by Marx's view of feudalism as a necessary stage in historical development, which on Marx's proposed time line leads toward the destruction of capitalism and the rise of socialism. Therefore, the ongoing scholarly question of whether the book is pro-feudalism or anti-feudalism, pro-chivalry or anti-chivalry, misses the point: the book was grounded in feudalism, not just historically, but also intellectually. Any next stage, whatever characteristics it demonstrated, would necessarily arise from feudalism, whether naturally or in direct reaction against it.

This argument not only portrays the text as an early-Enlightenment, explicitly political, work, but it also stresses the text as telling the story of Spain's highly fragmented nature. The polemics concerning specific economic practices, for example, do not confirm the interpretation of *Don Quixote* as primarily an attack on medieval manners and a call for modern, entrepreneurial thinking. Instead, they demonstrate an appreciation of the inevitability of such a shift, and thus they call for a smooth, proto-Burkean, non-violent substitution of older forms of order for newer ones, ones which would seemingly do less damage to the individuals making up this culture on the cusp of a modern economy. In the words of the historian of Spain John Elliott, "It was in this atmosphere of *desengaño*, of national disillusionment, that Cervantes wrote his Don Quixote."[15] It is in the passages on Sancho that this novel highlights these bleak economic choices.

2 Spain and the Intellectual and Literary Foundations of *Don Quixote*

Since the eighteenth century, Spaniards and scholars of Spain have taken the Spanish involvement in the Enlightenment and its shift toward the modern age for granted; however, Spanish theoretical ideas still tend to receive short shrift overall in the history of European ideas. This neglect of Spanish theory is, however, not the result of the lack of textual evidence. Just to give a few examples, Spanish thought is particularly strong in political theory and international law (that of Francisco Suárez and Luis de Molina), theology (especially that of the mystics Teresa de Ávila and Juan de la Cruz/John of the Cross), and economics (from the School of Salamanca). In addition, however common the practice today, dividing the work of early-modern writers (including the ones cited here) into modern academic disciplines is somewhat misleading, for there was remarkable overlap in their interests in the relationship between the individual and society, not just between the individual and God.

Admittedly, some of this intellectual isolation was due to the difficulty, both real and imagined, of crossing the Pyrenees, and thus the geographical remoteness of Spain. It is not clear, however, why the Italian Alps were not viewed as a similar barrier. The distinction between the treatment of Italy and Spain was primarily one of motivation, for generations of travelers on a Grand Tour, many of them young male aristocrats from Britain, made their way over the Alps into the Italian states—very often as far south as Naples, Capri, and Sicily—in search of large doses of ancient and Renaissance high culture.[16] The intellectual traffic across the Alps was not in just one direction. Italian writers and thinkers traveled and sought to engage other European thinkers in their concerns. However, post-Renaissance Mediterranean (specifically Italian and Spanish) thought and art were only appreciated outside of the Iberian and Italian peninsulas much later. Northern Europeans were almost exclusively concerned with Roman antiquity and the Italian Renaissance rather than with later Mediterranean intellectual contributions.

Nevertheless, there was some substantial cultural exchange across the Pyrenees, not just the Alps, even if this tends to be viewed as isolated examples rather than a pattern. French classical theater drew substantially from Spain. Pierre Corneille began with adaptations of Spanish plays, notably a reworking of *El Cid* (1637) and also *Le Menteur* (*The Liar*, 1644). Thus it could be said that French classical theater began by imitating Spanish plays. This is just one major example of many. There were also very early adaptations of Spanish plays by English playwrights, including those by John Fletcher, Philip Massinger, and even by Shakespeare. The English were among the first to translate a series of Spanish classics by Mateo Alemán, Antonio de Guevara, the anonymous author of the marvelous *Lazarillo de Tormes* (1554), and then the works by Cervantes himself. Fernand Braudel makes the case in *The Mediterranean and the Mediterranean World in the Age of Phillip II* that Spanish competed with Italian and French in European courts as a language of culture.[17] This point about Spanish literature could be extended to other fields, including, for instance, the sciences; however, the stress here will remain on the humanities and social sciences.

Although the Grand Tour was certainly focused on Italian antiquity, this does not mean that there was not intense curiosity about Spain. Young Englishmen making the Tour, at the very least, wanted and needed to know about their political enemies. At the same time, young Spaniards (and other young Continental Europeans) had a rich cultural life already grounded in Antiquity, and it might be argued, for this reason, they often did not travel as much abroad, certainly not as much as their opposite numbers from England.

And it is also the case that the relative isolation of Spain for over 30 years, under the authoritarian rule of dictator Francisco Franco, who died in 1975, has tended to color modern interpretations of the Spanish past and has exaggerated the isolation of Spain in earlier periods. Spain in the early-modern period was a transnational, multi-continental empire, and far more porous as a political entity than a modern state would be.[18]

The argument that *Don Quixote* is representative of the best of Spanish literature is often used as an implicit criticism of Spanish culture, as much as praise of this particular book. It often implies that early-modern Spain had little to offer in terms of theory, and had only this one book to contribute to great literature. The argument being made here is that substantial theoretical arguments were being made in Spain's most famous literary work, and that they were both drawn from, and representative of, other such projects by Spanish authors.

Thus *Don Quixote* draws from a long and varied Spanish literary tradition, as well as setting the parameters for much of modern Spanish-language literature. Spanish literary history is generally marked as beginning with the medieval period, with the anonymous poem *El Cid* (this Spanish work was, for example, favored over *Don Quixote* by seventeenth-century French playwright Corneille). *Don Quixote*, like *El Cid*, is characterized by a fascination with travelers, explorers, and diverse forms of government.

Renaissance Spanish literature, abounding in poems and ballads, in addition to the bawdy work by Fernando de Rojas, *La Celestina*, contains as well the seeds of modern literature. The beginning of the picaresque, sometimes called picaroon, tradition can be marked by the publication of the anonymous, highly popular work *Lazarillo de Tormes* in 1554. This picaresque tradition in Spain—into which Cervantes's novellas and some parts of *Don Quixote* fit, in terms of content, structure, plot, and the dating of these writings—encompasses two later works: Alemán's *Guzmán de Alfarache* (1599, 1604) and Francisco de Quevedo's *El Buscón* (*The Swindler*, 1626). Quevedo was the leading exponent of *conceptismo*, which, in stark contrast to *culteranismo* (favored by another leading Spanish poet of the same time, Luis de Góngora), was identifiable by a direct writing style free of grandiloquent language or literary flourishes. Quevedo's straightforward style, often found in first-person narrative, is a hallmark of the picaresque tradition. Both Góngora and Quevedo's writing are marked by the disillusionment that is often viewed as the distinctive feature of modern literature.[19]

The picaresque tradition was very much in demand across Europe in the sixteenth and seventeenth centuries. *Lazarillo de Tormes* was translated into English, Dutch, German, French, and Italian by 1633, and into Latin in 1652. The word *picaro* originally referred to ragged soldiers who fought in the historical Picardy region in northern France. The word was soon used to refer to the early anti-hero of European literature, generally low-born, extraordinarily poor, involved in crime, and dogged by persistent bad luck.[20] Later novels, including the German *Simplicissimus* (1668, 1669), the French *Gil Blas* (1715–1735) by René Lesage, and in English, Daniel Defoe's *Moll Flanders* (1722), and even Mark Twain's *Adventures of Huckleberry Finn* (1885), could all be argued to be part of the picaresque. Although Spanish books are usually taken as the starting point of the picaresque novel, it might make as much sense to date the tradition as far back as Petronius's *Satyricon* (c. 61 A.D.), the classic satire from ancient Rome, which emphasizes the working poor and their rebellious attitude toward authority.[21]

El Siglo de Oro, la Edad Dorada, the Golden Age of Spanish literature and the arts (which overlaps with, but is not identical to, Spain's Golden Age of imperial power), encompassed the Renaissance and Baroque, a two-century period that one could date from *La Celestina* in 1499 or else from Garcilaso's lifetime (1501–1536) to the deaths of Calderón and Velázquez in 1681 and 1660. This age is known not only for the mystic writers noted above, Teresa de Ávila and Juan de la Cruz (John of the Cross), but also for Cervantes's contemporary and rival, the accomplished Lope de Vega, as well as for Cervantes himself. Lope de Vega, still known for his poetry as well as for his much-admired plays (which were written in verse, in the Golden Age style), drew from ancient as well as modern sources; Lope was much more overtly intellectual in his style and commitments than was Cervantes.[22] These literary and theoretical works of early-modern Spain had a blend of secular and religious themes, both of which contained political content relevant to the civil realm.

In the century following *Don Quixote*, eighteenth-century Spanish literature is often viewed as being at a low ebb, partly because of a return to classical models without much innovation; however, by the nineteenth century, Spanish fiction indisputably developed a new emphasis on contemporary life. The best-known examples of this are the popular writings of Benito Pérez Galdós and the novels of Clarín (pseudonym of Leopoldo Alas y Ureña, 1851–1901), and Emilia Pardo Bazán (a novelist and short-story writer, and the first woman to be admitted to the Spanish Academy of Language). Galdós's novel, *Fortunata y Jacinta* (1887), is sometimes ranked as Spain's number-two novel, following only *Don Quixote*. However, many modern scholars now rank Clarín's *La Regenta* (*The Regent's Wife*) much more highly than the work of Galdós (although, to his credit, Galdós himself was one of the few contemporary admirers of Clarín). These two later books would, at first, seem to have little in common with their celebrated predecessor. In contrast to *Don Quixote*, both later novels are urban (one set in Madrid, and the other implicitly in Oviedo), have far more characters (the minor characters are often the best), and stress a mercantile society. Like *Don Quixote*, all three books stress family, rank, and democratic instincts in the form of allegorical fiction. The proto-free-enterprise spirit is not so surprising in the late nineteenth century, but it is jarring to some readers to find it as early as the early seventeenth century. The later two books are also, like *Don Quixote*, anti-clerical, yet at the same time stress the need for respectability in ways that are not always ironic. Clarín and Galdós were steeped in Cervantes and borrowed meta-fictional devices from him, among other characteristics. Galdós's renowned 1900 prologue to a third edition of Clarín's *La Regenta* traces the rise of the modern European novel from *Don Quixote* through the English, French, and Russian novelists, and then back to Spain, where he says that the Spanish novelists, Clarín and himself included, restored humor to the novel after it had passed through French and Russian hands.

In the twentieth century, much of the best Spanish literature was written in the Americas. However, Spain itself produced Miguel de Unamuno, Federico García Lorca, Camilo José Cela, and Juan Goytisolo, again to give just a few examples. In Latin America, Jorge Luis Borges, Gabriel García Márquez, and Mario Vargas Llosa created a new literary tradition, often called "magical realism," in which usually just one element of magic is added to a realistic setting.[23] Almost all of these Spanish-language authors have also written *homages* to *Don Quixote*. The connections apparently go backward as well as forward. In like manner, twentieth-century magical realism seems as if it could just as easily have started much earlier in the early seventeenth century with Cervantes, or half a century later with Grimmelshausen's *Simplicissimus*.

Many modern Spanish cultural debates have emerged from the scholarship on *Don Quixote*. Philosophers Miguel de Unamuno (in *Vida de Don Quijote y Sancho, The Life of Don Quixote and Sancho*, 1914) and José Ortega y Gasset (in *Meditaciones del Quijote, Meditations on Quixote*, also 1914) drew on the novel to explore what was valuable in Spanish tradition and what would need to be challenged or thrown overboard in a period of political crisis and rapid economic, demographic, and social transformation, post 1898.[24] There was an obsession with lost empire in this period of extremely rapid industrialization, urbanization, economic and demographic growth, and cultural flourishing in Spain. Unamuno and Ortega were responding to a time of great progress, not decline. *Don Quixote* is used as a touchstone in Spanish culture in both good times and bad. To give one key example, the influential scholar of Spanish literature,

Américo Castro, an exile from Franco's Spain, argued that Spanish national identity began only in the midst of the complexities and peculiar alliances during the Moorish occupation, and that Spanish cultural formation was slowed down by the reconquest of the Spanish peninsula by the Christians. Castro's claims led to a greater appreciation of the three cultures that formed Spain—Christian, Muslim, and Jewish.[25]

3 The Author: Miguel de Cervantes Saavedra (1547–1616)

For almost all his adult life, Cervantes considered himself to be a failure for not achieving artistic success or financial security. Cervantes's situation can be contrasted with that of his exact contemporary, Shakespeare, who achieved fame during his lifetime.[26] Yet in retrospect, it seems evident that Cervantes could not have written *Don Quixote* without his range of mostly miserable experiences as a soldier, as a slave, as a supplicant (when seeking compensation for his military injuries), as a minor courtier to the Spanish King Philip II, and as a tax collector. These colorful biographical details do not, however, sufficiently account for how Cervantes was able to present what is effectively a cultural history of his time, including not only Catholics, but also Jews, New Christians (also called *conversos*, converted Jews), *marranos* (converted Jews who nevertheless still practiced Judaism secretly, and there is some thought that Cervantes's own family members might have been *conversos*, if not *marranos*), Muslims, *moriscos* (Spanish Muslims who converted, or their ancestors converted, to Catholicism), Basques, and gypsies, all of whom were residents in some numbers in Spain at the time. In his acclaimed novel, Cervantes gives an account of a dry, poverty-stricken region of Spain, as an example of the collapse of traditional Spanish society overall—marked especially by the breakdown of aristocratic society, the rise of commercial enterprises, and the power struggle between very different ethnic and religious groups.

Most of Cervantes's life was spent in the same area. Miguel de Cervantes Saavedra was born in Alcalá de Henares, even then a famous university town, just northeast of Madrid, in 1547. Ignatius Loyola, the founder of the Jesuits, attended the university in Alcalá until he was imprisoned and tried for heresy. Indeed, the Quixote character could be linked to Loyola's presentation of himself, in his autobiography, complete with the story of a wandering penitent and an historical account of his life, including his aristocratic background, his profound education, and his ability to attract amazingly loyal followers.[27] Well-educated, dedicated to higher aims, and poor are descriptions that fit Loyola, the author Cervantes, and his character Quixote. Indeed, to pose an authoritarian interpretation of *Don Quixote*, the dictum sometimes associated with the Jesuits, to "know thy enemy," could be used to explain Cervantes's detailed scrutiny of all social groups in Spain. It would not be possible to control Spain unless one first knew it in all its forms. Whatever the author's conscious intentions, *Don Quixote*, in line with his own life experiences, is grounded in both detail of local life and also in a sense of a larger nation.

Unlike the case for many later famous authors, there is no danger that a fascination with Cervantes's life will take over from the study of his work, as it is still hard to piece together his life story at all. Cervantes's background was solid, but not grand.[28] It is well known that his father was a barber, which at this stage of Spanish history meant that he was also a surgeon, a poorly paid profession, and the family moved often. Typical of the time and of the family's social station, Cervantes's mother was presumably responsible for his education. There is a story that Cervantes was educated by a well-known tutor, who may even arranged to have some of the boy's work published for him. The transition to the next stage of his life is even less clear, and there is no direct evidence, for example, regarding how Cervantes became such a great reader. Overall, it seems that his young adult life was marked by poverty and adventure, his great expectations were encouraged by mixing with people of wealth and power, which together set the tone for the rest of his life. After his studies ended (he probably did not attend university, even though there were many fine universities in Spain at the time), he spent six years in Italy, mainly in Rome (where he served a future cardinal) and in Naples.[29] Apparently by this point, it had become prudent for him to leave Spain for some substantial time, perhaps because of difficulties following a duel.

Cervantes was no isolated scholar, indeed, but he was an active participant in one of the most famous battles in European history. It is known that he became a sailor on an Italian ship. He fought, apparently with some distinction, in the famous Battle of Lepanto. This battle is taken to be one of the turning points of Western European history, for on that day, October 7, 1571, the Venetians decisively beat the Ottoman Turks. The victory of the Battle of Lepanto is taken as effectively ending the threat of Turkish invasion in Western Europe. Titian, Tintoretto, and Veronese are among the artists who painted this crucial battle.[30] Cervantes lost the use of his left hand at Lepanto, as he (presumably right-handed) later, supposedly, and certainly immodestly, wrote,

Thy left hand shattered lost the active power
It once possessed, for glory of the right![31]

Thus he claimed that all that actually mattered was that he could write.

Sometime later, he and his brother Rodrigo were taken captive by Barbary pirates, at sea in the Mediterranean, and taken to Tunisia. Cervantes engineered several escape attempts; however, they all failed, and it took five years for family and friends to raise the substantial sum required to buy the brothers' freedom (kidnapping and then ransoming Europeans were substantial cottage industries in North Africa at the time). Cervantes returned to these themes repeatedly in his writing.

Ironically, this time spent in North Africa made Cervantes suspect of both treason and apostasy.[32] On his return to Spain, Cervantes was not able to get a typical job for a veteran, such as working for a noble family. He was, however, somehow able to write, ferociously, in many different genres (he had a love of drama in particular, but never gained fame as a playwright), and he slowly gained a substantial reputation as a writer. Financial problems plagued him throughout his life. He took various government jobs, but his overzealousness as a tax collector and then the disappearance of some of his takings meant that he was then no longer able to obtain government positions. He spent some time in jail—at least twice—perhaps partly for these financial improprieties, although his family seems to have been an easy target for lawsuits. It was in prison that he started to write *Don Quixote*.

Cervantes's personal life is likewise not easy to assess. He may have had a son in Rome. He had a daughter in Spain who lived with him. Soon after his daughter's birth, he married, but not his daughter's mother. He and his wife had no children. Overall, not much is known about the any of the women in his life—his daughter's mother, his daughter, or his wife. This lack of a detailed historical record of their lives is, sadly, commonplace for women, even for family members of famous men, in the early-modern period. There is also no record of his possible Italian son, although it is known that his daughter joined a convent. The persistent themes throughout Cervantes's life, as a child and then as an adult, professionally and personally, were isolation and serious financial difficulties.

It also seems clear, however, that Cervantes suffered from depression and felt he was prevented from having a full social and intellectual life. This isolation was at least partially contextual. He did not have the company of an academy, a confraternity, a university or, in later life, a royal court, any one of which might have made his inner compulsions toward writing literature seem more natural, even conventional. At several times, he decided he would not be able to make a living by literature, but nevertheless he returned to writing every time.

Cervantes wrote, almost compulsively, in a wide range of genres—all of them can be found, in capsule form, in *Don Quixote*. He wrote plays, poetry, and other fiction, notably *La Galatea (Galatea, A Pastoral Romance, 1585)*. His *Novelas exemplares (Exemplary Stories, 1613)* still receive attention in their own right.[33] They are compelling short stories, with substantial political and economic content, grounded in the complexities of seventeenth-century Spain. They are much more than simply the early work before *Don Quixote*. Less well known is that, following *Don Quixote*, Cervantes wrote an epic novel, *Persiles y Sigismunda (Persiles and Sigismunda)*, which he finished just days before his death (published posthumously in 1617) and which he considered his greatest work.[34]

In sum, Cervantes seems like one of the more outrageous, immoderate, uncivilized characters from his own fiction. His writing, especially in *Don Quixote*, is markedly autobiographical. Cervantes covered thousands of miles (although later in life, the same miles, as a tax collector), suffered multiple reversals of fortune, and somehow persisted in believing in his talent despite repeated rebuffs, including financial difficulties, outright poverty and debt, and imprisonment, right up until his death in 1616, which occurred soon after the publication of Part II of *Don Quixote*. This is of interest not only in term of theories of genius, but also in economic terms. The constant setbacks not only gave Cervantes more material to write about, but perhaps also intensified his resolve to write, precisely because he was seemingly being discouraged from doing so. (The process of recovery could be argued in economic terms to have made Cervantes stronger each time, for, like a business cycle, nothing was necessarily lost in a downturn that could not be more than recouped on the next upswing; however, much dross would have usefully been discarded at each downturn.) Thus, Cervantes's life could astonishingly be seen to fit into the ideal pattern for what he was to become, or what he seemed to be consciously on course to become: an author who reflected often-contradictory versions of being Spanish, indeed of being human. His supposedly indomitable qualities as a writer might be better viewed as flexibility combined with strength, which allowed him to achieve his personal goal, to write about abstract ideas in literature.

4 Historical Setting: The Age of Philip II (1550–1598)

Cervantes's life overlapped with the rule of Philip II and the Golden Age of Spain, roughly 1550–1680, during which time noble patrons supported writers and artists in a manner reminiscent of Renaissance Florence.[35] Spain was the greatest power in Europe in the sixteenth century. The Spanish conquest of Mexico began in 1519, and this was the age of widespread Spanish imperial dominance in the Americas. During Philip's rule, Spain was the wealthiest and most powerful country in the world. The characterization of Spain's economic circumstances as taken from *Don Quixote* on La Mancha must, once again, be contrasted with the historical economic fluctuations of this often-dominant nation. Philip II became King of Spain in 1556 (although he had been the boy king of Milan since 1540). One of the most remarkable rulers of European history, he was an absolute monarch, in a time otherwise marked across Europe by conciliarism, a reform movement that gained power *vis-à-vis* the pope, in a time when the pope wielded considerable political clout. The remarkably talented Philip II, did not, however, take advice from anyone, even from his own advisers, and he was not shy.[36] He suppressed Protestantism, and he made the entire Iberian Peninsula Spanish by taking over the Portuguese throne.[37] Although he was a patron to individual scholars, he also suppressed the arts, as Cervantes himself complained.[38] In short, the story about Philip II is mixed. Known for encouraging the Inquisition and approving of the expulsion of the Jews and the Moors (both groups had been expelled by Ferdinand and Isabella in 1492), he is also praised for rebuilding Toledo and for ensuring domestic security, making Spain a safe place to travel under his rule. Building on the legacy of his father, Charles V (who himself ruled over land in at least three continents), Philip II was then to rule over the first empire in history upon which the sun never set.[39]

Philip II was also responsible, against the advice of his admirals, for sending the supposedly invincible Spanish Armada to its defeat by the English navy in 1588. The defeat, so startling at the time, now seems inevitable, military historians having determined, among other reasons, that the English could discharge a full fusillade (a continuous, rapid discharge of firearms) once an hour, and the Spanish only once a day.[40] This seems to be a fitting metaphor for feudal Spain, which was unable to adapt to the changing political situation.

Allegorically, the character Don Quixote represents an archaic Spain unable to adapt to the new world. However, it could be argued that it was not "Spain" that was unable to adapt; after all, it had had a flourishing economy from antiquity through the Middle Ages and the Renaissance until the 1570s and 1580s. It was particular policies by specific monarchs, notably Philip II, Philip III, and Philip IV, who were intent on retaining hopelessly overstretched and far-flung dominions, that damaged Spain's economy, especially, oddly enough, that of powerful Castile, the region that claimed credit for the formation of the state of Spain (and the Spanish language is still often called *castellano*, Castilian). When Philip II died in 1598, just seven years before the publication of Part I of *Don Quixote*, taxation was oppressive, and the country was ruled by the power of the Inquisition, which Philip II had enthusiastically supported. After his death, the malignant image of Philip II was mixed in popular European consciousness with anti-Jewish and anti-Moorish sentiments, leading to a general disparagement of all things Spanish.

Spanish power continued to decline during the reigns of the next two monarchs, his son, Philip III, and his grandson, Philip IV. By 1655, France was the leading power on the continent, and Spain had lost most of its Lowland territories except Flanders, which, with the Peace of Utrecht, passed to Austria in 1713. Spain fought the Ottoman Empire to the south and increasingly was bested by France in Europe, and by the Portuguese, English, and Dutch overseas. Although Spain was a powerful military force when Cervantes was an adult, in many ways it could be judged to have been lagging behind some of the other European powers even by that time. Again according to Elliott, Cervantes's life "spans the two ages of imperial triumph and imperial retreat. . . . The crisis of the late sixteenth century cuts through the life of Cervantes as it cuts through the life of Spain."[41] This mixture of immense power and impending doom could also serve as a description of the backdrop of *Don Quixote* itself.

5 Link to Marcus Aurelius (121–180 A.D.)

Another European monarch could be linked, in a literary sense, perhaps even more strongly than Philip II to Cervantes: the ancient Roman Emperor Marcus Aurelius. In the history of ideas, there are some remarkable examples of the transcendence of ideas over personal, contextual circumstances. One such case is that of Marcus Aurelius, one of the three most renowned Stoic thinkers (the others are Epictetus, a former slave, and Cicero, one of the greatest Roman orators and writers). Stoicism was marked by self-knowledge and detachment from the world, even from emotion itself. There is the pronounced sense in Marcus Aurelius's writings that his day job (being emperor of the Roman Empire) took him away from his favored activities of intensive reading and writing, most of which he did at night, often when he was on a military campaign. In his *Meditations* (written in Greek, also known as *Thoughts* or *Writings Addressed to Himself*, and sometimes simply as *To Myself*), Marcus Aurelius wrote as a means to make sense of his own place in the world, a process that is itself part of Stoicism.[42] Marcus Aurelius's work can be compared to John Donne's early seventeenth-century poem beginning "Death be not proud," and also to Rudyard Kipling's poem "If" (1910), beginning "If you can keep your head when all about you/Are losing theirs and blaming you," and ending "You'll be a Man My son!" Marcus Aurelius has remained a perennial favorite through the centuries. He was, for example, one of John Stuart Mill's favorite writers. Mill is the author of *On Liberty* (1859), which codifies the classical liberalism of that century and shows evidence of decided Stoic leanings. Yet for all of Marcus Aurelius's reflective tendencies and later, liberal connections, it has been suggested that if good Roman emperors killed some Christians, then Marcus Aurelius was a very good emperor indeed.[43] A remarkable military tactician, Marcus Aurelius was also uncommonly shrewd at spotting talent and employing similarly gifted people, personally recruiting some of the great minds of his time.

Marcus Aurelius's written work can be linked with profit not just to other works of Stoicism, but also to the even earlier work of Lucretius (1st century B.C.), whose *De Rerum Natura* (*On the Nature of the Universe*), is the classic statement of Epicureanism, putting forward early articulations of both atomic theory and the cyclical view of history.[44] *On the Nature of the Universe* and Marcus Aurelius's *Meditations* remain, as well, marvelous books for pleasure reading. Marcus Aurelius's emphasis on developing a sense of oneself, perhaps in direct opposition to the qualities of those nearby, was linked to a belief that the universe is internally coherent. For Marcus Aurelius, it is not only possible for the individual to develop a distinct sense of oneself in the universe, it is also useful, for this sense can be so strong that it can hold off even the horror of death, which for him meant non-existence.

Returning to *Don Quixote*, although the title hero is in a great many respects a fool, not a powerful or wise man, his story could also be read as a record of the dark doubts of a highly reflective individual born at the wrong time. Thus *Don Quixote* can be argued to embody the qualities of two celebrated European monarchs, the self-assurance of Philip II of early-modern Spain, and the self-doubt of Marcus Aurelius, Emperor of Rome and Stoic philosopher.

6 Synopsis

In *Don Quixote*, the intellectual messages are conveyed not just through farcical false dichotomies and silly straw-man fallacies, but also through the presentation of abstract ideas from the mouths of the most ludicrous advocates, Sancho Panza and Don Quixote. This novel is grounded in the rich intellectual and literary history of Europe, not just of Spain. The author lived a colorful if impoverished life that gave him the opportunities, however unsought (for example, as a captive in North Africa, and as a prisoner at home in Spain), to investigate social worlds unlike his own. Yet *Don Quixote* is grounded not just in high culture and low culture, but also in the political realities of a country in decline from the affluence that had so marked the age of Philip II. Part I of *Don Quixote* was published just seven years after the death of Philip II. The novel is grounded as well in the Stoic tradition of Marcus Aurelius, which was presented in the form of memoir and philosophical reflections. Claims about the theoretical content in Cervantes's novel could, however, be made even for much earlier literary works, certainly including the writings of Lucretius and Marcus Aurelius. In this chapter, the emerging economic theories of mercantilism and physiocracy will be examined in order to trace some of the intellectual contributions of this illustrious work, a book that is usually hailed as a masterpiece for entirely different reasons.

II *DON QUIXOTE* RECONSIDERED: SANCHO PANZA ON GOOD GOVERNMENT; JOHN LOCKE, AND THE ORIGINS OF MARKET CAPITALISM

1 Economic Setting: Mercantilism

Don Quixote is, in part, a reflection on older patterns of economic thought circulating in Spain and elsewhere in Europe in the early seventeenth century.[45] The roots of Spanish mercantilism, in particular, are to be found in Spanish economic thought since the Middle Ages. Spanish ideas, especially from the medieval School of Salamanca—known for its substantial contributions to theology, law, and economics—provide an immediate context for what we find in *Don Quixote*.

    Don Quixote was written during the early phase of mercantilism in the seventeenth century; in the next century, mercantilism was the economic policy of the rising nation-states across Europe.[46] Mercantilism was thus the *de facto* economic system of Europe in the early-modern period and then the explicit economic system at the time of the shift to the modern age. Most obviously, mercantilism was identified with strong leadership, usually that of the king, and flamboyant displays of wealth at court—whether in London, Paris, or Madrid. There was no separation between political and economic decision making, and it was always centralized. Mercantilism was a means of displaying the strength of the country, financially and in other ways, such as in the creative arts, which each country wished to celebrate.[47] More precisely, mercantilism was distinguished by an emphasis on money— gold, silver, and bullion—over wealth in any other form, be it land, capital, or labor. National wealth was thus determined by the amount of money a nation possessed. Nations actively sought to amass wealth in the form of money, often from the Americas, the new source of treasure.

However, mercantilism was marked not just by tremendous amounts of wealth, but was further demarcated by very particular government policies: a strong preference for exports over imports, by tariffs, and by the protection of infant industries. The early-modern period was dominated by an unexpressed yet virtually wholesale belief in absolute advantage, a concept codified that maintains that each nation trade the goods for which they have an advantage to produce (for example, a geographic advantage). This injunction was difficult to follow, especially because of the high demand for foreign luxury items, which were wholly unavailable in Europe and only produced in Asia (for example, silk and spices) and the Americas (for example, gold and silver), and later for commodity items (such as tea from Asia, and tobacco from the Americas). Thus mercantilism was driven by two opposing forces—the desire to support domestic industry and yet a parallel equally strong desire for foreign, much-sought-after goods. Mercantilism remained the dominant, if loosely organized economic approach in Europe during the seventeenth and eighteenth centuries.

Perversely, it is Adam Smith, who, although opposed to mercantilism, actually coins the term "mercantilism." Smith still supports absolute advantage (the theory that nations should be self-sufficient, not reliant on imports), although he discards not only the more ostentatious aspects of mercantilism and, more crucially, the extensive role of the government in the economy. These ostentatious qualities included, but were not limited to, sumptuous buildings, decorations, costumes, and fanfare at the royal court. The peculiarity of Smith's formulation of the theory of absolute advantage is that his work overall more accurately foreshadows the slightly later approach of David Ricardo on the same subject, rather than the mercantilist approach. The belief in absolute advantage was, in the early nineteenth century, replaced by Ricardo's counter-intuitive notion of comparative advantage (the argument that it is best for nations to divide up the goods to be traded, even if one nation seems to have the absolute advantage in all the relevant items). This shifted the emphasis in trade to specialization and a global division of labor. Adam Smith's 1776 *Wealth of Nations* is rightly understood as a major attack on mercantilism. Nevertheless, although it is generally assumed that mercantilism died out after the ascendancy of market capitalism, often marked by the publication of *Wealth of Nations*, this is not actually correct.

There is no shortage of examples of the ongoing influence of mercantilism. The first example is that Adam Smith himself approved of the English Navigation Acts, a fierce case of mercantilist protectionism enacted by Cromwell—who was, if not the king, very much the strong ruler during the English Civil War in the mid-seventeenth century—as necessary to build up the English navy; the expansion of the English navy would lead directly to the rise of British imperialism. In terms of ongoing influence, many economists today, economists of various stripes, still accept the protection of infant industries. The second example of the ongoing influence of mercantilism is the mercantilist emphasis on data. This is understandable in historical terms, as so many mercantilist writers were themselves merchants and government officials rather than professors.

However, Smith and other classical economists rejected both the mercantilist, and later physiocrat, emphasis on the collection and use of data in favor of theory.[48] (Later social scientists would almost never regard it as necessary, or beneficial, to choose between theory and data; quite the reverse.) Particular mercantilists are still cited for their contributions; for example, Thomas Mun, an early-modern merchant and the best-known mercantilist writer, is credited with putting emphasis on services, that is including labor (not just land or even trade) in the overall evaluation of the economy.

Most tellingly, the lasting impact of mercantilism can be traced to John Maynard Keynes, the major economist of the twentieth century, who not only wished to return to various mercantilist premises, but also to rehabilitate the term "mercantilism" itself.[49] He failed on this later point, however. The connections between John Locke and Keynes are well known; this chapter proposes a connection between *Don Quixote* and John Locke, and thus implicitly also between *Don Quixote* and Keynes.

Amusingly, the most lasting example of ongoing mercantilist influence begins with Keynes, who employed substantial elements of mercantilist thought in his own attack on *laissez-faire* economics in the first half of the twentieth century.[50] Here in accord with the mercantilists, Keynes emphasized the money supply and stressed not only the utility, but the necessity of government intervention in his own time, that of the Great Depression, a time of extraordinarily high unemployment rather than high inflation. The recent view of Keynes as concerned more with institutional change than with business cycles implicitly highlights his mercantilism. Keynes's embrace of mercantilism is—perversely, as they are assumed to be antithetical in their economic views—not wholly unlike Smith's usage of some elements of mercantilism. Smith's desire for a new economic system in the late eighteenth century was not so strong that he was willing to jettison what were for him the most appealing aspects of mercantilism.

Smith was not unaware of the logical inconsistencies in his thought; rather, this compromise is best viewed as a practical and shrewd move on his part. It is a clear indication that he was outlining an emerging system, not writing the manifesto for a system already solidly entrenched. Smith's work is rightly understood as the statement of the British industrial merchant classes (although not the merchant classes that invested in the slave trade) in the eighteenth century, but his capitalist approach was underpinned by the elements of mercantilism that still made this relatively new economic system most profitable for these same merchants.

2 The Morisco Ricote, the Missing King, and Mercantilism

There is a telling example in *Don Quixote* of the notion of a polity, which emphasizes the autonomous role of individuals, not just an authoritarian form of government. This incident features a *morisco* (again, a Spanish Catholic of Muslim descent), Ricote, Sancho's former neighbor, who first makes an appearance in Part II, Chapter 54. Ricote, who had been a shopkeeper in Sancho's village, has now been reduced to begging, following the anti-Moorish royal edict. Ricote and Sancho meet on the side of the road, during Quixote and Sancho's travels, and Ricote tells Sancho of his failed attempts to find a new home for his family; Ricote becomes the center of a reflection on religious toleration and on what it means to belong to a polity. As their conversation continues, it becomes clear that their fellow villagers were sad about the forced departure of Ricote, his family, and the other *morisco* exiles, thus distancing themselves from the royal expulsion decree. However, the villagers hold back from expressing their disapproval, or from even harboring Ricote's beautiful daughter, whom they genuinely like, for fear of repercussions.[51] Nevertheless this brief story emphasizes the role of individual decision making separate from the power of an authoritarian government; the state may dictate the villagers' actions, but not their sympathies.

This episode has long been regarded as key evidence for a conception of *patria*, a homeland, a sorely missed homeland, that set aside religion and emphasized shared language and customs, such as food and drink. In this scene the *morisco* drinks wine and eats ham, forbidden by his religion, and the drinking accompanies food and conversation with Sancho; this Epicurean style is in marked contrast to the German pilgrims nearby, who get drunk and pass out. Ricote is viewed as a good neighbor, one who is being driven from the region for his religious and cultural background, not because he is an economic threat, and in this story, this is deemed peculiar.[52]

This small episode in *Don Quixote*, perhaps the quintessential story of the novel, oddly foreshadows the call of the eighteenth-century *philosophes* (Voltaire in particular) to the rulers of Europe to enact fundamental, social change leading to a more egalitarian society, free of the control of the Church. Voltaire had some limited success in this regard with both Catherine the

Great in Russia and Friedrich the Great in Prussia. The references to kings in *Don Quixote*, however, go beyond kowtowing to the notion of the divine right of kings, even when one knows the king to be wrong or unnecessarily severe. They point in particular to the king as being much more than a mere embodiment of a form of government, and to his role as the chief financial officer of the country. The king is thus the operating force of mercantilism in a practical, not just symbolic manner. The character Quixote is not trying to bring down the king, he is trying to change the role, the function, of the king. The novel *Don Quixote* shows a particular interest in ferreting out sources of wealth, and controlling the cycles through which this wealth filters through society.

It might be surprising in a work on individual lunacy that the reader also finds not only a detailed exploration not only of economic relations, but also of the limits of national power. To a great extent, the king is merely a figurehead in this story. The priest, the barber/doctor, and to some extent, the younger Bachelor (the university graduate) hold the real power in Quixote's village of La Mancha. These supposed friends of Quixote, presumably the only other educated men in the village, function, in effect, not unlike the friends of the biblical Job. They make Quixote's life very much worse, not just by burning his books (perversely the books are chosen for destruction by size, and some of the choices for burning are, by accident, religious books) but also by designing complicated tricks to play on him (at one stage binding his hands and bringing him back from his travels in a cage), supposedly for his own good; and, almost up to the time of his death, by restraining him, putting him under effective house arrest, so that he cannot live out his quest.

In contrast to this small, claustrophobic group of friends, the remoteness, the starkness, of this region of La Mancha is surprising, even now; likewise the emphasis throughout the story is on power at the local rather than national level, and on suspicion of all authorities—especially ones that cannot be seen—notably, the king. All of this would seemingly lead to criticism of organized religion; however, this is done in only the gentlest ways in the text, perhaps indicating an affection for religion, as much as fear of it. In *Don Quixote*, one can discern a very healthy, Mediterranean respect for the power of the ruler (both religious and political), deference that is genuine, but not naive, certainly not servile. Quixote repeatedly compares himself to a medieval warrior knight, presumably on a royal mission; this bolsters the reading of Quixote as a major political force, on a mission to revamp his country in many diverse spheres.

The Quixote figure could indeed be explained by the notion drawn from medieval theology of "The King's Two Bodies," from Ernst Kantorowicz, as a means to understand the developing notion of national sovereignty in Europe in the early-modern period.[53] *Don Quixote* is riddled with repeated references to the protagonist's skinny legs and his unclean shirts. Yet even the most literal reading does not use the body of Quixote as grounds for dismissing his message altogether. Indeed, Quixote's wholly unprepossessing physical appearance to some degree makes his mission even more persuasive. In the Middle Ages, the era that preoccupied Quixote much more than his own, it was assumed that if the lower body of the king is corporeal, earthy, then his upper body is taken to be divine, for he is "God's Lieutenant on earth," to use a phrase favored by James I of England.[54] For the Quixote figure, the lower body is certainly that of a fool, albeit one with perhaps a mystical connection to God. Even while Quixote is falling, sometimes without even being pushed, he is often mouthing words that transcend his time and place. His upper body is that of a leader who uses his foolishness, his lower body, to win over the people for a higher purpose. Quixote draws on older sources—in this case not only that of chivalry, but also on the medieval political theory of "the King's two bodies"—in order to change the world in which he lives.

The theme of the divine right of kings, of the constructive rule of the king for all his people, and the comingling of Church and state, is not just medieval. It can be fully found as late as the compelling writings of James I of England in the early-seventeenth century. James, an exact contemporary of Cervantes, is best known for commissioning, and perhaps contributing toward the translation of the 1611 Authorized Version (also known as the King James Bible), and he had a vested interest in propounding the divine right of kings. Thus Quixote, simultaneously mocking and invoking the theory of the divine right of kings, claims to have transcendental approval for his project, in his case from medieval chivalric sources.

Continuing this metaphor, Quixote's upper body could also be taken to represent the state, an "imagined community," to use Benedict Anderson's term, a society that is not primarily delineated by common land, property, language, or even specific people (common lines along which nations form, according to Max Weber), but rather by the group's acceptance that it comprises a separate, autonomous (however little-recognized) society. Dispossessed peoples (such as those lost peoples described with care by Eric R. Wolf in *Europe and the People without History*) would have had just as much claim to be such an "imagined community" as, for example, the French, who possessed the only unified nation-state on the continent before the nineteenth century.[55] Just as the original concept of "the King's Two Bodies" was used to bind together the Church and state in western Europe, and thus to establish the rule of law, Quixote is implicitly calling on religious and secular forces to support him in his one-man, rather pitiful fight against modernity.

3   Windmills

The windmills and watermills are, in the most tangible sense, Quixote's explicit foes in his attack on developing industry. Tilting at windmills (this well-known phrase refers to one of Quixote's favored forms of attack, called tilting, as derived from the medieval sport of jousting) is not just a means of demonstrating, in choreographed form, Quixote's desire to bring back a medieval sensibility.[56] The choice of mills—used for grinding grain, and forming the base of an agricultural economy—as his particular, *modern* enemy is slightly perverse, because mills had existed for at least a thousand years at the time that *Don Quixote* was written. (Mills powered by horses and donkeys have been found in the ruins of Pompeii, destroyed in the first century A.D., and the first horizontal windmill was believed to have been in Persia, in the seventh century A.D.)[57] Windmills are, more crucially for the purposes of this story, also examples of the more developed technology of the medieval period, and by 1605, when Part I of *Don Quixote* was published, they were widespread in Persia, Tibet, China, and throughout Europe.[58] Thus windmills were a potent symbol of successful emerging technology, even though they were also part of a much older industrial framework.

For all these ancient and medieval connections, the windmills symbolized, even for most seventeenth-century readers, both a mystical Enchanter (for Quixote, a specific one, who is so immediate that Quixote calls the Enchanter by a particular name, albeit a nonsense name, Friston) and certainly an established profession, but also the economic shifts that were later identified as emerging capitalism. It is the representatives of this economic shift staff the windmills. The millers (along with Sancho) are put forward in *Don Quixote* as textual examples not only of a rough but vocal working class, but also (and here unlike Sancho) of an emerging skilled group outside of the cities. Early-modern guilds, made up of highly specialized artisans, existed primarily in cities. They generally functioned on a remarkably high skill level, both artistically and bureaucratically, producing, for example, the homes, furniture, and clothing for royals, aristocrats, and the slowly-developing *nouveaux riches*. However, the guilds employed relatively few people, and thus did not, on their own, mark a shift in overall economic activity, much less in economic and social class, for most Europeans, throughout the Middle Ages. The millers, who were primarily rural, not urban, and not members of a traditional guild, represent a new, more widespread form of labor specialization.

Quixote is, however, doubly occupied; he is at war not only with modern sensibilities, but also with the magical forces that a medieval knight supposedly would have pursued. Even if, in the novel, the Enchanter is the real enemy for Don Quixote, the windmills are, for him, the obvious manifestation of a multitude of evil, unavoidable giants all around. Therefore, for Quixote, and clearly also for many readers, the windmills represent all that is outwardly profitable, yet spiritually vacant. This combination is anathema to Quixote, someone "who does not need breakfast, only savoury memories."[59]

It is not that the physical world holds no fascination for Quixote. He has not chosen to be a monk, but rather a knight, in pursuit of what he so very much wants. He is surely on a quest for love, but he also desires a radically altered society in which life is easier for all, not because of a new democratic arrangement but rather because the old order, based on equity rather than equality, is finally working the way it should, albeit in an Aristotelian, patriarchal sense. For Quixote, this society would interact similarly to an early-modern, functional family, with the parents making decisions for young children, and the father making the ultimate decisions for them all.[60] Quixote is not unaware of his surroundings; rather, he believes that the physical, economic, and political world in which he lives can only be reformed when the abstract ideas that support it have been rearranged. He viewed the world as a puzzle, with all the necessary pieces present to make it a beautiful whole, but with substantial work needed to make this happen.

Although tilting at the windmills (now often taken to represent failed enterprises, and a resistance to all change) clearly indicates a rejection of the growth and expansion of modern technology and science, yet the message of the book is more complicated. The Quixote story is set in an agricultural economy, not an urban one, be it medieval or modern. Yet the agricultural sector is attacked regularly throughout the story. The book targets patterns of abuse, oversight, and foolishness more than the particular institutions themselves. In this manner, *Don Quixote* can be distinguished from *Candide*, which attacks both social institutions and human nature. This does not necessarily make the earlier, Spanish work any less radical in political and economic terms, but instead indicates that its means of reform were from the inside rather than the outside. Thus *Don Quixote* calls for reform within existing institutions, not for the overthrow of them.[61]

Returning to Quixote's windmills, Quixote grasps that the windmills are a threat, (whether or not they are enchanted); over and over he cites the value of experience in making economic progress, and this is clear in the historical case of the windmills. However, he notes this as a part of expanding common wisdom, not simply as the accrued benefit of a single established system, even that of chivalry. At one stage, for example, the millers recognize Quixote as a threat to their livelihood, or they are simply annoyed, and they knock Quixote into the water.[62] They save him when it becomes clear that he cannot save himself, given his armor and, of course, because of his general ineptitude. This is a straightforward example of the reformer being dependent on those he is attacking. The book repeatedly cites the need to conserve the high and low culture, the efforts of intellectuals and of the working people, even when their ideas are seemingly in conflict, in order to move successfully into the future.[63]

Regularly overlooked in *Don Quixote* (especially by modern readers consciously seeking abstract ideas in the text) are the tales and verses (often modern readers' least-favorite part of the novel) that actually provide substantial material on economic thought, itself a modern preoccupation. One way of understanding the many, many songs in the novel, including, for example, "The Despairing Verses of the Dead Shepherds and other

Unexpected Matters," (Part I, Chapter 14), written, like most of the book, purportedly only about love, as indicating cultural, often-repeated reference points for a shifting economic system. In this section of the novel, Cervantes's own strong concern for the pastoral and for story lines from antiquity is evident. The songs reflect both the upper-class troubadour tradition of the Middle Ages, and likewise directly set up many of the concerns of the working classes, such as personal injuries that are often not recognized, and for which the transgressors are not forced to atone. The shepherds represent the agricultural workers (favored by physiocracy, to be discussed below) as being the most productive workers in the economic system. The isolation of the shepherds does not dilute either the fundamental importance of their work or their ability to pass on their message in songs over generations, much like, in oral tradition, the Greek rhapsodes, the wandering Greek storytellers of antiquity, known for reciting Homer (although they are now believed to have collectively composed the two great works of Homer). The book praises the simple work of agricultural workers as not only somehow more virtuous than that of city workers (and note the distinction here from Aristotle's disdain for farmers in particular, which remained into the early-modern period) but also highly productive. Thus many of the icons of this work, windmills or shepherds' songs, often have multiple purposes, playful and sometimes also intellectual.

4 Physiocracy

A pre-Adam Smith challenge to mercantilism arrived in the form of earlier eighteenth-century French physiocracy. This system of thought, perhaps the first organized economic system, emphasized the land, agricultural workers, and agricultural products over all other factors in the economy. Both mercantilism and physiocracy developed out of very specific financial circumstances, not out of preexisting economic theory. Thus, the physiocrat emphasis on agriculture over industry did not indicate a lack of prescience on the part of these French writers. It was instead a direct attempt to better the actual situation of France, a country almost wholly dependent on agriculture as its main source of wealth. France had no emerging industries, even in this period of the supposed high-cultural ascendancy of the French Enlightenment, in the decades leading up to the French Revolution.[64] (And, it is often said, not entirely as a joke, that France had its industrial revolution after World War II. The lack of demand for women workers in industry in France before 1945 helps to explain why women were late to join the work force in France, and also, partially, to account for why women received the vote in France only in 1944; France was the last country in Europe to make this change.) In any case, France, in the early-modern period was dependent on agriculture to a debilitating extent; or, on a more positive note, it was a leading exporter of food in Europe. In theoretical terms, physiocracy challenged the emphasis on money—bullion, which is money in the form of gold and silver, in the case of mercantilism—and put the emphasis on the agricultural sector: land, goods, and services.

The physiocrats contributed much more toward emerging capitalism than to the establishment of a separate, long-lasting school of their own. As they are rarely noted together as part of the same movement, it is well worth noting in passing several of the most influential physiocrats in order to show the scope of physiocracy. *Le Tableau économique* (1759, the same year as the publication of *Candide*), written by, arguably, the leading physiocrat writer, François Quesnay, had an influence on thinkers and merchants across Europe. This work stressed that only agricultural workers were productive, and all other laborers, including merchants, were sterile in economic terms, a concept that did not win general acceptance outside of the countryside. More constructively, this work stimulated debate about the relationship among the various sectors of the economy, forcing recognition that there were, to begin, various sectors. Quesnay recognized that the wealth of the country and the population is tied to the health of the agricultural sector. In this he disagreed with Richard Cantillon (following William Petty on this point; Petty was, otherwise, perhaps the first proto-*laissez-faire* writer). Cantillon was the well-known author of *Essai sur la nature du commerce en général* (1732). Generally known for his early articulation of long-term equilibrium, a critical component of both physiocrat and capitalist thought, and of a quantity theory of money (a theory that assumes a direct relationship between money supply and price), Cantillon also wished to discourage agricultural exports. The agricultural sector was at the heart of early-modern debates about the expanding market economy. Ancillary industries—such as shipping, for example, as well as the individual parts of the agricultural sector, including grain production—were at stake in these contemporary debates regarding exports. These debates were focused primarily on the immediate situation and not on establishing an ongoing theoretical school. Cantillon's own thought is perhaps best understood as anti-mercantilist, leading toward classical economics, and stressing entrepreneurship by bolstering the notion of a natural, short-term price. Later, in the nineteenth century, William Stanley Jevons rehabilitated Cantillon's work in his utility theory. Anne-Robert-Jacques Turgot, yet another author sometimes labeled a physiocrat (more precisely a capitalist figure), put new emphasis on the entrepreneur and was a major influence on both Condorcet and Adam Smith. Turgot, regarded by many as the greatest French economist of this period, anticipated classical economics in his stress on selfishness as the prime economic motivation for the individual, and in his emphasis on both demand and free trade. Jean-Baptiste Colbert (later called the very worst French economist because of his economic decisions that led directly to the chaos that allowed the outbreak of the French Revolution) was one of the major exponents of mercantilism. The influence of these intricate, and sometimes surprisingly well-written (especially in the case of Ferdinando Galiani) debates about trade, tariffs, and especially agriculture, went far beyond that of mid-eighteenth-century *économistes.*[65] In other words, these economic ideas were both to be located in non-academic and academic writings of the time, and their influence went far beyond scholarly circles.

Don Quixote anticipated these physiocrat writers by over a century by placing the emphasis on the land as a productive force, yet doing so without isolating agriculture from other forms of economic activity, and crucially, by stressing the role of the human will (later to be termed selfishness) in economic gain. This novel gives sharp examples of how attitudes toward the land are not neutral, but rather that they determine the health of the larger national economy overall. Remembering that much of Spain's previous international dominance, and its vast wealth, had come in the form of gold, silver, and other precious metals from the Spanish colonies in the Americas, this novel's emphasis on the productive capacity of Spain itself, including Spain outside of the cities, and even in its apparently most remote, impoverished, and hottest region, is a statement of faith in Spain's ability to thrive economically even without its colonies.

5 John Locke and Emerging Capitalism

Although Adam Smith's *Wealth of Nations* is generally taken as the marker for the advent of the capitalist age, a better indicator might be the work of John Locke in the previous century.[66] Although Locke's work now tends to be studied in segments—with twenty-first-century scholars dividing up his texts into political theory, economics, psychology, and philosophy—this fragmentation is an unintended consequence of later specialization in the university world. Perhaps the best example of the unity of Locke's thought and his major contribution to the history of economic thought can be found in his concept of property.[67] Locke joined social contract theory together with an analysis of the economic underpinnings of society in a manner consistent with his theory of the workings of the human mind.

For Locke, property was created at the point when one "mixes land with one's labour," thus putting emphasis on capital in the form of land and labor, both factors that are missing from the mercantilist concern for money.[68] This is a labor theory of property, and at its core it spurns monopolistic tendencies. Locke's definition of personal, and indeed institutional, property thus defied the notions of inherited wealth and the divine right of kings, and also rejected other perhaps more modern forms of accumulated wealth. The core of Locke's thought on this subject can be found in the extraordinary Chapter V, "Of Property," of his *Second Treatise of Government*, written during the Restoration (of the English monarchy, following the English Civil War), but was not published until 1690, after the Glorious Revolution of 1688 (which not only changed the royal line, but also mandated a more limited form of monarchy).[69]

Much later, in not altogether diverse ways, Marx, and then Keynes, developed Locke's emphasis on labor. Yet economic reasoning was not simply an intellectual hobby for Locke. Although he is often viewed as only a political theorist—granted that his work was used, along with that of Montesquieu, as the basis of the American founding documents—for Locke, economic relations are at the basis of all political arrangements, and indeed economic relations serve as the key to understanding Locke's philosophical and psychological work as well. The centrality of economic relations in Locke's thought is evident in his fundamental political ideas: that human beings have reason even in the state of nature, and thus, by extension, given that human beings are naturally rational creatures, they do not owe their social order to any specific government. For Locke this demonstrated that society is separate from government. Unlike Hobbes (the first of the social contract theorists, Locke being the second), Locke argued that a society could rebel against its ruler and then go on to form another legitimate and viable government. For Hobbes, there is no right of rebellion because without the strength of the original government the society would collapse.[70] The origin of this distinction goes back even further in their theories of society: Locke differed from Hobbes on the basic nature of human beings, and thus on economic motivation. Hobbes assumes that human beings have not changed much since the state of nature, where life was "nasty, brutish, and short," thus maintaining that human nature is base. According to Hobbes, all economic activity, even in a well-regulated society, is brought about by selfishness. (This approach is perhaps best exemplified by the subtitle of Bernard Mandeville's *The Fable of the Bees: or Private Vices, Publick Benefits*, 1714, 1732). Mandeville was the whipping boy of the Enlightenment thinkers, especially Rousseau, who instead tended to argue for some degree of human perfectibility.) Rather than emphasizing corrupt human nature or perfectibility, Locke stressed reason as an innate human endowment since the state of nature. The Lockean emphasis on reason shifts the nature of economic activity from something purely greedy and short-term to a series of decisions by the individual and by the state, which should be overseeing the interests of that individual. However, reason is clearly linked to financial profit by Locke. He did not separate intellectual ability from financial shrewdness.

An emphasis on economics also helps to explain Locke's notion of "tacit consent," that simply by living in a country one accepts its rules and regulations, which thus does away with the need for an actual historical agreement, a social contract (as put forward in the work of Hobbes). According to Locke, there is little fundamental difference in human nature and economic behavior regardless of the form of government in power. The benefits of the particular form of government that he proposes are a higher standard of living and a higher quality of life. Locke's emphasis on reason did not indicate *naiveté* about human nature. His system of checks and balances within the various parts of government (mainly in the legislature and the executive; Locke paid relatively little attention to the judiciary) was a realistic means of contending with the temptations of great power.

For Locke, it is the use of money that has caused inequality in society by allowing monopolistic behavior. This parallels Marx's later assault on colonialism. Marx declared that because money earned in one part of the world could be transferred easily to another part of the world, it was possible for the economic benefits to be enjoyed far from the people who had often suffered to earn that wealth.[71] Locke's concerns about money were specific as well as theoretical. For example, he wrote papers on the possible options regarding the metallic composition of coins, the major currency in Britain in his time, thus following Gresham's Law, the assertion that when there is a legal currency, bad money drives out the good.[72] Coins made of base metals will drive out coins made of more valuable metals because the more intrinsically valuable coins will be sold for their metallic value, not traded for their legal value. Even silver in relation to gold could play the role of the base metal. This is a system of bimetallism, and indicates the use of price control. Locke's notions of the social contract, innate reason, tacit consent, the division of power within government, and his theories of money for a democratic form of government all are based on the premise that there are basic patterns of economic behavior that are, for him, grounded in the relationship between labor and property, which will be discussed below.[73]

6 Sancho Panza on Good Government

As early as Book I, Chapter 10, of *Don Quixote*, Quixote promises Sancho an island to govern at their first meeting as master and squire. And, as soon as their first major fight, against the Benedictines (members of a Catholic religious order) and the Basque (a man from the ancient ethnic group from northern Spain and southern France), was over, Sancho wants to be given his island.[74] A few minutes after his request, however, Sancho suggests that he would be willing to trade the governorship for the recipe for a particular liqueur. Nevertheless, the island remains a stable part of their ongoing conversation, symbolizing a time when Sancho, as the everyman, would have both autonomy and political clout.

Chapter 51 of Part II of *Don Quixote* (1615), on Sancho Panza's time as governor of an island (he does not realize that he was set up as part of an aristocratic prank), is a gift to political and economic theorists.[75] In a work about individual lunacy, the reader also finds a detailed exploration of the limits of national power and the basis of a capitalist economy. In the previous chapter and then specifically in this chapter, ideas of democratic government and of a modern capitalist economy with limited, but some decided, government intervention are put forward 75 years before Locke published his *Two Treatises of Government* in 1690.[76]

Sancho's bewilderingly prescient comments on good government are actually more than partly derived from Quixote's advice to Sancho, before Sancho leaves for his island.[77] Indeed, the quixotic spirit has also been embraced by readers of markedly different types. James March, a professor of International Management at Stanford Business School, argues persuasively that Quixote should be used as a model for good leadership, as he embodies persistence, imagination, discipline, joy, a love of beauty, and a strong sense of self. *"Yo sé quien soy"* ("I know who I am"), Quixote declares without apology early in his adventures, and he is no more apologetic even later, toward the end of Part I, when he is imprisoned in a cage by his supposed friends.[78] This is in line with the argument above about Quixote and "The King's Two Bodies." It assumes a logic of consequences based on a logic of identity. The relationship between Sancho and Quixote is thus a unifying line through the book, binding together both the abstract ideas as well as the story line. This interpretation of good leadership is that of a visionary ruler, and is a most positive view of a Machiavellian prince.

However, it is Sancho who sets up a government that could function even with an ordinary person in charge. This is not necessarily an argument that Sancho himself is pedestrian. Instead, rather extraordinarily, Sancho is outlining a balanced political system that would function over time, even without gifted rulers. The document by Sancho on good government, a portion of which appears below, is worthy of ongoing theoretical debate. It is grounded in the letter from Quixote to Sancho—"Visit the prisons, the slaughterhouses and the markets" and also "Do not show yourself to be greedy"—which, in a clearly Machiavellian mode, indicates the symbiotic relationship between a concern for appearances and apprehending the truth. The letter is both Platonic in its concern for "the whole"—all of society— and also Machiavellian in its sharp assertion that appearances are the same as truth for most people. Thus Quixote's advice to Sancho on the best form of government relies wholly on the mercantilist image of a strong ruler, and thus Quixote's ruler would help the people only to the extent that doing so would bolster his public image as the governor. Sancho, in this chapter, shows that a good ruler is aware of both appearance and reality, thus blending rationality and common sense.

It is of interest that Sancho's return letter to Quixote begins with pages of relatively trivial complaints; however, after all these expressions of dissatisfaction, in the next paragraph, Sancho institutes many aspects of good government, not all of them culled from Quixote's earlier letter on the same subject. This mixture of policy and problems supports the view that the workings of government have to do with the organization and easing of very minute activities in daily life. The English *Magna Carta* (1215), the American *Declaration of Independence* (1776), and the French *Déclaration des droits de l'homme et du citoyen* (*Declaration of the Rights of Man and of Citizen*, 1789) are all definitive examples of such an admixture of commonplace complaints with sweeping political claims.

This crucial paragraph in Part II, Chapter 51, directly predates many key aspects of Lockean thought; it highlights the role of private property as a fundamental part of civil society, stresses the need for balance of power in government, and directly attacks mercantilism. Monopolies are forbidden, free trade is encouraged, price fixing is disallowed, a wage rate is set (albeit to fight inflation), and the position of an inspector of the poor is created both to protect the poor and to catch any fraud. This is the quintessential passage in *Don Quixote* on properly functioning government, addressing the specific roles that the leader should fulfill. In a different political mode, it could even be argued that embedded in this paragraph is a case for the abolition of private property. One key point of similarity between Cervantes and Locke is that they both forward aspects of a modern state. The state outlined in Sancho's ordinances was organized by a benevolent dictator and could be argued to be a proto-welfare state, however far it might be from having a Lockean form of representative government.

Here is the core of that paragraph:

> That evening Sancho spent drawing up some ordinances touching on the good government of what he supposed to be his isle. He decreed that there must be no cornering of provisions in the state, and that wine could be imported from anywhere at all, on condition that its place of origin was declared, so that it could be priced according to its value, goodness and reputation. . . . He fixed the rate of servants' wages, which were mounting unchecked at a headlong pace. . . . He created and selected an inspector of the poor, not to prosecute them but to examine whether they were genuine; for under the disguise of poverty and counterfeit sores go sturdy thieves and hale drunkards. So good, in fact, were the laws he ordained that they are kept in that place to this day under the name of '*The Constitutions of the great Governor Sancho Panza.*'[79]

This extraordinary chapter represents a break from mercantilist government intervention to benefit the ruler and the wealthy. The change is toward a more open market, albeit one with government regulation, designed to protect the individual consumer (not the king). Thus it is not through the character Quixote, but through Sancho as supposed governor of the island of Barataria (from *barato* or "cheap," as Sancho gets the island for free) that the book poses the most direct questions regarding which type of government would be best for the people, and thus for the state and the whole, and also which personal qualities that are essential for a leader to govern effectively. This chapter gives two reasons why the illiterate character Sancho could potentially be a very good governor. He is grounded in the common sense of the working class, a mixture of "*discretos y tontos*" ("shrewdness and simplicity"), which is needed for a strong, stable state.[80] He has also taken into account Quixote's advice, sent by letter, thus indicating Sancho's ability to assimilate new knowledge quickly. Despite his lack of formal education, Sancho has had a remarkably wide variety of previous experiences, including time at court and at a monastery. In much the same way as Quixote earlier, again invoking the notion of "the King's Two Bodies," Sancho the fool is used for a higher purpose, that of proposing a new form of government—capitalism—in this farcical passage. A link could be made here to Locke's *Letter on Toleration* as well, which argues that people had to agree to the overall system of belief (monotheism, for Locke) in order for the overall political and social system to work. Cervantes and Locke both stressed the interworking of a grand system with its own theory as grounded in preferences from everyday life.

However, there has been little work on the connection between Cervantes and Locke in later scholarship on Locke. Nevertheless, Locke himself acknowledges his debt to this specific chapter in *Don Quixote*, in his *First Treatise of Government*. Locke declares:

> And if *Don Quixote* had taught his Squire to govern with Supreme Authority, our A. [Author, that is Robert Filmer—see below], no doubt, could have made a most Loyal Subject in *Sancho Panza's island*: and he must needs have deserved some Preferment in such Governments, since I think he is the first Politician, who, pretending to settle government upon its true Basis, and to establish the Thrones of lawful Princes, ever told the World, That he was *properly a King whose Manner of Government was by Supreme Power, by what means soever he obtained it*; which, in plain *English*, is to say that Regal and Supreme power is properly and truly his who can, by any Means, seize upon it: and if this be *properly a king*, I wonder how he came to think of, or where he will find, an *Usurper*.[81]

Locke later uses this chapter from *Don Quixote* in order to bash Robert Filmer (although now forgotten, except for Locke's attack on him, Filmer was a major figure in the defense of the theory of the divine right of kings in seventeenth-century Britain). Most crucially, this passage makes it manifestly clear that Locke not only had read *Don Quixote* (and this is a book that many people cite without reading it with care, or reading it at all), but also that Locke was familiar with this particular chapter from late in this very long novel. There are numerous constructive links here in terms of political and economic theory between Cervantes's *Don Quixote* and Locke's *Two Treatises of Government*—especially a core emphasis on property and a system of, if not yet checks and balances, at least an established system of responsibility on the part of the government toward those most vulnerable in society. Perhaps the reason so little attention has been given to this connection is that later generations of scholars and readers have automatically ignored any references to literature as having any substantive connection to the theory (and also because Locke's *First Treatise* is itself virtually ignored in favor of his *Second Treatise*) not just out of lack of interest, but because very few people read both the literature and theory of the past.

7 Link to Carlos Fuentes, *Terra Nostra (Our Land,* 1975)

Many modern novels stress similar themes of authoritarianism and corruption accompanied by a fierce desire for freedom, which is often expressed by characters who outwardly seem downtrodden by their political system. A fairly recent example has immediate political relevance to the Spanish-speaking world, especially to Latin America, yet its message is universal. *Terra Nostra (Our Land)*, by Mexican writer Carlos Fuentes (1928–2012), demands comparison to *Don Quixote*, and not just for its length—783 pages in Spanish.[82] The action of Fuentes's dense book starts in late-twentieth-century Paris, although it is set primarily in fifteenth- and sixteenth-century Spain, as well as in ancient Rome and in the early-modern New World. The present-day Paris that Fuentes depicts is literally plagued with a magical, wholly destructive disease that threatens only men, not women, thus implying a targeting of victims in structural terms. In the early-modern setting, there are almost preposterous psychological tensions not only between the members of the Spanish royal family, but also between the members of the royal family and their servants, their animals, and their hobbies, such as cathedral building. The cruelty—toward enemies, servants, family, animals, or any living obstacles—that oozes out of the pages of this book is at times genuinely revolting. If there are messages in the work of Fuentes, who has written on Cervantes, they are as ambivalent yet undeniable as those of Cervantes: contempt for arbitrary power, whatever its source; the joy of simple diversions; and a sense of destiny that is present in the most unlikely characters. In a particularly disturbing section Fuentes contends with, among other topics, the Spanish Inquisition (which began as early as 1478, and officially ended only in 1834), the expulsion of Jews from Spain (1492), and the Spanish conquest of Mexico (again, which began in 1519 and continued in full force throughout the next century). Much of *Terra Nostra* is set in the century just before *Don Quixote* was published (1605, 1615). *Terra Nostra* is comprised of political rebellion, personal dissatisfaction, manufactured families, dream sequences, and killings done solely in order to produce religious relics, bones, and other body parts. This is fiction writing on a grand scale.

Fuentes's novel, modeled directly on that of Cervantes, manifestly contains a call for nationalism. Its pragmatic agenda is to provide a forum for Latin Americans to confront their own history, and it is also a device by which to prod them into taking a more active role in the ongoing shaping of the future of politics in Latin America. *Terra Nostra* offers another classic, if fictional example of the power of colossal selfishness in building monuments and even nations, destroying the lives of countless individuals, and enabling only the few survivors to develop satisfying lives, even to become wealthy themselves. *Don Quixote* mixes material concerns and grand, abstract concepts that are delivered together by the least likely characters, and in *Terra Nostra* even by loathsome protagonists who are nevertheless not always wrong about the internal workings of their own societies. If *Don Quixote* tests the readers' willingness to find theory in fiction, *Terra Nostra* vexes readers by giving horrific characters the best insights. Both books make high demands on their readers, yet both offer the hope of raising the standard of living and the quality of life for individuals and their countries.

8 Synopsis

In *Don Quixote*, with its two strong lead characters spending most of their time wandering, not settled in their own village or even relocated in any neighboring city, it might perhaps seem a little disappointing that the book's dynamic repeatedly returns to that of small, tight groups, and not more to the internal life of these two characters; however, this highlights the utility of the characters as types. Early textual examples in the novel include Quixote's relationships with his housekeeper and his niece, both of whom live with him; and the grouping at the inn, particularly the short-tempered innkeeper, who functions as the not-very-subtle symbol of the fussiness and rules-oriented approach of the emerging, muscular middle class. The text seems based on the assumption that an autonomous individual—a child, woman, or man—must function within a group with its own rigidly defined regulations and *mores*. This leads to the encouraging conclusion that individuals can create great works, in any field, even when surrounded by a group that does not encourage them, and might even persecute them, but that at least does not fully take away their means of expression (for example, writing fiction). *Don Quixote* stresses the emergence of group identities and their relationship to the individual. The novel can be taken as a statement on the new relationship of the individual and society in the modern age. There is a shift away from the ancient and the medieval Christian perspective on the individual. Certainly Augustine's *Confessions*, in late antiquity, was indeed the story of one man's relationship to God, but the shift more broadly from the medieval to the early-modern perspective was precisely a shift in the relationship of an individual not just to his (almost always his) God, but now between the individual and society at large. *Don Quixote* has at times been viewed as a simple, direct—if long—call for a return to the principles of chivalry at a time of the encroachment of industrialization and its corresponding set of new social customs and priorities.[83] However, this book is perhaps best understood as an attack on both medieval and early-capitalist conceits and assumptions. Its genuine contribution, in a political sense, could be regarded as its unwillingness to argue in a wholesale fashion for any political system as being ideal, or even wholly admirable. Even the proposal of the new economic system of capitalism must be limited by government intervention for the greater good. This is perhaps the strongest modernist aspect of *Don Quixote*: rather than advocating one particular form of government and/or one economic system for all times and places, instead it tests the strengths and weaknesses of many.

Written in the years after the death of the powerful King Philip II of Spain, this Spanish novel portrays the dominant economic system of mercantilism, alongside emerging physiocracy and capitalism, in the early seventeenth century. The emphasis is on economic systems that can provide the foundation for new forms of government. It may be startling for some readers to find proto-Lockean, English notions of property, the labor theory of value, and political consent in this southern European, early-modern work. However, it is not so surprising if both Cervantes's Spanish intellectual context and John Locke's own reading of *Don Quixote* are taken into account. Yet throughout the book (and not just in Part II, Chapter 51, on Sancho's supposed governorship of an island), there is the outline of good government, of a state that would provide for the needs of all people, giving particular attention to the poor, especially the working poor. This basis of this *largesse* is rationality.

However, *Don Quixote* both mocks rationality and celebrates it. Remember that Quixote is most likely to talk about freedom in scenes dominated by magic. Likewise, Carlos Fuentes's *Terra Nostra* could be used as much more modern literary evidence for the claim that it is the fascination with magic, not the emphases on rationality and on politics in a straightforward sense, that is the key not only to writing successful literature, but also to comprehending the working of society, including the economic relations within that society. Both *Don Quixote* and *Terra Nostra* force recognition of the power, and inevitability, of non-rational aspects of human experience, and thus the need to find rational ways to comprehend them, often in reference to economic systems. Through its attention to topics as varied as forms of government, the philosophy of history, madness, and indeed the emergence of free trade and the market economy, *Don Quixote*, sometimes called the very first novel, can be argued to have set the intellectual agenda, with its emphasis on the abstract individual, for Europe, and the world, for the next four centuries, and perhaps beyond. Overall, *Don Quixote* still has the power not only to make us laugh and smirk at the failings of others, but also then to force us to stare directly into our own rigid belief systems.

NOTES

1 The most authoritative edition in Spanish is now Miguel de Cervantes, *Don Quijote de la Mancha*, ed. Francisco Rico (Barcelona: Galaxia Gutenberg, 2004). A very useful separate volume summarizes the scholarship episode by episode with bibliographical references: Miguel de Cervantes, *Don Quijote de la Mancha: Volumen Complementario*, Francisco Rico, ed. (Barcelona: Galaxia Gutenberg, 2004). Recommended English translations include the excellent John Ormsby 1885 translation, revised by Joseph R. Jones in the 1980s, for Norton: Miguel de Cervantes, *Don Quixote*, Joseph R. Jones and Kenneth Douglas, eds., and John Ormsby, tr. (New York: Norton, 1981). Among the many modern translations, I have chosen the eminently readable Miguel de

Cervantes Saavedra, *The Adventures of Don Quixote*, J. M. Cohen, tr. (London: Penguin, 1950) for the citations in English.

Thank you to Geoffrey Parker and Giuseppe Mazzotta for their close reading of this chapter. I am grateful to Michael Armstrong-Roche. This first, "Background" section draws extensively from his comments.

2 The direct quotation in the list is from Cervantes, *The Adventures of Don Quixote*, Cohen, tr., I.1.33. Hereafter as *Don Quixote.*

3 More specifically, Quixote believes this helmet to be Mambrino's helmet, thus alluding to the Christians fighting the Moors, during the Crusades, from the epic fifteenth-century poem by Ariosto.

4 Anthony J. Cascardi, "Genre Definition and Multiplication in *Don Quixote*," *Cervantes: Bulletin of the Cervantes Society of America.*

5 See Barbara Fuchs, *Mimesis and Empire: The New World, Islam, and European Identities*, and *Passing for Spain: Cervantes and the Fictions of Identity*. Also see William Childers, *Transnational Cervantes.*

6 Cervantes, *Don Quixote*, II.5, is well worth reading for more on the dynamic of this early-modern, proto-working-class marriage. For a rare, constructive reading of Sancho's wife, see Louise Ciallella, "Teresa Panza's Character Zone and the Discourse of Domesticity in *Don Quijote*," *Bulletin of the Cervantes Association of America.*

7 *Pace* Dan Tobin. On the proto-bourgeois economic and political implications of Cervantes's fiction, see Carroll B. Johnson, *Cervantes and the Material World.*

8 The Parts are sometimes dated 1604 and 1614; apparently the confusion is that the publication process began at the end of the year.

9 See also the work of Marjorie Grice-Hutchinson, including *The School of Salamanca: Readings in Spanish Monetary Theory, 1544–1605*. Also see David Hume, *Writings on Economics.*

10 Cervantes, *Don Quixote*. Rico, ed. II, XVIII.846, and esp. I.25.315. Cohen, tr., II.18.583.

11 See Carroll B. Johnson, *Madness and Lust: A Psychoanalytic Approach to Don Quixote.*

12 Aristotle, *The Politics*, 1317b2, p. 239: "One principle of liberty is for all [all citizens] to rule and be ruled in turn."

13 Cervantes, *Don Quixote*, I.20.

14 See Cervantes, *Don Quixote*, I.20, for a financial argument between the two.

15 John Elliott, *Imperial Spain, 1469–1716*, p. 299.

16 On the Italian connection to this novel, see Mazzotta, "Modern and Ancient Italy in *Don Quijote*," *Poetica: Zeitschrift für Sprach- und Literaturwissenschaft*, 38 (2006), pp. 91–106.

17 Fernand Braudel, *The Mediterranean and the Mediterranean World in the Age of Phillip II*. Written in French, and first published in 1949.

18 See Geoffrey Parker, *Europe in Crisis, 1598–1648*. And David Ringrose, *Spain, Europe, and the 'Spanish Miracle', 1700–1900*, which reviews earlier historiographical patterns in the study of Spain (particularly, the "rise and fall" myth and the "eternal Spain" myth). Ringrose argues that the successful post-Franco Spanish transition is the result of much earlier political and economic, going back as far as the eighteenth century). Also Henry Kamen, *Empire: How Spain Became a World Power, 1492–1763*. Thank you to Michael Armstrong-Roche.

19 Parker, *Europe in Crisis, 1598–1648*, pp. 146–147.

20 *La Vida de Lazarillo de Tormes*, Aldo Ruffinato, ed. and *Lazarillo de Tormes and The Swindler: Two Spanish Picaresque Novels*, Michael Alpert, tr., p. ix. The

author of *Lazarillo de Tormes* is anonymous. *El Buscón (The Swindler, 1626)* was written by Francisco de Quevedo. These two Spanish and English editions both have worthwhile, remarkably different, introductions by the editors.

21 *The Encyclopaedia Britannica* (New York: The Encyclopaedia Britannica Company, 1911), 11th edition. The 11th edition, published in 1911, is still prized, mainly because many of the articles were written by major nineteenth-, early-twentieth-century writers.

22 Lope de Vega, *Three Major Plays*.

23 However, not all twentieth-century Latin American writers should be categorized as part of magical realism, not even all of the Boom generation of the 1960s, which is most closely associated with magical realism. Just to cite writers noted above—Borges, García Márquez, and Vargas Llosa—only García Márquez, and later Isabel Allende, can be fully associated with magical realism. Neither Borges nor Vargas Llosa is connected with magical realism, however defined. Since the Boom generation, there have been at least two generations of major Latin American writers that have distanced themselves from this term.

> And see *Magical Realism: Theory, History, Community*, Lois Parkinson Zamora and Wendy Faris, eds. Also Roberto González Echevarría, *Alejo Carpentier: The Pilgrim at Home*. The Cuban writer Alejo Carpentier, along with the Venezuelan writer Arturo Uslar Pietri, is often credited with the first use of the term "magical realism" (or variations on it, such as the "marvelous real") to describe a certain tendency in some Latin American writers from the 1920s to the 1960s.

24 Miguel de Unamuno, *Vida de Don Quijote y Sancho*; and Ortega y Gasset, *Meditaciones del Quijote*.

25 Américo Castro, *La realidad histórica de España*.

26 This is not the place to consider the question of "Who was Shakespeare?" However, for those who wish to pursue this and other questions regarding Shakespeare's biography, see, for example, Stephen Greenblatt, *Will in the World: How Shakespeare Became Shakespeare*.

> And see David Armitage, Conan Condren, and Andrew Fitzmaurice, eds., *Shakespeare and Early Modern Political Thought*, for many themes regarding politics and literature that complement this present volume.

27 Roland Barthes made a connection among three contradictory life stories—those of Loyola, Fourier, and Sade—which could be extended to include Cervantes's fictional Quixote, who might also be discussed as demonstrating a form of masochism, of suffering taken on deliberately in the name of a particular ideology. Roland Barthes, *Sade, Fourier, Loyola*, esp. ch. 2 on Loyola.

28 See especially Jean Canavaggio's biography, *Cervantes*. The original is in French; the book was then revised for the Spanish and English editions.

29 Fernando Cervantes, "Cervantes in Italy: Christian Humanism and Visual Impact of Renaissance Rome," *Journal of the History of Ideas*.

30 The Turks were attempting to take the Italian island of Cyprus, which would have given them power over the eastern Mediterranean. This victory retains its symbolic significance, even though the Venetians gave Cyprus back to the Turks two years later.

31 English translation from Miguel de Cervantes, *Journey to Parnassus*, ch. 1, p. 25.

32 Nina David, "Ways of Remembering: Cervantes and the Historians, *Don Quijote*, Part I," in *1605–2005: Don Quixote Across the Centuries*, John P.

Gabriele, ed., pp. 153–160, esp. 153. On the impact of Cervantes's captivity on his writing, see María Antonia Garcés, *Cervantes in Algiers: A Captive's Tale.*

33   Cervantes, *Exemplary Stories.*

34   Armstrong-Roche, *Cervantes' Epic Novel: Empire, Religion, and the Dream Life of Heroes in Persiles.*

35   Geoffrey Parker, *Philip II.*

36   Parker, *Philip II*, ch. 2.

37   Parker, *Philip II*, chs. 3, 8–9.

38   Parker, *Philip II*, ch. 3.

39   Geoffrey Parker, *The Grand Strategy of Philip II*, "Introduction," p. 1.

40   Jeremy Black, *European Warfare, 1494–1660*, pp. 183–186.

41   Elliott, *Imperial Spain, 1469–1716*, p. 319.

42   Marcus Aurelius, *The Meditations*, "Introduction."

43   Marcus Aurelius, p. xxi.

44   Lucretius, *On the Nature of the Universe*, Ronald Melville, tr. (Oxford: Oxford University Press, 1997) is an excellent verse translation. This title of this work is usually translated, more literally, as *On the Nature of Things.*

45   Johnson, *Cervantes and the Material World.* See also Grice-Hutchinson, *The School of Salamanca: Readings in Spanish Monetary Theory, 1544–1605.*

46   An earlier version of this section was presented as a paper for the Social Science Workshop, Grinnell College, Grinnell, Iowa, on October 1, 2009. Thank you to Gemma Sala. Previously this paper was given at the Market Institutions and Economic Processes Colloquium, in the Economics Department, New York University, on January 29, 2007. Thank you to Maria Pia Paganelli, David Harper, and Sanford Ikeda. Other aspects of this section were developed in my comments as a participant at a "Special Roundtable on Liah Greenfeld's *The Spirit of Capitalism: Nationalism and Economic Growth*" (Cambridge, MA: Harvard University Press, 2001), at the ASN (Association for the Study of Nationalities) 9th Annual World Convention on "Nation, Identity, and Conflict," Harriman Institute, Columbia University, April 16, 2004. Thank you to Peter Rutland. And see David Levy, *The Economic Ideas of Ordinary People: From Preferences to Trade.*

47   A similar emphasis can be seen today in the desire for, and even the fetishism of, a strong exchange rate, which is now implicitly taken to demonstrate the strength of a people beyond the economic and financial spheres, and thus often shading into some area of national, moral superiority.

48   See the later section in this chapter on "Physiocracy."

49   Thank you to William Butos for his help on this section. For Keynes on mercantilism, see Allan H. Meltzer, *Keynes's Monetary Theory: A Different Interpretation*, a technical treatment of Keynes's monetary theory. More recent studies include Roger Garrison, *Time and Money: The Macroeconomics of Capital Structure*, esp. ch. 9. Garrison's work has in turn been reevaluated by William N. Butos, "Garrison and the 'Keynes Problem,'" *Quarterly Journal of Austrian Economics*, 4, No. 3 (Fall 2001): 5–16, esp. pp. 6–11.

50   The classic work on mercantilism is E. F. Hecksher, *Mercantilism.* Written in Swedish, first English translation in 1955. For more recent work, see Roger B. Ekelund, Jr. and Robert D. Tollison, *Mercantilism as a Rent-Seeking Society: Economic Regulation in Historical Perspective.*

51   See Johnson, *Cervantes and the Material World* on the incident, esp. pp. 51–71. Cervantes, *Don Quixote*, II, p. 63.

52   Thank you to Michael Armstrong-Roche for directing me to this section on Ricote and its implications.

53   Ernst H. Kantorowicz, *The King's Two Bodies: A Study in Mediaeval Political Theology.*

54 A useful source is *Divine Right and Democracy: An Anthology of Political Writing in Stuart England*, David Wootton, ed., pp. 99–109, on James I, esp. p. 108. More accurately, he was James VI of Scotland and James I of England.

55 Eric R. Wolf, *Europe and the People without History*. Thank you to Ayse Turkseven.

56 Cervantes, *Don Quixote*, I.VII, in particular.

57 Richard L. Hills, *Power from Wind: A History of Windmill Technology*, esp. ch. 2, "The horizontal windmill.

58 Hills, *Power from Wind*, esp. ch. 2.

59 Cervantes, *Don Quixote*, Rico, ed., I.8.10, and Cohen, tr., I.8.70–71.

60 This emphasis on the mixture of family and economics was developed much later by Friedrich Engels, and then again by Charlotte Perkins Gilman: Friedrich Engels, *The Origin of the Family: Private Property, and the State*, first published in German, in 1884, and Charlotte Perkins Gilman, *Women and Economics: A Study of the Economic Relation between Men and Women as a Factor in Social Evolution*, published in 1898.

61 Thus, once again, this demonstrates a closer connection to the slow change for society later sanctioned by Burke than to a call to revolution, as attributed to Rousseau.

62 Cervantes, *Don Quixote*, II.24.

63 Thank you to Gemma Sala.

64 Ekelund and Tollison, *Mercantilism as a Rent-Seeking Society: Economic Regulation in Historical Perspective*.

65 See Richard Pipes, *Property and Freedom*, on changing patterns of property ownership and a shift to a new economic system. The core of Pipes's argument is "that while property in some form is possible without liberty, the contrary is inconceivable," from p. xiii.

66 As an example of the shift in economic thinking among thinkers at this time: Adam Smith's *Wealth of Nations* was read with great pleasure by his friend David Hume on his deathbed in 1776. Hume's own economic contributions were noted above.

67 Although unity is certainly not a requirement for the ideas of a strong thinker, with Rousseau, the third social contract thinker, as a colorful example of disorganized brilliance.

68 *Pace* Thomas Mun.

69 John Locke, *Two Treatises of Government*, Peter Laslett, ed., from *The Second Treatise of Government*, ch. 5, #25–51, pp. 303–320.

70 See Susanne Sreedhar, "Defending the Hobbesian Right of Self-Defense," in *Political Theory*, for a more expansive interpretation of the right to rebel in Hobbes.

71 This is a good example of Marx's remarkable shrewdness as a critic of market capitalism, albeit most readers are distracted from this because Marx's stress is almost always on formulating an alternative economic system.

72 On Gresham's Law, see von Mises, *Theory of Money and Credit*, pp. 90–93. Thank you to Richard Adelstein and Steven Horwitz.

73 Thank you to Alan Nathanson for this information on coinage. Locke's was hardly the first European work to comment on economics in a sophisticated fashion. Chaucer's "The Shipman's Tale," in *The Canterbury Tales* (from the fourteenth century) gives an early account of double exchange, and Goethe's *Faust* on money (in the nineteenth century) are just two famous examples. See also Georg Simmel, *The Philosophy of Money*. And see Foucault, *The Order of Things: An Archeology of Human Sciences*, on connecting through resemblances.

74 Cervantes, *Don Quixote*, I.10.

75 The Rico edition of *Don Quixote*, in the supplementary volume, summarizes the major political texts that underlie these episodes, including the advice given

by Quixote; it includes princely mirrors and reflects ideas recorded at least as early as thirteenth-century Alfonso X of Castille's major juridical work, *Las Siete Partidas (The Seven-Part Code).*

76 Laslett argues (in Locke, *Two Treatises of Government,* Laslett, ed., "Introduction," pp. 3–120) that most of Locke's 1690 publications, including *The Essay Concerning Human Understanding,* the *Letters on Toleration,* and *The Two Treatises of Government* were written earlier, before the Glorious Revolution in 1688.

77 Cervantes, *Don Quixote,* II, p. 51, and II, pp. 42–43.

78 Cervantes, *Don Quixote,* Rico, ed., I.5.79; and Cohen, tr., I.5.54. James March and Steven Schecter, a film titled *Passion and Discipline: Don Quixote's Lessons for Leadership,* a Stanford University Business School DVD, 2003. Thank you to Mark Zbaracki.

79 Cervantes, *Don Quixote,* Rico, ed., II.51.1149–1150, Cohen, tr., II.51.804.

80 Cervantes, *Don Quixote,* Rico, ed., II.51.1141, and Cohen, tr. II.51.797.

81 Locke, *Two Treatises of Government,* Laslett, ed., from *The First Treatise of Government,* ch. VIII, #7–19, p. 219. Robert Filmer was an immensely popular seventeenth-century English political writer who staunchly defended the divine right of kings. Filmer is best known now for Locke's attack on him. Nevertheless, it is in Locke's less well-known *First Treatise,* his attack on Filmer, that the arguments about *Don Quixote* and Filmer are to be found. This is one of many examples being made here about core Enlightenment notions developing out of public intellectual debate.

82 Carlos Fuentes, *Terra Nostra* (Mexico City, 1975,1976). Carlos Fuentes, *Terra Nostra,* Margaret Sayers Peden, tr., (1976). See David W. Price, *History Made, History Imagined: Contemporary Literature, Poiesis, and the Past,* ch. 2, on Carlos Fuentes.

83 This could be viewed as similar to more recent calls from Christian Socialists and back-to-the-land advocates.

REFERENCES

Aristotle, *Aristotle's Politics,* Benjamin Jowett, tr. (Oxford: Clarendon Press, 1905).

Armitage, David, Conan Condren, and Andrew Fitzmaurice, eds., *Shakespeare and Early Modern Political Thought* (Leiden: Cambridge University Press, 2009).

Armstrong-Roche, Michael, *Cervantes' Epic Novel: Empire, Religion, and the Dream Life of Heroes in Persiles* (Toronto: University of Toronto Press, 2009).

Aurelius, Marcus, *The Meditations,* G.M.A. Grube, tr. (Indianapolis, IN: Hackett, 1983).

Barthes, Roland, *Sade, Fourier, Loyola.* Richard Miller, tr. (New York: Hill and Wang, 1976).

Black, Jeremy, *European Warfare, 1494–1660* (London: Routledge, 2002).

Braudel, Fernand, *The Mediterranean and the Mediterranean World in the Age of Philip II,* Siân Reynolds, tr., 2 vols. (New York: Harper & Row, 1974).

Butos, William N., "Garrison and the 'Keynes Problem,'" *The Quarterly Journal of Austrian Economics* 4, no. 3 (fall 2001): 5–16.

Canavaggio, Jean, *Cervantes,* J.R. Jones, tr. (New York: Norton, 1990).

Cascardi, Anthony J., "Genre Definition and Multiplication in *Don Quixote,*" *Cervantes: Bulletin of the Cervantes Society of America* 6, no. 1 (1986): 39–49.

Castro, Américo, *La realidad histórica de España,* 3rd ed. (Mexico City: Editorial Porrúa, 1966).

Cervantes, Fernando, "Cervantes in Italy: Christian Humanism and Visual Impact of Renaissance Rome," *Journal of the History of Ideas* 66, no. 3 (July 2005): 325–350.

Cervantes, Miguel, *Adventures of Don Quixote*, J. M. Cohen, tr. (London: Penguin, 1950).

———. *Don Quixote*, Joseph R. Jones and Kenneth Douglas, eds. John Ormsby, tr. (New York: W.W. Norton & Co, 1981).

———. *Don Quijote de la Mancha: Edición del Instituto Cervantes, 1605–2005*, Francisco Rico, et al. (Barcelona: Galaxia Gutenberg, 2004).

———. *Don Quijote de la Mancha: Volumen Complementario*, Francisco Rico, ed. (Barcelona: Galaxia Gutenberg, 2004).

———. *Exemplary Stories*, Lesley Lipson, tr. (Oxford: Oxford University Press, 2008).

———. *Journey to Parnassus*, James Young Gibson, tr. (London: Kegan Paul, Trench and Co., 1883).

Chaucer, Geoffrey, *The Canterbury Tales*, Nevill Coghill, tr. (London: Penguin, 2003).

Childers, William, *Transnational Cervantes* (Toronto: University of Toronto Press, 2006).

Ciallella, Louise, "Teresa Panza's Character Zone and the Discourse of Domesticity in *Don Quijote*," *Bulletin of the Cervantes Association of America* 23, no. 2 (2003): 275–296.

David, Nina, "Ways of Remembering: Cervantes and the Historians, *Don Quijote*, Part I," in *1605–2005: Don Quixote Across the Centuries*, pp. 153–160, John P. Gabriele, ed. (Madrid: Iberoamerica/Frankfurt am Main: Vervuert, 2005), pp. 153–160.

Divine Right and Democracy: An Anthology of Political Writing in Stuart England, David Wootton, ed. (Harmondsworth, U.K.: Penguin, 1988).

Ekelund, Jr., Roger B., and Robert D. Tollison, *Mercantilism as a Rent-Seeking Society: Economic Regulation in Historical Perspective* (College Station: Texas A & M University Press, 1981).

Elliott, J. H., *Imperial Spain, 1469–1716* (Harmondsworth, U.K.: Penguin, 1975).

The Encyclopaedia Britannica, 11th ed. (New York: The Encyclopaedia Britannica Company, 1911).

Encyclopedia Britannica, Online: http://www.britannica.com.

Engels, Friedrich, *The Origin of the Family: Private Property, and the State.* Ernest Untermann, tr. (Honolulu, HI: University Press of the Pacific, 2001).

Foucault, Michel, *The Order of Things: An Archeology of Human Sciences*, translator not given (New York: Vintage, 1994).

Fuchs, Barbara, *Mimesis and Empire: The New World, Islam, and European Identities* (Cambridge: Cambridge University Press, 2004).

———. *Passing for Spain: Cervantes and the Fictions of Identity* (Urbana-Champaign: University of Illinois Press, 2003).

Fuentes, Carlos, *Terra Nostra* (Mexico City: Joaquin Moritz, 1975).

———. *Terra Nostra*, Margaret Sayers Peden, tr. (New York: Farrar, Straus, Giroux, 1976).

Garcés, María Antonia, *Cervantes in Algiers: A Captive's Tale* (Nashville, TN: Vanderbilt University Press, 2002).

Garrison, Roger, *Time and Money: The Macroeconomics of Capital Structure* (New York: Routledge, 2000).

Gilman, Charlotte Perkins, *Women and Economics: A Study of the Economic Relation between Men and Women as a Factor in Social Evolution* (Boston, MA: Small, Maynard & Co., 1898).

Goethe, Johann Wolfgang von, *Faust*, David Luke, tr., 2 vols. (Oxford: Oxford University Press, 1998).

González Echevarría, Roberto, *Alejo Carpentier: The Pilgrim at Home* (Austin: University of Texas Press, 1990).

Greenblatt, Stephen, *Will in the World: How Shakespeare Became Shakespeare* (New York: Norton, 2005).

Greenfeld, Liah, *The Spirit of Capitalism: Nationalism and Economic Growth* (Cambridge, MA: Harvard University Press, 2001).

Grice-Hutchinson, Marjorie, *The School of Salamanca: Readings in Spanish Monetary Theory, 1544–1605* (Oxford: Clarendon Press, 1952).

Hecksher, E. F., *Mercantilism*, Mendel Shapiro, tr., rev. ed., 2 vols. (London: George Allen & Unwin, 1955).

Hills, Richard L., *Power from Wind: A History of Windmill Technology* (Cambridge: Cambridge University Press, 1994).

Hume, David, *Writings on Economics* (Madison: University of Wisconsin Press, 1970).

Johnson, Carroll B., *Cervantes and the Material World* (Urbana and Chicago: University of Illinois Press, 2000).

———. *Madness and Lust: A Psychoanalytical Approach to Don Quixote* (Berkeley: University of California Press, 1983).

Kamen, Henry, *Empire: How Spain Became a World Power, 1492–1763* (New York: Harper Perennial, 2004).

Kantorowicz, Ernst H., *The King's Two Bodies: A Study in Mediaeval Political Theology* (Princeton, NJ: Princeton University Press, 1957).

La Vida de Lazarillo de Tormes, Aldo Ruffinato, ed. (Madrid: Clásico Castalia, 2001).

Lazarillo de Tormes and *The Swindler: Two Spanish Picaresque Novels*, Michael Alpert, tr., 2nd ed. (London: Penguin, 1969, 2003).

Levy, David, *The Economic Ideas of Ordinary People: From Preferences to Trade* (London: Routledge, 1992).

Locke, John, *An Essay Concerning Human Understanding*, Roger Woolhouse, ed. (London: Penguin, 1997).

———. *A Letter Concerning Toleration* (Indianapolis, IN: Hackett, 1983).

———. *Two Treatises of Government*, Peter Laslett, ed. (Cambridge: Cambridge University Press, 1960).

Lucretius. *On the Nature of the Universe*, Ronald Melville, tr. (Oxford: Oxford University Press, 1997).

Magical Realism: Theory, History, Community, Lois Parkinson Zamora and Wendy Faris, eds. (Durham, NC: Duke University Press, 1995).

March, James, and Steven Schecter, film entitled "Passion and Discipline: Don Quixote's Lessons for Leadership," Stanford University Business School DVD, 2003.

Mazzotta, Giuseppe, "Modern and Ancient Italy in *Don Quijote*," *Poetica: Zeitschrift für Sprach- und Literaturwissenschaft* 38 (2006): 91–106.

Meltzer, Allan H., *Keynes's Monetary Theory: A Different Interpretation* (Cambridge: Cambridge University Press, 1988).

Mises, Ludwig von, *The Theory of Money and Credit*, Harold E. Batson, ed. (Indianapolis, IN: Liberty Press, 1981).

Ortega y Gasset, José, *Meditaciones del Quijote* (Madrid: Cátreda, 1990).

Parker, Geoffrey, *Europe in Crisis, 1598–1648* (Glasgow: Fontana, 1979).

———. *The Grand Strategy of Philip II* (New Haven: Yale University Press, 1998).

———. *Philip II* (Boston: Little, Brown and Company, 1978).

Pipes, Richard, *Property and Freedom* (New York: Vintage, 2000).

Price, David W., *History Made, History Imagined: Contemporary Literature, Poiesis, and the Past* (Urbana and Chicago: University of Illinois Press, 1999).

Ringrose, David, *Spain, Europe, and the 'Spanish Miracle', 1700–1900* (Cambridge: Cambridge University Press, 1998).

Simmel, Georg, *The Philosophy of Money*. Tom Bottomore, tr., David Frisby, ed. (London: Routledge & Kegan Paul, 1978.

Sreedhar, Susanne, "Defending the Hobbesian Right of Self-Defense," in *Political Theory* 36 (2008): 781–802.

Unamuno, Miguel de, *Vida de Don Quijote y Sancho* (Madrid: Cátreda, 1988).

Vega, Lope de, *Three Major Plays*, Gwynne Edwards, tr. (Oxford: Oxford University Press, 1999).

Wolf, Eric R., *Europe and the People without History* (Berkeley, CA: University of California Press, 1982).

2 *Simplicissimus* (1668, 1669), Religious Toleration, and Friendship

I BACKGROUND

1 The Fool

The immense success and then decline into obscurity of *Der abentheurliche Simplicissimus Teutsch* (*The Adventurous Simplicissimus Teutsch*, 1668, 1669), even in the German-speaking world, denote a sea change in literary and intellectual tastes.[1] Two decades after the end of the Thirty Years' War, in the late seventeenth century, Germans rejoiced in this story of someone even more average than themselves, someone who survives moral hazards and multiple death threats, manages to thrive economically, and sires countless children across central Europe, all in the midst of the most inauspicious circumstances. Simplicissimus's attractiveness is grounded in both his ordinariness and his exceptionality, even when young. It was not just his gamine qualities, and thus his appeal to the child within all of us, but also his strident proto-capitalist leanings and abilities that accorded with the tastes of late-seventeenth-century German readers. This is the life story that the first readers would have wished for their fathers, uncles, and grandfathers during this extended debacle, the Thirty Years' War, which, not surprisingly, was actually longer than 30 years. However, the title character Simplicissimus is also the perpetrator of countless killings and rapes, an active force for evil in the horror of this war, not just a victim of the war.

Narrated by an active, albeit initially reluctant, participant in the Thirty Years' War, this book metes out harsh criticism to all established authority: political leaders; established views of marriage; and traditional loyalties, including those to both Catholicism and Protestantism. (And the author, Grimmelshausen, from a Protestant background, was an adult convert to Catholicism in the midst of a religious war.) Yet this book is not just about war; the topics of courtly love, the extreme pain of childbirth, idolatry, cross-dressing, love potions, witchcraft, fortune-tellers, ghosts, exorcism, necromancy, alchemy, poisoning, sorcery, brigandage, immorality (especially in the upper class), duels, numerology, physiognomy (judging human character from facial features), palmistry, minor trickery, as well as several easily discernible major Freudian psychoses, are all mentioned, at least in passing, and many of which are manifested by the title character himself.

Although still debatable, *Simplicissimus* has often been cited as a direct model for Voltaire's *Candide*, perhaps most markedly in terms of the detailed violence, the wandering lead character, the resurrections, and the reassembling of family in the conclusion. Like so many other powerful war novels, including the much later, post–World War I, German work, Erich Maria Remarque's *Im Westen nichts Neues* (*All Quiet on the Western Front*, 1929), the question of whether *Simplicissimus* is best understood as an anti-war novel remains unresolved.[2]

Simplicissimus is sometimes ranked as one of the three greatest works of German literature, along with Wolfram von Eschenbach's *Parzival* (c. 1200–1210) and Goethe's *Faust* (1806–1832). *Simplicissimus* also echoes many of the earlier popular themes from medieval German legends about a young trickster called Till Eulenspiegel and from Sebastian Brandt's *Das Narrenschiff* (*Ship of Fools*, 1484). Nevertheless, *Simplicissimus* is not drawn directly from oral culture. Grimmelshausen's work comes midway between the German Medieval (exemplified by Eschenbach's *Parzival*) and the German Classical (as exemplified by Goethe's *Faust*) literary periods. Much more recently, and denoting a renewed interest in *Simplicissimus*, Bertolt Brecht and Günter Grass have used the Thirty Years' War setting, and *Simplicissimus* directly, as part of their own political statements, on stage and in fiction.[3] These productions and other books help to define the particular German qualities to be found also in *Simplicissimus*, even if these other works are of markedly different literary styles and would thus usually be studied in terms of separate literary criteria.

The title character Simplicissimus starts from the bottom of society: an idiot, from a most undistinguished background, who, nevertheless, through formal academic and military training, becomes a shrewd leader of men and a most successful thief. His name changes as do his fortunes: from lad, to Simplicius, to Simplicius Simplicissimus, to the Calf (when he is playing a fool), to Sabina (when he is pretending to be a young girl), again to fool, to the Wee Huntsman, to the Huntsman of Soest, to Beau Alman, back to Simplicissimus, and then finally, simply, to the hermit. The symbolism of his name functions on many levels. As in John Bunyan's *The Pilgrim's Progress* (1678, 1684), names correlate directly to personality types. In this case, all these names have a mutual relationship with Simplicissimus's multiple personality types.

Simplicissimus' name works on two, opposing levels. It means "the most stupid one" in Latin. In English it would effectively be Simple Simon. Yet, at the same time, ancient sages and scholars have directly claimed simplicity as their means to the truth, and at times to this word as their own personal name. For example, Simplicius is also the name of a learned mathematician and a scholar of Aristotle and Epictetus from Cilicia, in present-day Turkey, of the sixth century A.D. Much later Aristotle is mocked in Galileo's *Dialogues Concerning Two Chief World Systems: Ptolemaic and Copernican* (1632) through the utterances of an Aristotelian philosopher named Simplicio.[4] There is also a marvelous line from Peter Lombard (born c. 1100), the Italian Archbishop of Paris, who wrote one of the main theological texts of the Middle Ages, in which he declares that *Deus non est simplicissimus* ("God is not the most simple"), thus implying, as does Thomas Aquinas, that God is not limited in any way.[5] These classical and religious allusions are altogether deliberate in the novel: "*Sancta simplicissimus*," (holy, highest simplicity), also known as *ad docta ignorantia*, ("on learned ignorance"), both phrases invoke the simplicity of the good Christian, yet they are also imply genuine lack of knowledge.[6]

Yet for all these allusions, this work of fiction is certainly not wholly academic or spiritual. The book is decidedly not erudite at all stages, as can be inferred from this almost randomly chosen quotation (there are several hundred other passages in the book that would serve equally well):

> When day broke I ate some more wheat then went straight to Gelnhausen. There I found the gates open. They were partly burnt, but still half barricaded with piles of dung. I went in but could see no living person. On the other hand the streets were strewn with dead, some of whom had been stripped naked, others down to their undershirt or petticoat.[7]

This passage is arguably the quintessential summation of the entire work, encompassing famine, war, death, corruption, and isolation in crisp, forthright observations. This simple description by the narrator, Old Simplicissimus, shows the inevitable results of the breakdown of morals in society. It represents the individual's shift from the state of nature to civilization, for Simplicissimus is, in this passage, leaving the forest and entering the city for the first time. However, unlike the various versions of this transition provided by Hobbes, Locke, and Rousseau, the example here is wholly negative, particularly for these former residents of Gelnhausen, strewn around, dead on the street.[8]

The novel *Simplicissimus* is a mixture of erudition and debauchery on an astounding scale. The accounts, for example, of Simplicissimus's time as a male prostitute in the upper-class *bon ton* of Paris give the work a tone not dissimilar to the calculated, logical farce in *Candide*, but perhaps like the straining of the sensibilities within an alcoholic daze. Long passages that refer in surprising detail to bodily functions—sections that would have made even Jonathan Swift blush—remain jarring even today. Yet many readers have enjoyed the coarse references to the basic workings of the human body, and these passages do help to account for the book's initial popularity. Even in the late seventeenth century such detailed discussions were designed to shock and did not simply indicate the frankness and coarseness of that time.[9] Popular taste, however, has not changed altogether over the centuries; some of today's readers still find these sections highly amusing. More seriously, these references stress the commonality of the human experience across time, place, education, and even class.

The book offers no apologies for the subject matter, indeed it is likely that the repeated and direct references to farting and defecating, just part of the book's anal fixation, are also a deliberate attempt to impart a forthright tone. This, rather oddly, indicates a sense of responsibility to others as individuals and groups, of solidarity with the human condition, which is especially clear when the narrator dispassionately describes subhuman existence during wartime. Vomiting, gas, bloating, and burping are mentioned as normal topics of conversation. At the same time, the assumption is also clear in the text that the narrator would not hide the truth about other, more crucial subjects from the reader, however uncouth or unattractive. Thus the unrelenting vulgarity of the subject matter might actually be used as evidence that the story could be generally trusted on more substantive subjects as well. The narrator claims that he will not hide his vices or his virtues from his reader, although he is a master at hiding both from those around him throughout his story. Compared to most of the characters, however, Simplicissimus is, especially when young, substantially more transparent. Overall, frankness and sincerity, sometimes by their absence, are the qualities desired by all parties involved in this story, and thus this widespread and profound desire for frankness and sincerity partly accounts for Simplicissimus's extraordinary popularity throughout his adventures.

As the character Simplicius grows up, he becomes increasingly attractive to countless women across Europe. Simplicissimus (Grimmelshausen's character, presumably not the Aristotle scholar) litters central Europe with his many, generally unacknowledged, illegitimate children, all of them apparently sons. During his life, his occupations take him around Europe, and these life experiences span almost the entire social scale. These jobs include: stable boy, student, court fool, soldier, musketeer, *Regimentschreiber* (regimental clerk), prisoner, petty thief, page, gang leader, writer of religious books, gigolo, itinerant salesman of quack medicine, fraudulent doctor, masquerading, out-of-work organ-player, sorcerer, prisoner (again), and hermit. The last occupation of hermit, narrating his story as Old Simplicissimus, is crucial because it mixes the categories of literacy and stupidity, not just because it is his final role. The loss to smallpox of his celebrated boyish looks, including his curly hair, the almost simultaneous loss of several fortunes and a few close friends, the brief rediscovery of his closest friend who is thought to be long dead, a visit to an underwater utopia, time spent with Hungarian Anabaptists, and a pilgrimage around the world, however, change the hardened soldier Simplicius Simplicissimus, by the end of the book, into a religious hermit. He thus follows the model of an earlier hermit, his first teacher, who is eventually revealed to have also been his natural, and aristocratic, father. Simplicissimus can be argued to an early example of an anti-hero, a major character without the traditional qualities of a hero, including idealism and courage.

Simplicissimus's travels, in Book V, briefly highlight the preoccupations of his time: Moscow (symbolizing despotism and technology), Japan (exoticism), Portuguese Macao (ethnic mixing), Alexandria (ancient learning), Rome (the fallen Roman Empire now subsumed by the failing Holy Roman Empire), and Loreto (oracles and mysticism). Thus, Book V makes clear with these examples that national eccentricities, proclivities, and vices are more correctly understood as indicative of universal human inclinations and failings. The knee-jerk attacks on the French, and corresponding praise of the Germans in the first four books of this German novel, make the traditional rivalry between these two peoples evident. In addition, Book V also shows that Simplicissimus is as lost, literally and personally, in Macao, off the southern coast of China, as he is in the Black Forest, his original home, where his family farm was attacked, leaving him alone for the first time in his life.

Unlike the later conflicts of nineteenth-century nationalism, the rivalries in the seventeenth century take place between the states, on the one hand, and vernacular-speaking heirs of antique erudition, on the other. In addition, the religious rivalry was taking place at a time when the split between Protestants and Catholics—the Protestant Reformation and the Catholic Counter-Reformation—was not fully complete (even though the Protestant Reformation was taken to have started over a hundred years earlier with Martin Luther's Ninety-Five Theses), and there was still the suspicion of heresy. The splits are ironically apparent in Simplicissimus's unlikely, friendly interactions with groups with fervently antagonistic views.

Overall, the many southern German states were, at the time of the war, loosely connected by the remnants of what was still called the Holy Roman Empire, which was based in Regensburg. (And it is always worth quoting Voltaire on the Holy Roman Empire—that it was never holy, Roman, or an empire.) However, the fractured composition of the Holy Roman Empire did not completely diminish its institutional role.[10] In any case, it is incorrect to view the Thirty Years' War as either a wholly religious or a wholly German war. In this book the religious tone of Old Simplicissimus invokes suffering as part of life in the world. Likewise, in political terms, the book dovetails between an early-modern and modern understanding of the state.

2 Gruesome Breakdown of Society

In *Simplicissimus*, some vestiges of political organization remain in the midst of the Thirty Years' War, but they are located not in the city but in the woods. The brigands, both those with and those against Simplicissimus, form tightly organized groups that function extremely well in a limited region for short periods of time. This type of political grouping can be linked with profit to the organization of convicts in prison.[11] The presence of well-run groups of brigands in *Simplicissimus* indicates that there were new, functioning alliances in the warring German states, but there is no hope that such unions would last even for years, much less decades or centuries. These groups were instead goal oriented in the short run. Although relatively traditional organizational systems were not wholly abandoned, it seems that only those using these systems for evil purposes (for example, the brigands) were able to make them work; this was because there was no greater political culture that recognized the legitimacy of functioning groups.

Understandably, readers of this book in the late seventeenth century were acutely aware that during the Thirty Years' War the German states had gone from a situation of extreme social control to one in which there was a wholesale breakdown in even basic public services. Policing and the army, services that the local lord generally provided, broke down or disappeared entirely. It is worth drawing parallels here between the German states and Britain, which was also in the midst of civil war in the mid-seventeenth century. Despite the devastation of the English Civil War, in Scotland and Ireland as well as in England, many British institutions continued to function, including, for some time, Parliament and the seven universities in Britain at that time, Oxford and Cambridge in England, St. Andrews, Glasgow, Aberdeen, and Edinburgh in Scotland, and Trinity College, Dublin, in Ireland. In addition, the alternative government in power in Britain during the Interregnum (after the execution of Charles I, and when Oliver Cromwell ruled as Lord Protector) functioned relatively smoothly, if with little toleration for the Royalists. However, in the German states at this same time there appears to have been little government or policing at any level at all. The comparison to Britain, itself in chaos in the seventeenth century, in the midst of the Civil War, gives some sense of how stark, how lawless, the situation was in the German states at the time when *Simplicissimus* was set.

3 The Thirty Years' War, 1618–1648

The Thirty Years' War, initially a battle between the Catholic South and Protestant North of the German states, became, with the introduction of foreign support, a testing ground for pan-European dominance.[12] The conflict grew out of the 1555 Peace of Augsburg, which legitimated the rights of Lutheran rulers in addition to those of the Catholic rulers but did nothing for many rulers who embraced Calvinism. Thus four decades after the Protestant Reformation, the dominant Protestant group on the Continent (Lutherans) but not smaller Protestant groups (such as Calvinists) were recognized as politically legitimate. However, the complexities were not just religious. The ongoing rivalry between France and the Hapsburgs continued on the battlegrounds of the German states on the Italian peninsula, and Spain joined the players as well (although the fighting never extended to Spain).

In 1618, the year taken to mark the outset of the Thirty Years' War, the German states were divided into seemingly countless states and principalities. (It was unlike France, which was already an early-modern territorial state, a unified nation-state, although still divided into various lands or regions.) There were German-speaking areas with non-German rulers, and areas such as Alsace and Lorraine, which were then, and are still now, difficult to classify as either wholly German or French.[13] There was some rough agreement on the frontiers of the German states (plural), but there was no German state (singular), if we understand "state" as a nation-state or territorial state (albeit Bavaria and Prussia were already states in a more limited sense).[14] In 1600, eighteen years before the start of the Thirty Years' War, the total population of the German states was between sixteen and seventeen million people, and there were perhaps 2,500 political rulers in the German states; a few were Imperial Knights, a few others ruled Free or Imperial States.[15] Although most rulers and people in the North were Protestant, and most rulers and their people in the South were Catholic, this kept changing, particularly during the war. The Protestants were not united; Calvinism had become increasingly popular by 1600, and was hated by the Lutheran Church (the dominant German Protestant Church) as well as by Catholics.[16] Religious toleration had not been a major feature of German culture at any time since the Reformation. Nevertheless, for some time Catholic rulers simply ignored the waves of Protestant defections, and only in the late sixteenth century (almost a century after the start of the Protestant Reformation) was there a concerted effort among Catholic rulers to stamp out the Protestant threat. The Catholics had much more luck reincorporating Lutherans than Calvinists, who represented the newest, one could say, more potent Protestant threat.[17] To bolster these claims, there existed a Catholic League of princes and a Protestant League of princes, each of which advanced only its own interests. Economic disparities also divided the German-speaking peoples; at this stage, the south was much more prosperous than the north, and certainly more prosperous than the northwest, of Germany. *Simplicissimus* is set right in the middle of this division, in the west, at about the mid-point of modern-day Germany.[18]

However, the Thirty Years' War became pan-European, transcending German domestic divisions. The major international contention, late in the war, was between the Bourbon French and the Hapsburg Spanish (at this point the Hapsburg Viennese were still active, if less powerful than their Spanish relatives), and was mainly played out on German soil. Protestants in both parts of the Hapsburg Empire were living on borrowed time; at times the Hapsburgs worked in tandem with the Turks against their own Protestant peoples.[19] Gaspar de Guzmán y Pimental Olivares (1587–1645) was the key player on the Spanish side as he was in charge of Spanish foreign policy. All of this was further complicated by the direct involvement of the King of Sweden in support of the German Protestants. The most famous Swedish general was the Swedish King himself, Gustavus Adolphus (Gustav II Adolf), the "Lion of the North," who wished to establish Protestant dominance in the German lands. Only after the death of Gustavus, late in the war, when the Swedes were beginning to feel the full brunt of its financial cost, did Sweden start to retreat. One of Gustavus's great rivals was a Habsburg general, the Bohemian Albrecht von Wallenstein, who at times negotiated clandestinely with the Swedish Protestants and was then murdered for this by his followers. Those unfamiliar with early-modern Europe are often surprised to learn that the Swedes and the Spanish were major players in this war, as well as in seventeenth-century, middle-European politics. No side was fully innocent in this war.

The overriding character of this war, even allowing for gross exaggeration, was one of shocking brutality of the soldiers on all sides against the people, especially in the countryside, and this had long-term implications. The war was marked by killings, coarse brutality, and torture. Rape and slaughter of women and children were not uncommon during these decades. One of the most famous, and disturbing, artistic representations of the war is of a hanging tree, from which at least 50 dead bodies are dangling.[20] Although there is some debate whether 75, 50, or 20 percent of the German people died during these years—modern estimates are on the lower end—there is apparently no doubt about the war's outright savagery, not to mention the toll of the famine and disease resulting from it.

Soldiers on all sides, most of them mercenaries, were apparently driven not only by greed but also by a love of cruelty for its own sake. This response was thus not even explicable in terms of a desire for personal revenge, as mercenaries were so often involved. The consistency of the war's unrelenting cruelty, from all participating nationalities and religions, could not have been accidental, even if it was not all ordered by military leaders.

Yet, some would argue, that the soldiers of the Thirty Years' War were not necessarily more brutal, just more efficient, than those in both earlier and later wars. Changes in technology between the Hundred Years' War (1337–1453) and the end of the Thirty' Years' War in 1648 were responsible for a new ease in killing. Just as there was no single cause for the war, there is also no single explanation for its brutality. Ever since its first publication, many have found the graphic descriptions in *Simplicissimus* to be a better memorial to this extended bloodshed than statistics.

Clearly the high death toll was caused not just by battle deaths in direct warfare but also by famine and the plague (as well as a low birthrate), all of which had an impact on both the citizenry and soldiers.[21] Germany had suffered from lack of food before 1600, and Europe as a whole was in the midst of what is often called the General Crisis of the Seventeenth Century.[22] All this was accompanied in the German states by high emigration (which was already a trend in this area, if not yet widespread). The number of battle deaths was relatively low; however, the figures do not even include the kind of hideous skirmishes described in detail at the outset of *Simplicissimus* when the title character's family farm is attacked.[23] Some modern scholars also doubt whether there was much violence by the military against the people: one hopes they are correct.[24]

However contentious the human toll—the figure of one-third of the entire population dead during these years is still being debated—the results of the Thirty Years' War were stultifying for German business, and perversely, this is more difficult to argue away.[25] It does seem odd (and certainly very sad) that it is easier to track the decline of the economy than the number of dead people.

It is clear that agriculture did not revive in the archetypal "breadbasket of Europe" for at least a century after the Thirty Years' War. More cattle and livestock than human beings had died. Food shortages were so extreme that mice were regularly sold for food in the later years of the war. The war undoubtedly gave France, Germany's rival, the commercial advantage for the next century, although the political and economic independence of the German princes led, two hundred years later, to the successful *Zollverein*, customs union, which was established by Prussia in 1834, leading eventually to free trade throughout Germany. The *Zollverein* is often taken to be the first stage in the process of German unification (thus presupposing the final end of the Empire to be at the beginning of the nineteenth century, and culminating with the rise of Otto von Bismarck late in the nineteenth century). However, even after German Unification in 1871, the German economy continued to experience economic depression, scarcity, and lack of capital, a trend since the outset of the Thirty Years' War.

Modernization cannot be judged in terms of politics and economics in any straightforward manner. Many questions remain. To what extent was modernization in the German states manifestly retarded by the war? Did the German states even have the appropriate emerging economic infrastructure to modernize before the war? And, for our immediate purposes, to what extent does *Simplicissimus* help or hinder the untangling of the evolving concepts of nationalism and economic modernization in the German states?

The Peace of Westphalia in 1648 ended the Thirty Years' War. Crucially, it also recognized the sovereignty of small states, thus breaking the waning power of the Holy Roman Empire. In effect, small states were given sovereignty, recognized by all the European powers involved, and thus were also given the right to choose their own religion. The Peace of Westphalia extended religious freedom beyond the Lutherans to the Calvinists (the Catholics needed no such extra coverage). The Peace of Westphalia (unlike almost any other aspect of the Thirty Years' War) is still cited regularly by scholars, politicians, and human rights activists. It is taken to be a watershed for the rights of all nations, rights that are not based on size, power politics, economic or military strength, or religious preferences.

Much of the interest in *Simplicissimus* in the centuries since its publication has been in its value as a source of information regarding the brutish, confusing Thirty Years' War. The term "Thirty Years' War" was probably coined by Samuel Pufendorf (1632–1694), best known for his work on natural law and international law; he, in line with later seventeenth-century European writers in almost every field, tried to make sense of the war's havoc.[26] Much later, in 1949, C. V. Wedgewood, for years the English-language expert on this war, made only two references to *Simplicissimus* in her classic work, and they were used, first, to give detailed, gruesome examples of the violence of the war, and then, in the footnotes, to cast doubt on the historical accuracy of *Simplicissimus*.[27] Yet history books, and certainly also later literary accounts of this time, including one by Friedrich von Schiller, are generally indebted to *Simplicissimus*. Wedgewood was right to identify *Simplicissimus* as a crucial source of historical information about the war, but at the same time, not to trust it wholly as a source.

Geoffrey Parker, in his 1984 revisionist work on this war, neither places attention on *Simplicissimus* primarily as a source of gruesome historical examples of the war nor ignores the book because it is embellished. Parker stresses this work of fiction because Grimmelshausen was certainly an eyewitness to, most probably a participant in, the war, and also because, at the very least, Grimmelshausen has shaped the way later writers and scholars have approached the life of the soldier in this war.[28] Just as historians now might use film, they have for centuries drawn on fiction, for both sources help them better grasp their historical subjects in a different way. Parker notes the major sources for the novel are low born and unnamed, thus demonstrating that the book is not wholly autobiographical. Parker evokes the almost domestic scene at the camp:

> So Grimmelshausen's characters smell unmistakably of the campfire, not of the headquarters, as they are shown brawling, gambling or darning socks as they wait for action; and although the events in *Simplicissimus* may be imaginary, the actors are not.[29]

In addition, Parker senses that the real enemy in this book is not from elsewhere in Europe, or of another religion, but rather is someone of higher rank.[30]

Indeed the war did little to change the pre-existing, highly aristocratic class structure. Class distinctions, which broke down during the war (dramatized in this novel by the ostensibly low-born Simplicissimus as a major war figure) were reasserted as soon as the hostilities ended (and even in the novel the main character is at the end revealed to be an aristocrat). Despite the stupendous loss in human lives during these decades—even given the lowest estimate of 20 percent of the total population dead—almost none of the dead civilians, Catholic or Protestant, were aristocrats. In addition, the South of Germany remained Catholic and the North remained Protestant. Thus, despite the carnage and economic devastation, many of the strict pre-war class and religious divisions survived the war intact.

4 The Author: Johann Grimmelshausen (1621?–1676)

Relatively little is known of Johann Jakob Christoffel von Grimmelshausen's own life. He was born in Gelnhausen, Hesse, near Hanau (the same city Simplicissimus enters in Book I, where he at first finds no one left alive after "imperial troops [on the side of the Holy Roman Empire] had surprised a company of Weimar dragoons"), in 1621 or 1622.[31] After his father's death, and his mother's remarriage when he was five years old, Grimmelshausen stayed on in Gelnhausen with a relative, probably his grandfather. His grandfather, Melchior Christoph (the character Simplicissimus's revealed Christian names), at this stage working as a baker, had dropped the "von" from their family name, thus demonstrating the same tension between aristocracy and poverty shown by his grandson's title character. Raised a Protestant, in 1634, at age 13, Grimmelshausen was in Gelnhausen when it was attacked by Imperial, Hessian (that is Catholic) soldiers in one of the great battles of the Thirty Years' War; this battle is not only brought forward in *Simplicissimus*, but it is also developed in the sequels to *Simplicissimus* (especially in *Tearaway*). It is assumed that Imperial soldiers kidnapped young Johann Grimmelshausen, and that he was in the regiments of several of the officers mentioned in the novel, most often on the Catholic Imperial side. This is the point historians repeatedly make when they note the autobiographical aspects of this novel. Apparently Grimmelshausen later served with the Hessian army, this time by choice, and was employed part of this time as a regimental clerk. After the war, having returned to his home area near Strasbourg, and he married (adding the "von" back into his name on the marriage document). His primary profession was not as a writer. He worked as an innkeeper, publican (this profession is also developed in *Tearaway*), and steward. He also held several local political offices. Thus Grimmelshausen himself did more than survive the war; he prospered on the local level.

During these years he started writing. He wrote popular calendars (guides and lists, not unlike Farmers' Almanacs), horoscopes, satirical and moral pamphlets, and then the Simplician Cycle of books. There are so few records about his life that it is not possible to determine the extent to which Grimmelshausen was a self-educated, lonely intellectual, with no friends or even university within which to debate, or whether he was part of a lively academic or literary grouping of which we are unaware.

Perhaps most crucially, Grimmelshausen was an adult convert to Catholicism, the religion of the Imperial Hessians (generally implying Catholic mercenaries) whom he had served with in the army. Although there are other classic examples of this, in the seventeenth-century German states this religious conversion was regarded as much more aberrant, beyond a private preference, a personal epistemological break; it was a clear, traitorous sign of shifting political allegiance.[32] The story of Grimmelshausen's adult conversion in the midst of a country torn by a supposed religious war is of interest, but there is insufficient primary evidence to pursue this in depth.

Studying Grimmelshausen by way of the history of the book is one way to tease out the secrets of this elusive author whose life and preferences are still hidden in the wreckage of the aftermath of the Thirty Years' War. The publishing history of *Simplicissimus* is problematic, but it helps at least to track down aspects of his life. It is known that Grimmelshausen first published *Simplicissimus* in 1668, and that it was published in its entirety in 1669.[33] The later additions to *Simplicissimus*, that is the ones written by Grimmelshausen, were all produced by the same publisher. Grimmelshausen's obscurity is actually a little surprising, given the success of his writings. In any case, the major points to be gained here seem to be: the publication date of *Simplicissimus* was 20 years after the Thirty Years' War ended; Grimmelshausen's own geographical location was far away from any major European capital or university; and his pursuit of his subjects was done seemingly on his own, albeit with substantial reference to printed sources. Only in the nineteenth century, with the revival of interest in *Simplicissimus*, was it even determined that all the diverse works mentioned above—including the horoscopes and moral pamphlets—were even written by Grimmelshausen. These themes of religion and war, freedom and anarchy, come in and out of focus more starkly in *Simplicissimus* than in any other early-modern work on the Thirty Years' War, and help to explain its popularity, if not the obscurity of its author.

5 Literary Genres

It would be wrong to consider *Simplicissimus* only in terms of seventeenth-century politics; this book can also be easily characterized by literary type. It is a classic *Bildungsroman*, a growing-up story of a boy reaching maturity in the midst of a world over which he had little control, and of a young man searching not only for his destiny, but even for his true name, both literally and metaphorically.[34] *Simplicissimus* is also assuredly part of the picaresque, the early-modern tradition recounting adventures of young men marginalized by society.

In the German tradition, the two genres of the picaresque and the *Bildungsroman* are opposed to each other in important respects, although certainly they both concentrate on the journey of a young hero through space and time. Nevertheless, they are different in the sense that the picaresque hero generally contends with complicated situations without changing, developing much himself, whereas the *Bildungsroman* is predicated on the education of the hero, who develops in essential ways through the course of the novel. Both are present in *Simplicissimus*. This book is a very peculiar case of a picaresque novel, but it is also true that in the tradition of German literary history, people tried to treat Grimmelshausen's novel as a *Bildungsroman*. This is a consequence of a later explanation—an interpretation based on the premises of modern nationalism—when scholars tried to extend the categories of the Goethe period across all of German literature.

Simplicissimus is manifestly a political satire. Yet rather than attacking just one side or one set of policies, the book pillories all participating countries, political systems, and forms of organized religion (predating both Swift and Voltaire, although following Cervantes, in this respect). Certain elements, however, such as Simplicissimus being revealed as the son of aristocrats, and the strong religious *motifs*, are reminders that the book also draws on much older, medieval traditions, especially medieval romances and passion, mystery plays.

Hence, *Simplicissimus* is associated with several established literary genres, yet it does not wholly fit into any one of them, instead breaking from these classic types in several respects. The distinctiveness of *Simplicissimus* is that it both draws from the context of a highly specific society in chaos and also produces a universal story of growing up, and of succeeding, at least for a while, despite the odds. Yet the character does not so much develop intellectually as he develops the social skills that allow him to make it clear to the rest of the world what his ideas are. He is never stupid, even when he is still wholly uneducated. This emphasis on Simplicissimus's growth also demonstrates that this work gives priority to the individual—children, women, and men—over society. *Simplicissimus*, if not a classic *Bildungsroman*, is nevertheless a story of the coming of age of one young person and is also arguably the coming-of-age story of the German people, indicating a pre-nation-state notion of national as well as cultural identity.

Although the book fits perhaps most neatly into the picaresque tradition, there is a more decided emphasis on classical learning and political debate in *Simplicissimus* than even in the picaresque.[35] The political banter in the Spanish picaresque novels, often in the form of classical allusions, is present in a substantive and nuanced form in the political analysis in *Simplicissimus*. The classical quotations are used for color, but also are an integral part of arguments being made in the book, including an effort to break down the barriers between high and low culture, with people of every social class presenting insights about disparate lifestyles. With the protagonist's quick assimilation and then application of classical sources, the supposedly dim leading character is revealed to be both an able intellectual and an entrepreneur.

In this first-person account, the older Simplicissimus plays the role of a narrator, and at times speaks directly to the reader, especially at the beginning and end of descriptions of a particular adventure. Many of the best lines are to be found in the first and last sentences of seemingly random chapters. The supposedly uncomplicated personality of the title character is reproduced almost wholly in the book's forthright writing style, which is, nevertheless, generously sprinkled throughout with Simplicissimus's erudite and entertaining quotations from ancient texts, often in asides to the reader. These references, invoked especially in terms of theoretical issues, such as epistemology and political philosophy, give classical, academic authority to the common-sense pronouncements that Simplicissimus makes at every age and stage.

Both the book and the main character are revealed to have much more depth than the reader would expect. Even when addressing contemporary mayhem, the narrator's education is revealed. This text—employing the techniques of both a *Bildungsroman* and the picaresque—asserts the utility of formal learning for the average person in a manner that is generally associated with the later eighteenth century.

6 Shifting Popularity of This Book and Later Usages of the Character Simplicissimus

Few books have had such a varied reception. Placed on the Catholic Index of Forbidden Books, and debated in the Prussian Parliament even as late as 1876 as possibly being worthy of censorship, the book has had strong allies and detractors at almost every stage.[36] Although rarely read today by Germans, and until the publication of an up-to-date English translation in 1999, even more rarely by non-Germans, the image of the not-so-simple, eponymous hero—a Candide who grows up, if not quickly, certainly substantially—remained alive in Germany. Even now in the twenty-first century, German students preparing to go to university to study the humanities often read at least parts of *Simplicissimus*. This was even more common in the GDR, the former East Germany.[37] This is a good example of the stress on assimilating classic books at school and at university that was an impressive element of education in the former East Germany, which is now lost. Appropriately, and in line with the attention to the book in the former East Germany, it would be easy to argue for *Simplicissimus* as a model for the emerging proletariat. This novel could feature prominently in a study of the development of pre-Marxist thought, of Marxism before Marx, in the pre-modern German states.

One somewhat odd but telling example of the character's lasting impact is that many German cities today have both expensive restaurants and bars,

Kneipe, named after Simplicissimus. In addition, both a German computer system and a Canadian library scripting system, are named in his honor. His name is still regularly invoked to denote spirit and especially rebellion against authority, as well as, to give one striking example, for name recognition for advertising purposes.

Previously *Simplicissimus* was thought to have been lost for most of the eighteenth century, and then rediscovered by the Romantics (a good example of Romantic concern for *Simplicissimus* is Carl Maria von Weber's opera *Der Freischütz*, first performed in Berlin in 1821), but this is now considered to be too sweeping a judgment, as the book was never wholly forgotten.[38] Much later, in the mid 1930s there was an anti-war opera adaptation of *Simplicius Simplicissimus* by Karl Amadeus Hartmann (1905–1963). However, the best-known link comes from Munich, from 1896 to1944, where there was a satirical magazine, with innovative graphics, named *Simplicissimus*, explicitly named to honor the seventeenth-century character. This magazine published such distinguished authors as Thomas Mann and Rainer Maria Rilke. Replete with marvelous, sharp political cartoons that directly attacked bourgeois values and the growing militarism in Germany, this journal— especially the political cartoons—is still startlingly amusing and worthy of attention in its own right.[39] All these later usages of Simplicissimus's name (perhaps especially the frequent choice of his name for slightly seedy German bars) indicate a rebellious spirit, the quality that allows an individual to succeed even in dreadful circumstances, which Germans, at least collectively if not individually, rightly remember as Simplicissimus's identifying characteristics.

A number of literary renditions of the Simplicissimus story, some of them deliberate updates, have attempted to reproduce the title character's indomitable will to survive; for example, there is a link to Büchner, that is not often explored. Georg Büchner (1813–1837) is generally categorized as an early German Expressionist writer, whose writings, especially the play *Woyzeck*, put forward political and social criticism in the vein of Thomas Paine.[40] Büchner's own work is devastating in its sharp criticism of all manifestations of human behavior, not only of social and political institutions. Notably, it does not put forward constructive political alternatives.[41] Büchner's work, distinctively for its time, asserts the right of the individual reader to make judgments and does not lead the reader toward set conclusions.

Yet, overall, it is Bertolt Brecht's name that comes up even more appropriately in conjunction with *Simplicissimus*. To begin, Grimmelshausen and Brecht share a fascination with the Thirty Years' War. Brecht, a follower of Büchner, was an East German playwright, literary critic, and Marxist public intellectual. Brechtian values include "fatalism, irony in the face of the Establishment homilies, [and] the tenacity of self-preservation."[42] It is not surprising that one of Brecht's plays is based on a later installment of Grimmelshausen's *Simplicissimus*, Grimmelshausen's second most-famous work, *Die Landstörtzerin Ertzbetrügerin Courasche (Courage, the Adventuress*, 1669). The Brecht version was entitled *Mutter Courage und ihre Kinder (Mother Courage and Her Children*, 1941).[43] Criticism from the left and right, even when the play was first performed in Berlin, charged that the character Mother Courage seemed stunted, continuing the debate about the character development in Grimmelshausen.[44]

Mother Courage and Her Children adheres exactly to Brecht's own principle of drama: that the core intellectual and political concerns of the play are not to be resolved in a manner that allows the audience to go home convinced that there is nothing left for them to do after they leave the theater.[45] There are multiple examples in *Mother Courage* of Brecht's dramatic principle of forcing the audience, not the characters, into action.

7 Grimmelshausen's Own Sequels

However, it was not just later admirers who continue the Simplicissimus story; even for Grimmelshausen himself the story seemingly never ends. The 1668 edition of *Simplicissimus* by Grimmelshausen contains only Books I–V; in 1669, Book VI was added. In Book VI—generally not treated as part of the core book—it is nevertheless of interest that the central character leaves his religious isolation and again travels the world—this time to the South Seas, refuses to go back to Europe, and dies a hermit. In the sequels to Grimmelshausen's original novel, the character is also traveling, but closer to home and in the company of many of his original companions. Most readers treat Books I through V as the core of the novel, which is not surprising, as most editions and translations only include Books I–V; Book VI and Grimmelshausen's sequels are at times unwieldy, but are rewarding to read in their own right.[46]

Grimmelshausen's own books, *Simplicissimus*, and the later sequels, *Courage, Tearaway*, and *The Enchanted Bird's Nest*, are perhaps best viewed as a unit, each one telling the same Simplician story but in a different genre each time. If *Simplicissimus* is a growing-up story, *Courage* tells the same story from a woman's perspective; *Tearaway* tells it from the view of a veteran, focusing on military history, and *The Enchanted Bird's Nest* tells it as fantasy. The first sequel, *Lebensbeschreibung der Ertzbetrügerin und Landstörtzerin Ertzbetrügerin Courasche (Courage*, 1669) is the retelling of the Simplicissimus story through the adventures of a female lead character.[47] The character Courage, like Simplicissimus, is also highly attractive, intelligent, and wily. Yet at all stages her lot is even harder than his for she must constantly negotiate for husbands in order to increase her wealth and to gain respectability. Even her remarkable abilities in both soldiering and money-making are not marketable unless she has the cover of a supposed male authority figure. The plight of the marginalized is also played out in the appearance of gypsies for the first time in the Simplician Cycle (all the books by Grimmelshausen on Simplicissimus) in *Courage*. This adds the element of race to these stories, and also puts forward the notion of an entire nation that exists separately from the German states, one that is even removed from the Thirty Years' War. After Courage loses her looks and the ability to attract new officers to become her husbands (she has many), she becomes a gypsy queen. The gypsy community presents one of the few viable, peaceful alternatives to nation-states in this book, and it fulfills Kant's two criteria for civilization: hospitality and peace. Despite her own wildly changing circumstances, Courage's desire throughout her story is always for vengeance on the one lover who spurned and tricked her, Simplicissimus himself. This adds a personal dimension, a tension lacking in Grimmelshausen's other two sequels, and reminds the reader that individual concerns can be even more galling than the horrors of war, the loss of social status, and growing impoverishment.

In Grimmelshausen's second sequel, *Der seltzame Springinsfeld* (*Tearaway*, 1670), Tearaway, Simplicissimus's fellow soldier, the sometime husband of Courage, is the main character and he tells his story as a military history.[48] For the first time, there is an emphasis in the Simplician Cycle on trying to get the sequence of military actions correct, not just using battles as markers of the changing fortunes of the main characters. Also for the first time in these three works, the lot of the victim is viewed as much worse than that of the victors. Tearaway's reunion with the main characters— Simplicissimus on a break from being a hermit, his Da and Ma, his bastard son Simplicissimus (not the son of Courage, but of Courage's maid)—first takes place in a tavern. But this reconnection becomes more substantial; eventually Tearaway dies, apparently peacefully, on Simplicissimus's farm. This reunion can be seen as foreshadowing the end of *Candide*, with the surprise reconnection of all the major characters on the farm outside Constantinople, a controversial ending taken to represent the limits of human happiness and achievement in a most imperfect world.

Grimmelshausen's third sequel, *Das wunderbarliche Vogelnest* (*The Enchanted Bird's Nest*, 1672), turns on a magical object that grants supernatural power to its wearer, but it also controls its wearer.[49] Set after the Thirty Years' War, in peacetime, this novel especially emphasizes social interactions, primarily adultery, although this is not a new theme in the Simplician Cycle. Coming in last in the series, the destruction of the enchanted bird's nest adds to the finality of this last book in the Simplician set of stories.

8 History of the Book

Even though it is generally accepted that this novel was popular when it was first published, some recent scholarship suggests that the price of the first editions of the book was too high, and the number of copies too low, to account for its widespread popularity.[50] This would cast some doubt on the *Märchenzeichen simplicianisch* (Simplician tales, a term often used for those books not written by Grimmelshausen). Yet, without a doubt, the original book spawned an industry of *simpliciana*, of which Grimmelshausen's own later additions, generally viewed as substantially inferior to the first five books of *Simplicissimus*, form just one portion.[51] For example, *Die Lanstörtzerin Courage,* noted above, is not an insignificant literary work in its own right. Overall, the general dismissal of all of Grimmelshausen's later writings seems too severe; in the same way, one could argue that minor works by Cervantes, Swift, and Voltaire, as well as Manzoni, also deserve attention.

In any case, at the time, even if all interested parties could not afford the book, the seventeenth-century market was able to sustain substantial sales of both Grimmelshausen's many sequels as well as their unauthorized counterparts. Both his own books and the versions of them written by other authors sold very well throughout the late 1600s. Much of the recent German scholarship on *Simplicissimus* focuses on the novel in terms of the history of the book.

The translations of the book appeared very late (wholly unlike the publishing history of *Don Quixote* published in Spanish in 1605, and first translated, for example, into English in 1612, even before Cervantes published Part II of *Don Quixote* in 1615, followed by a 1620 English translation of Parts I and II). The first translation of *Simplicissimus* was into English in 1912, followed by French in 1923, and later translations into Italian in 1958, and Spanish in 1978. Overall, almost all the copies of *Simplissimus* have been published in German, including Grimmelshausen's sequels and sequels written by those purporting to be Grimmelshausen.

The examples of *fausse simpliciana* (false versions of *Simplicissimus*) seem instead to have been written soon after the original book and follow strands of the original, admittedly complex, story, and do not put forward a separate message. The hope, in the German case, seems to have been that these versions would be taken as written by Grimmelshausen, if not by Simplicissimus himself. Thus, apparently, most Germans in the late seventeenth century had read, or more likely, had listened to, *Simplicissimus* and/or one of the books that followed *Simplicissimus*, which may or may not have been written by Grimmelshausen. Although most scholars now have a decided preference one way or the other, the term *simpliciana* is often used both for the later works by Grimmelshausen and also for those by other authors on the Simplicissimus theme. All these sequels, whether written by Grimmelshausen or not, confirm the power of the character Simplicissimus.

Perhaps more interestingly, a parallel tradition of unauthorized sequels exists for many famous works of fiction, including, of course, *Don Quixote.* The numerous *Simplicissimus* sequels by authors other than Grimmelshausen vary, for example, from the later case of *Robinson Crusoe* sequels. Much of the Robinsonia features the same story with a small, crucial difference: Crusoe as a woman, or the story as a learning tool for encouraging child literacy, or the story told in the form of a Baptist tract.[52] These three examples were themselves all competently written and widely distributed. The Simplicissimus stories, however, all continued the adventures of the same characters, sometimes minor characters, from the original volume. Thus in the German case the connection to the message of the original story was maintained by telling the story of the later lives of the main characters, whereas in the English case there was instead a repeated usage of the character Crusoe, with no substantial variations from the original plot, but done so for a range of ideological purposes.

9 Intellectual Traditions

This unusual novel, designed to shock as much as entertain, also contains strong elements of political thought, political theory, political philosophy, and modern political science more generally.[53] The book examines the motivation for political actions, examines political institutions, seeks better solutions for political problems, and outlines a system for studying such problems. First, the story could be read as an account of a Hobbesian state of nature (when Simplicius's family is graphically, yet not all permanently, killed); or as a depiction of a more enjoyable Rousseauian state of nature (during his years with the urbane hermit, whom he does not yet know to be his natural father); or as a display of Machiavellian wresting of power (when Simplicius shows decided skill in both ruling his troops and gaining popularity among the people, or at least, among certain, well-disposed young women); or, finally, as a utopian alternative (perhaps benevolent despotism; or a philosophical kingdom in the episode featuring the character called Jupiter, a schizophrenic; and certainly in the story of the fantastical underwater world of Mummelsee in Book V of *Simplicissimus*).[54] However, it can also be viewed as the logical, if perverse, extension of the theories of Adam Smith by showing the market in action: Simplicissimus's work as a mountebank—for example, his manufacture and sale of fake potions—is ludicrously profitable, he is able to make a significant amount of money from a ridiculous but well-packaged product. The eccentricities of the story, not just the central character, are used for satirical purposes in order to mock the political and economic structures and practices of the time.

One clear entertainment factor, which is part of the educational project of the book, is the employment of the title character as a fool. It might seem so obvious that there is humor in the employment of a simpleton as a title character that the utility in identifying the simpleton with a theory of early society is rarely considered by readers. However, each of the three main social-contract theories could be argued from Simplicissimus's personality. First, the Hobbesian sense of conflict, of warring in the human soul, which leads to perpetual fighting among individuals and groups, is evident not just in the set battle pieces in this work, but in all the human interactions that Simplicius is involved in once he is driven from his home in Chapter 1 of Book I. Second, a Lockean view of reason in the state of nature seems an ideal explanation for why even this supposedly dull-witted young man was able to master erudite and obscure books of ancient learning and also to become both a powerful military leader—a popular local figure, the Huntsman—and a successful business person. One clear example of this is when he learns from his mistake when swindled by the peddler for medicine that would supposedly cure his pock marks, in turn he almost immediately starts swindling others by selling worthless medicine, which would not cure them, but which did make him briefly (and all of his stages in this book are brief) very wealthy. Third, it is more difficult, but possible, to use Simplicissimus as an example of the Rousseauian state of nature. His strong desire for self-improvement, which draws him into society, even when he recognized it as corrupt; his blaming of women for the extreme ills of society; and his cheerfulness could be read as a prototype for the stereotypical interpretations of Rousseau's noble savage by nineteenth-century Romantics. The absence of functioning government in the midst of war does not mean that there is an absence of political debate and speculation in this work. *Simplicissimus* can be read from all these perspectives. Even though the political theory quoted and discussed in the book itself is different from all three traditions noted above, the political theory in the book could be read as a forerunner of the three later social contract traditions. The notion of the fool is used deliberately in fiction and theory for both entertainment and instruction.

The book looks both backward and forward, drawing from ancient and early-modern thought. There is, for example, a strong concern for utopias in *Simplicissimus*, and three desirable utopias are presented, although ultimately all are rejected: that of the Anabaptists (who have a utopia moving toward heaven); Switzerland (which is apparently quite literally heaven on earth); and Mummelsee, the underwater society (which is described in perhaps too much detail by its king—clearly this is designed as a satire of the pomposity of utopian political philosophy). The lead character, the narrator, and the book dismiss all three utopias. Yet these repeated descriptions of a society that would be good for its inhabitants and visitors are presented not only for entertainment, but it might be suggested that they also demonstrate a concern for both abstract individuals and for actual people who might be reading this book.

10 Religion and the Slow Shift toward *Laissez-Faire* Economics

The theme of religion resonates throughout this work in ways that are often unattractive, both in economic and social terms. However, Simplicissimus shows a love of theology at all stages of his development. He is drawn not just to the hermit but also to the pastors he encounters from town to town. Simplicissimus has sustained conversations with Protestant pastors, perhaps because these pastors (and not the Catholic priests) have copies of the religious books Simplicissimus has written (these books are mentioned throughout *Simplicissimus*, but not much information is given about them). The book *Simplicissimus* displays surprising tolerance toward both Catholicism and Protestantism, but also exhibits great interest in (if supposed dismissal of) other Christian groups, such as Eastern Orthodoxy and Anabaptism. *Simplicissimus* is widely understood as putting forward a peaceful viewpoint that advocates the overcoming of the confessional, Protestant versus Catholic, split.

At the same time this book has regularly been used, over the centuries, as evidence for the standard interpretation of the Thirty Years' War: religious hatred started the hideous fighting, but was not fully responsible for the continuation of bloodshed for decades. Much of the fighting had to do with economic disputes, many triggered by famine: this might gesture toward the slow movement of Germany toward free trade and growing capitalism. Mercenaries did much of the fighting in the Thirty Years' War. Machiavelli's dire views on the deleterious effects for any state that employed mercenaries were certainly proved correct by the Thirty Years' War.

This was also the first major religious war within Europe. The marauding soldiers themselves could be viewed as an example of the new mobility of labor of the German working class (to employ a much later term), not free as much as forced to leave both the land and urban homes in order to earn sufficient income to feed themselves and their families. It was not just land or tangible capital that was being negotiated, but power over trade routes and the flow of labor markets. *Simplicissimus* does not privilege capitalism over all other economic systems, but certainly it is a descriptive report about the economic system at the end of the Thirty Years' War, a system that was at best no longer wholly feudal, but also showed signs, even in the midst of the destruction, of incipient (if tardy, by European standards) capitalism.

In *Simplicissimus*, the choice between economic systems is just as stark as in such classic works as *Robinson Crusoe* and *Frankenstein*; however, *Simplicissimus* puts forward an altogether different view of the economy. The other two works are generally read both as wholesale attacks on the unbridled egotism of capitalism, and as proto-Romantic or Romantic. A Romantic orientation is often taken to be a challenge both to the pure sciences and to technology and is often linked to a literal return to nature, the countryside as an escape from the sprawling urban centers. However, in this much earlier book, trade could be argued to be a possible means of recovering from war.[55]

Capitalism in the mid-seventeenth century had not yet developed sufficiently to be the economic system culpable for the horrors of these decades of war. Marx rightly latched onto *Robinson Crusoe* as an example of how the value of money is determined only by demand, or in other terms, by social context.[56] There is a strong emphasis on the disutility of "a parcel of money, as well as gold and silver" for Robinson Crusoe on what he called, at first, "this wretched island."[57] In distinction, in this much earlier German book, capitalism could be argued to be a possible means of postwar reconstruction, although most readers have seen only a strong interest in politics and the building of government and the state. Nevertheless, the emphasis on Simplicissimus's adoptive parents' creation of a successful new farm, years after their original farm was demolished, is just one example of the strong entrepreneurial spirit within the book, which is embodied most fully of course by their adopted son. This emphasis on entrepreneurialism should be viewed not primarily as innocence about the later abuses of capitalism, but it is perhaps not too farfetched to consider it as offering a possible means for overcoming the limitations of capitalism, that is, by not regarding capitalism to be the ultimate economic system, but as a useful stage of economic development. Although more overtly religious than most later political novels, at the same time, and at all stages, *Simplicissimus* weaves together the themes of religion, economics, and war, in a manner that is more familiar to twenty-first-century readers than it would have been to readers of the intervening centuries.

11 Link to Titus Livius (Livy, 59 B.C.–17 A.D.)

It would seem most natural to continue the comparison of *Simplicissimus* to the works of Machiavelli—the major writer on political power, vilified in the early-modern period, who is now celebrated as the thinker whose work marks the shift to modern political thought—who is often cited directly in *Simplicissimus*. (The odious character Oliver, for example, declares in Book IV: "I can see you haven't read Machiavelli, my dear Simplicius. I have my principles.")[58] However, links can be traced further back to one of Machiavelli's own *autori* [favorite authors], Titus Livius (Livy, 59 B.C.–17 A.D.), one of the three greatest historians of Rome. Livy's view of the development of Rome parallels the story in *Simplicissimus* so closely that at times one summation works as well for *Simplicissimus* and the German states of the seventeenth century as it does for that of Livy's history of first-century Rome, when Livy was writing, yet primarily of even earlier centuries of Roman history. A slightly irreverent reading of the first 10 books of Livy is the following. (1) This is primarily military history, then political history: these two forms of history culminate in the history of building a city, building by building, and area by area. The story is told through the actions of a series of great men along the way. (2) All Roman women are beautiful, or at least all Roman women worth mentioning by name. Some Roman women are even articulate (young girls, as well as old women) and brave (including a servant girl who has a statue put up in her honor, with examples from Books I to V). Thus outer appearances do reveal inner moral qualities. (3) According to Livy, pesky neighbors such as the Etruscans, Samnites, and Volscians should realize that they are not a genuine threat to the growing might of Rome. The Romans must realize their own power. (4) Some plebeians, by virtue of being Roman, are as naturally talented as patricians. Thus, for

Livy, Roman plebs get the better of foreign aristocrats, if not in every battle then in some overall reckoning; and all plebs in Rome should have a share in the political and financial rewards of the city. National allegiances are more powerful than class distinctions. (5) The emphasis on superstition and signs, especially in the form of casual comments by servants or lower-level soldiers, could be taken, during crises, as direct manifestations of the will of the gods. People of the lower classes have information that could be used for the good of all, and such information could be crucial in times of crisis. The concern is to learn how to read the minds and discern the insights of the uneducated. (6) It is not cowardly to cede to mob pressure, but rather expedient. The Forum is one of the best places to judge the immediate mood of the city, especially in the midst of a crisis. In these situations, this is not a sign of the weakness of men, but rather of their profound involvement in Roman affairs. Military stoicism is sometimes inappropriate. (7) Although Rome suffered from plague, and the plebs from debt, the real problem of Rome was lack of unity, civil strife, and political intrigue—for a united Rome could not be beaten by disease or by foreigners. Thus any invasion of Rome had much more to do with Roman failing than with Gallic valor. Thus the people are also responsible for their own problems, for their have the power to change, to better, their society.

All of these broad notions can be found in *Simplicissimus*. They help to establish the intellectual grounding of the German novel more fully, as the links are to the classic Roman work, not just to the popular conception of Machiavelli as a devil in the early-modern period. Machiavelli made clear his own debt to Livy in the subtitle of his own marvelous work: *Discorsi sopra la prima deca di Tito Livio* (*Discourses on the First Ten Works of Livy*, published posthumously in 1531). Thus the emphasis on the working people is not new in *Simplicissimus*, but can be located much earlier in the ancient Roman history of Livy and the Renaissance political theory of Machiavelli.

What is new in *Simplicissimus* is a strong emphasis on economic factors over forms of government. Overall, these seven points from Livy are reworked in an early-modern setting in *Simplicissimus*. Both books are reflections on the chaos, yet also the particular creative spirit, of a nation in its formative stages. Even though Livy's work is history and Grimmelshausen's book is fiction, in content, tone, and political message they are surprisingly similar.

12 Synopsis

This German story of a young fool who becomes a stupendous success, an abject failure, and then a hermit is used to show the gruesome breakdown of society in seventeenth-century Middle Europe. The story can be explained partly by an examination of literary genres. The shifting popularity of this book, and yet the ongoing name recognition of the title character, indicate not only changing tastes but also readers' desire for a superhero, perhaps even a role model, who can overcome the most preposterous adversities. Grimmelshausen's own sequels to *Simplicissimus—Courage, Tearaway,* and *The Enchanted Bird's Nest*—all develop themes he alludes to in the first novel, including the plight and perspicacity of women and the marginalization of veterans by society, as well as non-judgmental comments about belief in magic in the midst of a supposedly modern society. The autobiographical aspects of this story are manifest when one examines the life story of Grimmelshausen. A study of this work in terms of the history of the book indicates both the obscurity of the author and the astonishing popularity of a book when it was first published, a book written by someone from outside of the traditional educated classes.

Indeed, the appeal of Grimmelshausen's series of books was so strong that countless people who have never read this book, or even one of the later sequels written by other authors trying to take advantage of the success of *Simplicissimus*, from the seventeenth century to the present, are still able to identify the character Simplicissimus, a peasant boy who is more than a survivor, he is at times a winner. Simplicissimus has become a folk hero to the Germans, and even though he was created first in a novel rather than as part of an oral tradition, he is treated like a Robin Hood figure. This explanation exists despite, or perhaps because of, Simplicissimus's wholesale lack of concern for others, including his own love objects. There was much robbing from the rich, but little giving to the poor by Simplicissimus. Thus, although the Simplicissimus story does not wholly come directly from the oral tradition, it actually produced an oral tradition.

Yet the connections to high culture are always there as well. Intellectual traditions from Aristotle in particular are referenced directly by the title character, even when he is supposedly a fool. This indicates the need for both common sense and classical education for all—two key concepts for Aristotle, and by simply using Aristotle's name, the classics are invoked. At all stages of the story, religion, especially Protestantism, is linked to the shift toward what would later be termed *laissez-faire* economics. This predates Max Weber's theory of the Protestant work ethic by over two centuries. Nevertheless, it may well be Livy (who lived 16 centuries before the Thirty Years' War), not the later Machiavelli (who lived only a century before Thirty Years' War), who may provide the best way of examining the intellectual content of this early-modern German war novel.

II EASING THE PILGRIMAGE: MONTAIGNE, COOKED PEAS, AND ENVIABLE FRIENDSHIP

1 The Friendly Deception

Friendship is perhaps the one abstract notion, certainly the one type of relationship, that Simplicissimus responds to positively at all stages, whether he is wild and wandering, or educated and privileged. Indeed, it is somewhat surprising that friendship—the desire for friendship—manages to dominate Simplicissimus more than does greed, suspicion, and extreme self-interest, all of which he wallows in for much of the time, polluting his personal relations. His innate desire for friendship is perhaps nowhere as striking as in the story of the cooked peas at the end of Book IV and into Book V. To be sure, Book V, Ch. 1, is also about genuine penance, self-improvement, moral debate, piety, the inability to reform oneself, and the loss of innocence, but it is manifestly about friendship.

Simplicissimus has just located his dear friend, Young Ulrich Herzbruder (Brother-of-the-Heart), whom he had believed to be long dead. (Herzbruder's father was the first to spot Simplicissimus's true abilities when Simplicissimus is still literally acting the fool.) Actually Simplicissimus at first does not recognize his friend, who appears as a smelly beggar (perhaps a link forward to Pangloss in *Candide*), but once Herzbruder identifies himself, Simplicissimus treats him royally, even though those around them cannot understand at all why Simplicissimus would host such a down-and-out. Herzbruder, the erstwhile stylish and successful commander, has become not only poor, but also exceedingly religious in the meantime, and he wants Simplicissimus to accompany him on a religious pilgrimage, which Simplicissimus proceeds to do.

Herzbruder plans a pilgrimage to Einsiedeln, outside Zurich, still a place of pilgrimage, with a tenth-century Benedictine abbey built on the site of the ninth-century martyrdom of St. Meinrad, and famous for its relic of the Black Madonna. Simplicissimus's motivation for the trip is to see the Swiss Federation, the only place he knows in the region that has peace. He also very much wants to be with Herzbruder.

By this stage, their sincere desire is to accommodate each other: "Each of us maintained he had not done as much for the other as a friend should."[59] Typical of close friends, they fight most tenaciously when they are attempting to help each other, almost always in ways that the other does not desire, indeed cannot abide. They have multiple squabbles about the logistics and premises of the pilgrimage, which is even more amusing when one realizes that at this point they are wearing long black robes, using pilgrim's staffs, carrying rosaries. They have paid off the guide, apparently so they can be alone to get on with these disputes. Their quarrelling, verging on that of lovers, continues as the trek advances, and Herzbruder notices with rage that Simplicissimus is not praying as much as he is. Simplicissimus sighs:

> He thought I should be praying all the time like him, but I just couldn't get myself into the habit.[60]

And then Simplicissimus cooks the peas.

The cooked peas are not a break from the ordinary food for pilgrims, but rather the result of Simplicissimus's inability to withstand the pain of walking with uncooked peas in his shoes, as his friend Herzbruder was doing as penance throughout the journey.

This is how it happened: one day, after one long day of rugged hiking, Simplicissimus takes the raw peas out of his shoes, cooks them, and then walks on mashed peas the next day. Once Simplicissimus admits to Herzbruder why he is walking so freely, after Herzbruder praises Simplicissimus for his greater fortitude in withstanding the peas (Simplicissimus is unable to lie to Herzbruder), Herzbruder threatens that his love for Simplicissimus might disappear because of the cooked-peas incident.[61]

> 'Oh Simplicius', he said, 'peas or no peas, I can see you have strayed far from the path of salvation. May God lead you to better ways, otherwise our friendship is at an end.'[62]

After this outburst, as the pilgrimage continues, Herzbruder will no longer talk to Simplicissimus; he will only look at Simplicissimus and sigh.[63]

It is worth contemplating again Simplicissimus's reasons for making this journey at all. Perhaps Simplicissimus accepts the idea of a pilgrimage as fitting, not just as penance for his scattered nature but also as a constructive and orderly response to, and as a means of redeeming, his utterly disorganized life. He thus sees the trip as a corrective not only to his nature but also to his own lack of nurturing as a child. At first Simplicissimus is not invited on the spiritual trek; Herzbruder initially wants to make the pilgrimage alone, but Simplicissimus wants to be with Herzbruder all the time. The marvelous test case of the cooked peas in the pilgrim Simplicissimus's shoes does not necessarily indicate that he was being sacrilegious, as Herzbruder hotly charged, but rather that Simplicissimus, unlike Herzbruder, has no interest at all in participating in the self-tests of pilgrims. Simplicissimus instead is using this as a way to exert some minute degree of control in the midst of a life of continued upset and chaos. Although the book has many partially hidden endorsements of Catholicism, this episode certainly could also be read as an attack on the Catholic tendency to value performance and ritual over both the practical application and symbolic meaning of the ritual, a Protestant theme.

Assuredly, Simplicissimus put peas—and when they hurt too much, cooked peas—in his shoes as a way to participate with his friend in the pilgrimage. This demonstrates not only the title character's literalist bent but also loyalty and some degree of belief in abstract ideas, as well as single-mindedness. Herzbruder is correct to ask why Simplicissimus does not simply take the peas out of his shoes, instead of cooking them and returning them to his shoes. However, Simplicissimus is so delighted to be reunited with his friend that he wants to participate in all aspects of his friend's pilgrimage. Yet he does not want to fight with Herzbruder about the parameters of the trip, and he does not want to feel any pain in the process.[64]

The emphasis here is only partly on the desire for creature comforts in the midst of a sacred journey; it also reveals the internal resolve in this young character, even while he is markedly irreligious. Despite his religious debates with countless pastors, and the book's many calls for religious toleration of both Catholics and Protestants, Simplicissimus's determination to set off on a pilgrimage, and to persevere until the end of that pilgrimage, is not necessarily religious in origin. This constancy stems from a relationship, not an ideological commitment. If it is ideological at all, it extends only to the idea of intense personal association. Friendship seems to be the paramount reason for Simplicissimus's participation in this uncomfortable hike, for the reader assumes, especially at this stage, that Simplicissimus would have followed young Herzbruder equally happily to places that offered more immediate diversion, such as the nearby spas in the Black Forest.[65]

2 A Craving for Friendship, or Just a Craving

Yet this friendship is linked with a desire for luxury, and also with feelings of a more intense nature. A more cynical view is that Simplicissimus, with soft peas now inserted in his boots, is allowing Herzbruder to suffer when he does not. This would indicate that Simplicissimus's feelings for Herzbruder are closer to infatuation than genuine love, and that the desire for self-sacrifice is not present in Simplicissimus. If, as Freud argues, the desire for proximity, identification, and self-sacrifice are the three factors indicating love of a sexual nature, then according to this rubric, Simplicissimus is only expressing the first two of these three factors.[66] Simplicissimus's idea of friendship, however, includes allowing his friend to do what he wants and to accompany him, but without too much pain. Thus, again in Freudian terms, this is a concern most fully between ego (Simplicissimus) and object (Herzbruder, or the idea of Herzbruder). Making Herzbruder happy is not the central concern here at all. In more literary, somewhat less direct terms, the same dynamic is most evident in medieval, courtly love literature, which features a knight and his lady love.

The peas themselves, not just Simplicissimus's cooking of them, are symbolic. The peas could represent the small items of life, that it is best to judge someone by his behavior in small situations over time, in particular the consistency of his work ethic, such as Simplicissimus's commitment to a prolonged pilgrimage. The peas might demonstrate the small vices that attract all people, confirming that the vices craved most are the small, secret ones, never mind if they are not very grand in comparison to other people's more colorful vices. The peas could even suggest an outrageous claim regarding the necessity of full political participation, especially in the small German states that did not have adequate civil protection (this would thus reflect the Peace of Westphalia, which gave sovereignty to small states) for the little people, those even less talented and fortunate than Simplicissimus, who nevertheless have decided views that are never part of official calculations. Another somewhat preposterous suggestion might be made that the peas could stand for how the voice of the small person will in some way be heard, even if not through official channels. This is oddly manifested in both Herzbruder's righteous rage and, shortly later, in the howling condemnation, by a madman possessed by a devil, that Simplicissimus has cooked the peas. Even war-hardened Simplicissimus is shown, finally, to have a normal conscience that bothers him for the behavior he finds most loathsome, such as tricking his friend, much more than for his more indisputable crimes, including murder, rape, and plunder. Overall, in almost all these readings, these symbolic meanings of the peas demonstrate that Simplicissimus responds to the crises in his life in ways that are somewhat counterintuitive, and these non-intellectual responses are what allow people, especially the less well educated, to live in the midst of dire circumstances, even poverty and war.

Another suggestion is that cooking the peas indicates the lengths to which people in trauma will go to maintain long-standing relationships. Instead of taking this to imply that people turn to friends only during crisis, rather it could show that the dynamic of friendship can be understood only when worldly distractions, including any outside requirement for the relationship, are stripped away. Thus, the need for human connection, only partly determined by family connections, is innate, and can also be blocked. The deliberate nature of cooking the peas could represent the myriad decisions and actions taken by those who have suddenly had an epistemological break, indicating how they should live from that point on. Thus, the shift here in the theoretical reading of the book might be from psychological theories of Simplicissimus as an everyman to a theory grounded in association, necessary as a basis for civil society: that is, a theory of friendship.

This is an Aristotelian model of friendship that places substantial demands on friends. For Aristotle, friendship is always between just two people (for Aristotle, in fourth century B.C., only between two men), and should last throughout their entire lives, for there is only a limited number of reasons that a friendship could ever be terminated. According to Aristotle, "most differences arise between friends when they are not friends in the spirit they think they are," for example, when one of the two has failed to develop intellectually.[67] This classical model of friendship, most fully expressed in Book IX of Aristotle's *Nicomachean Ethics*, puts forward the model of friends as equals, similar in terms of personal qualities and thus balanced in terms of rank, who are able to give each other constructive criticism as well as support for life. Distinct from a lover or a business partner, although these categories could overlap, this is not a relationship that would always give pleasure. This type of friendship can often be awkward, for there are no inherent benefits to be accrued besides the existence of the friendship itself. Nevertheless, for Aristotle, this highest form of friendship is the basis for a constitutional system, in which one would be comfortable "ruling and being ruled in turn." For Aristotle, friendship is the basis of the society that could be ruled without tyranny or anarchy. Aristotle's consideration of when friendship should be broken serves as a pre-Lockean (and anti-Hobbesian) model of changing rulers without destroying the very fabric of society; this dynamic is directly mimicked in Simplicissimus and Herzbruder's bickering.

3 The Evil Spirit

Shortly after the boiling of the peas, in the next chapter (Book V, Chapter 5), Simplicissimus and Herzbruder are in a church, where Herzbruder (but not Simplicissimus) prays, and where they encounter a priest exorcising a demon from a madman. This beastly spirit proceeds, uncannily, to be both authoritative and accurate in his multiple condemnations of Simplicissimus. To begin, the spirit is surprised to see Simplicissimus; he declares that he had assumed that he would instead see Simplicissimus with Oliver in hell. (Oliver is a soldier, an acquaintance of Simplicissimus, who appears throughout the story; he is indeed a more hideous version of Simplicissimus, and wholly without Simplicissimus's charm.) For perhaps the first time in his life, Simplicissimus experiences guilt (not just annoyance) that he is failing to achieve his goals. This evil shade accuses Simplicissimus, again perceptively, of being a monk (remember that he is wearing religious attire, although it is just a ruse). This also makes sense because of his early connection to the earlier hermit, revealed to be his biological father. Simplicissimus is, perversely, also charged with being an Anabaptist (part of a splinter Protestant group), not even a Lutheran (which was the established Protestant Church, for German-speaking states that were not Catholic), and this is perhaps a reference to his adoptive parents, who are rural farmers. Further, he is charged with being an atheist. All of these multiple, somewhat accurate attacks come out of the mouth of the man possessed by an evil spirit. The evil spirit within the man shrieks, and Simplicissimus assumes that it is wholly because he walked on cooked peas that the dark spirit in the church condemns him. At this point, unlike the previous days since Herzbruder discovered the cooked peas, Simplicissimus does not even consider that the shrieking has to do with the other evil deeds he has so consistently committed. He takes breaking the sanctity of the pilgrimage to be much more vile than all the other things that he has done, including mass murder and multiple rapes. It is apparently the combination of contempt for religion plus, most strongly, betrayal of a friend that make this particular action the most loathsome to Simplicissimus. There is no need for sophisticated analysis by Simplicissimus regarding why he has lost God's grace: the demon explains with multiple condemnations, albeit without direct mention of the peas, but complete with howls.

Simplicissimus and the man with the evil spirit are both behaving as holy fools. There is a long tradition of this, especially in Eastern Europe. Patristics and Byzantine scholar Mary Cunningham considers deliberate lunacy used by the holy fool as a teaching tool for the Christian life:

> This group of ascetics turned all the rules of Christian life, so to speak, upside down. Saint Symeon pretended to be half-witted, acting in outrageous and unpredictable ways. According to his seventh-century biographer, Leontios of Neapolis, Symeon entered a church one Sunday and began throwing nuts at the candles. When the congregation tried to chase him out, he went up in the pulpit and began pelting the women with nuts. As Symeon finally left the church, he overturned the tables of the pastry chefs (presumably selling cakes at the front of the church). Many other incidents in the life of this holy fool seem to mock the customs of the church, but also to recall events in the life of Christ.[68]

She continues:

> There can be no doubt that Symeon mimics in this scene the entrance of Christ into Jerusalem, reversing the story, however, by making himself an object of ridicule rather than celebration. The holy fool, basing his way of life on the passage 'We are fools for Christ's sake' (I Corinthians 4:10) experienced humility more completely than even the most impoverished and hungry ascetics could ever do. The tradition of 'holy fools' survived through the later centuries of the Byzantine era and was adopted in Orthodox Russia. . . . in Russian literature the concept is treated most famously in Dostoevsky's *The Idiot*.[69]

Cunningham's Byzantine and Russian examples help to clarify the bizarre setting, including the general acceptance of wise madmen, in this German book.

This scene in *Simplicissimus* functions on at least two levels. Even though the others present in this Swiss church are not too concerned about holy shouting and do not understand why the possessed man is accusing this particular religious pilgrim, Simplicissimus comprehends nevertheless that it has to do with the overcooked vegetables. Herzbruder (inaccurately) defends Simplicissimus against the charge of ever having been a monk. (It is not explained why this should be a problem for a mendicant Catholic, but perhaps the implication is that he is a disgraced monk.) Herzbruder stresses instead that Simplicissimus has been a soldier. Outwardly, this incident is not substantial problem for Simplicissimus, despite his own fears and Herzbruder's trepidation, for no one believes the spirit, because Simplicissimus is dressed as a pilgrim.

In order to mute the evil spirit, and however much against his will to begin, Simplicissimus goes through the religious rites. The result is unexpected: he feels genuine regret for his sins, he goes through confession and absolution, and the evil spirit in the man stops screaming at him.[70]

The ritualistic benefits of confession and then communion need not be completely dismissed. This incident shows Simplicissimus willing to try any option, even a religious one, and receiving indeed some sense of peace, even though there is no lasting change in his character.

The encounter concludes, as so often is the case, with an almost story-book ending, for the two then spend two weeks rejoicing in Simplicissimus's conversion. He wrote later, however, that his conversion did not last because it was never genuine.[71] Thus, even though the possibility of a Christian life is not demonstrated by even one lay example (as presumably Herzbruder is now fully in the Church), the theme of saintliness is heralded throughout this book. This celebration of the renunciation of the life of the flesh is a means of reminding the reader how attractive, not just difficult, life in the world is. For far from being mocked, the lead father-and-son hermits (Simplicissimus and his birth father) and the Anabaptists who appear toward the end of the book are invariably noted with respect by the narrator, Old Simplicissimus, who is no disinterested observer of this story. The hermit and the Anabaptists, indeed, bookend the story, and there is very little saintliness between them, until the lead character himself becomes a hermit in Book V. Simplicissimus is innocent or righteous only at the beginning and end of the book. However, in Grimmelshausen's three sequels to the book, Simplicissimus leaves his island retreat where he lived as a hermit to wander in his former homeland in an almost idle, no longer frantic or spiritual, fashion. In the sequels, the most preposterous incidents seem to be the repeated times when he supposedly accidentally meets up with his former acquaintances. Yet at the same time, it is the other-worldliness of deeply religious figures, their mystical qualities, that seem palpable to the young and the Old Simplicissimus alike; the renunciation of earthly riches, honors, and power seems to be a necessary factor in achieving such pronounced piety.

Piety and magic are mixed throughout *Simplicissimus*; the book is not reluctant to mix a genuine belief in magic with fantastical literary elements. The theme of magic as essential to basic human survival is asserted in ways most readers since 1750 would view as puzzling. There is, indeed, more mention of magic in this book than in *Don Quixote* (assuming that Quixote is misled on the theme of enchantment). All the characters believe in magic in *Simplicissimus*, and only one does in *Don Quixote*. There is also less magic in this book than in the later works *Gulliver's Travels* or *Candide*, even though the latter two are built upon such fantastical premises such as the inability of the central characters to die natural deaths, and the human-like lifestyles of non-human species. There is magic even in the Italian novel *The Betrothed* (published in 1827, revised in 1840), a reminder that even though it was written in the nineteenth century, it was set in the seventeenth century. In *The Betrothed*, the belief in enchantment—in this case, that widespread confidence that plague is spread by black magic deliberately practiced on unsuspecting victims—is roundly criticized by the presumably Catholic Liberal narrator.

The magic in *Simplicissimus*, however, embraces not only superstition but also actual witches and warlocks (several spotted by the central character near Magdeburg), stories of the witches' sabbath, and performing magicians (one of whom casts spells on Simplicissimus, who admittedly had been toying with the magician), all of which are noted as natural parts of the story. Necromancy, sorcery, and alchemy are referred to at regular intervals. Casual comments compare the extraordinary activities of the war to the regular activities of peacetime "as if they were extracting confessions from witches before burning them."[72] There is no condemnation of witchcraft whatsoever in this book even though it was set in a time of mass witch hunts in early-modern Central Europe, approximately 1450–1700, which lends an aspect of toleration. The magical elements in the story intensify late in the story. There is an underwater society, Mummelsee, with its own Prince, and, adding to the preposterousness of this deep-sea culture, the Prince of Mummelsee is the only character in the entire work to deliver an extended lecture, the subject of which is good and evil. This section of the book is, predictably, useful and dull. Nevertheless, all the small, magical elements in Book I through IV (such as the three witches in Book II, Chapters 17) become dominant in the underwater society in Book V. The deliberate addition of magical elements throughout the story makes it necessary for the modern reader to remember that, in contrast, the extent of the violence in the story, throughout the seventeenth-century German states, was not fabricated. Most modern accounts, such as Keith Thomas's *Religion and the Decline of Magic*, tend to equate the move toward modernity with a growing hatred of superstition.[73] However, if *Simplicissimus* is taken to mark a conscious transition toward the modern age, this supports the argument that not only religion, but also magic, or at least toleration of those who practice magic, remain part of the modern landscape.

4 Magical Realism

Simplicissimus's ability to survive numerous hideous attacks is an example of what would much later be called magical realism.[74] He alone seems to possess this ability, although some key characters he assumes to have died later reappear relatively unscathed. (Voltaire's *Candide*, of course, develops this theme to preposterous lengths.) In *Simplicissimus*, Young Herzbruder appears for a final bow. Da and Ma are resurrected, not just to tell Simplicissimus that he is not their natural son, but also so that they can run their new family farm, funded by Simplicissimus, in a highly efficient, proto-Weberian manner. Even Simplicissimus's natural mother reappears in a fashion through stories: from Da's stories, layered onto the Governor's earlier story of his own sister, whom Da much later reveals to Simplicissimus to have been his birth mother.[75] Resurrections, if only through stories of dead biological (and aristocratic) parents, give the older Simplicissimus a sense of personal history. Thus this early version of magical realism helps to give the reader a vicarious sense of personal history as well.

The style of magical realism of *Simplicissimus* is now associated with the best Latin American literature in the twentieth century, especially the "levitating grandmothers" of Colombian writer Gabriel García Márquez, and the work of Argentinean Jorge Luis Borges. This term is also highly appropriate for some of the work of Salman Rushdie, especially *Midnight's Children* (1981). There is indeed a link between Grimmelshausen and Rushdie: the German novelist Günter Grass, who declares himself a follower of Grimmelshausen, is also admired by Rushdie.[76]

Simplicissimus was directly influenced by the magic inherent in the German folk songs, folktales, and fairy tales later collected by the Brothers Grimm, and by other German folk tales of the Huntsman, echoes of which can still be found in modern German literature, and which hearkens back to a simple literary style of decades, even centuries, earlier. There exist, in *Simplicissimus*, both an urge to ground the work in high culture—especially Aristotle—and the perhaps stronger pull of popular beliefs.[77] The modern examples of magical realism and *lo real maravilloso* (the marvelous real) force a reevaluation of the much earlier *Simplicissimus*, which weaves magic into a story of the evisceration of feudalism by soldiers from opposing sides, united only by their mutual desire for rape, torture, pillaging, and destruction, who seemingly leave no structure in place in which capitalism, or any other economic system, could flourish.

5 A Model of Friendship: Jupiter and Simplicissimus

Yet in the midst of the lawlessness, tumult, and destruction, there are many models of friendship in *Simplicissimus*; the most absurd demonstrates that Simplicissimus is in such close touch with supernatural powers that he supposedly even encounters gods in his ordinary life. The colorful character Jupiter has arguably received inordinate attention from readers and scholars of this work over the centuries, yet Jupiter's ongoing attractiveness to others (including generations of readers) is still hard to deny. Jupiter is, of course, the Latin version of the Greek name, Zeus; he is the highest god in charge of order in the entire world. Jupiter, a character in *Simplicissimus*, is "a strangely foul-mouthed god," in Simplicissimus's estimation. Jupiter nevertheless becomes a camp follower in Simplicissimus's brigade when Simplicissimus first encounters him:

> I saw a single man come along the road, respectably dressed, talking to himself and shadow fencing with the cane he had in his hand. All that

I could hear was that he said, 'If the world won't recognize my divinity then I shall just have to punish it.'[78]

Simplicissimus later saves Jupiter from the less-than-friendly horseplay of another group. The character Jupiter symbolizes a direct personal connection to the spiritual dimension, one that cannot be hidden even in the working world of vagabonds and self-appointed soldiers. Those around him fear and deride his connection to the other side of reality, but no one wholly dismisses it. Jupiter apparently has a power, at least the force of personality that is awe inspiring; he is not dismissed easily like some insane fellow whom these soldiers would have known in their hometowns before their wanderings. Jupiter's message is much more diluted than those of some of his predecessor; indeed, he has no specific message to pass on. He is to be understood both in terms of the history of madness as an actual victim without appropriate custodial care and should also be counted among the great literary madmen with a message, such as Quixote.

Jupiter can be viewed as an anti-model for Simplicissimus regarding how to be a demagogue; Jupiter also demonstrates that friendship can occur even between two people who are not equals (*pace* Aristotle). Jupiter calls Simplicissimus his Ganymede, the symbol for beautiful youth and homosexuality (later the theme of homoerotic love comes out more fully in Simplicissimus's feelings for Herzbruder than even in Jupiter's feelings for Simplicissimus). Jupiter, the character in the novel, is either the Roman god reappearing in the seventeenth century, or evidence of a fascinating case of multiple personality disorder. In symbolic terms, he contrasts with the Epicurean view, and later the eighteenth-century Deist view, of the gods as uninvolved in human affairs.

The reader wonders at times whether the personality disorder is Jupiter's or Simplicissimus's, as demonstrated by lines such as "I could not get rid of my Jupiter."[79] Most of the time Simplicissimus's first reaction to this man never changes: "he has not caught a prince but a lunatic who had studied too much and had been driven mad by poetry."[80] Like Quixote, Jupiter is not reluctant to pull down his trousers in public, and he does so regularly to scratch his fleas. The possibility exists not only that Jupiter suffers from serious derangement, but also that he and Simplicissimus are the same person. The political implication of this might be that the common sense of the German people must be linked through Jupiter to the ancient wisdom of the past in order to achieve new and lasting political clout. This final possibility, that Jupiter exists only in Simplicissimus's mind, demonstrates, at the very least, the range of ways that heroic characteristics could be useful to all those in the hero's circle even though they were harmful to the hero himself. Jupiter attaches himself so firmly to Simplicissimus that the obligation is not that of a high-ranking officer of the other side, but rather a much deeper, almost primal one of family obligation. This is more than a father–son relationship, however quixotic; rather it is akin to the affection of an atheist for the gods of his parents. In any case, if Tearaway is part of Simplicissimus's *débutant* stage, in the same section of this book, Book III, Jupiter symbolizes Simplicissimus's own shift toward becoming a demagogue, again if only as an anti-role model. Simplicissimus wants to become a leader without being as crazed as Jupiter.

However, the figure of Jupiter shifts attention backward as well as forward in time. Jupiter serves as a symbol of a past civilization at a time when all civilization had crumpled. Keeping him alive and talking was thus an easily justifiable task for Simplicissimus. Given that there are only hints of folk tales and myths in the book, it might be speculated that this was a time when each person was caught up in a series of adventures that in ordinary years would be viewed as mythic in proportion. Perhaps only a figure as outrageous as one claiming to be the classical god Jupiter could be taken seriously in such a chaotic historical period.

In the midst of warring and pillaging, Simplicissimus himself also seems in need of diversion, and "my Jupiter," as he calls the older man, certainly provides that, no doubt especially when "he was in one of his moods."[81] The reference to "his Jove," who was "in one of his deranged phases," implies that there were manifest aspects to Jupiter's madness, and thus the degree of his madness could in a theoretical sense indicate that only through such a marginalized character as Jupiter could the authority of the classical past, and of classical leadership, be asserted. There were no modern models to take the place of the ones from antiquity.

Simplicissimus, who is in the role of the Huntsman at this stage, does not take Jupiter on as his fool permanently. Simplicissimus leaves Jupiter in the company of Tearaway for his next adventure. Simplicissimus is disappointed nevertheless, at least at a later stage, not to be able to have proper contact with Jupiter. When Simplicissimus sees him on a return visit, Jupiter, then demonstrating no superhuman qualities, does not recognize him. Jupiter is no better than anyone else at seeing through Simplicissimus's post-Paris, ravaged face to find the person inside whom he had known so well before. This may symbolize the inability of rivals to recognize the merits in each other's approaches as much as each other's achievements. It could also represent the desire by the wild, ungovernable German people for divine approval of their way of life, which even without much reflection appears to them unlikely to be granted. Just as Simplicissimus has mentors for his more rational side (Da, the hermit, and Old Herzbruder), so Jupiter is his guide to accepting the non-rational aspects of the world. Jove himself, in all of his roles and in his symbolic playfulness, represents parts of Simplicissimus that are unfulfilled. This psychological interpretation of Simplicissimus stresses that he is not uninhibited in all respects—that there are aspects of his character that he hides away. This leads to the political interpretation that Simplicissimus and Jupiter together represent the most extreme versions of the responses to the Thirty Years' War. A union of such extremes could be positive or negative, a constructive linking of rationality and emotion, or of laws in a world where the strongest employed the laws for their personal benefit. The friendship between Simplicissimus and Jupiter is one of loyalty, not equality, but seems even more powerful for this.

6 Yet Another Model Friend: Tearaway as the True Working-Class Hero

It could be argued that the minor character Spring-ins-feld (translated as Tearaway), Simplicissimus's early friend, is the true working-class hero of the book. Tearaway can be likened not so much to a friend but rather to a flea in Simplicissimus's life (Jupiter is called "the god of the fleas").[82] It is not just that Tearaway is a nuisance, but that for Simplicissimus his irritating presence is something normal in the midst of all the transience and tumult. Thus, Tearaway, as a flea in Simplicissimus's life, is similar to Simplicissimus in relation to the upper classes. This reinforces that the deepest source of conflict in the not-yet-united German states was not so much that between the aristocracy and the princes (as in early-modern France between the King and the aristocrats), but rather between those who had to work for a living and those who did not, a much more primal, proto-Marxist division. It is this rather forgettable character, Tearaway—albeit one of the sequels is named after him—who demands this type of political analysis.[83]

Tearaway, a gawky companion in arms, could at first be dismissed as a warm-up character for Jupiter, as just another soldier whom Simplicissimus encounters during his time as the Huntsman; however, this shortly changes. Simplicissimus introduces Jupiter as his fool now, when a year ago Simplicissimus had been a fool himself: "Not long ago I was being tormented by lice and now I had the god of fleas in my power."[84] Yet it could be argued that Tearaway as a *débutant*, and then Oliver, the evil companion, as a demagogue, outstrip Simplicissimus in these roles. Tearaway may be a flea, but he is one whom Simplicissimus was willing to tolerate. Tearaway represents an un-regenerated version of Simplicissimus himself. If the reader thinks that Simplicissimus is grasping, then Tearaway is useful in his self-presentation of ambition with no reflection whatsoever. Tearaway thus represents an annoyance in Simplicissimus's life, not a domestic or farm animal, but a wild animal, an independent creature, perhaps a parasite, who has a far too intimate and lasting relationship with his host.[85] Shifting to a military explanation for Tearaway as the book's working-class hero, he could be viewed as the type of enlisted man without whom no army can function and no battles can be won. He is highly competent, but could never be a leader of men. He functions on the cusp of enlisted man and officer.

Tearaway is not mad like Jupiter; he has, for example, no inclination toward self-education; no times, however brief, of vast wealth; no mystical side; and no talent for friendship, especially close friendship. All of these characteristics are presented as examples of being mad in this book. For this reason, Simplicissimus's relationship with Tearaway is the best way to judge Simplicissimus's daily interactions, for Tearaway is never the dear friend that Young Herzbruder is to Simplicissimus. (Remember that at one stage, Simplicissimus describes Herzbruder and himself as "drunk on each other's affection.")[86] Tearaway is not revealed later to have highborn parents, and is thus the true working-class symbol and survivor. Further, Tearaway, more than Simplicissimus, is the abstract individual of this rollicking and raunchy story. Simplicissimus has too much control and power to represent the average person. The book could also be seen as a pro-aristocratic, anti-peasant novel, conforming to the old stereotypes, and following Luther's rebuke to the people in the midst of the Peasants' Revolt (which was particularly galling to the peasants, as Luther had already challenged them to choose their own form of religion). In this regard, the abstract ideas to be taken up in terms of Tearaway as an insect are relativism and royalism. Embedded within the most trivial details in this book are miniature commentaries on political theory.

It is not wholly preposterous to think of this other working-class boy, Tearaway, in terms of the conversion strategies of the two best-known Church Fathers. Tearaway is the type of convert whom Aquinas, rather than Augustine, sought. Augustine wants the best of each generation to come forward to rule the Christian city-state, the "city of God." However, Aquinas recognizes that all individuals work within systems, and that it is will as much as intellect that is required for proper leadership and good government, indeed for proper Christian government on earth. Thus, practical theories of leadership from Augustine and Aquinas can be used to balance the idiosyncratic qualities that also seem necessary for a successful leader.

7 Return to Herzbruder and Simplicissimus's Pilgrimage

Immediately following Simplicissimus's supposed conversion, Simplicissimus and Herzbruder take a break from their pilgrimage, find quarters for the winter, and turn their attention toward Simplicissimus's long-abandoned wife and one of their favorite senior colleagues, Imperial General Count Götz, who pops up regularly throughout the story. The good rapport between Count Götz, an authority figure of the Thirty Years' War, and Herzbruder, indicates the possibility of associations beyond class lines, even before Götz's own difficulties.[87] Götz represents the possibility of friendship with someone supposedly unlike oneself who nevertheless possesses the core characteristics required in Aristotelian friendship.

Yet it is the love, not just friendship, binding Simplicissimus and Young Herzbruder that not only serves as a goal for Simplicissimus in his random, often painful, wanderings, but also fully demonstrates his ability to form at least one lasting personal attachment. Remember that even when Herzbruder reappears as a beggar, Simplicissimus is instinctively kind to him (which is not always his way) even before he recognizes that this is his dearest friend.[88] Herzbruder is the only person whom Simplicissimus recognizes after a long separation, and Simplicissimus comments on "his Herzbruder" throughout the book.

The homoerotic theme is not suppressed in *Simplicissimus* (and, in this respect as well, it can be linked to both Plato and Aristotle), indeed it is part of the political approach of the book. "I loved Herzbruder almost more than myself," is one of the countless declarations Simplicissimus makes about Herzbruder.[89] Their relationship is presented as if they are lovers, even as if they are in an enviable marriage. In terms of actual marriages, Herzbruder's insistence that Simplicissimus take care of his wife implies not that the relationship with the wife is primary, but rather that Herzbruder is so involved that he cares even for Simplicissimus's wife. She is not at all viewed as a threat to their relationship.[90] Certainly neither Simplicissimus's wives nor his other women are ever mentioned with the passion with which he regularly speaks of Herzbruder. This homoerotic attraction also symbolizes the breakdown of conventional relations on almost all social levels in this time and place, as well as obviously evoking both Platonic love between men and Aristotelian friendship.

8 Death of Herzbruder and Worldly Distractions

But when Herzbruder dies, Simplicissimus abandons his religion—which he had adopted briefly in order to join his friend on the pilgrimage—and seemingly he forgets Herzbruder as well, for he never mentions him again. This experience could be contrasted with profit to the death of the unnamed friend of Augustine, in Augustine's *Confessions*, IV, 4.[91] In each case, the death of the friend can be argued to be the major shift in the life of the central character. Likewise, Simplicissimus finally becomes a religious hermit (although in Grimmelshausen's sequels, he is back on the road again). Simplicissimus's transitions within paragraphs of the narration of the death of Herzbruder are particularly staccato, even for this book, confirming the view that Simplicissimus responds only to experience rather than to any internal plan.[92] Soon after, Simplicissimus encounters an unnamed woman, the most beautiful person he has ever seen. They are both in mourning, but soon marry.[93] Thus, extraordinary physical beauty is the necessary stimulation to distract him from his feelings of extreme loss at Herzbruder's death.

Much earlier, the beauty solicited was Simplicissimus's own, and there was less emphasis on friendship. As a young man, he often receives extravagant compliments on his looks. The German maid, for example, perhaps best understood as the madam or at least the procuress, speaking for her mistress in Paris, is the most eloquent of his admirers. She assures Simplicissimus that if her mistress's wishes are not pure, they certainly are not meant in any way to harm him:

'She feels she will die if she does not soon have the pleasure of seeing your divine body and being revived by it.'[94]

Simplicissimus is presented as a German national treasure on tour, currently on exhibit in Paris. There is a strong undercurrent of beauty defeating good manners here, as if the French had to invent systems of behavior because they had no dazzling beauty in their land. Thus the Germans are presented, even in this German work, as beautiful but not noble savages, and the French are portrayed as jaded members of modern society eager to be jolted, perhaps not out of their current mode of behavior, but out of their *ennui,* their profound boredom.

Prostitution is surprisingly profitable for Simplicissimus in Paris. He was not at all a typical prostitute, and the assumption is not that he was not just a gigolo, but rather that he was, very briefly, a minor celebrity in Paris.[95] His following was made up of aristocratic and royal women in Paris. As he leaves Paris, he falls ill, following this period of intense activity and stress. Initially, he fears that he has the French disease, which was probably syphilis (brought back from the New World, the name was used by non-French people for sexually transmitted diseases; similarly, the French still call it *la maladie anglaise,* the English disease). According to a modern historian of disease:

> The new disease (the French disease) manifested itself in sharp pains in the joints, fever, sores, and swelling. Pustules formed on the body and cases then progressed to destruction of the tissue, and the body seemed to rot. The victims gave off a powerful stench.[96]

The book gives Simplicissimus many of these characteristic symptoms even though he is then identified as having contracted smallpox (which apparently, historically, primarily struck children); the childlike Simplicissimus is thus an adult victim. However, similar to those of the French disease, Simplicissimus's symptoms are chronic: they might change, but would last for a lifetime.[97] Like lepers, the victims of the French disease were hideously recognizable for the rest of their lives.[98] The result is that Simplicissimus loses his celebrated looks and his face is pock marked forever. To add even more insult to what he takes as a personal injury, he loses his curly hair, and his remaining hair has even changed texture, no longer retaining its former luster. He is once again poor (he has been robbed), and he cannot even sell his fine clothes until he can find someone as unscrupulous as he, for people were rightly concerned that his clothes were diseased. He also loses his beautiful singing voice.[99] Thus prostitution and rapid loss of beauty to the point of physical disfigurement are unashamedly bound together in this section of the story. This does not, however, imply that this incident is meant as a brief, potent morality tale. Instead it suggests that prostitution is deadly not in a moral sense but because it indicates a (generally financial) lack that precludes the leisure Aristotle—and thus the narrator Old Simplicissimus— deem necessary for proper study and friendship.

Yet just as he loses his looks, Simplicissimus starts to worry that he is being cuckolded, although he recognizes that this is somewhat unfair given his own behavior in Paris.[100] This indicates that on one level Simplicissimus understands that there should be equality between the sexes, but that his response was somehow instinctive, not just patriarchal. Initially, the book offers no questioning of traditional male and female roles. Simplicissimus neither forms a lasting relationship of any sort with any one woman nor mentions that he has seen any strong relationship that includes a woman. His emphasis is wholly on his friendships with other men, especially with one man. However, thinking of Simplicissimus as a *debutant*, on the brink of adult life, is itself a means of reevaluating gender roles as a means of identifying power lodged in the most unlikely places, even in the early-modern period.

This book shows women caught up in the exigencies of war at least as much as their men. There is no home front in the Thirty Years' War; the war is fought in the countryside and the villages, as well as the major cities. Far from leaving women in their traditional roles as caregivers, this book delineates in broad terms the breaking apart of the social bonds that would allow families to survive on the income of the male head of the household alone. Times of domestic and international crisis force women to consult other women for advice. The text indicates grudging respect for women, including unmarried and old women, and for their contributions to the remaining members of the family. Although there is no direct textual evidence in *Simplicissimus*, respect for strong women is played out, oddly, but directly, in Grimmelshausen's own sequels, especially in *Courage*, in which there is a power-hungry central female character, who for some time acquires countless men and much wealth. Thus, if women are not playing heroic roles in this story, they are at least no different from the men, for even Simplicissimus's time as a heroic figure is short-lived, indeed scarcely longer than his time passing himself off as a woman. The desperate need for subsistence does not necessarily raise the position of women but instead brings all to the lowest level, because women, at least as much as men, are too busy to develop substantive friendships.

9 Quest for Friendship in a *Bildungsroman*

Earlier, when confronted after cooking the peas, Simplicissimus bewails the loss of his innocence. His personality change is assuredly evident even to the reader, but this spiritual reform lasts only as long as Herzbruder is alive. In both secular and academic terms, Simplicissimus is distressed by his own unclear thinking. He views his conflicted impressions as a sign of failure, not as a sign of growing intellectual maturity. He shifts between several world systems (rural and working class, religious and military), never reaching a point where he is able to hold ideas from several of them at the same time. Rather, it is exactly when he might have gained some intellectual maturity that he has his intellectual and emotional crises.

The issue could be posed whether Simplicissimus wants to avoid love because love is sinful or whether it ends up costing him money. After

Herzbruder's death he realizes that he needs distraction.[101] Throughout his adventures, Simplicissimus is motivated most strongly by his ideal of friendship, and perhaps by the hope for (even more than the presence of) a devoted friend. Scornfully, it could be argued that what he wants most is not an actual friend, for only in the absence of such companionship does he become concerned with the category of friendship. In this case he is concerned more with the notion than the reality.

Yet in this incident, Simplicissimus is forthright, concise, and determined even in the midst of profound loss. He knows his own needs and works to meet them. He recognizes that he needs someone to love (and also an enemy) in order to live a worthwhile life. In Freudian terms, he has lost the love object that his ego craves in order to pursue such an unconventional lifestyle. The passage above, about the need for "a sworn enemy or a good friend," continues: "Unfortunately all I had was my money."[102] This reinforces Simplicissimus's *naïve* but fundamental lack of interest in material goods. His search for fortune has as much to do with his search for satisfaction and security as it does with greed.

Simplicissimus's ongoing quest for friendship and its long-term benefits become starkly evident, even to him, after Herzbruder's death. He notes, for example, ways to walk off the noxious parts of human nature, but also acknowledges that there were qualities he desired to find and even return to, not just other qualities he wished to escape:

> The longer I walked, the farther away I went, without realising it, from the place I most wanted to be.[103]

Simplicissimus was on a quest not for personal fulfillment but rather to find the family and then friends that he had lost, preferably the original ones, not the replacements. Late in the story, he recognizes that he also has strong connection to places and to the land itself, and he comments that peace must be on its way as he is seeing wandering scholars once again.[104] He instinctively realizes that a sign of a country at peace is that it can sustain the luxury of thinking and wandering for a small portion of its population. The chaotic state of war-torn Central Europe is evident here. It cannot afford to have even the smallest, most expendable percentage of its population wandering, for there is no safe passage. In war and in peace, the presence of an intellectual class is the sign of a healthy nation. Simplicissimus seems to recognize that friendship cannot exist in a fluid situation, and that only a society that makes room for those on the margins, such as scholars, will be secure enough to allow for ordinary friendships.

10 Literary Sources on Suffering and Friendship

Simplicissimus is in need of consolation after Herzbruder's death, but he does not invoke key classic and modern books on the subject as he does on so many other subjects. Despite his real need, he fails to seek from books the comfort they are able to offer. *Simplicissimus*, crammed full of references to classic texts, strikingly, does not mention the one classic text deliberately written about managing isolation and pain.

For all the classic works cited in *Simplicissimus*, there is one text that the reader would expect to find there that is actually missing. The character Simplicissimus could have benefited from Boethius (c. 475–525 A.D.), who wrote the remarkably popular medieval work, *Consolatio Philosophiae* (*The Consolation of Philosophy*), in prison (in Pavia, Lombardy, now northern Italy) as he awaited what was to be a particularly hideous execution.[105] (Boethius's failure was as a politician, and he was too much of a thinker for the time of Theodoric, King of the Ostrogoths.) However, contrary to what might be expected from the title, the female character named Philosophy, in *The Consolation of* Philosophy, has little sympathy for Boethius's self-pity, and instead gives him a crisp refresher course in philosophy (as Boethius is the central character of his own book), which is presented in both prose and poetry. The character Philosophy reminds the character Boethius that he—not his circumstances—is responsible for his own state of mind. Although this text is best understood as Stoic, implying that its message is for the individual, to encourage self-control, nevertheless this work is now most often discussed as Neo-Platonic, for it also stresses the belief in universal ideas. In the Middle Ages, *The Consolation of Philosophy* was used as a vehicle for popularizing both Stoicism and Neo-Platonism. For Simplicissimus, there is little sense that he should be learning lessons, practical or philosophical, from his range of bizarre experiences, yet *Simplicissimus* is written so that readers, so inclined, might learn them. Sadly, the character Simplicissimus lacks such constructive, much less supernatural, coaching, designed for those in hideous circumstances they cannot control.

Overall, it is the well-known early modern work on reflection, friendship, and isolation written by Michel de Montaigne that, perhaps surprisingly, aligns best with this raucous work by Grimmelshausen.[106] Montaigne's concern for other cultures and his incipient relativism, most famously in his essay "On Cannibalism"—which one might take as the most anti-social form of behavior—can be found in bits and pieces throughout the *Essays* (published in 1580). His desire to carve a life for himself is grounded less in Renaissance concerns from Castiglione's *Il Cortegiano* (*Book of the Courtier*, 1528) or even from Erasmus's *Institutio principis Christiani* (*The Education of a Christian Prince*, 1516), although he admired Erasmus, but from the Ancients as well as from the common people, thus the same sources as for *Simplicissimus*.[107] This is perhaps not surprising, as Montaigne's self-proclaimed, most cherished personal characteristics are idleness and frankness, again Simplician qualities.[108] His emphasis on behavior is based on inner motivation, not on learned routines or the opinions of others. He is blunt about human nature, and thus the often amusingly idiosyncratic examples drawn primarily from classical and European literature—especially

Aristotle, Lucretius, and Seneca—support rather than subvert his outlook. These stories of exceptions to the rules make his *Essays* perhaps more similar to the work of Herodotus than to any other single work of European literature. Montaigne's contentious attitude toward Stoicism, and especially toward Cicero, indicates his desire to institute a life for himself that was not wholly robbed of joy; thus his more substantial link is to the Epicureanism of Lucretius. His connection to the Ancients is so strong (he was raised, mostly unusually for his time, to speak Latin before French) that it is as if he is discussing them as older brothers, and this is part of the practical side to his ruminations. Montaigne was able to articulate thoughts that most people would never tell anyone. The deeply psychological elements of his *Essays* include Montaigne's dismissal of the notion of (almost all) innate ideas, the desire to isolate the component parts of every individual, and the wish to understand how the mind tangles itself up.[109] His book lingers on the theme of death; he is, for the most part, not obsessed with death in terms of power, in the manner of Machiavelli or Nietzsche, but more in line with the Stoic Marcus Aurelius. Overall, Montaigne tries to make sense of his life, and the life of his father, in terms of old age, death, and precious friendship.

Friendship is one of the oldest European political models for good government; this notion comes directly from ancient Greek thought. Again, the Aristotelian notion of friendship, specifically from Book IX of his *Nicomachean Ethics*, sets out a relationship formed by two equals that is not based on pleasure or advantage.[110] Distinct from a lover, and distinct also from an advantageous business partner, although the categories could overlap, the friend, instead of regularly bringing profit or pleasure, might at times cause discomfort, for there is an obligation inherent in friendship. Friendships, for Aristotle, can occur only between equals. This is far too intense a relationship to enter into with anyone not capable of functioning at the same level. The distinction here is on the basis of personal quality, not age (the model in Athens was between an older man and a much younger man), although Aristotle assumes friends will be equal socially. The notion of inherent equality between friends deserves attention (even putting aside the requirement of equal social class). Indeed, the quality of the relationship between the friends, the close nurturing and pushing each other to improve—not the seeking of promotion, fame, or wealth—is itself the reward of the relationship; again, this relationship could indeed be at times awkward and even painful. The political key here is that government for Aristotle was to be composed of these friends, once again, "ruling, and being ruled in turn," and the political obligation was just as strong for those out of office as for those ruling.[111] This is a crucial theme for *Don Quixote* as well as *Simplicissimus*.

Although anti-Platonic and pro-Aristotelian in most respects, Montaigne follows Plato in *The Symposium* on the craving for intense friendship.[112] For Montaigne there is no reason to desire a different form of government, or even to study politics (Aristotle's particular contribution); rather, one should cultivate an ideal friendship, or at least the memory of it after the death of such an exquisite friend, for friendship is the most perfect form of association. The following lines could almost have come from Plato's *Symposium* (or from *Simplicissimus*), but are from Montaigne's *Essays*:

> In a truly loving relationship—which I have experienced—rather than drawing the one I love to me I give myself to him. Not merely do I prefer to do him good than to have him do good to me: it is when he does good to himself that he does most good to me. If his absence is either pleasant or useful to him, then it delights me far more than his presence. . . . It was for me he lived, and saw and enjoyed things: and I for him—more fully than if he had been there. When we were together part of us remained idle: we were merged into one.[113]

For Montaigne, friendship has almost magical, long-term benefits: simply having had this type of association, even in the distant past, allows the survivor to live a rich life, even when aging and alone, and even in the midst of suffering.

11 A Theory of Aging

The suffering that Simplicissimus endures is not all war related; much of it is internal and physical. To this point, the Aristotelian theory of friendship challenges the traditional view of aging, for Aristotelian friendship should trump any other obligation or relationship at any stage of life, thus putting the lie to any theory of natural shifts in individuals and in their relationships over time. This supposed contradiction calls for a specific theory of aging to be used in both political theory and fiction that accounts for factors in the individual that do not change over time.

The character Simplicissimus is, as the story unfolds, a classic example of angry youth, of disenchanted mid-life, and then, as an old man, the desire to find consolation as a hermit, not in love. Yet the Aristotelian concept of friendship confronts this typical view of growing old. Perhaps one of the reasons that Simplicissimus is such a fool, for example, even during him demagogic phase as the Huntsman, is that he allows a few core ideas, so crucial that he believes them to be innate, to dominate all aspects of his thinking and behavior. In this respect he is closer to a character in a utopian novel than to what the reader might expect in a burlesque of the Thirty Years' War. Although outward factors contrive to make him much more successful at some stages than at others, Simplicissimus is driven by a desire for intense friendship: this is shown by his willingness to change his lifestyle markedly for Herzbruder and even to go on that wretched pilgrimage.

This same sense of determination and inner drive is used in psychological theories to explain genius. It might be proposed that a theory of aging would be geared not so much toward exceptions (for example, geniuses) but instead toward the average person. In this novel, Simplicissimus is very much worse or better at every activity than the average person over a lifetime. However, it is also of interest to view him as an exception to his age group. This most average of people is functioning almost exclusively because of his innate beliefs: there is substantial textual evidence that he cares more about friendship than even self-interest, and not just because of his eventual dwindling fortune.

A theory of aging for literature and political philosophy is needed, if only so the prejudices and inevitabilities attached the aging process can be identified. As with other such theories, such as those regarding gender differences, such propositions generally have little to add about specific individuals who are at one end or the other of the spectrum of their group.[114] However, such a theory could be useful in linking an individual not just to one set personality type, but rather to substantive changes, both positive and negative, over time, that are not only to do with chronological age.

Early-modern fiction stresses the common factors that appeal to all generations. The emphasis on wild youth, for example, in early-modern literature (not just in *Simplicissimus*) leads to the implication that the appeal of the adventures of wild, young, working-class men had an appeal that crossed class, as well as age, and gender boundaries. This implies that wild young men simply have the opportunity, briefly, to act out the desires of the many, not just the few. A clear linkage exists among the attitude, plot, and concerns of the Spanish picaresque tradition and the Cony-Catching pamphlets in Renaissance England (Cony is a type of rabbit; Cony-Catcher means cheat, sharper, deceiver). Overall, the Simplicissimus story, for example, fits exactly into the tradition of these pamphlets in England at the turn of the seventeenth century, which centered on the exploits of the low life of the big cities, especially London. These pamphlets detailed the tricks that con men might play on unsuspecting citizens. The raucous, vulgar tracts were sold as handbooks with detailed instructions on how to avoid such thievery. These stories of conmen also appealed to a general reading audience, not just as morality tales, but also as colorful adventure stories. There is also evidence that some thieves used the booklets to improve and update their skills. The story, *Simplicissimus*, could also be put in all three of these categories—a warning against thievery, an adventure story, and instruction manual for thieves—although it falls short on how, for example, to be a successful thief.[115]

Yet *Simplicissimus* also shows strong concern for the title character, a wandering, homeless youth, not just for the character as an example of a social phenomenon. He is not-quite-living proof of what early-modern northern Europe, with its Protestant system of social control, had tried so hard to suppress—young people realizing the joys of prodigality, gambling, prostitution, and get-rich-quick schemes.[116] The shock effect of these stories was thus used to bring young people back into the urban fold by recognizing their places in the hierarchy. The stories do not diminish the thrill of sex with strangers, drunkenness, or winning large sums of money through no skill of one's own. Yet the emphasis in the British "Cony-Catching" pamphlets and in the Simplicissimus story is more on the ephemeral nature of such pleasures than on the punishments attached to them. This puts forward a Lockean rather than Hobbesian view of basic human nature, which would appeal to the rational nature not dependent on fear of punishment for motivation. Thus these pamphlets were based on the assumption that the wild youth involved in such activities could rationally sort out which activities would be best for them.

The theme of social control in pamphlets and in works of fiction is not surprising, that crime does not pay; what is unexpected here is the social assumption that all individuals, no matter how much, how often, or even how cheerfully they have sinned, can and should be brought back into the social network, not just back to the Church. It is thus social *mores* as much as religious connections that presumably make social rehabilitation possible, the individual eventually realizing the best means of behavior and adopting it naturally, even if somewhat later in life than might have been thought normal.

The possibility of redemption, perhaps as a natural, even pleasant, stage for old age, is one of the major themes of this work. Thus if Simplicissimus, a sinner on a level that could be called world-historical (Hegel's term for those few powerful leaders who can shape history to their will), can become a genuine religious, even a hermit, himself, then anyone else could easily achieve the same status. The conversion story of Simplicissimus is so grand (in terms of the sinning), and so natural (in terms of the eventual move toward religion), that it makes the process seem easy for anyone else. This work of debauchery, grand larceny, and gross warfare could thus be argued to be a seventeenth-century tract in line with the only slightly later work by Bunyan, *The Pilgrim's Progress*.[117] Bunyan's work, deliberately written as a religious tract (he wrote it while in prison for his religious views), also functions as one of the last examples of folk tradition, before both the Enlightenment and the later push towards mandatory school education for all. There is, in *Simplicissimus*, a double emphasis, one grounded in Aristotle, and the other drawing from religion, on stages of life as separate from the aging process.

Simplicissimus also emphasizes (usually through ghastly stories of the need for this) that only if the young develop multiple strong relationships will they later as individual adults remain committed to their society. The Rousseauian, social contract argument for monogamy as one of the three reasons for the shift from the state of nature to society (Rousseau's other reasons are farming and metallurgy) can, for example, be found in this novel. Instead of being simply a connection to one other person through a profound friendship, or through marriage to an extended family, society binds multiple families through a series of friendships. This smacks both of the Platonic view of society as a whole (one part cannot be damaged without damaging it all) as well as of the Aristotle's emphasis on the responsibility of government best being shared, much more than it resembles the early-modern, Protestant and Catholic commitment to a nuclear family. The text contrasts German reality with ancient Greek political standards as a means of bettering Central Europe, and not necessarily to bring about a religious conversation. *Simplicissimus* is still most overtly a confessional story by an old man about his wild youth.[118]

12 Link to Michel Tournier, *Le Roi des aulnes* (1970, as *The Ogre*)

A literary link can be made between Simplicissimus and a relatively recent book, Michel Tournier's 1970 *Le Roi des aulnes* (published in English as *The Ogre*, dedicated to the slandered memory of Rasputin), a book that might strike the reader initially as simply repulsive.[119] In this twentieth-century novel, the main character's preoccupation with his own body; his developing sense that he has evil qualities and is becoming a monster; his disturbing obsession with carrying small, wounded children; and his identification of potential rape victims make this the kind of book that most readers would not ordinarily choose to read, even though it is perhaps one of the best written novels in the last 50 years, thus making it similar to Vladimir Nabokov's *Lolita* (1955) in both respects. After much violence, the final sacrifice in this story comes as an intellectual surprise, for the main character, Abel Tiffauges, seems to be a highly unlikely savior.

The reader slowly recognizes the progression in the book not only of a fascist state, but also of a fascist mode of thinking, the latter of which is inspected in remarkable detail, both directly by the corrupt, central character and then by the reader when analyzing this character. The cyclical aspects of the story (the main character Abel returns to the same themes of alienation and sacrifice at all phases of his life) are akin to Nietzsche's theory of eternal recurrence (and are a less clear example of Vico's "course and recourse of history").[120] Tournier's book is most conspicuously in line with Nietzsche's analysis of power, and reflects Nietzsche's excesses as well as his constructive contributions to Western thought.[121]

The Ogre challenges the restrictions of conventional views about the limits of myth and history for modern readers. The title is taken from Johann Wolfgang von Goethe's symbolic ballad, *Der Erlkönig* (*The Erl King*, or *The King of the Elves*, 1782), in which nature reels from the violent impact of unconscious forces. Similarly, in Tournier's novel, the internal, psychological struggle in the basic, indeed base nature of the central character reflects his hope for possible reconciliation within, or among, his own social groups more than it represents acts of nonconformity and dissension within society. The characters want to be accepted but also appreciated by those around them; they do not wish to bring down their social world. Thus despite his sense of ostracism, even the most aberrant character, Abel perhaps predictably defines himself at all stages in terms of his conventional social group. These include his classmates, and to a lesser degree, his masters at school, his jailers, his customers, and his lovers. The main character never functions without reference to his social groups.

The Ogre presents an analysis of what brings about and sustains a pathological psychology for both an individual and for a culture. However, this was not Tournier's only purpose; perhaps he also wanted to prove that he could still jolt a jaded, modern audience. In *Simplicissimus*, by the time Simplicissimus, following the pox, looks like a monster, the reader already has full sympathy for him. Thus without even realizing it, for much of the book the reader takes the side of the monster, not just because of sympathy for the character's disfigurement, but also because of his lack of contrition for his own violent actions the reader forgets his violent actions. Perhaps it takes books of this type, with so many distinct means of shocking the reader, to warn that any person has the potential to be as vile and hideous as the narrator of the Tournier story, a self-declared ogre, or that a charming, attractive hero like Simplicissimus could be responsible for multiple deaths and mayhem. Thus the goal of both *Simplicissimus* (remembering that the character Simplicissimus was a rapist and mass murderer) and *The Ogre* could be that it is necessary to disabuse the reader that such monsters are necessarily in the minority in human society, and also that monsters are in a category separate from ourselves.

13 Synopsis

Simplicissimus's friendly deception of Herzbruder, walking on cooked peas during their pilgrimage, comes about because of Simplicissimus's craving for friendship, or just his desire for Herzbruder. Eventually reconciled with Herzbruder after his deception is revealed, once Simplicissimus claims a religious experience, he is then condemned as a fraud by an evil spirit, even though he has managed to fool everyone around him. The evil spirit is used as a classic, early example of magical realism. Beyond Herzbruder are plenty of other models of friendship—unequal but oddly constructive relationships—notably that of Simplicissimus with the deranged Jupiter, who symbolizes a particularly perverted version of demagoguery. Another model of friendship is presented by Tearaway, who is perhaps the most apt working-class hero of the book, thus implying perhaps that Simplicissimus's education, however delayed (and even more than his eventually revealed aristocratic parents), separates him from the real concerns of the people. After Herzbruder's death, Simplicissimus returns with a vengeance to worldly distractions, abandoning religion one last, if prolonged, time before he himself becomes a hermit. This is a story of an unrelenting quest for friendship, all contained within a *Bildungsroman* (a growing-up story). It is based on literary sources about suffering and friendship, gesturing toward Boethius and Montaigne. The book makes clear that there is a need for a theory of aging, if only so the exceptions to the theory (such as the youthful character Simplicissimus, and the later fictional character Candide) can be identified. A comparison to Augustine's *Confessions* indicates the overt religious quality and the conversion element of the later German work. Yet, it is not clear, as most modern readers at first would assume, that the religious content of *Simplicissimus* was simply a guise for putting forward the crucial political and economic messages. It was likely to have been the other way around. The book advocates religious toleration (often by showing what happens in its absence) and echoes Aristotle in its call for friendship as the basis of good government. Yet reading Michel Tournier's *The Ogre* reminds the reader of *Simplicissimus* that the character Simplicissimus too is a monster—raping and killing throughout much of the story—however beautiful he is when young, and however repentant he is later. Throughout *Simplicissimus* there is a sense of monstrosity, and of being always isolated. The multiple perspectives in *Simplicissimus* on friendship and the hunger for friendship indicate a desire for social connection that is both Aristotelian and also resonates with the creation of the modern state and its emphasis on the relationship of the abstract individual and society.

NOTES

1   I wish to thank Rüdiger Campe and Geoffrey Parker for their close readings of Chapter 2 and for their overall assistance. The Background section draws extensively from comments from Rüdiger Campe. Thank you to Ursula Sampath for help on German literature, especially on Kaspar Hauser.

An early version of this section was given as a College of Social Studies (CSS) Monday Lunch Talk at Wesleyan University, Fall 2003.

The critical edition of *Simplicissimus* is now Hans Jacob Christoffel von Grimmelshausen, *Simplicissimus*, Dieter Breuer, ed., 3 vols. (Frankfurt am Main: Deutscher Klassiker Verlag, 1989). Affordable German editions of several of Grimmelshausen's works are available from Reclam. For a marvelous English translation of the novel, see Johann Jakob Christoffell von Grimmelshausen, *Simplicissimus*, Mike Mitchell, tr., ed. (Sawtry, U.K.: Dedalus, 1999). Quotations and citations are from the Breuer German edition and the Mitchell English translation. For a bibliographical study of Grimmelshausen's works, see Dieter Breuer, *Grimmelshausen Handbuch* (Munich: Fink, 1999).

The word *Teutsch* in the title of the novel is an antiquated form of "deutsch" or "German." It is also a reference to the satirical writings of Johan Michael Moscherosch who wrote during the Thirty Years' War. Grimmelshausen also wrote a piece called "Teutscher Michel," published in 1670. Grimmelshausen's phrase is still used in Germany today, as "der deutsche Michel," often by politicians, to indicate a simpleton, one who does not learn from experience. See Alan Menhennet, "Cutting Linguistic Capers: The Title-Sequence of Grimmelshausen's *Teutscher* Michel," German *Life and Letters*, 48, No. 3 (2007): 277–291.

2 One alternative interpretation of *All Quiet on the Western Front* is that it is primarily an attack on the World War I German military command, not on war overall. *All Quiet on the Western Front* is also a powerful 1930 American film.

3 Günter Grass views Grimmelshausen's novel as the birth of modern European literature, and rightly places *Berlin Alexanderplatz* (1929), by Alfred Döblin, his favorite author, in this same picaresque tradition. See Reiko Tachibana Nemoto, "On Two Interviews between Günter Grass and Ōe Kenzaburō," *World Literature Today*, 67, no. 2 (Spring 1993): 301–305. See below on Bertolt Brecht.

4 Thank you to Mary-Hannah Jones.

5 St. Thomas Aquinas, *Summa Theologica*, vol. 1, pt. 1, question 7, pp. 30–34.

6 Nicholas of Cusa, author of *Ad Docta Ignorantia* (c. 1440) stresses the role of imagination when attempting to merge rationality and spirituality, and this is a source for Pico della Mirandola in his *De Imaginatione* (*On Imagination*, 1501), a classic work of the Italian Renaissance. In a different vein, see Avital Ronell, *Stupidity*.

7 Grimmelshausen, *Simplicissimus*. Breuer, ed., book I, ch.19, p. 69. Mitchell, tr., book I, ch. 19, p. 60.

8 Thank you to Aaron Slavutin. Also, similar to Kaspar Hauser, the boy who had grown up in the wild in nineteenth-century Germany, the subject of so much academic and popular interest once he was discovered, the character Simplicissimus for a time lives as a feral child. Using German scholar Ursula Sampath's categories for analyzing Kaspar Hauser—as a paradigm for the "outsider," a Rousseauian noble savage, a Christ figure, a Lockean *tabula rasa*, and a tool for social criticism—the links between the earlier fictional character Simplicissimus and the historical feral child Kaspar Hauser are manifest. See Ursula Sampath, *Kaspar Hauser: A Modern Metaphor*. There is a chapter on each of these five categories in Sampath's book.

9 See Norbert Elias, *The Civilizing Process: The History of Manners*.

10 For example, at one stage of the war, in 1630, the powerful Albrecht von Wallenstein lost his position as Imperial General because he was suspected of trying to take over the Holy Roman Empire. Wallenstein nevertheless returned to power soon afterwards, mainly because of the need for strong military leadership.

11 William Godwin, in *Caleb Williams* (1794), uses a prison community as a means of presenting his own constructive theory of anarchy. William Godwin, *Caleb Williams; or, Things as they are.*

12 J. C. D. Clark, " 'In Denial': Wars of Religion in English Discourse, 1639–2007," unpublished article, on the interpretive secularization of wars of religion, including the Thirty Years' War.

13 John Gagliardo, *Germany under the Old Regime, 1600–1790*, p. 2.

14 Gagliardo, *Germany under the Old Regime* p. 3.

15 Gagliardo, *Germany under the Old Regime* pp. 2–4.

16 Gagliardo, *Germany under the Old Regime* p. 13.

17 Geoffrey Parker, ed., *The Thirty Years' War*, p. 21.

18 Parker, ed., *The Thirty Years' War.*, p. 14. Thank you to Rüdiger Campe.

19 Parker, ed., *The Thirty Years' War*, p. 8.

20 For example, see the print by Jacques Callot (1592–1635). Callot's series of 1633, called "*Les Grandes Misères de la Guerre*," is the source of this image. See "*La Pendaison*," #1349, in *Jacques Callot: Catalogue Raisonné de Oeuvre Gravé* (*The Complete Etchings & Engravings*) 2nd ed., vol. 1, p. 76, "*La Pendaison*," #1349; vol. 2, #1349. First published 1924–1927. Thank you to Susanne Javorski and Rob Lancefield.

21 See Quentin Outram, *Dearth, Disease and Death in Germany during the Thirty Years' War*.
22 See Geoffrey Parker and Lesley M. Smith, eds., *The General Crisis of the Seventeenth Century*.
23 Outram.
24 Outram, pp. 9–12. A century earlier, Montaigne, commented on how less spectacular circumstances are often more dangerous than the battlefield in wartime. Montaigne, *The Complete Essays*, II.16, "On glory," p. 308.
25 Outram, esp, pp. 3–4.
26 Parker, ed., *The Thirty Years' War*, p. xii.
27 C. V. Wedgewood, *The Thirty Years' War*, p. 257.
28 Parker, ed., *The Thirty Years' War*, pp. 199, 299–300.
29 Parker, ed., *The Thirty Years' War*, p. 300.
30 Parker, ed., *The Thirty Years' War*.
31 Grimmelshausen, *Simplicissimus*, Breuer, ed., book I, ch. XIX, p. 69; Mitchell, tr., book 1, ch. 19, p. 60. On Grimmelshausen's life, see Karl Otto, ed., *A Companion to the Works of Grimmelshausen*, "Introduction," pp. 1–21.
32 To give one example, there was a trend of British writers in the later nineteenth and twentieth centuries turning away from what they considered bland Anglicanism toward the Catholic Church in Rome and its high-church orthodoxy.
33 His publisher was, according to the title page, Wolf Eberhard Felsecker in Mompelgart (Montbéliard, now in France), but the book was probably published in Nuremberg, which is also listed on the title page.
34 To clarify, *Bildungsroman* and the picaresque novel are, again, two different categories, and not synonymous. It is, however, true that both terms have been applied to *Simplicissimus*. The picaresque novel is certainly the right category, whereas *Bildungsroman* is rather anachronistic, its use due mainly to national literary historians who deemed *Bildungsroman* as specific to the German tradition and tried to apply it throughout German literary history. Thank you to Rüdiger Campe.
35 On the picaresque, see Chapter 1, of this volume, on *Don Quixote*.
36 Otto, ed., *A Companion to the Works of Grimmelshausen*, "Introduction," pp. 1–21, esp. pp. 9–10.
37 The DDR (*Deutsche Demokratische Republik*, the German Democratic Republic, GDR). This concern had to do with the concept of a *kulturelles Erbe* (cultural asset) on the one hand, and the interest in early-modern, pre-bourgeois developments on the other.
38 On the reception of *Simplicissimus* as well as the sequels written by Grimmelshausen, in the seventeenth and eighteenth centuries, see Peter Hesselmann, *Simplicissimus Redivivus: Eine kommentierte Dokumention der Rezeptionsgeschichte Grimmelshusens im 17. Und 18. Jahrhundert (1667–1800)*.
39 Arnold Fritz, *One Hundred Caricatures from Simplicissimus, 1896–1914: An Exhibit of the Goethe-Institut*.
40 In terms of literary theory, this comparison is problematic as it is not altogether clear whether *Simplicissimus* or Büchner's writings are indeed realist. However, although the later expressionists (such as Franz Kafka) were not realists, there is an idea of a non-idealist tradition that begins with Büchner and continues with expressionism that to does resonate with the much earlier *Simplicissimus*. Georg Büchner, *Complete Plays, Lenz, and Other Writings*.
41 In Büchner's *Woyzeck*, a wife suspected of infidelity is murdered by her soldier husband, and yet the text manages both to defend the poor and yet to recognize other classes in society as just as socially constituted, and thus to some extent powerless, as the working class. Büchner's own scientific training is most evident in his literary work in his commentary, which is written like the field

observations of Herodotus and Aristotle in antiquity, not like laboratory reports evoked by Bacon's early-modern empiricism. Büchner does not set out to test human beings, but to learn about them.

42 E. P. Thompson, *The Making of the English Working Class*, p. 59.

43 Bertolt Brecht, *Mutter Courage und ihre Kinder*. Brecht, *Mother Courage and Her Children*, John Willett, tr. Olympia Dukakis wrote the Foreward to this edition. In it she makes the point: "The Greeks and Brecht are intentionally instructional. They mean to show us how *not* to live, in order to show us how to organize our life and society through certain values."

44 Brecht, *Mother Courage and Her Children*, Willett, tr., Introduction," p. 13. Most audiences of *Mother Courage* would disagree with the early criticism. Brecht's collaborator and wife, Helene Weigel, gave one of the most famous renditions of Courage on stage. This is still a prime role for a leading actress, comparable to a leading Shakespearean character for an actor. Weigel is still remembered for this role by those who lived in the former East Germany at the time of this performance. Courage, a minor character in *Simplicissimus*, is still discussed today in a natural manner at some dinner tables in East Berlin. Five days before the play was first produced in Germany, in January 1949, Brecht was summoned to the office of the Mayor of East Berlin. In a surreal discussion, Brecht was encouraged to change the script in order to give a final warning denouncing the man-hungry, impossibly successful, female lead character named Courage, and to give a less pessimistic, supposedly more edifying, and certainly more proletarian ending to the play. Somehow Brecht was able to resist making these changes, and he produced the play with performances in the spirit of Grimmelshausen, or rather Simplicissimus, as well as making his own political point regarding socialism as altogether superior to capitalism. Thank you to Burgel Schmidt for information on the production of this play in the Deutsches Theater in East Berlin in 1949.

45 Mother Courage, the stage character, shows flashes of the spirit of the original Courage. Her children, who are an addition to the story by Brecht, seem like material possessions of the original Courage. In the play, she allows one to die— Swiss Cheese is his name, the not very bright one, who dies with 11 bullet holes in him—as a result of her reluctance to sell or even pawn her cart in order to bribe the officials to release her son who is about to be executed, and who then is executed. This occurs in Scene 3. However, it is the end of the play, Scene 11, that is repeatedly praised, by Tennessee Williams among others, for the marvelous irony of the mute, but not deaf, daughter Katrin, who plays the drum to warn the villagers of the marauding soldiers who kill her soon thereafter. And see Bertolt Brecht, *Brecht on Theatre: The Development of an Aesthetic*, esp. #18, "Indirect Impact of the Epic Theater (Extracts of the Notes to *Die Mutter)*," pp. 57–62.

46 Other famous works of and about German literature such as Goethe's *Wilhem Meister Lehrejahre* (*Wilhelm Meister's Appreticeship*, 1795–1796), or Henry James's *Golden Bowl* (1904), were less likely to have continuations because of the plotting, thus implying, in contrast, the multiple possibilities for individuals inherent in the writing and character of *Simplicisimus*. Thank you to Rüdiger Campe.

47 Grimmelshausen, *Werke I.2*, Breuer, ed., *Courasche*, pp. 9–151; and Grimmelshausen, *The Life of Courage: The Notorious Thief, Whore, and Vagabond*, Mitchell, tr.

48 Grimmelshausen, *Werke I.2*, Breuer, ed., *Springinsfeld*, pp. 153–295; and Grimmelshausen, *Tearaway*, Mitchell, tr., ed.

49 Grimmelshausen, *Werke I.2*, Breuer, ed., *Das Wunderbarliche Vogel-Nest, Erster Teil & Zweiter Teil*, pp. 297–650. Menhennet, *Grimmelshausen the Storyteller: A Study of the "Simplician" Novels*, especially ch. 6, pp. 141–159.

50 This can be seen as both a justification for doing a textual study such as this, and also a strong argument against some of the dominant views of the reception of this work in the seventeenth and eighteenth centuries. It is necessary to differentiate the book known through reading or having been read out loud in the seventeenth century and the book as an artifact.

51 Hesselmann, *Simplicissimus Redivivus: Eine kommentierte Dokumentation der Rezeptionsgeschichte Grimmelshausen in 17. und 18. Jahrhundert (1667–1800).*

52 There are multiple examples of Robinsonia, including, for example, the ones cited above, at the Beinecke Rare Book Library at Yale University.

53 Thank you to Tammy Pelli and Terence Poon.

54 Mummelsee refers to the Undersea, and is also the name of a large lake in the northern Black Forest in Germany.

55 This was also the view of Cesare Beccaria, a theorist of legal reform in the eighteenth century.

56 Marx, *Capital*, Ben Fowkes, tr., Ernest Mandel, ed., vol. I, ch. 1, #4, pp. 169–177, esp.169–170, on Robinson Crusoe.

57 Daniel Defoe, *Robinson Crusoe*, p. 81.

58 Grimmelshausen, *Simplicissimus*. Breuer, ed., book IV, ch. 15, p. 407. Mitchell, tr., book IV, ch. 15, p. 326.

59 Grimmelshausen, *Simplicissimus*. Breuer, ed., book V, ch. 1, p. 44. Mitchell, tr., book V, ch. 1, p. 357.

60 Grimmelshausen, *Simplicissimus*. Breuer, ed., book V, ch. I, p. 449. Mitchell, tr. book V, ch. 1, p. 359.

61 Grimmelshausen, *Simplicissimus*. Breuer, ed., book V, ch. I, p. 450. Mitchell, tr., book V, ch. 1, p. 359.

62 Grimmelshausen, *Simplicissimus*. Breuer, ed., book V, ch. I, p. 450. Mitchell, tr., book V, ch. 1, p. 360.

63 Grimmelshausen, *Simplicissimus*. Breuer, ed., book 5, ch. I, p. 451. Mitchell, tr., book V, chap. 1, p. 360.

64 Grimmelshausen, *Simplicissimus*, book V, ch. I, and there is more on the cooked peas in book V, ch.10. At several points the text refers to peas and pebbles, both of which could be interpreted as religious icons.

65 A useful source on religious themes in this novel is Janet Bertsch, *Storytelling in the Works of Bunyan, Grimmelshausen, Defoe, and Schnabel*, ch. 3.

66 Sigmund Freud, *Group Psychology and the Analysis of the Ego.*

67 Aristotle, *The Complete Works of Aristotle, Nicomachean Ethics*, in vol. 2, book 9, pt. 3, lines 5–7.

68 On Patristics, the study of the early Church Fathers, see Mary Cunningham, *Faith in the Byzantine World*, ch. 6, "Holy Places, Holy People," p. 97. Thank you to Peter Kilby and Karen Kilby.

69 Cunningham, *Faith in the Byzantine World*, Ch. 6, "Holy Places, Holy People," esp. p. 97.

70 Grimmelshausen, *Simplicissimus*. Breuer, ed., book V, ch. II. Mitchell, tr., book V, ch. 2.

71 Grimmelshausen, *Simplicissimus*. Breuer, ed., book V, ch. II, p. 453. Mitchell, tr., book V, ch. 2, p. 362.

72 Grimmelshausen, *Simplicissimus*. Breuer, ed., book I, ch. IV, p. 29. Mitchell, tr., book I, ch. 4, p. 26.

73 Keith Thomas, *Religion and the Decline of Magic: Studies in Popular Beliefs in Sixteenth and Seventeenth Century England.*

74 On *Faust*, the economy, and magic, see Hans Christoph Binswanger, *Geld und Magik: Deutung und Kritik der modernen Wirtschaft anhand von Goethes Faust.* Thank you to Erik Grimmer-Solem.

75 Grimmelshausen, *Simplicissimus*, book V, ch. VIII.

76 Both Jorge Luis Borges and Salman Rushdie's magical realism remains grounded in realism in a specific time and place, and he adds a few curious, supernatural elements. Excellent earlier examples of this category, from long before the term "magical realism" was coined, include Matthew "Monk" Lewis's lurid, carnal, and entrancing tale, *The Monk* (1796), and James Hogg's surprisingly intellectual as well as intensely psychological thriller, *The Private Memoirs and Confessions of a Justified Sinner* (1824). Much more recently, the limitations of the magical elements in this genre have been criticized for being a manifestation of post-colonialism, of a sign of embarrassment about indigenous beliefs. The result of this criticism was a more recent movement called *lo real maravilloso* (the marvelous real or reality) and can be attributed to more recent Latin American authors such as Cuban Alejo Carpentier (who devised this term) and Guatemalan Miguel Ángel Asturias. *Simplicissimus* can be tied to both magical realism and to *lo real maravilloso.*

77 For example, in the remarkable work of Heinrich Böll, *Der Zug war pünktlich* (*The Train Was on Time*, 1949).

78 Grimmelshausen, *Simplicissimus*. Breuer, ed., book III, ch. III, pp. 252–253. Mitchell, tr., book III, ch. 3, p. 206.

79 Grimmelshausen, *Simplicissimus*. Breuer, ed., book III, ch. VIII, p. 271. Mitchell, tr., book III, ch. 8, p. 221

80 Grimmelshausen, *Simplicissimus*. Breuer, ed., book III, ch. III, p. 253. Mitchell, tr., book III, ch. 3, p. 207

81 Grimmelshausen, *Simplicissimus*. Breuer, ed., book V, ch. V, p. 464. Mitchell, tr., book V, ch. 5, p. 369, for both quotations.

82 Grimmelshausen, *Simplicissimus*. Breuer, ed., book III, ch. VIII, p. 271. Mitchell, tr., book III, ch. 8, esp. p. 221.

83 Tearaway reappears in a sequel named after him, and then in the second sequel, *Courage*, as Courage's favorite of a great many husbands, as well as in the third sequel.

84 Grimmelshausen, *Simplicissimus*. Breuer, ed., book III, ch. VIII, p. 271. Mitchell, tr., book III, ch. 8, esp. p. 221.

85 Contrast this with Giorgio Agamben, *The Open: Man and Animal*, ch. 11, pp. 45–48, "Tick." Thank you to Chris McDonald and Tristan Chirico.

86 Grimmelshausen, *Simplicissimus*. Breuer, ed., book V, Ch. III, p. 455. Mitchell, tr., book V, ch. 3, p. 364

87 This is also a clear example of the fictional characters (Simplicissimus and Herzbruder) as major characters and the historical character (Götz) as a minor character. This allows the reader to identify fully with the fictional, major characters as they are bit players in the war in this story.

88 Grimmelshausen, *Simplicissimus*, book V, ch. 25.

89 Grimmelshausen, *Simplicissimus*. Breuer, ed., book V, ch. I, p. 447. Mitchell, tr. book V, ch. 1, especially p. 357.

90 This somewhat parallels the feelings at one stage of the tedious love triangle— Anselmo, Camilla, and Lotario—at the end of Part I of *Don Quixote.*

91 Augustine, *Confessions*, R. S. Pine-Coffin, tr., book IV, ch. 4, pp. 75–76.

92 Grimmelshausen, *Simplicissimus*, book V, ch. VII.

93 Grimmelshausen, *Simplicissimus*, book V, ch. VII.

94 Grimmelshausen, *Simplicissimus*. Breuer, ed., book IV, ch. IV, p. 363. Mitchell, tr., book IV, ch. 4, p. 292

95 Grimmelshausen, *Simplicissimus,* book IV, chs. III–IV.

96 J.N. Hays, *Epidemics and Pandemics: Their Impacts on Human History*, pp. 69–77, esp. p. 69.

97   Hays, p. 72.
98   Hays, pp. 72–73.
99   Grimmelshausen, *Simplicissimus,* book IV, chs. VI–VII.
100 Grimmelshausen, *Simplicissimus,* book IV, ch. XIV.
101 Grimmelshausen, *Simplicissimus*. Breuer, ed., book V, ch. VII, p. 473. Mitchell, tr., book V, ch. 7, p. 377.
102 Grimmelshausen, *Simplicissimus*. Breuer, ed., book V, ch. VII, p. 473. Mitchell, tr., book V, ch. 7, p. 377.
103 Grimmelshausen, *Simplicissimus*. Breuer, ed., book V, ch. XVII, p. 517. Mitchell, tr., book V, ch. 17, pp. 409–410.
104 Grimmelshausen, *Simplicissimus*. Breuer, ed., book V, ch. XVII, p. 519. Mitchell, tr., book V, ch. 17, p. 410.
105 Boethius, *The Consolation of Philosophy*.
106 Montaigne, *The Complete Essays*. Thank you to Peter Hagan.
107 Erasmus was a major force in what could be called the early Catholic Counter-Reformation—the Catholic response to the Protestant Reformation—and he was, at the same time, in correspondence with Martin Luther, who is considered to be the father of the Protestant Reformation.
108 Montaigne, *The Complete Essays*, III.9, "On vanity," p. 1097.
109 Montaigne, *The Complete Essays*, II.14, pp. 692–693.
110 Aristotle, *Nicomachean Ethics*, book IX, pp. 1839–1852, in *The Complete Works of Aristotle*, Jonathan Barnes, ed., vol. II.
111 Montaigne, *The Essays*, 1.28, esp. pp. 207–210. Aristotle, *Nicomachean Ethics*, book IX, in *The Complete Works of Aristotle*, vol. II, Barnes, ed.
112 Plato, "The Symposium," in *Plato: The Collected Dialogues Including the Letters*. pp. 526–574.
113 Montaigne, *The Complete Essays*, Screech, tr., III3.9, "On vanity," p. 1105. And see Weller, "The Rhetoric of Friendship in Montaigne's *Essais*," in *New Literary History*.
114 This argument was prompted by a talk by Craig Horton, from La Trobe University, Australia, on "The Uses of Prodigality: Errant Youth and the Metropolis in Early Modern London Plays," at the Literary London Conference, Goldsmiths College, London, July 25–27, 2003. Horton made a direct call for a theory of aging in Literary Studies. Morton argues that working-class young men of London were viewed as the primary threat as they made up the mob element, of early-modern London. This fear makes sense, given the population explosion of that time; half the population of London was under the age of 21 in 1600. Horton's talk gave a new perspective on the dynamic of mob mentality, social bonds, and aging, topics that are often only discussed in terms of the models of ancient Rome and revolutionary Paris.
115 See Nandini Das, "Romance and the Development of Prose Fiction in Renaissance England," unpublished Ph.D. thesis, Trinity College, Cambridge University, esp. pp. 97–106.
116 Thank you again to Craig Morton.
117 John Bunyan, *The Pilgrim's Progress*.
118 Augustine, *Confessions*, Pine-Coffin, tr., books I–IX.
119 Michel Tournier, *Le Roi des aulnes*. Tournier, *The Ogre*. Much of Part I is centered on the narrator's fat, powerful, beastly (but not evil) friend Nestor, who dies when they are at school. In Part II, the central character, as an adult, is taken as a prisoner to East Prussia during World War II, before becoming a sub-gamekeeper for Hermann Göring. This part of the novel is certainly more palatable than the first, perhaps because it concentrates, indirectly but not accidentally, on abuses perpetrated by others, not on the violence that the main character (in the first

person in Part I) wants to inflict on others and to experience for himself. At the novel's conclusion, Abel carries a Jewish boy out of a concentration camp; the last page alludes to Abel's death, to the Jewish boy's survival, and to a Christian reading of salvation as the novel's ultimate message.

120 Giambattista Vico, *The New Science*, books IV–V.

121 David Price, *History Made, History Imagined: Contemporary Literature, Poiesis, and the Past*, ch. 8 on Michel Tournier.

REFERENCES

Agamben, Giorgio, *The Open: Man and Animal*, Kevin Attell, tr. (Stanford, CA: Stanford University Press, 2003).

Aquinas, St. Thomas, *Summa Theologica*, 5 vols. (Westminster, MD: Christian Classics, 1948).

Aristotle, *The Complete Works of Aristotle*, Jonathan Barnes, 2 vols. (Princeton: Princeton University Press, 1991).

Augustine, *Confessions*, R.S. Pine-Coffin, tr. (Harmondsworth, U.K.: Penguin, 1961).

Beccaria, Cesare, *On Crimes and Punishments*, David Young, tr. (Indianapolis, IN: Hackett, 1986).

Bertsch, Janet, *Storytelling in the Works of Bunyan, Grimmelshausen, Defoe, and Schnabel* (Rochester, NY: Camden House, 2004).

Binswanger, Hans Christoph, *Geld und Magik: Deutung und Kritik der modernen Wirtschaft anhand von Goethes Faust* (Hamburg: Thienemanns Verlag, 1985).

Boethius, *The Consolation of Philosophy*, V.E. Watts, tr. (London: Penguin, 1969).

Brecht, Bertolt, *Brecht on Theatre: The Development of an Aesthetic*, John Willett, tr., ed. (New York: Hill and Wang, 1964).

———. *Mother Courage and Her Children*, John Willett, tr., John Willett and Ralph Manheim, eds. (New York: Penguin Classics, 2007).

Breuer, Dieter, *Grimmelshausen Handbuch* (Munich: Fink, 1999).

Büchner, Georg, *Complete Plays, Lenz, and Other Writings*, John Reddick, tr. (London: Penguin Classics, 1993).

Bunyan, John, *The Pilgrim's Progress* (Oxford: Oxford University Press, 1984).

Campe, Rüdiger, "Conversation, Poetic Form, and the State." In *A New History of German Literature*, David E. Wellerby (Cambridge, MA: Harvard University Press, 2004), pp. 1622–1624.

Clark, J.C.D., " 'In Denial': Wars of Religion in English Discourse, 1639–2007," unpublished article.

Clowns, Fools and Picaros: Popular Forms in Theatre, Fiction and Film, David Robb, ed. Amsterdam: Rodopi, 2007.

Cunningham, Mary B. *Faith in the Byzantine World* (Oxford: Lion Publishing, 2002).

Das, Nandini, "Romance and the Development of Prose Fiction in Renaissance England," Unpublished Ph.D. thesis, Trinity College, Cambridge University, English Faculty, 2002.

Defoe, Daniel, *Robinson Crusoe* (London: Penguin, 1985).

Döblin, Alfred, *Berlin Alexanderplatz: The Story of Franz Biberkopf*, Eugène Jolas, tr. (London: Continuum, 2004).

Elias, Norbert, *The Civilizing Process: The History of Manners*, Edmund Jephcott, tr. (Oxford: Basil Blackwell, 1978)

Freud, Sigmund, *Group Psychology and the Analysis of the Ego*, James Strachey, tr. (New York: Bantam, 1965).

Fritz, Arnold, *One Hundred Caricatures from* Simplicissimus, *1896–1914: An Exhibit of the Goethe-Institut* (Munich: Goethe-Institut, 1985).

Gagliardo, John, *Germany under the Old Regime, 1600–1790* (London: Longman, 1991).

Godwin, William, *Caleb Williams, or, Things as they are* (London: Penguin, 2005).

Grimmelshausen, Hans Jacob Christoffel von, *The Life of Courage: The Notorious Thief, Whore, and Vagabond.* Mike Mitchell, tr., ed. (Sawtry, U.K.: Dedalus, 2001).

———. *Simplicissimus*, Mike Mitchell, tr., ed. (Sawtry, U.K.: Dedalus, 1999).

———. *Tearaway*, Mike Mitchell, tr., ed. (Sawtry, U.K.: Dedalus, 2003).

———. *Werke.* Dieter Breuer, ed., 3 vols. (Frankfurt am Main: Deutscher Klassiker Verlag, 1989).

Hays, J. N., *Epidemics and Pandemics: Their Impacts on Human History* (Santa Barbara, CA: ABC Clio, 2005).

Hesselmann, Peter, *Simplicissimus Redivivus: Eine kommentierte Dokumentation der Rezeptionsgeschichte Grimmelshausens in 17. und 18. Jahrhundert (1667–1800)* (Frankfurt am Main: Vittorio Klosterman, 1992).

Jacques Callot: Catalogue Raisonné de Oeuvre Gravé (The Complete Etchings & Engravings), Jules Lieure, ed., 2nd ed., 2 vols. (San Francisco: Alan Wofsky Fine Arts, 1989).

Marx, Karl, *Capital*, Ben Fowkes, tr., Ernest Mandel, ed. (New York: Vintage Books, 1976).

Menhennet, Alan, *Grimmelshausen the Storyteller: A Study of the "Simplician" Novels* (Columbia, SC: Camden House, 1997).

Mirandola, Pico della, *On the Dignity of Man*, Charles Glenn Wallis, Paul J. W. Miller, and Douglas Carmichael, trs. (Indianapolis, IN: Hackett, 1998).

Montaigne, Michel de, *The Complete Essays*, M. A. Screech, tr. (London: Penguin, 1993).

Nemoto, Reiko Tachibana, "On Two Interviews between Günter Grass and Ōe Kenzaburō," *World Literature Today*, 67, no. 2 (Spring 1993): 301–305.

Otto, Karl F., ed., *A Companion to the Works of Grimmelshausen*, (Rochester, NY: Camden House, 2003).

Outram, Quentin, *Dearth, Disease and Death in Germany during the Thirty Years' War* (Leeds, U.K.: University of Leeds, Leeds Business School, March 1998, E98/04).

Parker, Geoffrey and Lesley M. Smith, eds., *The General Crisis of the Seventeenth Century* (London: Routledge & Kegan Paul, 1978).

Parker, Geoffrey, ed., *The Thirty Years' War* (London: Routledge & Kegan Paul, 1984).

Plato, *The Collected Dialogues of Plato, Including the Letters*, Lane Cooper, tr., Edith Hamilton and Huntington Cairns, eds. (Princeton: Princeton University Press, 1982).

Price, David W., *History Made, History Imagined: Contemporary Literature, Poiesis, and the Past* (Urbana and Chicago: University of Illinois Press, 1999).

Ronell, Avital, *Stupidity* (Urbana and Chicago: University of Illinois Press, 2001).

Sampath, Ursula, *Kaspar Hauser: A Modern Metaphor* (Columbia, SC: Camden House, 1991).

Thomas, Keith, *Religion and the Decline of Magic: Studies in Popular Beliefs in Sixteenth and Seventeenth Century England* (New York: Oxford University Press, 1971).

Thompson, E. P., *The Making of the English Working Class* (London: Victor Gollancz, 1963).

Tournier, Michel, *Le Roi des aulnes* (Paris: Gallimard, 1970.

———. *The Ogre*, Barbara Bray, tr. (Baltimore, MD: The Johns Hopkins University Press, 1997).

Vico, Giambattista, *The New Science of Giambattista Vico*, Thomas Bergin and Max Fisch, trs., eds. (Ithaca, NY: Cornell University Press, 1948).

Wedgwood, C. V., *The Thirty Years War* (London: Pimlico, 1992).

3   Gulliver's Travels (1726, amended 1735), Science, and Social Class

I BACKGROUND

1 Intellectual Foundations

The intellectual foundations of *Gulliver's Travels* (1726, 1735) can be distinguished in Swift's English: his clever, seemingly effortless writing stems from his familiarity and confrontation with established ideas and institutions.[1] Swift's writing is simple, the style easy, yet his tone is barbed, and his bias is outwardly fiercely anti-intellectual. This anti-academic bias is perhaps most strikingly evident in his descriptions of the new sciences, especially in Part III, which spoofs disciplines that offer nothing of substance for any particular time and place. Tellingly, the text rails that useless inventions are all that scholars offer at a time of gross economic inequalities.[2]

This supposed children's story features Lemuel Gulliver, a surgeon, who goes to sea in the early eighteenth century to see the world. He spends much of the story interacting with non-human species who often seem to be more intelligent, or at least more rational, than human beings. Gulliver's own mental state deteriorates throughout his four long voyages, but his powers of observation do not.

This preposterous story is not just for entertainment—it is about science, and also about social class in Britain as examined in terms of imperialism abroad. The imperialism most often addressed in the book has to do with the slave trade and with Ireland. The book is not primarily about the British colonies in North America or the Caribbean, or about the tiny holdings that Britain had in India in the early eighteenth century. However, in numerous ways the book gestures toward these larger colonial themes as well. Within the frolicking and mayhem of *Gulliver's Travels* these theoretical themes of science, social class, and imperialism can be identified clearly.

Thus the core of both the European Enlightenment and the Counter-Enlightenment can be discerned in this deceptively simple work, published three decades before the apex of the French Enlightenment, which is often still viewed as identical with the European Enlightenment. Nevertheless, Swift tended to identify with past intellectual sources, not with the current attacks on them. In terms of the European Quarrel of the Ancients and Moderns, Swift emphasized learning from antiquity and considered himself to be an Ancient. However, later generations, not inaccurately, viewed Swift as the best of the Moderns because of his slashing social criticism. Swift was not just an early Enlightenment figure but also (along with Rousseau) a proto-Romantic because of his awareness, often expressed via disdain, for the tremendous power of science, technology, and heavy industry to create good or evil. This is not the first example in the history of ideas of a thinker being ranked by later generations as the best exponent of a group against which he was relentlessly fighting: in Swift's case, the Moderns. Yet often, and certainly in the case of Swift and his contemporaries (who were many times his targets, especially the scientists in the Royal Society), both sides in these debates were discussing the same subjects. These subjects subsequently became the intellectual markers of their place and time.[3]

It would be wrong, however, to exaggerate the linkages between Swift and his enemies. In regard to Swift's views on religion, he was, at the very least, not anti-religious, thus making him an unlikely Modern. "A Full and True Account of the Battle of the Ancient and Modern Books in St. James's Library," an appendix to *A Tale of a Tub*, exemplifies his own inner tension on these themes.[4] In this short story, after all the staff and patrons have left the library late one Friday evening, the physical books literally fight with each other for dominance. The battle is partly a class issue: gentlemen and Ancients versus upstarts, technicians, experts, and Moderns in a time when expertise was generally viewed as vulgar. In *Battle of the Books,* there are mock-heroic battles: Homer, Plato, and Aristotle against Francis Bacon and René Descartes, thus the inductive method (reasoning that goes from the specific to the general, as from the Ancients) is pitted against the deductive method (reasoning that goes from the general to the specific, theories developed from data, as from the Moderns). This brief work powerfully addresses topics that philosophers and theologians had debated over centuries, since antiquity, and yet it also reflects, in an astonishingly natural manner—although remembering that it features heavy volumes talking and fighting late at night—many of the immediate concerns of Swift's time. In this case, unlike some of Swift's other fiction, the battle is not about forms of religion, but about abstract, mainly secular ideas relevant to Swift's own time.[5]

The relationship between form and content in Swift's writings is vexed as well as delightful. Many literary scholars, including some specialists on *Gulliver's Travels*, deem Gulliver, the main character, to be a thin character, with relatively little character development, and consequently they consider this book to be a formless type of fiction. Some literary scholars go so far as to argue that this is a Menippean satire, such as Rabelais's *Gargantua and Pantagruel* and Voltaire's *Candide*. The literary form of Menippean satire is itself formless, marked by wild attacks on all types of willfully ignorant groups of people—generally priests and intellectuals, but also successful businessmen and politicians—all in a hyper-intellectual manner. And, certainly, *Gulliver's Travels* is crammed full of fantastical elements, so this book is not a novel (by definition a novel cannot have any nonrealistic elements). Literary scholars today are no more united than readers in the eighteenth century about the true message of *Gulliver's Travels*. However, there is agreement, then and now, that the content of this work of fiction is delivered through its clever format, and thus that that format must be broken like a code.

Gulliver's Travels, perhaps more than any other work of fiction of the eighteenth century, can be viewed as a time capsule of the intellectual concerns of Western thought at that time. Swift's complicated, often contradictory, views resulted in writing that is not just entertaining but also a source for ongoing theoretical arguments. Thus one of the ongoing curiosities of this book is that serious readers of *Gulliver's Travels* continue to interpret it in astonishingly different ways. There is not, for example, such a wide debate among scholars about the political message *Don Quixote*. Later references to *Gulliver's Travels*, from various, modern scholars interpret the book as differently as proto-democratic or fascistic, and anti-religious or deeply spiritual. Swift's ideas cannot simply be reduced to an arch, extremely well-written summary of the failings of his times, for they are also grounded in political and economic theory as well, and they have direct implications for his own time and for later generations, thus reflecting the concerns of both the Ancients and the Moderns.

2 Structure of the Book in Terms of Abstract Ideas, Especially from Plato

The structure of *Gulliver's Travels* can be outlined in terms of major categories of political theory since Plato.[6] Part I, for example, set in Lilliput, is both Machiavellian and Hobbesian, stressing two varieties of royal rule, both of which admit a limited, two-way relationship between the ruler and the ruled. The initial emphasis in *Gulliver's Travels* is on the Machiavellian Prince, but this is linked to the Hobbesian assumption that human nature does not change with the shift from the state of nature to that of society, or even within society itself. In the specific cases presented in *Gulliver's Travels*, this all-too-human nature is shared by almost all the other species Gulliver encounters. Part II, featuring the gargantuan Brobdingnagians, is Augustinian in substance, blending classical learning with New Testament morals in order to make one's own society victorious over its enemies. Further, based on an understanding of an Aristotelian reworking of Platonic theories, Part II is on properly functioning government, which is Aristotelian, but also on defending one's own particular way of life against one's enemies, which is Augustinian. Part III, on mathematics and the scientific academy, could be viewed as modeled on both Lucretius and Francis Bacon, with its theoretical explorations of the very nature of nature, reminiscent of

Lucretius's notion of the atom. In addition, there are often farcical scientific experiments that, although consistently derided in *Gulliver's Travels*, are nevertheless examples of a willingness to take intellectual risks that were, for Francis Bacon, the backbone of the scientific tradition. What can be viewed as the shift in emphasis in *Gulliver's Travels* from Hobbes to Lucretius (albeit very much out of chronological order) is of interest, specifically in terms of Gulliver and his possession of his own body. The Hobbesian view affirms the right of the person to defend oneself, even against one's own sovereign. However, the cynical view, from Lucretius, is that human beings have virtually no control whatsoever over material objects, even over their own bodies, thus making possible only a theoretical understanding of one's material circumstances. Gulliver becomes less rights oriented as his travels continue. His view of private property, including his own self, becomes more concentrated on philosophical and political interpretations of control. Part IV, on the Yahoos and Houyhnhnms and on Gulliver's decline into madness, can be linked to the classic utopian works: Plato's *Republic* and Thomas More's *Utopia* (1516). There are clear links among Plato, Thomas More, and Jonathan Swift to the later works by Edward Bellamy's *Looking Backward* (1888), William Morris's *News From Nowhere* (1890), and Charlotte Perkins Gilman's *Herland* (1915).

However, all these later usages could perhaps be set aside and a concentrated comparison—as much as a contrast—between *Gulliver's Travels* and Plato's *Republic* is perhaps most appropriate. Both *The Republic* and *Gulliver's Travels* follow a set pattern: beginning in *Gulliver's Travels* with negotiations within a set social setting in Part I; leading, in Parts II and III, to extended theoretical discussions regarding good government and justice, and offering specific case histories of these concepts; presenting models of good leadership; offering diverting, highly amusing moments provided by minor characters, which both mock and uphold the authority of the central characters and political leaders; and ending, in Part IV, with the most abstract and rarified form of knowledge, and thus Swift's and Plato's supposed best form of government. Even if *The Republic* and *Gulliver's Travels* both present the republic as the best form of government, at the same time both works deride this alternative as not only impossible but insufferable. Swift's work of fiction leads in the final section, Part IV, to a modern rewriting and update of Plato's *Republic*, with its emphasis on the Forms.[7] The same stress on the superior power of rationality in the Houyhnhnm culture is presented in *Gulliver's Travels*. The two books could thus be read as parodies of formal decision making in even the best possible form of government.

3 Gulliver as Not Wholly Gullible?

Lemuel Gulliver—who at times seems very smart and at other times very foolish—wishes to travel and talk, and he manages to do much of each.

Educated at Cambridge and then Leiden, in Holland, married with children, and a great reader (apparent from his erudite asides), he does not fully come alive as a character until he starts traveling. He has an "insatiable Desire of seeing foreign Countries," so much so that he disappears as a distinct personality during his visits back home.[8] He begins to talk not so much during his years as a ship's surgeon, and then ship's captain, but rather during the times in between voyages, when he is unable to pursue gainful employment at home and abroad, sometimes when he is a literal prisoner of one of the shockingly foreign, sometimes non-human, cultures he encounters around the world, mainly in the South Seas.

Although Gulliver may exaggerate his social skills (something he is not slow to accuse other travel writers of doing), nevertheless he is not foolish or easily manipulated. He is a marvelously competent traveler, even in the midst of the most inauspicious circumstances. The cultures he encounters are indeed bizarre; to give two examples, one is on a Flying or Floating Island, and the inhabitants there have a remarkable facility in mathematics (which is far more remarkable to Gulliver than that the creatures on this Island have heads that permanently tilt to the right or left); and yet another culture has equine rather than human rulers and humanoid slaves, thus the horses rule the proto-humans. Countless shipwrecks, mutinies, encounters with pirates, and repeated misfortunes result in his capture by peoples and creatures of wildly varying physical sizes and types. Although his early travels begin to wear down his conviction that the European, specifically English, political model is the best, albeit flawed, Gulliver retains this belief until the very last of the new cultures he encounters. Only twice does he even think about staying in any of these societies; he briefly considers this when he visits the Struldbrugg Immortals, and then he lives, surprisingly happily, for over five years, with the Houyhnhnm horses. Almost all of his other visits are initially imprisonments, and during these times, he inwardly resists being a captive, regularly demanding his liberty (although with less pugnacity on each subsequent voyage and imprisonment). At the same time, Gulliver is, in an instrumental way, gracious, fawning, even obsequious to his hosts, who are manifestly, certainly by toward the very end of the story, also his warders.

The book trenchantly criticizes major institutions, with attacks on political parties, marriage and family, research and technological institutes, the army, national government, the civil service, the university, religion (both Catholicism and Protestantism), and colonization. Despite these implicit criticisms, the rules-oriented Lilliputians whom Gulliver first encounters, the mercantilist Brobdingnagians, and the talented, if mad, scientists of Laputa are all unable to convince Gulliver of the folly of his role as self-appointed ambassador—even in the midst of his constant misadventure—for the western European way of life. Gulliver's lack of intellectual development is supposedly demonstrated by his regurgitation of seventeenth-century British principles. However, his Lockean pronouncements have no practical application, and thus, at core, are not actually Lockean. This work of fiction itself repeatedly makes the point that theory is not sufficient on its own; rather it must be applied directly for it to have any utility at all.

For all the theoretical depth of *Gulliver's Travels*, it is, sadly, nevertheless easy to read the main character as fracturing throughout the story. This is far from a story of personal growth, as in a *Bildungsroman*. Decline, rather than personal growth, can be found as early as Part I to Part II. For example, the only overt demonstration of war in this book is between the Lilliputians and the inhabitants of Blefuscu. In these battles, Gulliver is used as a foot soldier (he is at this stage very large) and at least once as a secret weapon by the tiny Lilliputians, for he wades into the sea to steal the Blefuscudian ships from their harbor and carry them away as if they were toy boats. However, he stoutly refuses to be the weapon of mass destruction that the Lilluputians wish him to be in order to wipe out their enemy completely. However, Gulliver apparently learns more about power politics than about his own beliefs from this particular experience, for if he makes the right moral decision here, he often does not. Already, by the time Gulliver is in the next society, in Part II of IV, he wants to give the King of Brobdingnag the secret of gunpowder and cannons, and he is amazed and offended when his offer is declined. Thus increasingly Gulliver craves ancient and modern theory (for he searches for stability as much as adventure in his travels), turning to theory for reassurance in the midst of his own tumultuous life, especially as he slowly loses his own sense of judgment. Although Gulliver's personality is molded for satirical ends, it should also be viewed as part of larger tendencies within society.

Certainly the goal of the work is not to demonstrate intellectual development in its hero, but rather to encourage intellectual development in its readers. Thus the question of whether Gulliver is gullible or passive is moot. In Part III, Gulliver visits with Immortals and then, in a separate visit, he meets the great men of the past, who are brought to life simply for his diversion. In one incident, while visiting the great dead men of European history, Gulliver realizes that Homer and Aristotle are separated from the rest because of a collective guilt among the others about how the works of these two Ancients have been treated by commentators; Homer and Aristotle are perhaps too lofty to notice the others, or they are simply surprised by being followed by such a mass of virtual mutes, as the later great thinkers will not speak to them. However odd these encounters, they underline Gulliver's desire not only for guidance but actually to locate the truth.

Gulliver repeatedly searches for lofty models, as a contrast to his own failings. When he is later forced to realize his own physical similarity to the wild, disgusting Yahoos, he turns to the stately, rational, equine Houyhnhnms—that is, horses—who offer, in his view, the only viable alternative civil society. Soon after his arrival in the Land of the Houyhnhnms, Gulliver is wearing the skins of Yahoos as shoes; the shoes are made by him, and are of Gulliver's own design.[9] This foreshadows the genocidal tendencies of Houyhnhnm culture. Gulliver is so devoted to, even deferential toward, his final hosts, one of whom he calls Master (as he had earlier referred to the giant farmer in Part II, who takes Gulliver into his home but then later shows off tiny Gulliver for profit); however, the title seems more profound in the final Part IV). Gulliver's motivation for embracing the Houyhnhnms' aristocratic form of republican rule is that it provides a means of making up for his own Yahoo skin that he could never change. His first thought is that the Yahoos are ugly cattle, and that their young smelled like something between a weasel and a fox. The Yahoos, he is told—and he starts to agree—are the "most unteachable of all Animals."[10] There is no pity for the disgusting Yahoos; their Houyhnhnm masters treat them like slaves, sometimes like beasts of burden. Likewise there is no contempt for the Yahoos, for they are considered to be incapable of behaving in any other way. These hierarchical tendencies are to be found even within Houyhnhnm culture, where social distinctions are based on color. At the time the book was written, in early-eighteenth-century Britain, the point of contention was social class, not race; there were not enough non-whites in Dublin or London for race to be much of a political issue in the modern sense; however, the race implications are fully exploited by modern readers. In the story, there is a sorrel horse (a yellowish or reddish-brown color, and for reasons unexplained in this work of fiction, supposedly not a desirable color), and the sorrel is effectively a fellow servant, along with Gulliver, not a Houyhnhnm leader. This horse is the only creature to regret Gulliver's eventual departure from Houyhnhnmland). Merit according to color is fully acknowledged by Gulliver's fascistic master.[11] At first Gulliver does not want to see this gross elitism. Later he makes excuses for it. Eventually he enthusiastically accepts this entire system based on racism and imperialism. The story clearly links this to Gulliver's growing sense of personal insecurity.

Gulliver slowly realizes, with rage, no longer disbelief, that in the Yahoos he has finally found a society of human beings. Much to his great displeasure, Gulliver is eventually forced to leave the Land of the Houyhnhnms, even though this time he has no wish to escape. Gulliver is devastated when his master tells him that the Assembly of Houyhnhnms has decided that Gulliver must go. However, this is a relatively mild decision, given that the Assembly had discussed the outright extermination of all Yahoos, and they regard Gulliver as a high-functioning Yahoo. The Assembly fears that as a rational Yahoo, Gulliver might start a revolution among the Yahoos, against the Houyhnhnms. So Gulliver, extremely reluctantly, returns home to England for the last time. Gulliver leaves by boat—the construction of this boat is Gulliver's master's idea, and the boat is built by Gulliver and the sorrel. The covering of the boat is made of Yahoo skins, and the mast is made specifically of the skins of young Yahoos. Genesis 6:7—"And the Lord said, I will destroy man whom I have created from the face of the earth; both man, and beast, and the creeping thing, and the fowls of the air;

for it repenteth me that I have made them."—is quoted almost verbatim in *Gulliver's Travels*.[12] The point of debate is whether God is genocidal, or whether humans deserve punishment. However, even on his departure, Gulliver still does not recognize the genocidal tendencies of his Houyhnhnm hosts, although they are stark for the reader.[13]

When Gulliver is in Houyhmhmland, his condemnation of colonialism is implicit, not explicit. Once at home in England, Gulliver sulks and refuses to talk to, much less be touched by, his family. He views them all as "European Yahoos."[14] He chooses to move into the family barn, where he converses for four hours a day with his two horses. The only human he can tolerate is the groom, as he smells like a horse. Deemed insane, not surprisingly, by his family and neighbors (and they had wondered about this even when he arrived home for the next-to-last time), he is, at the end of the book, no longer able to travel, and no longer able to interact with human beings. Nevertheless, in the midst of his personal trauma, and in a long paragraph, to be found eight paragraphs from the end of the book, when Gulliver is uneasily settled back home in England, there is a sharp denunciation of imperialism, clear enough for any casual reader who might have missed this major theme in the story.

However, the short piece at the outset of the book, "A Letter from Capt. Gulliver, to his Cousin Sympson," rarely discussed in commentaries on *Gulliver's Travels*, puts forward a rational, if somewhat whining, Gulliver who has already capably negotiated the publication of this book, and who is now trying to manipulate the reception of it. This suggests that Gulliver recovers from his madness, or that at least that he becomes involved in a more specific form of it, the publishing trade. Even more clearly, in the following fictional note from "The Publisher to the Reader," Gulliver is said to have now moved house, away from the curious neighbors in Redriff (Rotherhithe in London) to Newark, in Nottinghamshire, "where he now lives retired, yet in good esteem among his neighbours."[15] Thus the reader's final glimpse of Gulliver (from these two short pieces at the start of the work) is not of him living in the family barn, alone with the horses, but happily relocated to a comfortable new area, with a book in print, squabbling with the printer about the production quality of the book. Rather than diminishing the theme of madness, this suggests that madness need not be a permanent state.

In any case, questions could still be asked: To what extent should *Gulliver's Travels* (despite its presentation as a satire) be read as a pre-psychoanalytical exploration of the development of the abstract individual, and indeed, what is the relevance of this for the formation and maintenance of nation-states?[16] This shifts the emphasis away from the book's explicit attacks on particular individuals in power in London in the 1720s and from early-eighteenth-century institutions in London, and more toward theoretical concepts. Overall the major theme in *Gulliver's Travels*, and a unifying theme of the Enlightenment, is an emphasis on individuality as expressed through rationality.

The individual is the focus in *Gulliver's Travels* in at least two ways. First, the individual might obviously be Gulliver himself. He can be read as a character who tests the boundaries of individual elasticity so repeatedly that he eventually snaps. In a closely related, yet still negative, interpretation, Gulliver can be seen as a man who never develops an adult personality, and who thus collapses when his set, adolescent role is taken from him, when the familiar props are removed. Second, he could be taken to be the abstract individual, perhaps even the abstract reader. For example, the issue of whether science is a target in this work only when it impedes the development of the abstract individual, the abstract reader, will also be examined. (This would oppose the view of *Gulliver's Travels* as an attack on the evolving system of post-Cartesian science as a whole.) The often-contradictory answers that will be raised in response to these debates do much more than solidify the classic status of this work, indeed they help place this work into yet another category—that of political theory, specifically theory to do with the notion of the abstract individual.

Overall, *Gulliver's Travels* can be read with profit as an active addition to numerous ongoing intellectual and theoretical traditions, not just as a response to a very particular set of political circumstances in early-eighteenth-century British political history. Classic examples of the historical particularity of this book certainly include, for example, references to the development of the two-party system in the British Parliament, and as high entertainment, attacks on specific, powerful politicians by praising the skills of their mistresses (at one point in the story, one of the *"King's Cushions"* breaks the fall of a less-than-acrobatic minister).[17] However, the multiple academic tensions in this work affirm the fundamental role of abstract ideas, especially those from political and economic thought, all in a work still taken by many to be only a children's story. The consideration of whether Gulliver is gullible cannot be fully resolved by deciding either how well developed he is as a character or how intelligent he is.

4 Popularity of the Book and Varieties of Interpretation

This is a book that many educated adults have never read for themselves, but had read to them when they were children; their connection to the story is no less strong for this, as many of the political arguments in this work are fully comprehensible by children. However, the version they heard as children was most probably only Part I set in Lilliputia, and it was generally an expurgated and bowdlerized version—that is cleaned up and cut down—of Part I.[18] *Gulliver's Travels* is distinct in several ways from later children's stories, such as Mark Twain's *The Prince and the Pauper* (1882) and Robert Louis Stevenson's *Kidnapped* (1886). In these later stories, the hero is a teenage boy who has an older male friend to depend on in the midst of forced travel, betrayals, loneliness, and varied distresses. In *Gulliver's Travels*, the central character is an adult, educated, and already married with two children, with another one conceived during one of his brief visits home. Most critically, Gulliver rarely has anyone to help him for long, not even through one, much less all, of his voyages. Perhaps most strikingly, *Gulliver's Travels*, unlike *The Prince and the Pauper* and *Kidnapped*, is rude bordering on cruel and delights in mentioning raunchy topics and anatomical references generally not alluded to even now in polite conversation. It offers no safe or easy answers that would supposedly soothe children to sleep, or about how to better the all-too-familiar-sounding societies that are parodied so fiercely.

Yet the political and theoretical appeal of this novel, across generations and now across centuries, is not attributable simply to some adults reading beyond Part I and thus discovering a richer, more intellectual text. At all stages of this book, coarse humor and preposterous characters are mixed with strong political warnings, both immediate and long-term. The moral injunctions are discernible even in the tamest of the most censored children's versions of the story, usually lacking Part IV. Already in Part I, *"leaping and creeping,"* performed in order to gain political office, and the egg-breaking controversy, are used to describe the typical demeanor at court and the pressing, but fundamentally trivial, issues of the day at the Court of Lilliput (and, not coincidentally, also in the British Parliament in the early eighteenth century when this work was written).[19] Apparently in both cases, even when the issues were substantive, the political behavior demanded in order to make changes forced the participants to act as sycophants.

Gulliver's Travels goes back and forth between immediate and more long-lasting criticism, and thus represents its own time in many ways. It lacks, for example, a society ruled by a woman, a common trope in theory and fiction since Plato; perhaps because Britain had just been ruled by a woman, Queen Anne (who ruled from 1702 to 1714), and even more famously, almost two centuries earlier, by Queen Elizabeth I (who ruled from 1558 to 1603), a woman ruler would not have seemed preposterous. The rulers stand in for their states, and the states represent abstract individuals (or vice versa, keeping in mind the frontispiece of Hobbes's *Leviathan* in 1651, in which the state is made up of the little people, and the king is the head). The story forces a confrontation of the idiocy and small-mindedness not only in established institutions—for that would allow us as individuals to feel smug—but also in human nature, which for this book is not unchanged but contains recognizable components over time, in the individual psyche of each person. The most problematic aspect of the work is how to change society if human nature is both flawed and resistant to change, even if it is not wholly unchangeable.

Gulliver's Travels shares the adventure and travel themes of *Don Quixote*, *Simplicissimus*, and *Candide* (and *Robinson Crusoe* could well be added to this list), and it also stresses many of the same political concerns: the rejection of mercantile capitalism; the inability of existing legal systems to contend with immediate problems; and the unwillingness of people to change their material circumstances, even or especially for their own good, unless mercilessly forced to do so. Yet *Gulliver's Travels* is perhaps most appealing for the following contradictions, having been read as: an attack on European values and as an assertion of them; a warning against madness and a story about the inevitability of madness; and as a reminder of the inaccessibility of lasting love, and an implicit message that intense personal relationships are all that matter over time. In this book, as well as in *Don Quixote*, *Simplicissimus*, and *Candide*, the question could be posed whether madness or simplicity is the most crucial theme.

However, even if the immediate and visceral appeal for readers of all ages is the mad adventures of the title character, *Gulliver's Travels* would not have retained its classic status long after its publication in 1726 without the very different appeal of the abstract ideas it also puts forward. Recognition of the sophisticated presentation and sometimes development of political and economic ideas in this work helps to explain the astonishing popularity of the book—it has never been out of print—as opposed to that of almost all the other well-written and amusing travel and adventure stories of the time. These other works are now only to be found in rare-book libraries and archives, and are generally read only by scholars looking for forgotten classics, and/or by those establishing historical context for more famous novels. The eighteenth-century practice of reading books aloud to groups, large and small, publicly and privately, was driven not only by a desire to hear good stories but also because it provided mental puzzles of political life, puzzles that supposedly ordinary people—not just theorists and political leaders—craved.

The explanation of why this particular book was so often read aloud, and not just to children, has to do with the reading culture of this century (a later example being the reading out loud of political pamphlets in cafés and village squares in France before the French Revolution).[20] Overall, the increasing demand for reading material in the mid-eighteenth century was linked to the rise in female literacy; both the number of girls and women who read, often voraciously, increased, as did the number of girls and women who became writers. Somewhat later the interest in reading was bolstered by the growing political radicalism in England at the end of the eighteenth and beginning of the nineteenth centuries. Most famously, Christopher Hill makes this connection in *The Intellectual Origins of the English Revolution* (1965), as did E.P. Thompson in *The Making of the English Working Class* (slightly earlier, in 1963). There is no doubt that *Gulliver's Travels* in particular helped to spur interest in reading by the middle classes that was so marked by late in the eighteenth century.

5 The Author: Jonathan Swift (1667–1745)

Several contradictory interpretations of Jonathan Swift are generally recognized, two of which receive the most attention. First, there is Swift, the highly politicized and well-connected London journalist, later Dean of St. Patrick's Cathedral in Dublin, who wrote endless pamphlets, without demanding payment for them, in order to ambush politicians, clerics, and solicitors, in particular, on topical issues of the day. And, second, there is the author of *Gulliver's Travels*, almost the only piece of written work for which he, remarkably shrewdly, demanded royalties.[21] It is noteworthy that his most popular work is also the one that concentrates most fully on abstract ideas as well as on immediate social and political concerns. Remarkably, he recognized the potential market for such a distinctive mixture of theory and farce. Perhaps this indicates Swift's view of the high intelligence, albeit often accompanied by moral depravity, of the average reader. Thus the first interpretation stresses Swift as a professional success in both journalism and in the Church, while the second views Swift as a major writer, who was gifted, isolated, and shrewd.

There is an ongoing quest to find the origins of *Gulliver's Travels*. The casual reader might be tempted to regard Swift's voluminous, somewhat uneven, writings as merely rough drafts of, or later reflections on, this one brilliant work. Swift, however, would not have shared this view, for this would diminish his concern for changing specific practices in his own time, which is so most evident in his supposed minor works. Swift scholars would agree with him. One of his better-known works in his time, *A Tale of a Tub: Written for the Universal Improvement of Mankind* (1704), puts forward in its ironic subtitle a claim that Swift makes in most of his works. In this work, he attacks both rationality (thus French, Cartesian, scientific thinking) and common sense (the evolving emphasis of the Scottish Enlightenment). Many of his smaller works exhibit flashes of astounding acuteness and dexterity, erudition and entertainment. One small classic is "A Modest Proposal for Preventing the Children of Poor People in Ireland from Being a Burthen to Their Parents, or the Country, and for Making Them Beneficial to the Publick" (1729), which is read both as "an indictment of colonial landlordism in Ireland" and as a "response to the English financial revolution of the eighteenth century."[22] Even many of his less-well-known pamphlets contain sentences and ideas tossed out in the most unexpected ways, which most writers could only hope to produce. During his lifetime, and certainly at his death, centuries before Freudian analysis, commentators have not been reluctant to link to his childhood Swift's markedly strong personality, ambition, and fierce desire never to be harassed or hectored, all of which persisted throughout his life.

Yet in comparison to a great many other writers of distinction, Swift's childhood in most respects seems almost bland and conventional (despite his having been kidnapped as an infant by his nurse, and not returned home for three years). Although Swift was born into a family of ministers and solicitors, he was convinced that he had gained little from his seemingly worthy background, and there was apparently no warmth in his early family life. This seems to be the crucial element: he considered himself unloved by his family, and thus in return he chose not to love them. He spent years of his childhood away from his mother; his father died before he was born. As an adult, Swift's personal life was also ill defined. There is not space here to elaborate on his somewhat disturbing relationships with Esther Johnson (Stella) and Hester Vanhomrigh (Vanessa), the first of whom he might have secretly married. Surprisingly few personal details emerge from his voluminous writings, or from his substantial correspondence with each of these women. Apparently he believed these two women both loved him too much, and in return he refused to love either of them. Personal relations were not his strong suit.

Overall, much of Swift's adult life was spent fighting for independence. He wanted freedom from his family and from the Scholasticism at Trinity College, Dublin, where he went to university. Throughout his life, he desired freedom and recognition, for himself and for others, from all who held arbitrary power. Later, he fought against specific individuals in authority over him (indeed, often against some who simply did not support him) and most certainly against particular political and social injustices. Marked especially in old age by a generous spirit toward those below him with no defenders (for example, the poor around his Cathedral in Dublin), he was nevertheless ruthless in attacking anyone he regarded as having more power than himself, and these attacks were not always propelled by the best of motives. He was at his best with those who needed him; he was not good with his peers, much less his superiors.

Similar to Voltaire, virtually all of Swift's causes were more immediate than long-term. Yet the type of analysis of this present study—which stresses the long-term theoretical implications of *Gulliver's Travels*—would, on one level, have appealed to Swift's vanity, and yet, on another level, would also perhaps have struck him as misplaced. For, as Swift wrote, the problems to attack are those of the moment; many of the problems he stressed are still immediate problems today.

Even as a young adult, Swift channeled his defiance and powerfully strong will into his writing. He spent years in London, from age 22 to 46 (punctuated by time spent in Ireland), writing for Grub Street (which was an actual place, now lost under the Barbican Centre for the performing arts in London, but also the term for the popular publishing industry exploding in Swift's time) and later as one of the writers for the celebrated (or, depending on one's outlook, notorious) *The Tatler* and *The Spectator*.[23] These two early eighteenth-century journals showcased the best writers of the time and made the lasting reputations of many writers, including Swift. *The Tatler* and *The Spectator* are crammed with philosophical essays, personal attacks, and advertisements (the latter often ignored by modern scholars, and, to be fair, the advertisements have been left out of many later editions). Many of the pieces in *The Tatler* and *The Spectator* are so well written that it is still a pleasure to hear them read out loud today. Swift wrote well in all three categories: philosophical essays, personal attacks, and charming advertisements. His advertisements were calls for specific political changes that he wanted, for example, for journalists, and especially for the poor in for Ireland. At this stage in his life Swift was an acknowledged force to be reckoned with in both journalism and politics.

Swift had high-ranking patrons and was sought after by many of the aristocratic women who ran political salons at this time. The famed hostesses of early eighteenth-century London invited politicians, while Parisian *salon* hostesses of this time sought out intellectuals, *philosophes*. This marks a fundamental distinction in the political concerns of these two countries in the eighteenth century. Swift himself was a driving force, even more so than his wealthy, well-connected patrons, in many behind-the-scenes political intrigues. Not incidentally, his company was sought out for both his astonishing wit and his cruelty, so often a winning combination in high society.

One stunning example of his political machinations involved no less than the Duke of Marlborough, who was perhaps the most powerful man in Britain at the time. Historian Michael Foot highlights Swift's relentless participation in bringing down the Duke of Marlborough and his remarkably politically savvy wife Sarah from their positions of power and influence in relation to Queen Anne.[24] Swift's involvement, leading to the self-imposed exile of the Marlboroughs to the Continent, is very much part of the story of the emergence of a two-party system in Parliament.

However, shortly thereafter there was a shift in Parliament from the Tories to the Whigs, followed in 1714 by the death of Queen Anne and the ascension of George I. Queen Anne's patronage of Swift's patrons was definitely not continued by George I. Swift left for Ireland, where he was to become Dean of St. Patrick's Cathedral in Dublin. This was not a move he made with any enthusiasm. He never returned to England or Wales (a great favorite of his) for any extended period.

Swift predicted that he would die in Ireland "like a rat in a hole"; he regarded his years in Ireland to be years of exile from London, the center of his literary and political existence. Yet it was in Dublin that he wrote *Gulliver's Travels*. He was not the first writer to produce his greatest work in exile from the city he loved. Dante and Machiavelli never forsook their love of Florence, and both wrote their best work in exile.

The "rat in a hole" image, however, is not an entirely unfair example of Swift's attitude toward Ireland, and of the ambiguity of his position as the leading Protestant figure in an overwhelmingly Catholic Ireland (where at this time the aristocrats, landowners, and authority figures were all Protestant) despite his impassioned defense of the Irish poor in many of his best-known pamphlets. Nevertheless, if Swift is on occasion treated as a British, even an English writer, rather than an Irish one, *Gulliver's Travels* is nevertheless a very Irish book in subject matter, especially on the traditional identification of the subordinate group, the Yahoos in Part IV, as the Irish.[25] Quite simply, as Swift scholar Claude Rawson writes: "Though resentful of his Irish exile, he [that is Swift] became very active in Irish politics."[26]

If Swift's attitudes toward Ireland are somewhat confusing, and similarly, if his views on religion seem internally coherent, it is because they do not add up to the traditional views of any one religion, even or especially his own, the Church of Ireland (Anglican/High Church Protestant). This might now seem odd for a man who had a living (the contemporary term for a salary from a particular church parish, but which tended not to require any specific duties, not unlike a postdoctoral fellowship today). Swift took Holy Orders at age 27, and held various Church positions culminating in becoming Dean of St. Patrick's Cathedral in Dublin at age 46. Yet there is virtually no extended discussion of religion in *Gulliver's Travels*. Explanations vary for the deliberate exclusion of one of the most vital of human activities and institutions—it could not have been an oversight, especially given his profession—in a work that skewers most of the other key institutions. One perspective is that Swift, even before he gained his august ecclesiastical position in Dublin, would not mock the Church at this stage, even though he had done so explicitly in earlier, anonymous works. However, even a cursory reading of his other works, including those written both before and after *Gulliver's Travels*, discounts this view. To give one example, Queen Anne, for example, was enraged by the anti-clericalism of his *Tale of a Tub*.[27] Other interpretations have posited that he was frightened to reveal the full extent of his religious doubts and his criticisms of the Church, with his *Tale of a Tub* used as evidence. Although this view must be recognized, it is difficult to sustain. It is also possible that Swift was a sincere believer, that he had an inner spiritual life, even though his religious views were not always in line with the official doctrine of his own Anglican Church. Thus he simply suppressed any slight deviations in thought, perhaps out of a desire for privacy.

It does seem likely that Swift was isolating, often targeting, religious topics in *Gulliver's Travels*, but doing so in his own creative, perverse ways, perhaps within the context of his own personal faith. Two examples are his discussion in *Gulliver's Travels* of the very long lives of some non-human creatures (in terms of an Augustinian sense of time), and also of an all-powerful head of a religious group. Thus it might seem that Swift was either too frightened to discuss religion directly and openly but did so in this work of fiction in his own twisted and delicious ways, and/or that his views on religion were never wholly conventional. Surely if his views were conventional, he would not have had to hide them, yet perhaps also any conventionality would be an embarrassment to him.

Swift was willing at times to make traditional usage of religion when it suited him in debates about social control and the possible creation of a better society. Certainly, it could be argued that there exists no overt form of public morality in *Gulliver's Travels*, one based on the utility of a state religion, such as that advocated by Machiavelli in *The Prince*. Swift drew on both religious and secular sources, not only classical references, to support his views, and took on religious and secular classic texts (not just living people) as his opponents in his ongoing debate about the limits of the humanity's ability to reform itself.

6 Historical Setting of the Book

Despite the intellectual grounding of *Gulliver's Travels* and the author's fierce embrace of older rather than modern books, it would be foolish to ignore altogether the contemporary influences on this book. When it was published in 1726, Scotland and England had been unified for only 19 years (although they had had the same ruler since 1603), and Ireland, Swift's home, was a dependency of England. England had had a bloodless revolution in 1688—the Glorious Revolution—that changed the form of government from an absolute to a constitutional monarchy. Many scholars claim that the Glorious Revolution was the reason Britain did not have a Revolution such as occurred in France in 1789. Others cite the English Civil War, which immediately preceded the Glorious Revolution and was marked by the execution of Charles I in 1649, as the English, earlier version of the French Revolution. The early eighteenth century in Britain was certainly marked by a sharp awareness of war and revolution.[28]

The 1688 Glorious Revolution can be seen, in broad terms, as a move away from the emphasis on the group, and the state as a whole, to a new emphasis on the individual. Various thinkers and political parties had their own starting points for the foundation necessary for the good life for the abstract individual. A century later the individual is defended in Edmund Burke's prescient attack on the French Revolution in his *Reflections on the Revolution in France* (written in 1790, three years before the start of the Terror).[29] Yet the Burkean emphasis on property, hereditary monarchy, and history (he was a Whig M.P.) gave way by the mid-nineteenth century, not only in Parliament, but also in political philosophy, to an even clearer stress on the rights of the abstract individual. John Stuart Mill, known now as a classical liberal rather than a conservative, wrote *On Liberty* (1859), rightly considered the major statement of classical liberal thought; Mill himself, in later life, was a Tory M.P.[30] The struggles of the Whigs and the Tories (marked especially by their antagonism toward each other, the Whigs tending to favor constitutional monarchy, and the Tories absolute rule) in the late seventeenth and early eighteenth centuries are told with glee by Swift in his overt mocking of the courtiers in every country Gulliver visits, but especially in Lilliput.[31] It can be puzzling to sort out these two parties, for, then as now, both major parties claimed at times to be the one which would best protect the individual. Overall the Glorious Revolution can be viewed as the intellectual backdrop to a growing concern for the individual over the state, a concern that could be found across the political spectrum in Britain.

Yet for all this nascent concern for the abstract individual, political power in Britain at this stage was wholly vested in the Church and state, and there was seemingly no difference between them. Thus, not only in practical but also in legal terms, only those in the state church had political influence. The Anglican Church of England was in 1726 the official church of the country. Only those who belonged to the Church of England (or the Presbyterian Church of Scotland or the Anglican Churches of Ireland and Wales) had the right to vote or to become members of Parliament. Women, Catholics, Jews, and other nonconformists, as well as non-landed men, could not vote, regardless of other factors such as wealth and birth. Catholics received the vote and the right to hold public office only much later in 1829 (thus bringing about full Catholic Emancipation), Jews in 1858, and women in 1928. Britain, at the time of the publication of *Gulliver's Travels*, following the Glorious Revolution of 1688, had a constitutional monarchy, a more limited form of monarchy, but it certainly did not have a fully representative form of government.

One contemporary movement was not strictly church or state, the Societies for the Reformation of Manners, was a force from the late seventeenth to the mid-eighteenth century. (The later revival movements, coming out of the Anglican Church but spawning many new churches, happened somewhat later in the 1740s.) The anti-drunkenness campaign, for example, was certainly a form of social control, but one that targeted a genuine problem for the new urban poor.[32] The appeal was not just to the destitute but also to the working poor, and in many respects to the displaced peoples in the cities, many of them having recently moved from the countryside in the century leading up to the Industrial Revolution. This was often the first sustained contact any of these people ever had with organized social movements or even with religion. Thus, in broad terms, even though, or perhaps because, the state Church had a monopoly on political power at this point, it also had an impact on daily life in the major industrial cities. Although substitute institutions for religious practice, beyond the Church of England, were increasingly available, the disparities in British society at the time were not limited to politics and religion but were perhaps starkest in economics.[33]

The early eighteenth century in England was indeed a difficult time to be poor. This is despite Phyllis Deane's reminder that England was much richer than other parts of Europe at this time. England faced particular problems. In the eighteenth century, London's population was in the process of doubling, from half a million to a million between 1700 and 1800. By 1800, it was the largest city in Europe and North America.[34] In the early-modern period, the Church and then the state had become highly involved in issues of social control, and correspondingly gave some limited help to the very poor.[35] However, even in the early eighteenth century, there were strident calls for the repeal of the Poor Laws and for the abolition of charity schools. The gist of this move was that the Church (in the view of Thomas Robert Malthus, now viewed as an economist) and the state (according to the earlier, highly successful pamphleteer, Mandeville, also now studied as an early economic thinker) should withdraw from the practice of propping up the lives of the indolent, over-breeding poor, which was, in this argument, directly responsible for holding back the development of the national economy. Oddly, these calls could be viewed as not having been explicitly directed against designated poor people, or even toward a certain social class. Rather, these attitudes represented the belief that people of any social class, if unmotivated, would become poor, and thus should not be propped up. It seems almost unnecessary to note, however, that, especially in the early 1700s, people of all social classes were born into their station in life, and were almost never, at any point of their lives, on a level playing ground that would allow the most talented and thus supposedly deserving to thrive. Thus, poverty levels were rising, and at the same time, the established early-modern, church-based means of support for the poor was being attacked in Swift's time.[36]

It was not until the following century that nineteenth-century reformers (notably Shaftesbury, the 7th Earl, Anthony Ashley Cooper, a politician and major advocate of social reform, and William Gladstone, both before and after he was Prime Minister) would begin to have an impact on the increasing crime, and on the distressing living and working conditions of the working class, especially in terms of public sanitation, most notably in the heavily populated and congested cities of London and Manchester.[37] Prostitution in English cities, for example, became an established means for girls and women from the countryside to make a living to support their families. The outrages outlined in stark detail by Friedrich Engels, Marx's collaborator, in his mid-nineteenth-century writings about factory life in Manchester, could already be found in incipient form over one hundred years before.[38]

There were, happily, some notable late-eighteenth-century exceptions to the trend of leaving the less fortunate to fend for themselves. John Howard, a Quaker, and Jeremy Bentham, the Utilitarian thinker, both successful agitators for the rights of prisoners, must be mentioned here. Like Edmund Burke, who also was Irish, Swift was outspoken about the abuses in both urban England and rural Ireland, a great many, but not all, in Swift's view, attributable to the English; Swift, however, did not advocate charity.

Even in the early eighteenth century, some of the features of what Phyllis Deane calls the "First Industrial Revolution," an agricultural Industrial Revolution, were already apparent.[39] In Deane's view, the eighteenth-century version was the harbinger of the mid-nineteenth-century Industrial Revolution that was also inextricably linked to the consolidation of the worldwide British Empire. There was a movement from the countryside to the cities and toward work in factories (even in the countryside, marked by the putting-out system, in which employees, generally women, would take work home or then deliver it to some centralized place), which became more common even 100 years before the Industrial Revolution itself.

British interests abroad were being tested in the eighteenth century, and Britons were intensely concerned about their country's place in the world.[40] Commercial development in this century, of factory work in particular, provided the base of the British Empire in the nineteenth century. It was repeatedly asserted, perhaps not incorrectly, that "the sun never set on the

British Empire," somewhere in Britain or its colonies it is always daytime.[41] The concern for world domination, in power politics as well as trade, is a major theme in *Gulliver's Travels*, perhaps surprisingly, as it was written over 100 years before the height of the British Empire.

Change in Britain was not limited to the economy; this was a time of literary explosion in print. Newspapers had become common in major British and European cities and often in the provinces as well.[42] Daniel Defoe, author of *Robinson Crusoe*, was the first famous journalist in Britain. Defoe was not alone in using the printed word for immediate political purposes.

Political pamphleteering, on both sides of the English Channel, long predated the 1789 French Revolution. This trend was growing in Britain as early as 1726, the first publication date of *Gulliver's Travels*. Both radical and conservative pamphleteering were major parts of the intellectual dynamic in Britain in the early eighteenth century.[43]

There was a demand for contemporary reading material, especially works of fiction. Scholars, starting with Ian Watt, have devised compelling, and often conflicting theories about which book, and thus which publication date, should be taken as the birth of the novel, in particular the English novel.[44] This is made all the more confusing now by the initial presentation of works, such as *Robinson Crusoe*, as nonfiction, as genuine travel narratives. Perhaps the best comment on this comes from English literary scholar David Nokes: "the emergence of the English novel in the eighteenth century is an episode to gladden the hearts of those who believe the best discoveries result from happy accidents."[45]

And, at the very time so often taken to mark the rise of the novel (despite the existence of numerous prose narratives in the sixteenth and seventeenth centuries), eighteenth-century British universities were regarded as stagnant, if not in decline. Modern scholars, with some qualifications, tend to agree with the contemporary, low assessment of eighteenth-century English universities.[46] Some of this laxness was related, as cause or effect, to the number of young aristocratic men going to university as part of their normal social trajectory, as the universities attempted to gain a solid financial base. Thus, for example, the number of young men from plebian backgrounds going to Oxford actually declined through the eighteenth century.[47] Overall, *Gulliver's Travels* was written in a century of powerful intellectual achievements (often reckoned to rate with the generations of Plato's Academy and the Florentine Renaissance, in terms of both literature and theory), although, notably, most of the work of the long eighteenth century was not written by professors or at universities. Some of these books were, however, written by women, particularly by one celebrated young woman.

7 Link to Mary Shelley, *Frankenstein* (1818)

Frankenstein, written when Mary Shelley was 19, is similar to *Gulliver's Travels* in that it tends to be read in remarkably dissimilar ways. In recent decades, *Frankenstein* has been taken as a feminist text; historically it has served as the manifesto for Romanticism, and thus also as the strongest statement of the nineteenth century regarding the inherent dangers of science and urbanization.[48] All these interpretations are drawn from the story of a high-strung young intellectual who decides to create life out of dead bodies and he succeeds. This book might be best viewed as an early example of magical realism as there is only one key, yet crucial element of fantasy in the story: the creation of Frankenstein's monster from dead body parts stolen from graveyards and slaughterhouses. His creation, "his monster," turns out to have many human qualities: violent tendencies, poor impulse control, high intellect, the desire to be loved, and the desire for an education. In many respects Frankenstein and his monster are remarkably similar. Likewise *Frankenstein* and *Gulliver's Travels* are similar—and unusual—in taking on the theme of corrupt human nature so directly.

Frankenstein never learns about the workings of his own psyche, even after multiple deaths in his inner circle and despite his own ravings, for he is often overcome by grand emotions that he cannot harness to his own advantage. The order of the deaths in this story—Frankenstein's mother, his younger brother, the family servant accused of murdering the brother, his best friend, his bride, and then his father, symbolize the stripping of the young man of his immediate circle, his future happiness, and his heritage. Given the book's fame (and of course, the many film versions of it), perhaps its subtlety and well-developed characters come as a surprise. Young Dr. Frankenstein, for example, is presented as a poor father to the monster, but not because he was neglected as a child himself. Instead, Frankenstein is shown as having had an ideal childhood; thus, the responsibility for his actions is his own and cannot be passed back to his parents. At no stage during the years of planning does Frankenstein contemplate the consequences of the possible success of his project. Likewise, Frankenstein refuses to recognize the existence of his own emotions, believing that he is wholly driven by rationality. His life is dedicated to his work to such an extent that he ignores his family for years and he is unable, or just too busy, to make friends when he goes to university. At the same time, the theme of longing for genuine friendship is infused throughout this work, from the very opening to the close. This work attacks the glorified notion of genius that does not recognize any needs beyond that of the work, and that is based entirely on a sense of rights without any responsibility. After the multiple murders, Frankenstein becomes mad; he is as lost in his emotions as a leading character on stage in the last act of a tragic opera. By showing the exact opposite of what is desired, this book codifies the Romantic ideal that every person should embrace the positive qualities of men and women and reject the stereotypical weaknesses of both, thus leading to the genuine possibility of both enhanced personal lives and constructive social relations, brought about by individuals' deliberate choices. At least on the first point—by showing the exact opposite of what is desired, the work makes its strongest points—*Gulliver's Travels* and *Frankenstein* are in agreement. Both books are about the compulsion to travel and the desire to change oneself, and both books propound the possibility of constructive change, even given the corruptness of human nature.

8 Synopsis

The intellectual foundations of *Gulliver's Travels* clearly parallel Plato's *Republic*, confirming the Ancient (not just Modern) nature of this novel. The character Gulliver demonstrates flashes of wry self-awareness, if not irony, and he certainly is not wholly gullible. Yet his flattened responses are in line with someone encountering change and distress repeatedly throughout his adult life. This book has been popular since its first publication. Its appeal could now be viewed as at the two extremes: as a children's story and a fantastical travel story, but also as an exploration of political theory. A study of Swift's life does not settle the complications inherent in *Gulliver's Travels*. Yet however complicated Swift's own thinking, *Gulliver's Travels* is part of the general shift in both eighteenth-century theory and fiction toward reflection on the abstract individual—children, women, and men—within a political group and changing economic system, not just on the political structure itself, which had been the approach in both genres (the established field of theory and the emerging field of fiction) throughout much of the early-modern period. Instead, many of the Romantic themes in Mary Shelley's *Frankenstein*, especially travel and isolation, can already be found in *Gulliver's Travels*. Gulliver, despite his lack of affect throughout most of the story, arguably embodies many of the shortcomings and hopes of both Frankenstein and his monster—a fierce desire for professional recognition, a rejection of his own family, and at the same time a strong desire for a family, a profound sense of loneliness, a collection of most remarkable talents, and limited internal reflection, despite the preposterous turns his life takes.

II WITH APOLOGIES TO JONATHAN SWIFT AND E. P. THOMPSON: GULLIVER'S RAKISH REFUSAL TO IDENTIFY HIMSELF AS A SURGEON, AND THE MAKING OF THE ENGLISH MIDDLE CLASS

1 Gulliver's Undistinguished Career as a Surgeon

The question of whether *Gulliver's Travels* is a work of fiction with distinguishable character development, or a satire, becomes more pressing when turning to the symbolism of Gulliver's profession as a surgeon.[49] To be sure, as noted, the distinction between these two categories—fiction and non-fiction—was still unclear when this book was published in 1726. Early-modern literature is generally dated from 1500 to 1750, with 1750 often taken as the starting point for literature's modern era. Defoe, Montesquieu, and

Voltaire (whose most famous work, *Candide*, was written just after 1750), to give three famous examples, all sought to present their fiction in the form of a somewhat believable travel story. However, the story-telling, the fantastical travel narrative, derives from a much older tradition, with Marco Polo, the famous Italian traveler to China, as one of its distinguished practitioners.

Gulliver's unwillingness to identify himself as a surgeon and his strong desire to present himself instead as a gentleman-scholar on a personal Grand Tour around the world might indicate a sense of shame about his professional background and, at the most fundamental levels, about his social background, and thus about himself. This sense of nostalgia about privileges lost before they were gained is almost to be expected in a time of great social upheaval. In the late seventeenth to early eighteenth century, when this work is set, the middle and professional classes in England were slowly gaining in status, wealth, and self-respect, yet Gulliver chooses an older mode. The brief description of his home life seems, in modern terms, solidly middle-class. Remember that Gulliver studied not only at Cambridge, but also abroad, in Leiden, Holland, a center for both medicine and law. He does not present himself as a businessman or a government envoy. Nevertheless, he poses as a touring politician or diplomat, a young aristocrat or the son of a plutocrat, apparently in an attempt to bolster his own sense of professional and personal self-worth.

For Gulliver, the training and relative status attached to being a surgeon are not enough to make him sufficiently confident while traveling abroad. At some stage, Gulliver develops a rakish attitude—a term often used in the eighteenth century for a "fashionable or stylish man of dissolute or promiscuous habits."[50] He senses that it would be better to reinvent himself as the kind of traveler who, he is persuaded, would be most welcome to the non-Western peoples and non-human creatures he encounters. For much of the story, he pines to be a sailor rather than a surgeon (at the very beginning of the story he is an apprentice surgeon, but he even then spends his father's money studying navigation); and later when he is a captive he wishes to be viewed as a visiting diplomat, not a prisoner. Even his desire to be identified as a sailor is more typical of a supposed upper-class longing for travel, as opposed to the sense of distance that a middle-class man would probably want from the working class. Gulliver deliberately, and regularly, chooses to present himself not as who he is, but as the person he realizes that the surrounding, ever-changing group, sometimes volubly, wants him to be. In almost every case, he wants to be what he is not.

In the eighteenth century, a surgeon had even lower social status than a regular physician, so there are multiple issues at play regarding status. In addition, Gulliver's lack of overt commitment to the medical profession leads, in a larger sense, to a discussion of class, wealth, and justice, and more specifically to a consideration of a medical, scientifically based search for the truth. It is through his story, as much as through the character, that these larger abstract ideas are examined.

Indeed Gulliver's initial embarrassment about being identified as a surgeon does seem to have much more to do with status than with the pursuit of truth. *Gulliver's Travels* could be an early demonstration of English historian David Cannadine's argument about late-nineteenth-century imperialism: class and rank trump color and race. More deliberately, alliances based on color or race are often jettisoned for professional advancement and/or a rise in social class. Throughout, the emphasis in *Gulliver's Travels* is on what Cannadine terms "Ornamentalism."[51] This desire for status is so profound that it allows even creatures of different species to interact easily, once the hierarchy between, and among, them is established. Not just Gulliver, but almost every creature he encounters is motivated by a desire for status (perhaps with the exception of the giant young girl, Glumdalclitch, who cares for Gulliver in Brobdingnag, first at her family farm and then at court; but even she fawns on the Queen of Brobdingnag, and she tattles on Gulliver once the two of them are brought to court), and the one characteristic they all have in common is a willingness to appear ridiculous for tiny gains in social standing. Gulliver, to note a delightful small example from Part III, is instructed on how to eat the dust before the King of Luggnagg, as is the custom in this court. In this chapter, Gulliver is told stories about how this deferential activity is sometimes used as a means of execution: poison is, on occasion, put on the floor. The servants must then take care to clean the floor carefully for visitors and for others still in favor, for they too will have to perform this gesture of extreme obeisance. Gulliver's consistent, obsequious behavior toward his royal hosts might also be viewed as a deliberate stab at the stereotype of Britons abroad, especially in their colonies, as overbearing, irascible, and rude. Over and over, in Gulliver's seemingly endless conferences with emperors, kings, and princes of various species, and in outlandish places, there is an internal logic for, in all these preposterous encounters, there exists an awareness that Gulliver is not a genuine threat but rather an indulged traveler within a set structure, one who wishes to curry favor in a time-honored fashion.

Claude Rawson, in *God, Gulliver, and Genocide: Barbarism and the European Imagination, 1492–1945*, reflects on Gulliver in terms of Montaigne's enlightened views on barbarism (Montaigne suggests that the behavior of American Indians was more civilized and courageous than the behavior of Frenchmen during the French Religious Wars), rather than in terms of Rousseau on the idealized savage.[52] Rawson begins by commenting that

> Swift's works are a meeting-house for some of the most troubling moral nightmares of European intellectual history in the last five hundred years: war, imperial conquest, the impulse to exterminate.[53]

Central to this dynamic are the Yahoos, with their thick lips and flat noses, who are supposed to seem human yet foreign. Rawson suggests that the Yahoos represent not only Indians (or Africans), but also country Irish

Catholics. The link to *A Modest Proposal* is evident. The Houyhnhnm solution to the Yahoo Problem is also similar to that found in Defoe's satire, *The Shortest Way with the Dissenters* (1702), which at the time of publication was taken seriously by both sides, those who advocated executing dissenters and those who parodied such an idea. The mass extermination of the Yahoos, debated hotly at the Houyhnhnm Council in Part IV, stands for the supposedly rational discussion of the killings of all substandard human beings, however the decision to do so might be made. The emphasis on wholesale evil in *Gulliver's Travels* echoes darker passages on elaborate tortures and enthusiastic killings performed by all sides in the Thirty Years' War in *Simplicissimus*. Swift's work varies in tone from that of Montaigne: Swift is suggesting barbarity as a natural part of human nature; in contrast, Montaigne is elegantly outraged.

In a somewhat different mode, there is now an interpretation that *Gulliver's Travels* is not just a criticism of the human craving for status and preferment but also, explicitly, an attack on the eighteenth-century slave trade.[54] This attack could be seen as at the core of the repeated jabs in the text about East India Stock (that is the Dutch West India Company), which had, in the early eighteenth century, primary control of the African slave trade.[55] This anti-slavery explanation helps to clarify the many anti-Dutch comments in this work of fiction (otherwise puzzling as they come from the central character who speaks Dutch, and who studied at one the great universities of Europe in the eighteenth century, Leiden, in the Netherlands, and who thus would presumably otherwise have pro-Dutch sympathies).

As part of this anti-slavery interpretation, Elaine Robinson argues that *Gulliver's Travels* does not ignore religion, but propounds a "real religion" that is marked by an emphasis on Christian charity and an attack on pomp and religious distinctions. She maintains that the text presents lectionary dates (the established dates that particular Scriptures are to be read out loud in an Anglican service) for Gulliver's travels as part of a series of allusions to African slave trade ports of call.[56] Also in *Gulliver's Travels*, Plato, Aristotle, and Aquinas (Aquinas primarily for codifying Aristotle's thought, especially on natural slavery and just war) are blamed for a ludicrous emphasis on rationality and the move toward secularism, away from natural Christianity. Thus, in this reading, anti-Dutch comments go well beyond the English–Dutch mercantile and financial rivalries of this time, and, according to Robinson, are meant instead to be part of a larger anti-slavery and a pro-spirituality emphasis in the text.[57]

However, there is a strong counter-argument, from F.P. Lock among others, that dismisses attempts to put *Gulliver's Travels* into the liberal, democratic, even libertarian traditions of later centuries, and views Swift as not only conservative but even reactionary. This approach also separates Swift from any interest in the problems of Ireland or of the excesses of colonialism in his own time.[58] In this reading, Swift's Irishness does not give him a sense of inferiority, or the makings of a social reformer, but rather a great fear of revolution, again linking him to Edmund Burke, who predicted the extreme violence of the French Revolution, and who was also Irish. Thus, Swift's Christianity can be viewed as both intellectual and conventional for his time, not personally or particularly spiritual. This approach further downplays the satirical nature of this work, and focuses on the supposed censorship of the first edition of *Gulliver's Travels*. This is not only a Tory reading of Swift, it is also an unabashedly authoritarian reading of *Gulliver's Travels*. F. P. Lock presents *Gulliver's Travels* as a text that, in effect, looks back not just to Hobbes but even earlier to Filmer, on the divine right of kings.[59] This conservative reading of Swift proposes that Swift feared social unrest and insisted on the traditional values of order, hierarchy, and stability.[60] Without a doubt, voluminous biographical information about Swift supports this interpretation.

However, whatever Swift's views might have been, this does not wholly subvert the more radical textual readings of *Gulliver's Travels*. Both elements, the cynical and even the hopeful, are to be found in abundance in the text. In general, contextual studies of Swift and his time favor a conservative reading, whereas a study of the text without repeated references to its contextual setting in early-eighteenth-century Britain often results in more radical readings. More precisely, it is the very dichotomies of the text—Ancient versus Modern, conservative versus radical, high church versus low church—that make this work still worth debating, as all of these interpretations can be supported not just from historical context, but also from the text of *Gulliver's Travels*.

2 Gulliver's Clothes

The symbolism of Gulliver's clothes offers evidence of multiple viewpoints on imperialism embedded in the story. Gulliver wears a variety of outfits in his travels, much like a performer on stage. This goes beyond even the primping of an aristocrat changing for dinner as part of a daily routine. The clothes Gulliver exchanges so regularly, and rapidly, are a metaphor for the shifts in the *mores* in these many distinct communities that Gulliver so often apes. It is not the actual cut or style of the clothes that are discussed in the story, but how appropriately sized, or merely clean, clothes are procured for Gulliver. Gulliver is confined at the beginning of many of his visits to these new countries, while new clothes are made for him. It is of interest that the gigantic tailors of Brobdingnag are noted to be better at approximating his size by comparing him to a ring (he is at this stage very tiny in comparison to all his hosts) than the Laputian tailors (remembering that they are the mathematicians, not to be confused with the tiny Lillliputians) in Part III, who use geometry and astronomy for the same task.[61] Thus physical disabilities (extreme littleness or bigness) can be overcome, but not by a hyper-intellectual approach.

Gulliver wants appropriate clothing so he will be given the respect he craves, and at the same his new hosts are repeatedly taken up with dressing him in style. The actual clothes he wears in these various societies seem to change less than the physical appearance of the humans or creatures themselves. However, the dynamic is similar each time: it is crucial that Gulliver has clothes made in the society he has just entered. Correspondingly, these diverse cultures, whether with stunningly different or virtually the same values, generally adhere to a set pattern of life and to their own standards as firmly as do their rivals.

New clothes offer Gulliver a way at least to demonstrate his pronounced attempt to make himself part of yet another group. Wearing the skins of Yahoos as shoes when he is a guest, never quite a family member, in Houyhnhnmland, is only the most obvious, and loathsome, example. At this point, he is willing to submit to the most outlandish acts of submission in order to separate himself from the Yahoos, whom he, unfortunately, from his point of view, resembles rather strongly. (Although he earlier views the tiny Lilliputians as human, their minute size seems to argue against this categorization; he is only at the beginning of his adventures when he first meets the Lilliputians, and he can think of them only as small humans). The only striking differences between Gulliver and the Yahoos, and this is noted repeatedly, are that Gulliver is rational, and less hairy in very particular, private places; again, the physical distinctions do not all have to do with clothes. The Yahoos, wild creatures who run about naked, look very much like human beings, and Gulliver is mortified by them. Perhaps only a Yahoo would be so squeamish about this striking resemblance. Gulliver's revulsion at the Yahoos perhaps indicates his unconscious desire not so much to export a new proto-middle-class version of British values, with himself on occasion as the model of the prosperous, self-made man, but rather a desire to hide behind the older, aristocratic stereotype of the young gentleman traveler who spurns his social inferiors. This tension is equally clear in his politics and in his professional preferences.

Some would argue that the character Gulliver only serves the purpose of aiding the learning experience of the reader; he is rarely the mouthpiece for the message of the book (and no other character wholly fills the role either). One striking exception is the strong anti-colonialism section written by Gulliver in the final chapter. This could be used to support the view that he had changed intellectually, even grown.

In a somewhat different sense, Erasmus's *Praise of Folly*, which itself could be viewed as a Menippean satire, is also a model here. Erasmus's main character Folly is not a normal character; she changes form and outlook several times in that short work in order to accommodate larger satirical and pedagogical purposes. E. M. Forster, in *Aspects of the Novel* (1927), devised a category for flat characters that he sums up briefly:

> In their purest form, they are constructed around a single idea or quality. . . . The really flat character can be expressed in one sentence. . . . One great advantage of flat characters is that they are easily recognized. . . .

A second advantage is that they are easily remembered by the reader afterwards.[62]

In contrast to such a flat character, Gulliver, although not showing a full range of emotions and emotional growth in line with many modern novels, sinks into a decline from which he then recovers. Thus neither Gulliver nor *Gulliver's Travels* can be dismissed so quickly, even in light of Forster's comment above. This genre debate—whether it is legitimate even to categorize *Gulliver Travels* as having a main character who shows development—is of interest for many reasons, not least because it forces a rethinking of the purpose of the work overall. However, there is enough information about Gulliver's development, and then his decline, to make at least an analysis about his personal details and his profession pertinent, as might be done for any novel. His character cannot be dismissed in a short summary.

3 The Rise of the English Middle Class: Class, Wealth Creation, and the Notion of Justice

The middle class in England was beginning to cohere in exactly the decades in which *Gulliver's Travels* is set, 1699 to 1715. Social historian E.P. Thompson argues that the English working class did not crystallize until almost a century later, beginning in the 1790s. Thus the emerging middle class in the early eighteenth century generally defined itself against the upper class, not the still-to-be-mobilized working classes. The Swift scholar Ronald Knowles cites an earlier scholar, Edward A. Block, on Swift's social class: "Swift deliberately made Gulliver the middle son from (very roughly) the middle of England, with a middle-class father, having a middle-class religion and receiving middle-class education."[63] The theme of upward mobility, a classic feature of the middle class, is demonstrated in the text by the character Glumdaclitch, the giant girl from the countryside who makes a smooth transition from farm life to court, when she accompanies Gulliver to court.[64] *Gulliver's Travels* repeatedly stresses talent over privilege in its relentless attacks on privilege by birth, connections, or income.

In a facetious tone, *Gulliver's Travels* makes its arguments by means of false dichotomies and projection by targeting, for example, blatant injustice and then proposing an impractical Houyhnhnm version of justice. One of the clearest textual examples is that imperialism abroad is not explicitly attacked until the conclusion, as if the reader could have missed the implicit attacks throughout the book. These charges are a means of projecting domestic problems onto faraway places in order to skewer imperialist attitudes at home.

Gulliver's Travels, written decades before Smith and more than a century before Marx, nevertheless foreshadows these two thinkers on the topics of class, wealth creation, and justice.[65] Justice encompasses both a theoretical understanding of fairness and also the workings of the legal system. This book has clear ramifications for the development of economic thought and early-modern notions of fairness and equality.

Pre-Smithian and pre-Marxist, *Gulliver's Travels* was nevertheless published during the time when Bernard Mandeville's highly contentious work, *The Fable of the Bees* (1714, 1732), the worthy precursor of Smith's *Wealth of Nations*, was receiving a remarkable amount of public attention. *The Fable of the Bees* was attacked with fervor by the *philosophes*, especially Rousseau, for its insistence of the economic necessity of the luxury spending of the super rich for economic growth in the national economy overall. It seems possible to distill some small, but new, understanding of justice in the work of Swift, Smith, and Marx by means of a study of all three authors in terms of the history of economic thought. The evolving notions of class, wealth, and justice were critical for the self-identification of a separate middle class in these years.

Gulliver's Travels can be set in a theoretical framework later to be identified with Marx and Weber. Marx was reacting against the lure of increasingly middle-class life, which developed markedly in the eighteenth century, and which, for Marx, kept workers from realizing their entrapment and lack of personal autonomy. Thompson, in *The Making of the English Working Class*, especially in Chapter V, on "Planting the Liberty Tree," documents English working-class agitators' deliberate use of theory (especially Thomas Paine's *Rights of Man*) as part of their crusade for political rights and rights in the workplace in the 1790s. However, according to Marx, a partial fix of the political and economic system (as advocated by radicals in London and throughout England in the 1790s), would only delay the revolution he believed to be the inevitable, sufficient, and necessary cause to usher in a new social order free from class distinctions. *Gulliver's Travels* thus predates Marx by more than a century in its identification of the middle class (for Marx, the *bourgeoisie*) and its condemnation of the materialism and lack of core values necessary to promote the individual within this middle class.

Later, Max Weber put forward the notion, inspired by Marx, of life chances (*Lebenschancen*) and the interplay of choice and chance for the individual.[66] Weber uses social class, and the expectations promoted by that class, as a means of predicting how individuals would fare in life. Sociologist Anthony Giddens has recently discussed a variation of this Weberian theory as "life chances," a probability-based method for figuring out the statistical chances of particular individuals improving their situation in life.[67] This is part of Giddens's recent emphasis on the positive and negative aspects of risk for the entrepreneur, and for capitalism. It goes beyond Marx in considering not only means of production but also social mobility and social equality. In this framework, it is possible for an individual's expectations and drive to change his or her personal fate. In like manner, *Gulliver's Travels* repeatedly shows social groups caught in the machinery of fate (perhaps especially the Struldbrugg Immortals in Book III), and also presents Gulliver as someone who at times seems to grasp the possibilities of his own life chances, and who has the will to change his circumstances.

Gulliver's Travels examines wealth not just in terms of land and treasure but also in terms of labor. The work has long lists of occupations, often including criminal professions. Adam Smith, in *The Wealth of Nations*, lists many of these same immoral or simply shady professions in gorgeous detail, albeit without moral censure. Earlier, Mandeville had recognized that these illegal activities are indeed partly responsible, along with spending by the rich, for national wealth. *Gulliver's Travels* maintains that the ruptures in daily life can be soothed and smoothed only by an inordinate input of cash or other material advantages. However, the overarching moral here is that even the middle class cannot live by hard work, or even financial prosperity, alone. This can be viewed both as a failing of society and as a direct criticism of what Weber later termed the Protestant work ethic, which views earned wealth as the outward manifestation of the correct inner attitude. Thus the book celebrates the rise of this social class, yet it also disparages the values of this same class, as if responding to the birth of a long-awaited child, which is then revealed to be deformed.

Gulliver's Travels features individuals on the way down the scale, personally and professionally. The book highlights the possibility of a member of the middle class, a trained surgeon, who needs substantial assistance. The relevance of Gulliver, a surgeon, on the receiving end of individual generosity is symbolic not just in terms of profession but also in terms of attitudes toward spending and the national economy. This implies that some type of social services must be provided in order to galvanize "the worthy poor" into a productive working life of their own. Certainly a destitute surgeon would seem to be a likely candidate for this sort of aid. Either massive savings or an indulgent patron desiring only entertainment through story-telling are necessary for Gulliver to return to middle-class life, thus implying that emerging middle-class *mores* are not so unforgiving.

Despite these warnings about the grasping nature and vapidity of the rising middle class, which is clearly aping its perceived betters, Gulliver does not turn instead to older economic models. It might seem that a young aristocrat, or even Gulliver as a Cambridge graduate, might have known about these older theories. However, in this text, there is no endorsement of the wealth of the court as by mercantilists, or of the land as by physiocrats; instead there is the *laissez-faire* approach similar to that of Mandeville and anticipating that of Adam Smith. There is certainly no time here for government propping up those who cannot work, a cynical view of much later Keynesianism. However, the assumption is that worthy members of the working population who are currently unemployed will naturally receive the help they need, perversely aided by an almost "invisible hand" that will give needy citizens just enough help, but no more, in order to jump-start their financial possibilities abroad, and especially at home.

4 More on Gulliver's Clothes

Returning to Gulliver's fashion sense, his concerns about clothing might be viewed as a critical part of his advanced social skills; he quickly develops the varied abilities necessary for chatting easily with kings and their courtiers. He ingratiates himself with people in positions of power by adopting a languid attitude, indicating that he is free of commitment to any causes—certainly free of any compunction to save the lives of the ill and wounded. He enjoys and actively participates in conversation as a natural part of court life. He fully accepts his role as the foreign expert. However, he is viewed as an expert on Europe, England, and culture, not on medicine. He tells colorful stories about English culture. They are his party pieces, which he deliberately designs to shock his listeners as much as to persuade his audience of the superiority of the European way of life. Even though he was primarily defending Britain while in Lilliput, and excoriating Britain in the Country of the Houyhnhnms, Gulliver is, nevertheless, almost always focused on Europe, especially England and thus his own social context, in all of his voyages. He starts the story by all but singing the praises of Britain, a country that bores him when he is there too long, and he ends his travels by rejecting Britain again and again. This could be seen as not simply Anglo-centric, but rather as the result of the limited pool of stories he had to draw from in his role of up-market entertainer. Telling stories with topics that fascinate and horrify him, he increasingly expresses his own insecurities and preoccupations, which he is better able to articulate the longer he is away from home.

Gulliver seems to assume that there is a transcendent truth—initially the righteousness of European, especially English, culture—that could be used to explain the complexities of any given situation abroad. He believes at first that he knows the truth, and then he goes in search of it. It appears that at various points he is looking for some explanation of the workings of his society, his social class, or himself. He is also looking for possible solutions for his own social and personal difficulties. Yet it is striking that there is little evidence that he ever expects to come back to his own country as a better person, much less as one who could help others by improving English life as a result of his travels.

Most of the questions raised in this book are explicitly intellectual and theoretical, rather than practical, the key one being: What is social justice? The practical one might have been: Is there a better means to house and care for the insane than Bedlam Asylum in London? Early in the story, Gulliver does not expect to make any personal adjustments, and by the end of the story he is so broken emotionally and mentally that he is most certainly not returning rejuvenated and of use to his homeland. There is virtually no textual corroboration to support the view that Gulliver learns from all the cultures he visits or that he tries to assimilate the best of each of these cultures until the point when he rejects England. Thus a possible reading is that Gulliver was too good a traveler: he tries to adapt to too many cultures, passes his limits, adapts too much, and snaps. The search for theory is not enough to ground him in the midst of the repeated attacks on his European worldview.

5 The Scientific Method and Professionalism

Gulliver's attention to detail is mirrored in the explicit structural aspects of the book. This parallel extends throughout the highly disparate four parts of the work, most strikingly, Gulliver's shifts in size relative to those around him as the story progresses, the repeated mention of exact dimensions, and the ridiculously detailed explanations of rules and regulations as linked to Gulliver's ridiculous emphasis on the truth. This stress on exactitude leads to a preoccupation with details, which then leads to an awareness of defects that only then can lead to truth, as distilled through the experimental method. Certainly, Gulliver's preposterous attachment to the truth is an attack on perverted science. The insistence on precision and exactitude is thus not used just for entertainment or even just to ridicule other systems of thinking, but rather is a means of testing ideas.

Gulliver, in Part II, Ch. 4, in Brobdingnag, makes professional choices about which subjects to study that would seem not to be in line with his training.[68] He notes two overt physical ailments here, a massive cancer in a giant woman and a gushing wen [an oozing cyst] in a giant man, and he expresses a desire for his medical instruments. However, his sudden desire for his medical instruments is not brought about by a wish to view the huge cancer or the dripping wen but rather to examine the frighteningly large lice that he is taken aback to see on the clothes of these two individuals. This might be viewed as intellectual curiosity; he cares more about learning the topic he presumably knows the least about, lice as opposed to cancer. Yet, in terms of psychohistory, it is also a sharp reminder of his own inner fears. "Lice crawling on their Cloathes" represents for him all that should be hidden coming out into the open—both his fears and his desires. The lice and moving vermin change the power structure; they now are an enemy rather than an annoyance. The insects thus represent the odious aspects of himself and his own country that have not been left in England but which are now magnified and moving around freely for all to see. His wish is to kill and "to dissect" a louse, thus gaining control over it and the moving, untamable parts of himself. He is overcome by unresolved personal concerns, and perhaps also by intellectual curiosity, and has no time for professional tasks.

Yet his attitude toward science is even more complicated in the following instance, occurring at the Academy of Lagado, during his voyage to Laputa (*la puta* means prostitute in both Italian and Spanish), in Part III. In this section, the approach is perhaps most like that in *A Modest Proposal*. This is the portion of the work in which the Royal Society, the science academy in London, is attacked most directly:

> I was at the Mathematical School, where the Master taught his Pupils after a Method scarce imaginable to us in *Europe*. The Proposition

and Demonstration were fairly written on a thin Wafer, with Ink composed of a Cephalick Tincture. This, the Student was to swallow upon a fasting Stomach, and for three Days following eat nothing but Bread and Water. As the Wafer digested, the Tincture mounted to his Brain, bearing the Proposition along with it. But the Success hath not hitherto been answerable, partly by some error in the *Quantum* or Composition, and partly by the Perverseness of Lads; to whom this Bolus is so nauseous that they generally steal aside, and discharge it upwards before it can operate; neither have they been yet persuaded to use so long an Abstinence as the Prescription requires.[69]

Although it is easy, enjoyable, and not always incorrect, to take at face value the book's mockery of old as well as new science, this passage, albeit in laughable detail, constructively notes in a straightforward manner a great many reasons why an experiment might fail. Without dismissing science, the passage also refuses to take science as invariably the highest authority. The passage indicates a sense of the impermanence and the chanciness of the experimental method. It signals that some people are better suited for scientific enterprises than others, and that it is only these well-suited individuals who should move forward in these areas, thus reinforcing meritocracy in the scientific, not just the political, realms. Swift is an equal-opportunity critic of education, doling out little praise for either Scholasticism or the emerging experimental approach.

At this mathematical school, fasting students, irrespective of ability or inclination, are forced to swallow wafers with mathematical propositions and demonstrations written upon them, leading, perhaps, to the implication that all individuals in society serve a larger purpose in amassing information about the group, even a great number of the individuals seem only to be part of the control group that makes no progress. The problem in this example is that the "thin Wafer" with writing done with ink made of "a Cephalick Tincture" (extract of brain) makes the students nauseous, not that the system itself was flawed. Thus, the "brain" of the fasting student guinea pigs is invested with multiple symbolic meanings. It could represent the resting places for dead experiments, a graveyard. There is some doubt regarding whether there is any individuality among these students, as literally all their stomachs are responding in chorus. Hence, this passage on a seemingly trivial, preposterous, pseudo-scientific experiment can also be used to support the critical development of science that is dependent on some degree of democracy (any of the students seems to be a useful experimental subject) and meritocracy (the appropriate people must rise to be the scientists).

To continue on a more religious note, this passage was clearly designed to invoke the rite of Holy Sacrament, communion. Here is Aquinas on the subject:

I answer that, Sacraments are necessary unto man's salvation for three reasons. The first is taken from the condition of human nature which is such that it has to be led by things corporeal and sensible to things spiritual and intelligible. Now it belongs to Divine providence to provide for each one according as its conditions requires. Divine wisdom, therefore, fittingly provides man with means of salvation, in the shape of corporeal and sensible signs that are called sacraments.[70]

The passage in *Gulliver's Travels* raises the possibility of science and professional life as replacing religion not just in terms of hierarchy, but also as offering a substitute form of worship. Crucially, the references to established institutions, such as science and religion, help to domesticate this consideration of the rise of what is often viewed as an emerging, pushy social class, a new elite, as well as to quiet fears about the creation of wealth on an altogether new scale, one never before thought possible.

6 Counter-Argument Regarding Gulliver's Embarrassment about Being a Medical Professional

Gulliver's pronounced attention to detail, whether as a result of his personality, medical training, or both, is that of a practicing scientist touring around the world. Even though Gulliver is not practicing medicine and not saving any lives during his world tours, he is able to get jobs on many ships exactly because he is a surgeon, despite his record of being on a surprising number of ships that were lost at sea. His skillful approach, not to mention his easy-going manner, must be part of the reason Gulliver is apparently in demand as a ship surgeon. He is, for example, sought out after only 10 days at home for a new job, at the beginning of Part III. And the stories of repeated storms at sea, shipwrecks, and mutinies give the reader some idea why so few physicians or surgeons, indeed people in general, were willing to leave home to serve on a ship with an expected itinerary of several years. It might be argued that technical training and applied scientific knowledge give Gulliver the appropriate frame of mind for investigating shocking customs in brand new cultures. This suggests that the training of the evolving middle class makes it possible for the variations of human social customs at first to be identified abroad, and then much more slowly at home.

Gulliver may best be viewed not as a glorified tourist or as a gentleman diplomat, but as a spy. From this perspective, Gulliver's services as a physician are needed only as a possible cover story, and so he contents himself with being instead a detailed observer of the cultures through which he briefly passes. At least one ruler is unpersuaded that Gulliver could have arrived in his country by accident. This interpretation of Gulliver as a possible spy does not suggest that Gulliver views himself primarily as a diplomat and a propagandist (although he falls into these roles with ease) but that his main concern is to collect information about other cultures in order to bolster his own homeland, as if he has a sense that he is the first of many Britons to explore the world, knowing that others would come later to exploit the riches of these foreign countries. The notion of Gulliver as a spy, perhaps even as a double agent, is also supported by the clamor from those hearing about his travels at the end of the story who demand that all the nations he visited should be claimed as British property. This occurs near the end of the story as part of the rousing statement Gulliver makes against colonialism. If Gulliver's training as a surgeon seems directly relevant only in the Western world, and is more of a qualification than a profession to which he is personally dedicated, Gulliver is nevertheless not reluctant to make use of this training when it suits him, especially when it helps him get back on board another ship. Presumably it is only because he is a surgeon that he is taken on and finally is able to become the captain of his own ship in the opening of Part IV (albeit very briefly, as he apparently did not acquire leadership qualities in his travels).

Yet, if not the requisite leadership skills, Gulliver does have compassion. Even he realizes, in retrospect, that he lacks the appropriate assertiveness and skills with his crew that would perhaps have prevented the mutiny on the ship he captained (probably because he hires some buccaneers to replace sailors he has lost to fever). He is thus not entirely wanting as a leader. Gulliver's comment about a young man, a junior surgeon, he took on board his ship, when he set out for the only time as captain, shows maturity, compassion, and a sense of the passing of time.[71] The passage has the tone of a senior medic, one who is saddened by wasted young talent, for the young surgeon is lost at sea, after he would not take Gulliver's advice. This passage about the young medic reinforces the view of Gulliver as sane, indeed with strong critical thinking skills, who is able to mourn for this young man "a little too positive in his own Opinions," who had been on his ship for awhile and who did not make it home. At this point Gulliver has returned home and is deeply unhappy, yet he recognizes that coming home would have been the best option for the young sailor who dies so needlessly. It presents Gulliver as a rational creature who knowingly acceded to the views of his many hosts throughout his travels, if only so that he would survive until he encounters the next society. In this sense, the sojourn in the Land of the Houyhnhnms would necessarily require a different mode of behavior from Gulliver than in the other foreign countries he visits, but its effect on him is not necessarily any longer lasting than his visits to any of the other cultures. He eventually is able, in the writing of this book, to ruminate on the benefits of coming home, at least for someone else, with such tenderness. A good leader would mourn his lost sailor in exactly this way.

Thus to play the devil's advocate, against the notion of Gulliver's desire to distance himself from his medical training, Gulliver can indeed be viewed as an early traveling doctor. He has a quirky personality and exhibits many of the stereotypical characteristics of his profession. He works hard, and would like to play hard, during these visits. Although he seemingly has no leisure activities of his own (or no opportunities to pursue them), he craves knowledge of the leisure activities of others.

Gulliver has a scientific spirit of observation and exactitude. Again, like a country doctor, he has an eye for daily life and for exceptions in power structures. Even though Gulliver craves the easy acceptance that would be given to a young aristocrat on his tours, it is his professional and related social skills, not any letters of introduction or connections of birth, that allow him so often to be accepted in this way.

Gulliver's style is much more indicative of the empirical approach of Aristotle than of the experimental approach of Descartes and Bacon. *Gulliver's Travels* is filled with precise measurement, exact arrivals and departure times, and references to startlingly different relative sizes of the groups he encounters. These authoritative references to particular numbers for times, size, or place give this work a genuine feel, the sense that this was indeed a travel journal by one Lemuel Gulliver, written after his return from his final journey. Certainly it adds to the dramatic tone that the last journey was so draining that it took even this most experienced traveler some time to recover completely. It is even unclear whether he does fully recover. Gulliver's sense of exactitude allows him to make sense of the fantasy worlds around him, to pigeonhole them into his own existing epistemological framework. Yet when the worlds he encounters seems to be grander than, even superior to, his own intellectual capacity, he at least temporarily has a mental breakdown.

Gulliver's qualifications as a surgeon are held in reserve, as a tantalizing additional skill, throughout this work. He never practices medicine or announces to his hosts that he is a surgeon. Yet, at the same time, his attitude is sometimes that of a medic. For example, he agrees with the Houyhnhnm horses that human drunkenness and sexually transmitted disease are in some respects self-induced afflictions, not manifestations of divine intervention.[72] At the outset, he has a surgeon's (or a later economist's) ability to identify patterns in bizarre circumstances, even anomalous behavior around him without making value judgments, and to make informed guesses about the problems he confronts. This analytical outlook makes the rationality of the Houyhnhnms immediately more appealing to him, and ultimately makes it altogether more traumatic for him that the Houyhnhnms are perhaps correct not only about good government but also about all those who cannot achieve it—the Yahoos, Europeans, and himself. At all stages, this work demonstrates the late-seventeenth-century Lockean fascination with rationality, tempered with awareness that there are limits to the power of rationality.

The emphasis on exactitude and precision makes the tone of the book oddly more vulnerable, as if control can be manufactured from knowing distances, measurements, dates, and times. This desire for precision can be linked to a growing sense of fragility, humility, and inferiority in the main character. These details not only establish a veneer of reality for a story that leaps from one non-human culture to another, they also ground Gulliver in a respected profession (a profession almost all readers and their families would need to call on at some stage).

In exactly the same way, the relevance of his book learning is rarely developed, implying that in terms of medical training, and indeed all forms of education, experience always trumps theoretical knowledge, however fully assimilated. Most of his stories are of British life in his own time, without historical or theoretical references. Even Gulliver's portrait, which serves as the frontispiece for the work, titled in the first edition as *Travels into several Remote Nations of the World. In Four Parts. By Lemuel Gulliver, first a Surgeon, and then a Captain of several Ships*, is part of the game.[73] The original 1726 title is a reminder especially to later readers that this book was supposedly written as a genuine narrative of a sea captain.[74] At this stage in European literature, the genre of fiction was just developing in the sense that we now recognize, and thus works such as this one were presented as accurate accounts of particular individuals. This not only gives necessary historical context about the development of the novel, and the use of travel diaries as a means of presenting invented stories, but it also shows in psychological terms how ideas are learned by thinking of them in terms of people other than oneself.

7 E. P. Thompson, *The Making of the English Working Class* (1963)

Thompson argues that the best means for understanding the experience of people unlike oneself is through the concept of class: he puts forward a definition of class that is not rigid, in the Marxist tradition, but rather a return to Marx's own definition of class as a series of personal interconnections and actual human relationships.[75] Thompson maintains that just as class cannot be tested in a laboratory, it also cannot be discussed apart from real people at a particular time, and needs to be looked at from an historical perspective. By the period that is Thompson's focus—England from 1790 to 1832—the middle class (and obviously the upper class) was firmly entrenched in English society. What was new was the growing realization of people from the working classes that they had political interests in common, distinct from those of the powerful upper class (which was fiercely opposed to change), and also distinct from the growing middle classes (much of which wanted greater Parliamentary representation and the repeal of the Corn Laws, that controlled the import and export of grain). The working classes began to realize that they too possessed some degree of genuine political clout, even though they were disenfranchised. Thompson notes that what the English feared most from 1792 to 1796 was not the French Revolution (and the fall of the only unified nation-state on the continent, and thus a change in European power politics) but rather the political agitation throughout England. It was the English riots—not the French Terror—that frightened the English propertied classes the most. In the early years of the French Revolution, there had been much thought that the French were simply, and finally, undergoing the equivalent of the English Glorious (and bloodless) Revolution of 1688. English radicals were initially annoyed with Edmund Burke (who had earlier supported the American Revolution and had criticized the suppression of the Gordon Riots in London in 1780) for condemning the French Revolution. However, Burke identified the potential for great violence—murder and the destruction of property—in the French case. All this served as the backdrop for the recognition by the English working class of their own potential, their ability to gain the attention of the authorities (never mind that their model was not the working class, but rather the French lower middle class, the *sans culottes*, in Paris). In the early eighteenth century, *Gulliver's Travels*, as well as *Robinson Crusoe*, was emblematic of the growing identification of the middle class as separate from the upper class; in the late eighteenth century, the emerging working class saw itself as distinct from the middle class. Evidence for changing attitudes toward class can be found in a range of sources, including fiction and nonfiction. Thompson is able to establish the appeal of Thomas Paine in 1790s England by simply stating briefly that *Rights of Man* (1791) was as popular as *Robinson Crusoe* and *Gulliver's Travels*. Thus, late in the eighteenth century, nourished by reading or listening to Bunyan's *The Pilgrim's Progress, Robinson Crusoe, Gulliver's Travels*, and Paine's *Rights of Man*, the English working class began to coalesce, to become aware of itself as a separate entity, partially because it was no longer willing to be told the truth by its betters, but wanted to determine the truth for itself. Earlier in the eighteenth century, *Gulliver's Travels* had accomplished much the same task by identifying the emergence of the middle class.

8 Multiple Rescues by Indulgent Sea Captains and the Captains' Puzzling Search for the Truth

To return to the story, all of Gulliver's social interactions are marked by his ambivalent feelings about his professional status—which as an early-eighteenth-century surgeon was somewhat dubious and, in terms of power, markedly below that of the officers on his ships—and by his deep and constant need to discern the truth. Just as he is unsure about his own place in the world, he also believes that the limits of the social and physical world seem wrong. His desire for truth is so strong it is as if he had retained the instincts to identify and validate the truth usually associated with early childhood. Gulliver is frustrated, for example, that the captains of the ships who repeatedly rescue him are slow to believe his stories of his fantastical travels. He is like a young child seeking the approval of his parents. Beyond a normal adult desire for validation of his sufferings, real and imagined, he seems never to doubt whether these experiences actually happened to him. Rather, he is concerned that if the people who first rescue him do not believe him, then surely no one else will either, and he desperately wants the truth to be known. Thus the point of contention here is not Gulliver's sanity, but his desire to get the story out to the general public.

The captain of the ship that picks up Gulliver after his time in Lilliput, at the end of Part I, for example, is convinced not by Gulliver's stories, but rather by the surprises Gulliver pulls out of his pocket: little cows and sheep.[76] In this case Gulliver actually persuades someone of the truth of his adventures, however it seems to indicate that only material evidence, rather than good public speaking skills, will suffice for most of his listeners.

This pattern is repeated over and over, and generally, Gulliver has no tiny objects to use as supporting evidence (partly because he sells them off—making a tidy profit, £600, by selling the miniature cows on his return home at the end of Part I, and he breeds the tiny sheep, at his home in England, for their fine wool).[77] In Part II, at the end of his second voyage, Gulliver once again craves the approval of the captain, another Englishman, who picks him up off Brobdingnag after his second voyage. This captain first speculates that perhaps Gulliver was a great criminal who has lost his memory after committing some spectacular crime, and that he had been pushed out to sea in a small boat. Nevertheless, this possibility does not diminish this Captain's interest in, or willingness to help, Gulliver.[78] Gulliver asserts that the Captain was convinced because the truth will win, especially if you are interacting with someone educated.[79] Gulliver's assertion here that "Truth always forceth its Way into rational Minds" is more optimistic than John Stuart Mill's later wry comments:[80]

> But, indeed, the dictum that truth always triumphs over persecution is one of those pleasant falsehoods which men repeat after one another till they pass into commonplaces, but which all experience refutes.[81]

However, Mill continues,

> The real advantage which truth has, consists in this, that when an opinion is true, it may be extinguished once, twice, or many times, but in the course of ages there will generally be found persons to rediscover it, until some one of its reappearances falls on a time when from favourable circumstances it escapes persecution until it has made such head as to withstand all subsequent attempts to suppress it.[82]

Gulliver here seems like an unworldly version of a classical liberal: he has admirable views, but, unlike John Stuart Mill, he is wholly unaware of the adversities in the way. Throughout these instances in the story, Gulliver is at least able to persuade himself that his rescuers accept his story, but there is no such pretense when he goes home to England (albeit he does discuss the price he gets for some of the foreign objects he collects).

Gulliver's status as a doctor may partly explain why these various sea captains and helpful foreigners accept the veracity of Gulliver's outlandish stories. They treat Gulliver indulgently. In his final rescue, Gulliver is taken home to Lisbon with his last sea-captain savior, the Portuguese Pedro de

Mendez, and has to be backed into his isolated guest room at the top of the house, for he now fully identifies himself as a horse. Mendez finally makes it clear that it is time for Gulliver to return home, because, he reasons with Gulliver, only in his own home can Gulliver arrange for the extreme privacy he demands. Thus Gulliver returns to his family, perversely the only place he can escape them and all other Yahoo humans. Before he leaves Lisbon, the captain loans Gulliver £20 sterling. Even taking into account how close Gulliver and Mendez have become at this stage, £20 is a most generous offer, requiring some degree of sacrifice on the part of the Portuguese sea captain. It is worth speculating on the motivation of these captains, the last one a foreigner, to help Gulliver return home. Surely Gulliver must have been so bedraggled that he was not seen as a threat, or as a symbol of Britain's growing dominance in the world. The final captain's generosity to Gulliver does not seem to indicate either that he believes or disbelieves Gulliver's stories. It could instead be viewed, linking back to Cannadine's theory of Ornamentalism, as the readiness of people of different cultures to help someone they perceive to be from their own professional and social background, especially if that person is entertaining and non-threatening.

The £20 that the Portuguese captain gives to Gulliver is presented in this story as easing the route toward a possible, normal, routinized, middle-class lifestyle. Perhaps the most intriguing aspect here is that the middle class itself is recognized as needing help, and receives this aid from "the kindness of strangers," to invoke Tennessee Williams.[83] Thus as the British Empire was growing, during what Phyllis Deane calls the First Industrial Revolution, Gulliver, the ambassador for English superiority, not only is instructed by non-humans about how to be human, he also needs to be helped home, in this case by a foreigner.[84]

Despite this untraditional reading of the end of Gulliver's story, that he was a highly competent, if eccentric, author who has moved house and is not incarcerated in his own barn, it could be suggested that the back-to-England parts of this story are not of much interest to the reader because the tension between the personal and professional sides of the main character are less evident at home. For Gulliver, who all by himself represents several ways, not all of them odious, for a Westerner to interact with a non-Western society, his visits back to England are clearly evident to the reader, but not to him, as furloughs rather than a permanent return home. Gulliver expresses nothing but frustration whenever he is at home, unable to settle down after any of his voyages. This was not only, or even for the first time, a problem in the conclusion of the work. Although this reluctance to come home is a trope of fantasy and travel literature, Gulliver's times back in England are richer than, for example, the final return to England for Robinson Crusoe after he is forced to leave his island. Perhaps stories about individuals who have made peace with themselves and their dreadful life circumstances do not make for good literature, even though they might be therapeutic for the reader. In this interpretation, the last glimpse of Gulliver is similar to the traditional reading of the conclusion of *Candide*, that a balanced life is possible, if a little dull.

In contrast to most tales set in a utopia, such as Charlotte Perkins Gilman's *Herland* (1915), there is speculation throughout *Gulliver's* Travels, from the narrator, about the return home.[85] In *Herland* there is no clear report at the end of the story regarding the success of the leading characters' projects. The utopia is designed to stay in the reader's mind, with almost no gesturing toward home. This level of ambiguity about practical results for travelers who have visited a utopia is in line with most fantasy and travel books. This underscores the role of *Gulliver's Travels* as political fiction rather than fantasy or utopia literature.

There is, however, a greater attraction in studying Gulliver's return trips home than that in most utopia literature, centering on the story of Gulliver's final madness, and the economic implications of his penniless, final return (if not for the generosity of all these captains). These two reasons might even be merged; perhaps his wife, or even Gulliver and his wife working together, realized that it was prudent for her to present him to their neighbors or even family as mad rather than penniless, and lacking in all social graces, after so many years abroad. This interpretation works both in terms of entertainment and economic theory; the twinning of insanity and great wealth still has appeal. This may imply that Gulliver's insecurities about his class background lead him to exaggerate his social class (for, truth be known, no visiting upper-class young man would have been so attentive, much less fawning, to foreign dignitaries), and also lead him to accentuate his professional skills in a non-threatening way. Thus the tension he is experiencing about both his social class and his professional training make him both accomplished and slightly unstable outside of a formal setting.

Rather than using these incidents as a way of finding out more about himself, Gulliver instead is wholly consistent in trying to use his own professional methods, the only ones he had developed to a high level, in order to resolve grave personal concerns. Thus Gulliver's awareness of the growing power of the middle class, this sea change in political power in Britain and on the continent, is predictably brought about by his own mode of medical, scientific thinking. The subject matter and the conclusions drawn by the reader are not only scientific but also political and economic. The emphasis on personal and psychological validation in this test case of Gulliver as a surgeon with a strong desire for social recognition should instead be on Gulliver's use of the scientific method, especially in a time of great personal crisis, in order to make sense of shifting political realities.

8 Link to Hanif Kureishi, *The Buddha of Suburbia* (1990)

Class, wealth, and justice remain major preoccupations in European theory, and in very recent British fiction. Hanif Kureishi's novel, *The Buddha of Suburbia* (1990) is a literary representation of the modern *Zeitgeist* that may well be the harbinger of future political and economic developments. It also serves as a time capsule of 1970s London, and the rise of punk.[86] The young narrator seems wholly occupied with sex, drugs, and rock and roll; in deft asides, however, he languidly reassesses British culture, often in a manner devastating to fundamental British beliefs. He does the same for India and America. He is an insider/outsider: born in London, a Muslim Briton with an English mother. It is only after he leaves school, wholly without distinction, and is offered jobs solely because of his skin color (which is beige, not black, he notes) that he begins to think much about race. Even the thuggery of the neo-Nazis in South London, where he grows up, seems to him to have as much to do with poverty as ideology. However, once the narrator and his new family (father and his father's new girlfriend) move to London, he realizes that in a country obsessed by class, he cannot even enter the debate because of his race.[87]

The Buddha in the *Buddha of Suburbia* is actually the narrator's father, who left India, did poorly at university in England, married an English girl, and is understandably bored by his low-level civil-service job. The father finds a new life, perhaps even true love, with an ambitious, rather impressive woman, Eva. She is also from the suburbs, but from a more upscale part than where the narrator's family lives; she hosts ".do's" where the father leads Buddhist meditations. Buddhism did originate in India, but the father is Muslim, not Buddhist. Buddhism is a very recently acquired interest of his; indeed, he began reading about it on his way to work in London. Nevertheless, Buddhism becomes the father's *entrée* into the lower-middle class, perhaps even middle-middle class English society, where he is viewed, especially after he has gained substantial weight, as a seer. He is also seen as an exotic object; he is "Orientalized."

The Buddha of Suburbia could be called the new *Great Expectations*, given the Dickensian extremes of astonishing hubris and the wholesale lack of opportunity for those with great talent in the more recent novel. Yet, to invoke a different literary link, *The Buddha of Suburbia* ends with a Voltairean twist, with the newly manufactured family drinking together, almost huddling together, in London, after the narrator's return from New York. The final line of the book is oddly convincing: "I thought of what a mess everything had been, about that it wouldn't always be this way." This final line perhaps works better than the last lines of *Candide* (on renouncing the world, and simply working in one's own garden) because the preposterous situations in *The Buddha of Suburbia* were not only possible, but were fully experienced by the 1970s generation rebelling against the postwar narrowness of their parents, and also against what it viewed as the posturing of the 1960s, although, at the same time, without having much of its own to offer. After religion, nationality, and even the desire for fame have fallen away, all the main characters have left is each other. By this point in the story, the main characters, most of them unrelated, have merged into one large, marginally dissatisfied family. This coalition, nevertheless, affirms the desire for community and continuity even among the most alienated of characters.

This is perhaps the element—the creation of community—most often left out in a discussion of *Gulliver's Travels*; even less time is given to the notion of community than to class, wealth creation, or justice. If community were to be the focus, it might be Gulliver's psychological makeup, rather than his medical training, that would be most pertinent. There might be enough material here to discuss Gulliver's profession, but many scholars argue, perhaps not enough to develop his psychological phases. However, it is clear that not all his voyages were made out of financial desperation, a desire for higher rank, or an obsession to find out about other cultures, and then about his own. Perhaps he undertakes his travels to find community, and a home. For these topics—class, wealth creation, justice, and community— the reader of *Gulliver's Travels* is led back to the political and economic theory that undergirds this supposed children's story.

10 Synopsis

Gulliver's Travels contrasts the precocious development and then the decline of the outwardly ordinary central character as a means of indicating how most people, even those who regard themselves as political, have virtually no control over their political and social environments. Yet *Gulliver's Travels* is not just a story about isolated individuals, or even just about empire, it is also the story of the rising middle class, and its sense of unease about its place in terms of the past, the present, and the future. E. P. Thompson's *The Making of the English Working Class* is useful here, not least for its careful examination of the creation of a *mentalité* that was both the result and the cause of social change. Thompson uses shared experience and the awareness that others often have wildly divergent ways of viewing the world to offer a non-rigid definition of class, which is still useful in a post-Marxist world. Feminist scholar Joan Wallach Scott rightly recognizes that Thompson's analysis of the rise of the working class for the most part leaves out women.[88] Yet both Thompson and Scott assume that the rise of the middle class had been somehow less controversial than the rise of the working class.

The same mistake was not made in eighteenth-century fiction. Gulliver, as a minor (not to mention, fictional) member of the evolving English middle class, is both a product of his background, and yet very different from most members of it. Although he leaves no journal (as does Robinson Crusoe), Gulliver expresses preferences. One strong preference is that he does not identify himself to his multiple hosts as a surgeon, instead he wishes to be treated as a visiting diplomat. Surgeons had low status in the eighteenth century. This could explain his sense of embarrassment about his relatively low professional status. Gulliver shows little interest in pursuing scientific study during his travels, and yet his proclivities are still those of a scientist. His multiple rescues by indulgent sea captains are each marked by the captains' puzzled search for the truth about Gulliver's experiences. On occasion, he obtains objects to confirm his stories (such as the tiny Lilliputian cows that fetched such a high price as curios back in England). Hanif Kureishi's *Buddha of Suburbia* (1970) demonstrates many of these same longings in a post-colonial world. *Gulliver's Travels* and *The Buddha of Suburbia* both indicate a strong desire for a sense of belonging that is personal, familial, and national, but one which is nevertheless attached to an awareness of the virtual impossibility of fulfillment on any of these levels. The emerging middle class and its strong interest in modern science in *Gulliver's Travels* indicate a stress on the creation of a social class that could potentially fulfill these desires for most people—children, women, and men—within a society.

NOTES

1 Thank you to Claude Rawson for detailed comments on this chapter. The critical edition of the novel is Jonathan Swift, *Gulliver's Travels*, Herbert Davis, ed. (Oxford: Basil Blackwell, 1965). See also Michael Foot's Introduction in *Gulliver's Travels*, Peter Dixon and John Chalker, eds. (London: U.K.: Penguin, 1985), and Claude Rawson's Introduction and Ian Higgins's Notes in Jonathan Swift, *Gulliver's Travels*, Claude Rawson and Ian Higgins, eds. (Oxford: Oxford University Press, 2005). Citations are from the Davis edition unless otherwise indicated.

2 See Brian Vickers, "Swift and the Baconian Idol," in *The World of Jonathan Swift: Essays for the Tercentenary*, Vickers, ed., pp. 87–128. Vickers argues that Swift was very knowledgeable about Bacon's writings, and that Swift's attitude toward Bacon (and thus seventeenth-century science) was more ambivalent than wholly satirical.

3 On this topic more broadly, see Roy Porter, *The Creation of the Modern World: The Untold Story of British Enlightenment*.

4 First published with Jonathan Swift, *A Tale of a Tub* in 1704, and can be found in Jonathan Swift, *Major Works*, Angus Ross and David Woolley, eds., pp. 1–22.

5 Thank you to Claude Rawson.

6 On Hobbes, see Sreedhar, *Hobbes on Resistance*.

7 *The Collected Dialogues of Plato, including the Letters*, Edith Hamilton and Huntington Cairns, eds. (Princeton: Princeton University Press, 1982), *The Republic*, book X.

8 Swift, *Gulliver's Travels*, Davis, ed., part I, ch. 8, p. 80.

9 Swift, *Gulliver's Travels*, Davis, ed., part IV, ch. 10, p. 276.

10 Swift, *Gulliver's Travels*, Davis, ed., part IV, ch. 8, p. 266.

11 Swift, *Gulliver's Travels*, Davis, ed. part IV, ch. 6, p. 256.

12 Genesis 6:7. Authorized Version.

13 This paragraph draws extensively from Claude Rawson, *God, Gulliver, and Genocide: Barbarism and the European Imagination, 1492–1945* (New York: Oxford University Press, (2001), esp. ch. 3, "Killing the Poor: An Anglo-Irish Theme?" and ch. 4, "God, Gulliver, and Genocide."

14 Swift, *Gulliver's Travels*, Davis, ed., part 4, chap. 11, p. 285.

15 Swift, *Gulliver's Travels*, Davis, ed., "The Publisher *to the* Reader," pp. 9–10.

16 See Norman O. Brown, *Life Against Death*, ch. XIII, "The Excremental Vision," pp. 179–201, on Swift.

17 Swift, *Gulliver's Travels*, Davis, ed., part I, ch. 3, p. 39.

18 See Nokes, *Jonathan Swift, A Hypocrite Reversed: A Critical Biography* (Oxford: Oxford University Press.

19 Swift, *Gulliver's Travels*, Davis, ed., part I, ch. 3, p. 39; part 1, ch. 4, pp. 49–50.

20 It is indeed England, not Britain, and certainly not France, which is Gulliver's concern. The 1707 Union of the Crowns of England and Scotland and the control of Ireland by England are not dealt with overtly in *Gulliver's Travels*. However, Swift's strong views about the treatment of the Irish by the English are not difficult to locate in this work of fiction once one looks for them.

21 On Swift's life, see, for example, Nokes, *Jonathan Swift, A Hypocrite Reversed*.

22 Consider *A Modest Proposal* as linked with Part III of *Gulliver's Travels* on the Academy of Lagado. See Swift, *Gulliver's Travels and Other Writings*, Starkman, ed. The two alternative interpretations are from Sean Moore, "Devouring Posterity: *A Modest Proposal*, Empire, and Ireland's "Debt of the Nation." Thank you to Jeanne Lakatos. See also Joseph Lennon, *Irish Orientalism: A Literary and Intellectual History*.

23 *The Tatler* and *The Spectator* made Joseph Addison and Richard Steele, in particular, very well known. *The Tatler*: 1709–1711. *The Spectator*: 1711–1714. For the critical editions, see *The Tatler*, Bond, ed.; and *The Spectator*, Bond, ed.

24 Michael Foot, *The Pen and the Sword: Jonathan Swift and the Power of the Press*.

25 See the classic 1919 article by Charles Firth on "The Political Significance of *Gulliver's Travels*." *Proceedings of the British Academy*, IX (read December 10, 1919). Note in particular the Lindalino episode, *Gulliver's Travels*, Rawson and Higgins eds., part 3, ch. 3, pp. 159–160. These five short paragraphs were dropped from *Gulliver's Travels* (beginning with the early-eighteenth-century editions by Benjamin Motte and George Faulkner, and continuing even in the 1965 Davis edition) apparently because they imply British repression in Dublin and Ireland more generally. The name Lindalino is taken to be a play on words for Dublin.

26 Swift, *Gulliver's Travels*, Rawson and Higgins, eds., p. ix.

27 Swift, *Major Works*, Ross and Woolley, eds., pp. 62–164.

28 On eighteenth-century Britain, see especially Linda Colley, *Britons: Forging the Nation, 1707–1837*.

29 Burke, *Reflections on the Revolution in France*.

30 Mill, *On Liberty and Other Essays*. John Stuart Mill (1806–1873), a major political theorist, along with his wife Harriet Taylor Mill (1807–1858), wrote *On Liberty* (1859), which stresses the primacy of the abstract individual.

31 On the party politics, see Colley, *In Defiance of Oligarchy: The Tory Party, 1714–60*.

32 Thank you to Joanne Madin Vieira Paisana. In a much later incarnation, this campaign, in the form of the Salvation Army, founded in London in 1865, offered food for the hungry and an alternative life style for new members.

33 See E. P. Thompson, *The Making of the English Working Class*, ch. 11, pp. 350–400, "The Transforming Power of the Cross."

34 Jeremy Black, *Eighteenth Century Britain, 1688–1783*, pp. 115–116.

35 See, for example, Keith Wrightson and David Levine, *Poverty and Piety in an English Village: Terling, 1525–1700*, esp. ch. 1, "The National Context."

36 On the relationship between literature and the economy, see Mary Poovey, *Mediating Value in Eighteenth- and Nineteenth-Century Britain*.

37 It was the first Earl of Shaftesbury who employed John Locke as his personal physician, and the third Earl who was the well-known philosopher and writer.

38 Friedrich Engels (1820–1895) was Karl Marx's collaborator, and they co-authored *The Communist Manifesto* (1848). Engels is the author of *The Condition of the Working Class in England in 1844* (1887). Much of Engels's

book was drawn from his own experience of running factories in Manchester owned by his wealthy German family.

39 Phyllis Deane, *The First Industrial Revolution*. First published in 1965.

40 Linda Colley, *Captives: Britain, Empire and the World, 1600–1850*.

41 See C. A. Bayly, *The Birth of the Modern World, 1780–1914*, esp. chs. 2–6.

42 Lucy Brown, *Victorian News and Newspapers*.

43 Darrin M. McMahon, *Enemies of the Enlightenment: The French Counter-Enlightenment and the Making of Modernity*.

44 Ian P. Watt, *The Rise of the Novel*.

45 David Nokes, *Henry Fielding, Joseph Andrews: A Critical Study*, p. 9.

46 There is no single work on seventeenth- and eighteenth-century British higher education. See the following sources: *The History of the University of Oxford, Vol. IV: Seventeenth-Century Oxford*, Nicholas Tyacke, ed.; *The History of the University of Oxford, Vol. V: The Eighteenth Century*, L. S. Sutherland and L. G. Mitchell, eds.; *The History of the University of Cambridge, Vol. II: 1546–1750*, Victor Morgan, ed.; and *The History of the University of Cambridge, Vol. III, 1750–1870*, Peter Searby, ed. On the early-modern period, see Hugh Kearney, *Scholars and Gentlemen: Universities and Society in Pre-Industrial Britain, 1500–1700*. Thank you to Laurence Brockliss.

47 See, for example, Linda Colley, *In Defiance of Oligarchy: The Tory Party, 1714–60*, p. 11.

48 Shelley, *Frankenstein or, The Modern Prometheus*.

49 An earlier version of this section was given as a talk for the English and Comparative Literature Departments, University of Texas at Austin, November 12, 2007. Thank you to Jeffrey Barnouw and Samuel Baker. And see Ronald Knowles, *Gulliver's Travels: The Politics of Satire*, ch. 1.

50 *Oxford English Dictionary/OED Online*: "rake" and "rakish."

51 David Cannadine, *Ornamentalism: How the British Saw Their Empire*. The title is a play on Edward Said's *Orientalism*.

52 This again draws extensively from Rawson, *God, Gulliver, and Genocide: Barbarism and the European Imagination, 1492–1945*, chs. 3–4.

53 Rawson, *God, Gulliver, and Genocide*, p. 1. Also see Robert Mahoney, "Jonathan Swift and the Irish colonial project," in Claude Rawson, ed. *Politics and Literature in the Age of Swift: English and Irish Perspectives*, ch. 11, pp. 270–289, which reads this portion of *Gulliver's Travels* as an explicit attack on the British treatment of the Irish.

54 Elaine Robinson, *Gulliver as Slave Trader: Racism Reviled by Jonathan Swift*.

55 Robinson, *Gulliver as Slave Trader*, p. 5.

56 Robinson, *Gulliver as Slave Trader*, p. 7.

57 See Simon Schama, *An Embarrassment of Riches: An Interpretation of Dutch Culture in the Golden Age* (London: Collins, 1987).

58 F. P. Lock, *The Politics of Gulliver's Travels*, "Introduction."

59 This again is drawn from Locke's attack on Filmer in Locke's *First Treatise of Government*, which has given Filmer lasting notoriety, due to his defense of the divine right of kinds, although F. P. Lock finds some merit in Filmer.

60 F. P. Lock, *Swift's Tory Politics*, ch. 3.

61 Swift, *Gulliver's Travels*, Davis, ed., part 3, ch. 2.

62 E. M. Forster, *Aspects of the Novel*, pp. 103–112, esp. pp. 103–105.

63 Edward A. Block, "Lemuel Gulliver: Middle-Class Gentleman," *English Language Notes*. Cited by Knowles, *Gulliver's Travels: The Politics of Satire*, p. 55.

64 Thank you to Sean Moorhead.

65 Thank you to Raffi Stern.

66 For an example of the ongoing usage of this concept, see William C. Cockerham, Alfred Rütten, and Thomas Abel, "Conceptualizing Contemporary Health Lifestyles: Moving beyond Weber," *Sociological Quarterly*.

67 Anthony Giddens, *Runaway World: How Globalisation is Reshaping Our World*. This book is based on Giddens's 1999 Reith Lectures on BBC Radio 4. See also Chris Armstrong, "Life-Styles, Life-Chances, and Radical Politics: Giddens on the 'New Egalitarianism,' " *Egalitarian Theory and Practice*.

68 Swift, *Gulliver's Travels*, Davis, ed., part II, ch. 4, pp. 112–113.

69 Swift, *Gulliver's Travels*, Davis, ed., part 3, ch. 5, p. 186. And see John Bender, *Ends of Enlightenment*, on the realist novel, philosophy, and science, especially anatomy, in the eighteenth century.

70 St. Thomas Aquinas, *Summa Theologica*, vol. IV, part III, question 61, "Of the Necessity of the Sacraments," first article, p. 2346. Thank you to Tristan Chirico.

71 Swift, *Gulliver's Travels*, Davis, ed., part IV, ch. 1, p. 221.

72 Thank you to Peter Hagan.

73 On the portrait: after the first edition, the rubric and portrait are changed, and in the final version (1735), the rubric calls Gulliver a liar. This is much discussed, and the resemblance or otherwise to portraits of Swift himself is one of the issues. Jonathan Swift, *Gulliver's Travels*, Introduction by Claude Rawson, esp. pp. xi–xxiii, xliv–xlvi, including reproductions of some of the portraits. Thank you to Claude Rawson.

74 For example, *Robinson Crusoe* was itself based on the account of a Scottish sailor, Alexander Selkirk, punished by being left by his captain on a desert island, where he languished for almost five years. See Woodes Rogers, *Cruising Voyage Round the World*. First published in 1712.

75 Thompson, *The Making of the English Working Class* (1963), "Preface," part 1, "The Liberty Tree," chs. I–V1–5, esp. the Preface on class formation and the marvelous ch. V, "Planting the Liberty Tree."

76 Swift, *Gulliver's Travels*, Davis ed., part I, ch. 8, p. 79.

77 Swift, *Gulliver's Travels*, Davis ed., part I, next-to-last paragraph of ch. 8, pp. 79–80.

78 Swift, *Gulliver's Travels*, Davis ed, the end of part II, ch. 8, p. 145.

79 Swift, *Gulliver's Travels*, part II, ch. 8, p. 146.

80 Swift, *Gulliver's Travels*, part II, ch. 8, p. 146.

81 Mill, *On Liberty and Other Essays*, *On Liberty*, "Of the Liberty of Thought and Discussion," II, p. 33.

82 J. S. Mill, *On Liberty and Other Essays*, *On Liberty*, part 2, "Of the Liberty of Thought and Discussion," p. 34.

83 Tennessee Williams, *A Streetcar Named Desire*, scene 11 (final scene), p. 178.

84 Deane, *The First Industrial Revolution*.

85 Charlotte Perkins Gilman, *Herland*, first published in 1915, a much later work, makes predictions for all three of the main male characters, who have deliberately sought out an all-women-and-girls utopia, particularly in respect to their new love interests in Herland. The three resultant love affairs represent three ways that an early-twentieth-century American man could comprehend a pre-industrial, yet in other respects highly advanced, non-Western society: as an explorer, as a Romantic poet, and as a scientist. Two of the men return home. One is expelled for his rough treatment of his wife. The poet chooses to stay in Herland with his new, pregnant wife. And the narrator returns home to California with a wife from Herland. This new couple is committed to using Herlandish, utopian, yet practical ideals to better life in America. See also Gilman's *The Yellow Wallpaper*, which was first published in 1892.

86 Hanif Kureishi, *The Buddha of Suburbia*. Thank you to Mark Kelley and Ursula Sampath.

87 Just as Gulliver, given the opportunity to reinvent his image, presents himself as a diplomat rather than as a surgeon, in Kureishi's novel, the larger-than-life character Charlie, the son of his father's girlfriend, Eva, desires status more than

anything else. At one stage, Charlie disappears from the book for some pages after he dives through the window of a car being driven away by a rock band, even though at least one member of the band has just vomited on him; as of that moment, Charlie instantly adores the band. Charlie later reappears in the story as an international rock star. He cares only for fame, not even for music. A different link could be made to Gulliver. Similar to Gulliver, the narrator who tells the story in *The Buddha of Suburbia*, the friend who watches Charlie, is never fully accepted by the many cultures that he repeatedly bends himself into contortions to entertain and please.

88 Joan Wallach Scott, *Gender and the Politics of History*, "Women in The Making of the English Working Class," part II, ch. 4, pp. 68–90.

REFERENCES

Aquinas, St. Thomas, *Summa Theologica*, 5 vols. (Westminster, MD: Christian Classics, 1948).

Armstrong, Chris, "Life-Styles, Life-Chances, and Radical Politics: Giddens on the 'New Egalitarianism,'" *Egalitarian Theory and Practice* 9, no. 3 (2007): 191–210.

Bayly, C.A., *The Birth of the Modern World, 1780–1914* (Oxford: Blackwell, 2004).

Bellamy, Edward, *Looking Backward, 2000–1887* (Boston: Ticknor and Company, 1888).

Bender, John, *Ends of Enlightenment* (Stanford, CA: Stanford University Press, 2012).

Black, Jeremy, *Eighteenth-Century Britain, 1688–1783* (Basingstoke, U.K.: Palgrave, 2001).

Block, Edward A., "Lemuel Gulliver: Middle-Class Gentleman" *English Language Notes* 68, no. 7 (1953): 474–477.

Brown, Lucy, *Victorian News and Newspapers* (Oxford: Oxford University Press, 1985).

Brown, Norman O., *Life against Death: The Psychoanalytical Meaning of History* (Middletown, CT: Wesleyan University Press, 1959).

Burke, Edmund, *Reflections on the Revolution in France*, J.G.A. Pocock., ed., (Indianapolis, IN: Hackett, 1987).

Cannadine, David, *Ornamentalism: How the British Saw Their Empire* (Oxford: Oxford University Press, 2001).

Cockerham, William C., Alfred Rütten, and Thomas Abel, "Conceptualizing Contemporary Health Lifestyles: Moving Beyond Weber," *The Sociological Quarterly* 38, no. 2 (1997): 321–342.

Colley, Linda, *Britons: Forging the Nation, 1707–1837* (London: Pimlico, 2003).

———. *Captives: Britain, Empire and the World, 1600–1850* (New York: Pantheon, 2002).

———. *In Defiance of Oligarchy: The Tory Party, 1714–60* (Cambridge: Cambridge University Press, 1982).

Deane, Phyllis, *The First Industrial Revolution* (New York: Cambridge University Press, 1979).

Firth, Charles, "The Political Significance of *Gulliver's Travels*," *Proceedings of the British Academy*, IX (lecture delivered on December 10, 1919).

Foot, Michael, *The Pen and the Sword: Jonathan Swift and the Power of the Press* (London: Collins, 1984).

Forster, E. M., *Aspects of the Novel* (New York: Harcourt, Brace, and World, 1955).

Giddens, Anthony, *Runaway World: How Globalisation is Reshaping Our Lives* (London: Profile Books, 2002).

Gilman, Charlotte Perkins, *Herland* (New York: Pantheon Books, 1979).

———. *The Yellow Wallpaper and Other Stories* (Mineola, NY: Dover, 1997).

History of the University of Cambridge, The, Vol. II: 1546–1750, Victor Morgan, ed. (Cambridge: Cambridge University Press, 2004).

History of the University of Cambridge, The, Vol. III, 1750–1870, Peter Searby, ed. (Cambridge: Cambridge University Press, 1997).

History of the University of Oxford, The, Vol. IV: Seventeenth-Century Oxford, Nicholas Tyacke, ed. (Oxford: Clarendon Press, 1997).

History of the University of Oxford, The, Vol. V: The Eighteenth Century, L. S. Sutherland and L.G. Mitchell (Oxford: Clarendon Press, 1986).

Kearney, Hugh, *Scholars and Gentlemen: Universities and Society in Pre-Industrial Britain, 1500–1700* (London: Faber, 1970).

Knowles, Ronald, *Gulliver's Travels: The Politics of Satire* (New York: Twayne Publishers, 1996).

Kureishi, Hanif. *The Buddha of Suburbia* (London: Faber and Faber, 1990).

Lennon, Joseph, *Irish Orientalism: A Literary and Intellectual History* (Syracuse, NY: Syracuse University Press, 2004).

Lock, F. P., *Swift's Tory Politics* (London: Duckworth, 1983).

———. *The Politics of Gulliver's Travels* (Oxford: Clarendon Press, 1980).

Mahoney, Robert, "Jonathan Swift and the Irish colonial project," in Claude Rawson, ed., *Politics and Literature in the Age of Swift: English and Irish Perspectives* (Cambridge: Cambridge University Press, 2010).

McMahon, Darrin M., *Enemies of the Enlightenment: The French Counter-Enlightenment and the Making of Modernity* (Oxford: Oxford University Press, 2001).

Mill, John Stuart, *On Liberty and Other Essays* (Oxford: Oxford World's Classics, 2008).

Moore, Sean, "Devouring Posterity: *A Modest Proposal*, Empire, and Ireland's 'Debt of the Nation,'" *PLMA* 122, no. 3 (May 2007): 674–695.

Morris, William, *News from Nowhere; Or, An Epoch of Rest; Being Some Chapters from a Utopian Romance* (Boston: Roberts Brothers, 1890).

Nokes, David, *Henry Fielding, Joseph Andrews: A Critical Study* (Harmondsworth, U.K.: Penguin, 1987).

———. *Jonathan Swift, A Hypocrite Reversed: A Critical Biography* (Oxford: Oxford University Press, 1985).

Oxford English Dictionary/*OED Online*, http://dictionary.oed.com/entrance.dtl.

Plato, *The Collected Dialogues of Plato, Including the Letters*, Lane Cooper, tr., Edith Hamilton and Huntington Cairns, eds. (Princeton: Princeton University Press, 1982).

Poovey, Mary, *Mediating Value in Eighteenth- and Nineteenth-Century Britain* (Chicago: University of Chicago Press, 2008).

Porter, Roy, *The Creation of the Modern World: The Untold Story of the British Enlightenment* (New York: W. W. Norton, 2000).

Rawson, Claude, *God, Gulliver, and Genocide: Barbarism and the European Imagination, 1492–1945* (New York: Oxford University Press, 2001).

Robinson, Elaine, *Gulliver as Slave Trader: Racism Reviled by Jonathan Swift* (Jefferson, NC: McFarland, 2006.

Rogers, Woodes, *Cruising Voyage Round the World* (London: Cassell, 1928).

Schama, Simon, *An Embarrassment of Riches: An Interpretation of Dutch Culture in the Golden Age* (London: Collins, 1987).

Scott, Joan Wallach, *Gender and the Politics of History*, rev. ed. (New York: Columbia University Press, 1999).

Shelley, Mary Wollstonecraft, *Frankenstein, or, The Modern Prometheus* (Harmondsworth, U.K.: Penguin, 1985).

The Spectator, Donald F. Bond, ed., 5 vols. (Oxford: Clarendon Press, 1965).

Sreedhar, Susanne, *Hobbes on Resistance: Defying the Leviathan* (Cambridge: Cambridge University Press, 2010).

Swift, Jonathan, *Gulliver's Travels and Other Writings*, Miriam K. Starkman, ed. (New York: Bantam, 1986).

———. *Gulliver's Travels*, Herbert Davis, ed. (Oxford: Basil Blackwell, 1965).

———. *Gulliver's Travels*, Peter Dixon and John Chalker, eds. (London: Penguin, 1985).

———. *Gulliver's Travels*, Claude Rawson and Ian Higgins, eds. (Oxford: Oxford University Press, 2005).

———. *Major Works*, Angus Ross and David Woolley, eds. (Oxford: Oxford University Press, 2003).

The Tatler, Donald F. Bond, ed., 3 vols. (Oxford: Clarendon Press, 1987).

Thompson, E. P. *The Making of the English Working Class* (London: Victor Gollancz, 1963).

Vickers, Brian, "Swift and the Baconian Idol," in *The World of Jonathan Swift: Essays for the Tercentenary*, Brian Vickers, ed. (Cambridge, MA: Harvard University Press), 1968, pp. 87–128.

Watt, Ian P. *The Rise of the Novel: Studies in Defoe, Richardson, and Fielding* (Whitefish, MT: Kessinger Publishing, 2007).

Williams, Tennessee, *A Streetcar Named Desire* (New York: New Directions Books, 1980).

Wrightson, Keith, and David Levine, *Poverty and Piety in an English Village: Terling, 1525–1700* (Oxford: Clarendon Press, 1979).

4 *Candide* (1759), Sexuality, and the Modern Individual

I BACKGROUND

1 Intellectual Setting and the Author: Voltaire (1694–1778)

Voltaire's overwhelming and lasting influence is the result of the spectacular success of his political novel, *Candide*, known since its publication as a brilliant satire not just of the philosopher Leibniz, but of European pretensions on a grand scale.[1] *Candide*, the most famous of the eighteenth-century *contes philosophiques* (philosophical stories), is often readers' favorite (or least favorite) work of fiction of all time.[2] Immediately after its publication, *Candide* was wildly popular (partially the result of Voltaire's shrewd business instincts), and it is cited as a source for both the French and the American Revolutions. The implications of Voltaire's arguments may well have been more radical than he even intended. In a time of no division between church and state, Voltaire's call for religious freedom, to cite one key example, was essentially a call to reform the entire social structure. *Candide* had appeal across different nationalities, and even across social class. It is often argued that, because of its high entertainment value, its length, and its precocity, this short book remains perhaps the single best exponent of Enlightenment thought. This book was quoted by the educated and by aristocrats alike. However, Voltaire (born François-Marie Arouet, 1694–1778), based on his early writings and his larger-than-life personality, was a celebrity even before he wrote *Candide*. Seemingly all Britons, for example, at least literary ones who met Voltaire during his almost three years in England, 30 years before he wrote *Candide*, were likely to mention this meeting repeatedly for the rest of their lives. Voltaire's admirers often demonstrated two of the qualities—kowtowing to authority and arrogance—that were to be mocked most fiercely in his most famous work.

    Candide was published, anonymously, in 1759; at this time, all books in France had to be passed by the censors before publication, and the censors would certainly not have passed *Candide*. The Catholic Church publicly categorized certain books, deemed particularly dangerous, as unacceptable. Nonetheless, the Catholic Index of forbidden books was taken almost as a required reading list by thinkers across the political spectrum during the long eighteenth century. Many authors were incensed when their books were not placed on the Index.

Therefore, most of the books of the Enlightenment were published anonymously and with false places of publication. Amsterdam was often listed as the place of publication as there was relative freedom of the press in Holland at this time, which was both cause and effect of the presence of so many writers there. This literary tradition from Holland, especially in the late seventeenth century, but also throughout Europe and North America in the late seventeenth and early eighteenth centuries, is often referred to as the Republic of Letters. There now exists a scholarly literature that asks if the Enlightenment should be viewed essentially as an outgrowth of the Republic of Letters.[3]

Unlike Swift, Voltaire considered himself to be a Modern rather than an Ancient in the Quarrel of the Ancients and the Moderns. Yet Voltaire was only marginally involved in the major French Enlightenment project, *l'Encyclopédie*—the great compendium of knowledge from the natural sciences to literature—which was primarily the work of his contemporaries d'Alembert and Diderot. Thus Voltaire focused his attention on his own writings, not on the group projects that were, even at the time, considered the great achievement of the eighteenth-century Moderns.

Indeed, Voltaire's *Candide* quickly won attention; it was placed on the Catholic Index of Forbidden Books in Rome in 1762, only three years after its publication. Despite the mere three-year time lag, it was perhaps a little late. Soon after its first publication, *Candide* was already deemed the quintessential Enlightenment work of fiction. *Candide* and the work by Voltaire's rival Rousseau, *Julie, ou La Nouvelle Héloïse (Julie, or the New Eloise*, 1761), a love story told in the epistolary style so popular with eighteenth-century readers, were the European bestsellers of the middle of that century.[4] In political terms, Rousseau's novel *Julie* shows passion and reason tearing at the hearts of all the main characters. In the end, as she is dying, the title character Julie admits that her sensible marriage has been a failure, and that she still loves another man, even given her great respect for her husband. Despite the heroine's attempts to live her life conventionally, the book was shocking to its first readers. This was primarily because the book offers no clears guide to life choices that involve virtue, including respect for one's parents, and personal authenticity. Rousseau's refusal to indicate the right path (or even the wrong path) highlights the complexity of modern life.[5]

However, in contrast, *Candide* was not conservative in any respect, rather it parodies the romantic genre so popular over the centuries. In *Candide*, the girl kisses the boy, the boy loses the girl, the boy, once he is a man, finally gets the girl, now a grown woman, and although he no longer wants her, he marries her anyway in order to spite her family. However, romance is hardly the only target of this book. Other targets, all adding to the preposterous humor of the book, include the military, the Church, the academic hierarchy, the publishing industry, and all teleological explanations of historical, present, and future events, and thus all theory—both Scholastic and enlightened.[6] The attacks on these ways of thinking added to the popularity of the book, even with some of the members of the groups Voltaire targeted.

It is crucial to realize that Voltaire's personal circumstances were not always privileged and that Voltaire was one of the very few *philosophes*, indeed public intellectuals (Swift was certainly another), who became involved in protecting defendants in infamous cases of judicial injustice. One experience brought about this determination. Educated by the Jesuits, trained in law, he spent most of his 20's as a minor public intellectual in Paris. However, at about age 30, Voltaire was first beat up and then imprisoned, without trial, in the Bastille, for almost a year, for insulting a young aristocrat. Voltaire, the son of a lawyer, was merely middle class, a major difference in pre-French Revolution France. As an alternative to indefinite imprisonment in France, Voltaire agreed to leave France and to go to Britain. Thus despite his extraordinary reception in Britain (and partially the reason for much of his success in Britain), Voltaire was an exile during these years—almost three years—abroad. Similarly, after he could return to France, he decided to settle in Geneva, partially in order to be over the border from France, and thus be perhaps safer all around, which continued to matter due to the explosive content of his writings.

Voltaire turned his anger about how he had been treated by the French judicial system not only into strong denunciations of institutional abuse, but also into personal involvement in particular legal cases. Much later in his life, Voltaire became involved in one of the most notorious cases of judicial injustice in French history. This was the case of Jean Calas, a Protestant cloth merchant, executed in 1762, for the murder of his son. The courts assumed that the Protestant father murdered the son because the son was seemingly in the process of converting to Catholicism. This occurred in the years following the Revocation of the Edict of Nantes in 1685, an edict that for 87 years, had granted religious toleration to non-Catholics. This was a textbook case for early tabloids as well as for thinkers of the time; Adam Smith notes this case in his *Theory of Moral Sentiments*.[7] The death of the 28-year-old Calas son and then the execution of his father produced a case that mixed issues of Church and state, and quickly became a national concern in France, and far beyond. The impact of this case in other countries, especially Britain, was substantial. Voltaire's celebrated defense of the Calas family—indeed his defense of religious toleration, *Traité sur la tolérance à l'occasion de la mort de Jean Calas*—appeared in print in 1763. This work and its social impact can be compared to that of the later work by Émile Zola, *J'accuse* (1898), a defense of the French army captain, Alfred Dreyfus, in the midst of the 12-year Dreyfus Affair, which centered on anti-Semitism. Voltaire, in sharp contrast to the classic stereotype of the disinterested intellectual, was heavily involved in specific cases of attempting to better his own time and place, which itself is now a stereotypical trait of the engaged intellectual.

In his unwillingness to wait for gradual social change, Voltaire could be seen as a forerunner of John Maynard Keynes, who had no patience for the Smithian "invisible hand" that would supposedly smooth out economic inequalities in the long run. According to Keynes, "in the long run we will all be dead." Yet one could argue that there are proto-Smithian as well as proto-Keynesian aspects to this novel (Voltaire's defense of the Huguenot, Protestant father could also symbolize a defense of the growing middle class). Voltaire's championing of Calas could be used as part of a contextual argument that any reading of *Candide* must recognize both theory and practice, as the author never separated the two.

The Enlightenment in Europe has, until very recently, generally been considered to have started in Paris in the mid-eighteenth century, and then to have spread from certain *salons* of very particular *arrondissements* (urban districts) of Paris to the rest of Europe and then throughout the world.[8] The French Enlightenment was in some crucial respects Voltairean, molded deliberately by him, his intellectual rivals, especially Rousseau, and his enemies, particularly the hyper-religious *anti-philosophes*.[9] The interplay of these competing individuals and groups was crucial. Though the Enlightenment may have once been thought of as primarily French and the *lumières* (Enlightenment figures) as primarily Voltairean, no *dix-huitièmiste* (eighteenth-century scholar) would make either of these claims now. In particular, Voltaire has not been a major focus of French Enlightenment studies for several decades. Montesquieu, Rousseau, and Diderot are now taken to be far more important to the present understanding of the Enlightenment and its legacy than Voltaire. However, at this stage, a return to Voltaire could be argued to be in order to understand the concerns of the eighteenth (not twenty-first) century, remembering the great popularity of this book when first published, and to comprehend the ongoing popularity of *Candide* over the centuries, and in addition, to understand better the outpouring of reform literature that followed in the wake of its publication.[10]

It is not an accident that Voltaire's work had such a widespread impact. Voltaire himself demonstrated many pan-European features: he was an Anglophile, he lived outside of France, near Geneva, for many years, and his ambitions were not just Parisian and French, but universal. His writing represents a blending of conservative as well as radical political preferences: the need for a strong ruler but also the right to criticize the existing political structure. Rationalist, pro-scientific, and dubious, at the very least, regarding religion, Voltaire's liberty was always negative liberty, stressing protection against harm rather than assertion of rights to be claimed and enacted. His life mirrored and, some would still argue, set the traditional dates of the Enlightenment. He attacked any type of institutional control over the individual. Voltaire saw no need to defend the utility of social institutions; rather he aimed his unforgiving blows at the entrenched sources of, what was taken to be, absolute power in his own time and place. Thus missing from his work was a discussion of positive liberty, of the specific rights that individuals should be able to claim from their government. His writing was always focused on immediate problems, and yet it had theoretical implications. Thus what he wrote as a political pamphlet in fictional form is now studied as political theory.

2 The Story Itself

All of this culminated in the writing of *Candide*. In this story, the character Candide, probably an illegitimate, certainly a poor, relation of minor German aristocrats in Westphalia, is thrown out of his menial existence in their home at Castle Thunder-ten-tronckh—an act that saves his life, for soon after, foreign soldiers attack the house, killing almost all the family. This is just one instance of the deep hatred between warring factions prevalent throughout *Candide*, in this case between Catholics and Protestants in the Thirty Years' War. If religious intolerance is the first target, the second is blatantly secular: the security of the 1648 Peace of Westphalia—which asserted national sovereignty, especially for small nations, and marking the end of the Thirty Years' War—is punctured simply by placing the castle where Candide was raised, and which was mercilessly raided, in Westphalia. Thus even in the area where this declaration was passed, there is no peace and security, even in one of the small states that the agreement was designed in particular to protect. The satire in this work operates for the most part through presentation rather than analytical criticism.

Only the minor characters, however, stay dead in this story. Using the religious imagery of resurrection, *Candide* puts forward a secular attack on the belief in the biblical resurrection of Christ simply by having so many flawed human characters in the story repeatedly resurrected. Established authority structures and boundaries of all types are attacked. The daughter of the house, who is perhaps Candide's cousin, the 17-year-old Lady Cunégonde (her name is a play-on-words on the Latin and French terms for female gentitalia, thus mocking the pretensions of the aristocracy), much loved by Candide, and because of whom he is thrown out of their house by her father; the tutor Pangloss, her brother (who becomes the new Baron at the death of his father, and then later he becomes a Jesuit); and a maid named Pacquette are all eventually revealed to have survived. Not only do they outlive this initial onslaught, the main characters later avoid other, if possible, more brutal deaths.

Pangloss and his Candide travel relentlessly in what could be understood as an anti-Grand Tour. However, the tutor is separated from Candide for some extended period, while Candide and Cunégonde, whom he has rediscovered with a companion, *la vieille* (the Old Woman), sail from Cádiz to Buenes Aires. The disappearance of Pangloss in the middle of the story suggests that there is no call for Panglossian rote learning in the New

World. Overall, the use of types in this book can be associated with both personality types as well as social classes, and they tend to show not the possible range but the usual narrowness of deviations within these types. Seemingly without interruption since leaving Castle Thunder-ten-tronckh, soldiers, Inquisitors, and Latin American native peoples, all of whom have, perhaps understandably, lost patience with the central characters, harass Candide. He is flogged, forced to run the gauntlet, and burned at the stake. It is, however, worth noting that there is substantially more violence in Europe than in Latin America. Throughout most of the story, in Europe and in South America, Candide and Pangloss seem to find peace, or more precisely, quiet, in prison, or outdoors.

Candide thus manages both to remain in close contact with his teacher for years, and also to be the worst student one can imagine. Candide, for most of the story, is seemingly incapable of learning, as evidenced by his belief that his teacher is always correct. He regards his own simple repetition of his teacher's words—both a paean (a triumphal song) to, and a parody of, optimism—to be the highest form of compliment, and his teacher does nothing to disabuse him of this notion. In this respect, the work could be viewed as deliberately anti-picaresque, as Candide is not from the poorer classes and he is supposedly not at all intelligent. Candide's name variously translates from the French as ingenuous, naive, blunt, forthright, and honest, thus mixing positive and negative characteristics. His relationship with Pangloss is also oddly mixed.

Similarly, Candide's rationalization of the dangers he encounters is not only highly repetitious, it is also dangerous for him at various points. His passivity in the face of assault is not rewarded, for the text's anti-war stance is not designed to encourage weakness. The book indicates no sympathy for weak logic, especially in regard to the issues that Voltaire supported. The book's attack on all things, and all persons academic is, for example, bolstered by encouragement, however vague, of pragmatic aims and practices. *Candide* is a panegyric against extremes, dogmatism, and fanaticism of all stripes.

Thus, as a foil for the notion of toleration, it is the tutor, Pangloss, the dogmatic character, who is based on a caricature of Leibniz's view that we are living in "the best of all possible worlds." Pangloss is perhaps best understood as someone educated far beyond his intelligence. He is easily viewed as the embodiment not only of undigested theoretical notions but also of the general need for authority figures, who will satisfy the general desire conclusively to categorize types of behavior and abstract ideas as good or evil. Pangloss's ideas are presented as potentially dangerous, especially if not fully understood before applied. In addition, Pangloss's vague but strongly held ideas are also emblematic of all the contemporary scholars whom Voltaire despised, especially those who directly criticized him on both large and small points.[11] However, to be fair, it might be worth speculating on what Voltaire might have learned if he had absorbed some of their criticisms, rather than writing repeated vindications of himself against the charges of the *anti-philosophes* in particular.[12] Or, perhaps *Candide* would have been even better if it had allowed for more nuances, rather than basing its great appeal on its starkly ironic treatment, especially of the character of Pangloss.

Yet the book's supposed failures in terms of character development, transitions, and credibility are generally accepted to be overshadowed by brilliant writing and unforgiving wit. The reader might wish that the book had given some clues about what to do next after the identification of social abuses and even the destruction of existing social institutions. However, many readers declare these supposed failures to be the work's very strengths. Unrealistically abrupt transitions and one-dimensional characters serves a clear purpose; in a constructive, Leibnizian sense, they can be interpreted as showing the striving, sometimes flailing, of free will in the midst of the seeming dominance of predestination.

For Candide, it is never clear what to do next. He kills Cunégonde's two lovers in Lisbon. She was forced to spend part of every week with each of them, a Grand Inquisitor and a wealthy Jew, Don Issachar. Following the double murder, Candide, Cunégonde, and the Old Woman flee to Latin America. Candide cannot even stay with the women in Buenos Aires, as the news of the murders has spread to the New World. So Cunégonde becomes an adored mistress of yet another powerful man, this time the Governor of Buenos Aires. Candide escapes to Paraguay. All of this happens by accident.

Candide finds two replacement tutors during his time away from Pangloss, thus fulfilling his personal needs, and demonstrating at the same time two larger theoretical trends. The first tutor is Cacambo, a servant from Cádiz, who is "a quarter Spaniard of half-breed Argentine stock."[13] Cacambo plays the role of both a Rousseauian noble savage and an enlightened Rousseauian citizen. Martin, an unemployed French intellectual, the second replacement tutor, fulfills the role of a grumpy Socrates, irritated with the lack of respect given to his pronouncements. Pangloss mirrors Folly in Erasmus's *Praise of Folly*, a creature who inadvertently gives sound instruction by providing counter-examples of what should be done. In contrast, Cacambo teaches by commenting on life experiences. For his part Martin provides high-level, if narrow, education in a traditional manner—he is thus a better-educated, more reflective Pangloss.

In the New World, Candide and Cacambo visit a utopia by accident, but then choose to leave it, purportedly because Candide is in search of Cunégonde (although his motivation is mixed), whom he still loves. Martin aids Cacambo in the role of Candide's tutor beginning just before Candide's voyage back to Europe. Martin, convinced that he has wasted his youth working for publishers in Amsterdam, is a remarkably intellectual companion for Candide. No doubt this is why so many readers have read Martin as the voice of Voltaire himself. However, neither Cacambo nor Martin is directly responsible for Candide's almost imperceptible but steady character development. Thus life experience is put forward over formal education as the most powerful factor in forming the adult psyche.

The characters slowly regroup. The story ends with them back in Europe after a most difficult journey from Surinam (bordered today by French Guiana, Guyana, and Brazil), on the Atlantic Coast of South America. Candide travels from Paris to Venice, and finally settles outside Constantinople. His later European stays involve losing at cards, being humiliated in intrigues, and being robbed in several sophisticated rackets, especially in Paris. Toward the end of the story, the cast of characters is reunited and living together outside Constantinople, thus outside Western Europe. Candide and Cunégonde are married, although not particularly happily. Pangloss, the wise Old Woman (who is, incidentally, the daughter of a Pope), and Martin are all with them. Two of the major characters have now been missing longer than most. Pacquette, the maid, disappears in Venice after Candide gives her some money. Perhaps no one told the maid she was a major character, and that she was welcome to remain with the group. Nonetheless, she and her friar/lover, *frère* Giroflée, do eventually show up at the farm, the final setting of the book. One character, who might possibly be regarded a major character, Jacques the Anabaptist, is instead the only one of the group who dies once and permanently. Perhaps this is because he finishes his task in the book quickly, presumably to provide solace to others, unlike the rest of the touring group, who fulfill little clear purpose, altruistic or selfish.[14] Next, Cunégonde's brother, who, as the symbol of the aristocracy, is never identified by his Christian name, reappears briefly. The brother's relative anonymity is in odd contrast to the picaresque novels that give ornate and amusing names to the few aristocrats that appear in those stories. When the brother once again will not allow Candide to marry his sister, the group sells the brother back to the Levantine captain. Although some readers might sympathize with this as a prudent decision in many respects, the brother's reasoning is seemingly based only on status, for he does not view the bastard Candide to be sufficiently, if at all, aristocratic. Earlier, in Paraguay, Candide had already killed the brother once, when he would not allow Candide to marry Cunégonde. The brother's repeated refusal to let his sister marry Candide, despite their much changed circumstances, parody familial injunctions that are never heard just once. The others, at the end of the story, are all working together on a farm outside Constantinople. The characters function with appropriate spontaneity as recognizable individual types and equally well as loyal members of a most improbable group. Many readers have considered this a happy ending. It can be argued, however, that the book mocks this option as well, in much the same way that it does for all the previous political and philosophical options it presents.

Unlike the character Quixote, who has followers who adore him with the ferocious, misguided devotion of early-modern hooligans, Candide, for all his supposed beauty, appeals to relatively few people in this story. He is a cipher. Even Pangloss is only dimly aware of Candide. Candide is apparently such a fool that the reader is taken aback, finally needing to reappraise the idiot, Candide, as if he is a decoy, happily distracting the reader until the deeper meaning of the main character is revealed. At the very least, he has many solid, if not stellar, qualities; this supposed fool respects his elders, is grateful for his education, practices sexual faithfulness to one woman (with one slip in Paris), believes in true love, is a loyal friend, is willing to learn new ideas but does not abandon all his old ones, and finally builds a home for the non-traditional family he collects throughout this story.

It is also worth asking whether the character Candide was meant as a caricature of Voltaire's rival, Rousseau, who can be understood in many of the same terms. Like Rousseau, Candide is clearly not upper class, has no formal education, no university connections, came from an area deemed peripheral in the European political structure, and lives a life that is not settled geographically, personally, or professionally. Unlike Rousseau, Candide has no tendency toward depression or paranoia, and no sense of isolation, although he did suffer extraordinary financial insecurity. Rousseau's positive characteristics are also present in the evolving character of Candide, although one wonders how deliberate this would have been on Voltaire's part: these attributes include a very agile and curious mind, receptiveness to new ideas, without being malleable, and a strong personality and sense of purpose that were not diminished by adversities. Both the theorist Rousseau and the character Candide could then be viewed as embodying the stereotypes of a wild, untamed European intellectual.

Cynically, the appeal of this book is that it is short, academic, and yet highly irreverent, invoking theories but with no extended discussion of them, leaving the reader feeling superior to every academic and political system, and indeed to everyone, except perhaps the author, who is recognized as an equal finally located. The conceit of the author brings the reader into a new and fashionable group. Similar works, such as Montesquieu's *Les Lettres persanes (Persian Letters*, 1721) and Godwin's *Things as They Are: or, The Adventures of Caleb Williams* (1794), arguably tax the reader with extended theoretical discussions. In contrast, the pacing of *Candide* is remarkable. No scene is drawn out, some might say finished, and there are a great many diversions. A surprising amount of ground is covered, not all of it geographical.

The abstract ideas raised in this book still need attention: suffering, tutelage, forays to the New World, and imperialism.[15] Readers are still drawn to this book not just for entertaining and challenging ideas about France, the Enlightenment, and the looming French Revolution, but overall, for the intellectual, teasing banter, indeed thrusts at all types of hypocrisy, much of it embedded in the authority structures, which resonate beyond the time and place of publication of this work.

The humor should not be ignored; it is not window dressing in this story. This is perhaps the most entertaining academic work ever written, with *Praise of Folly*, by Erasmus, as perhaps the first runner-up. This is humor for the Senior Common Room, for those who have no fear of losing their privileges, much less their jobs. Yet Voltaire somehow had the sense of assurance to write this without any professional backing or job security (albeit Voltaire was himself, by a certain point, financially secure, partially because of lottery winnings after he returned from England and then from an inheritance from his father).[16] Overall, at all stages, bite of his wit seems to be of the type that cannot easily be stopped, and perhaps only serious censorship rendered his writing this mild.[17] The major messages of the story are often delivered in the most amusing, outrageous passages.

3 Gottfried Wilhelm Leibniz (1646–1716)

Voltaire's characterization of Leibniz's view that we live in "the best of all possible worlds" certainly does no favors to the German thinker; indeed, it verges on caricature.[18] Yet both Leibniz and Voltaire were concerned with similar issues, including theodicy, the dilemma of why a loving God allows evil in the world. Perhaps Candide gives the clearest definition of optimism—*ou L'Optimisme (Or Optimism)* is the subtitle of the book—to the black slave at the Dutch sugar plantation in Surinam, in South America: "It's the passion for maintaining that all is right when all goes wrong with us."[19] Only the three main characters ever mouth these platitudes; even in the book the minor characters are not taken in by Pangloss's pseudo-philosophy. However, the blame here should not necessarily be ascribed to Leibniz. The Leibnizian dimension of *Candide* may in some respects be overstated; however, some perhaps constructive linkages between the two thinkers still need attention.

Leibniz would seem not to have been a natural enemy for Voltaire. Leibniz lived for some years in France, and he wrote in French as well as German. As was to be the case for Voltaire later, Leibniz had broader intellectual concerns than most of his contemporaries. Immersed in classical and medieval writers for most of his life, only during his time in Paris (in 1672, more than 20 years before Voltaire was born) did Leibniz first start reading contemporary authors. Leibniz was concerned to blend the best of Scholastic thought—then under heavy attack by Descartes's followers—with early-modern philosophical thinking in order to make sense of political life in a century, the seventeenth, now call a century of General Crisis.

Nevertheless, a single passage from *Candide* can be used to represent various aspects of Leibniz's thought, as well as Voltaire's own sharp criticism, indeed manipulation, of it:

> 'There is no effect without a cause,' replied Candide modestly. 'All things are necessarily connected and arranged for the best. It was my fate to be driven from Lady Cunégonde's presence and made to run the gauntlet, and now I have to beg my bread until I can earn it. Things could not have happened otherwise.'[20]

This short passage accurately portrays Leibniz's emphasis on cause and effect (part of the early-modern interest in bringing together theology and science), yet the absence of free will and the presence of predetermination in this passage.

Leibniz repeatedly stresses the role of free will, even though, granted, it did not work well in his overall system of monads. (Monads for Leibniz are living substances that possess consciousness; they are arguably Leibniz's replacement term for atoms.) At the very least, Voltaire's intellectual agenda—especially regarding free will, and cause and effect—was set out by Leibniz, and this is evident both when Voltaire is attacking Leibniz and when he is supposedly not discussing Leibniz at all.

For all Voltaire's scorn, Leibniz has been given credit in several distinct areas of the history of European thought. Regularly cited by post–World War II philosophers for his emphasis on personal identity, Leibniz is particularly known for his view that no two people are identical. He propounded this view long before the Enlightenment emphasis on the abstract individual, but this view is now, amusingly, viewed as a twentieth-century break from Enlightenment thought. In terms of political theory, Leibniz could be viewed as one of the early contributors to the subject of personal autonomy, even personal liberty, given his additional emphasis on free will. There is thus a strong parallel between Leibniz and Voltaire that the later writer presumably would not have appreciated.

Leibniz's work also inspired a second great response (in addition to *Candide*), for Immanuel Kant's writings overall can be viewed as an attempt to systematize problems that Leibniz had set out earlier in a much more haphazard way. Kant was the major thinker of the German Enlightenment. Given that the German Enlightenment followed the French, Italian, and most of the other national European Enlightenments by several decades, Kant's views gained additional status as he was taken to be presenting the best of the entire European Enlightenment, along with his own distinctive and grand additions. In addition, a great many other writers throughout the eighteenth and nineteenth centuries defined their own intellectual concerns both in comparison and in contrast to those of Leibniz.

Overall, *Candide* demonstrates Leibnizian qualities in its consideration of the balance between sufficient human reason and predetermination.[21] Nevertheless, Voltaire was not altogether misrepresenting Leibniz's work on the notion of pre-established harmony. However, the emphasis in Leibniz would be best viewed not as optimism, but as Stoicism in the midst of dreadful circumstances—and this is the popular reading of Candide.[22] Thus Leibniz and Voltaire both rejected the Christian view of man as corrupt.

It is speculated that Voltaire's concentration on the problem of evil had to do as well with the works of Pierre Bayle, a seventeenth-century French skeptic and a precursor of the *philosophes*, and also with Alexander Pope's poem *Essay on Man* (1733/1734).[23] Initially, Voltaire used Pope's poem to fight Christian orthodoxy, and later as part of his development of an overall philosophy.[24] During Voltaire's time at the court in Potsdam, Friedrich the Great tried to interest him in Leibnizianism.[25] In Voltaire's work *Zadig* (first published as *Mennon, Histoire orientale*, 1747), set in ancient Babylon, Voltaire first started to work on the question of evil. Over the next years, Voltaire was more convinced that human folly causes earthly woes. Soon, though, his attention turned to *"meilleur des mondes possibles"* ("the best of all possible world") drawn from Leibniz. By the time Voltaire writes *Candide*, Leibnizian thought is only caricatured. In *Candide*, even the character Martin's Manichaeism (which views life in stark dualities—good versus evil, to give the prime example), a system to which Voltaire was sympathetic, is dismissed. A rejection of Pangloss is not necessarily a move toward fatalism, and it can be argued that Voltaire rejects Leibniz's despair.[26] Voltaire is generally attacking Leibnizianism, or lack of intellectual rigor, not Leibniz. In any case, the choice of Leibniz over Pope as the object of ridicule is no doubt partially because Leibnizianism was much better known, if not fashionable, in France at this time (and also probably because Voltaire knew Pope during his time in London).[27] Throughout his life, Voltaire supposedly considered Leibniz incomprehensible, rather than a direct enemy. In any case, even though Leibniz worked on the problem of evil in a Christian manner, Voltaire did so in a Deist manner that was not wholly secular. However, there is a characteristically perverse element here. Voltaire scholar W. H. Barber speculates that although Voltaire outwardly attacked Leibnizianism, he favored the secure basis of hopeful individual activity that Leibniz had been anxious to provide.[28] Thus Voltaire's notion that human responsibility implies human freedom, and thus the possibility of free will, is drawn directly from Leibniz.[29]

4 The Lisbon Earthquake

However, not all of Voltaire's motivation for writing this book was philosophical and anti-Leibnizian. On the morning of All Saints Day, November 1, 1755, an earthquake, followed by a triple tsunami, hit Lisbon, Portugal, and the surrounding area, including Spain, and reached as far as North Africa. Five years earlier an earthquake had hit London. World-historical events can happen over centuries, in a few years, or in a few minutes. The reaction to this second major European earthquake, in 1755, so soon after the first, had an impact on European thought—even beyond the death toll, physical destruction, and economic decline—on the scale of that of the Fall of Rome in late antiquity, or of the French Revolution (occurring some decades after the Lisbon Earthquake) on the modern age. Relatively few natural disasters have had such direct impact on political and even scientific thought as the Lisbon Earthquake of 1755. Kant published at least three scientific works on it, and Walter Benjamin later gave Kant credit for developing a scientific interest in earthquakes. Areas unaffected physically by the Lisbon earthquake, such as Britain and

Germany, nevertheless suffered substantial financial losses. Even though Spanish and North African towns were destroyed as well, at the time, and certainly since, popular concern was fixated only on the admittedly wholesale devastation of the capital city of Lisbon. This had to do partly with the remarkable rebuilding of the city by the Enlightenment politician, Sebastião de Carvalho, marquis de Pombal. However, the focus was not all on reconstruction, it also indicated a shift in thinking. Ministers throughout Europe, and Jesuits in Lisbon itself, railed that the earthquake was punishment for the evil lives of the Portuguese. Somewhat more moderately, and yet with their own decided point of view, the founders of Methodism, John and Charles Wesley, to give one example, viewed natural disasters as social levelers, destroying entrenched class divisions and leading people, supposedly of all backgrounds, toward Methodism.[30] Voltaire was not the only one in this generation to exploit the Earthquake to further his own particular causes.

The popular reading of *Candide* in terms of this hideous event is the following: Voltaire, following the Lisbon earthquake, an event that rocked the optimism of the early eighteenth century, sought to find at least some middle ground between what he viewed as the naive optimism of Leibniz and the raw, unvarnished acceptance of whatever nature or society might deal out to a particular person.[31] Voltaire had already written a poem about the Lisbon Earthquake (1756) before *Candide* (1759), and *Candide* seems to be more of a return to his ongoing concern with evil, and with the impoverished means by which human beings try to reconcile themselves to natural disasters rather than simply accept their fates blindly.[32] The same tension can be found in the work of the Epicurean writer Lucretius in the first century A.D., who compares human behavior to that of atoms— regular, even predictable up to a point, but always subject to the whims of natural events as well as to aberrant human or animal behavior.[33] However, thinkers—ancient, medieval, and modern—have less regularly attempted to understand natural disasters (as distinct from disease, especially the plague) as part of human experience, and as part of political theory, than one might expect. Voltaire is most unusual—and to be praised—for his attempt to comprehend the role of natural disasters in terms of theories of society.

In contrast, Voltaire's 1756 poem on the Lisbon disaster, written three years before *Candide*, Voltaire mocks the beliefs of the poet Alexander Pope (a friend from his time in London) perhaps even more strongly than he attacked Leibniz, supposedly his major target in *Candide*. Part of the reason that this work had such instant success was certainly that it epitomized the feeling of the time.[34] At the very least, Pope's poem, *Essay on Man* (1733/1734), demonstrated a renewed interest in cosmology, theodicy, and Leibnizian optimism. Despite Dr. Johnson's wry comment on the poem, "Never were penury of knowledge and vulgarity of sentiment so happily disguised," the French translation of the poem was very popular in France and beyond.[35] Pope's poem emphasizes man as an individual, but as limited, both intellectually and morally. Thus both poems embrace some Christian themes, albeit from a secular perspective.

In *Essay on Man*, at the end of Epistle I, Pope advocates an optimism that apparently has no boundaries:

All discord, harmony not understood;
All partial evil, universal good:
And, spite of pride in erring reason's spite,
One truth is clear, whatever is, is right.[36]

The extent to which Pope meant this ironically is still debated. In any case, this poem gives some nuance to the view that Voltaire gained inspiration primarily from the English about the possibility of bloodless reform of authoritarian systems, as demonstrated by the Glorious Revolution, in England, in 1688. Thus Voltaire imbibed many English views during his visit, some of which he later felt compelled to reject. It could be argued that Voltaire rejected Leibniz and Pope so violently because they represented intellectual positions he had himself advocated in his own earlier phases. Overall, the Lisbon earthquake shifted Voltaire's thinking. Voltaire's poem on the Lisbon disaster was an effort to come to terms with divine providence, natural disasters, and the limits of human achievement.

Human perfectibility must then be viewed as separate from natural disasters: the human mind is not necessarily developing along with nature in some overall beneficent manner. Voltaire does not turn to a proto-Darwinian explanation of survival of the fittest as the proper understanding of natural disasters. However, he does stress human ingenuity as always necessary, particularly in times when nature and society are giving little help to the unfortunate.

5 Candide in the History of Ideas

In line with the other four major works being considered here—*Don Quixote, Simplicissimus, Gulliver's Travels,* and *The Betrothed*—the themes in *Candide* can also be found in writings since antiquity, continuing into twenty-first-century fiction and thought. The story that made Voltaire famous is from the outset a satire of the beliefs that good looks are all that is necessary for a happy life, and that being born in the right place, to the right parents, and at the right time, guarantees respect. This is a direct parody of the world evoked in Baldassare Castiglione's 1528 work, *Il Cortegiano (The Courtier)*, used for centuries as a manual for how to raise young gentlemen, and of manners and etiquette more generally.[37] Yet the eponymous hero of *Candide*, although he is present on almost every page, is nevertheless perhaps the one character most difficult to define, much less comprehend. Initially, Candide's simplicity, bordering on idiocy, makes him appear to be an odd choice as Voltaire's everyman or even every-boy. However, this book has been taken to support the view of the Enlightenment that considers the average person to be not only educable but also, to some extent, perfectible, and thus anti-Leibnizian in expecting the future to be better than the present. The book nevertheless certainly does not conclusively demonstrate such a shift in any of the characters, or at any stage. This is one of the criticisms of the Enlightenment already being addressed at the time, in this case even in the text of *Candide* itself. This book never proposes an enlightened solution that would resolve all of life's problems. Perhaps the book's argument is that even someone as amazingly dim as Candide has rights, and that even Candide recognizes the distinction between right and wrong, thus establishing a basis for justice that can be comprehended and enacted by the most ordinary of individuals. This interpretation goes some way toward explaining why it was this work by Voltaire, and not one of the many other works—including even more explicit fables and non-fiction diatribes against corrupt institutions—that became so hugely popular in the long eighteenth century. Thus the theory in the book should be viewed as part of its popular appeal, not as indigestible bits discarded by most of its contemporary and later readers.

According to the ancient writer Lucretius, in *On the Nature of the Universe*, it is best to dole out theory like medicine, which is given to a child in honey. This is not just a structural model for Lucretius and Voltaire— the hiding of a moral within a more palatable form (as can also be found in *Aesop's Fables*). Instead, in both Lucretius and Voltaire, pleasure is put forward as an essential quality of life, not just a fleeting feature of it, but rather as something that should be secured for oneself. Lucretius could be viewed as a precursor to Voltaire in a number of ways; both used shock effect in their writing and both stressed the duality of pleasure and pain in life. It is pleasure that is ignored by most serious writers. Both authors were concerned with the material and physical aspects of the good life. Politics and culture and everything else were just a means to having high quality of life for both of them. These themes can be found in works since antiquity and continue in both twenty-first-century fiction and thought (although there were many centuries during which there were no such books), thus making Lucretius's *On the Nature of the Universe* and Voltaire's *Candide* crucial texts in the long tradition of European ideas—and, it can be argued, this is because they stress pleasure as well as duty.

6 Link to *La commedia divina* (*The Divine Comedy*) by Dante Alighieri (1265–1321)

Although evidently not a spiritual venture, Candide's wanderings can nevertheless be compared with profit to Dante's journey. In both cases the actual route seems, if not predetermined, then at least to fall into a set pattern toward redemption. In almost every way Candide seems unworthy of both the punishments he suffers and the riches he occasionally receives.

Unlike Dante, Candide, sadly, has no sense of his inadequacy. Yet Candide is a survivor of a series of disasters. He has not left home by choice, unlike Dante, who, although lost, is also nevertheless in mid-life and is actively in search of a new way of life. Admittedly, Dante was also in exile like *Candide*. Candide is not on a hike or a climb in the sense of the fictional Dante, but rather he is a most-unprepared rambler. He is without a map, sufficient funds, appropriate clothes or boots, and certainly without a proper leader (Dante gets two: Virgil and later Beatrice, his earthly love who has transcended into a divinity herself, the Queen of Heaven; it is so marvelous when those we love do well).[38] Candide instead is a part of a game, but he is a pawn. Until the final chapters, he is not an active player in the game of his own life; he is a character with no rights whatsoever, with almost no opportunity to engage in decision making about the development of his own life. For most of this book, the demand for rights is made from repeated scenes demonstrating the manifest absence of rights. Candide is never in a position, mainly due to poverty, to make critical decisions that would test and hopefully strengthen him during the journey. He is not a pilgrim or a medieval knight, but rather a dispossessed, homeless person, with no way of knowing if his loved ones are even still alive, much less where they might be. Only in the conclusion does Candide begin to demonstrate some autonomy, even leadership, within his own sphere; only then is he in the proper state of mind to begin to demand his rights. It takes the entire book to lead him to that moment.

It certainly is easy, possibly even correct, to argue that the dominant theme of the entire work is suffering, and that the resurrections make suffering impossible to avoid. The endless, Dante-esque tortures, the non-stop poverty, pain, and loneliness of hell have started already on earth. The characters have little theory to turn to for consolation. Although Western theory is decidedly not a golden thread of optimism toward democracy and then perfectibility, nevertheless it can be described as a long, relatively unbroken tradition of study of the topics of justice and political arrangements, in particular, in this work. This is what Arthur Lovejoy termed the "great chain of being." Lovejoy further specifies that

> any unit-idea which the historian thus isolates he next seeks to trace through more than one—ultimately indeed, through all—of the provinces of history in which it figures in any important degree, whether those provinces are called philosophy, science, literature, art, religion, or politics.[39]

Scholars have repeatedly made use of this tradition in both their personal and professional lives, heeding a Platonic injunction that sensible men (and women, for Socrates) have a responsibility to reflect on good government and the good life itself. Thus reflection, even more than formal education, is necessary for any kind of political progress. The stress here is not so much on repeating theories, but on reflecting on them. All Candide has in the midst of strife, beatings, mockery, imprisonment, dashed hopes, and unwanted travel, are his own thoughts.

This book is so grounded in suffering that it seems to be the only universal experience. Yet the work indicates concern through direct and unwavering attention to the subject, not by way of overt sympathy. The possible release from suffering seemingly does not come from Western theory, but rather from participation in the developing modern economy (this is the case in Western Europe and in Latin America, even before the concluding chapter of *Candide*), partially because in the story (and of course in mid-eighteenth-century Europe), there are so few ways for the ordinary person to enter into the theoretical debate about suffering. In any case, for Candide the suffering is so great that easing it, at least, is his immediate concern, albeit on his way back to Cunégonde.

Yet in the midst of the many transit points, taverns, extended conversations with strangers, and the exhaustion of travel, Candide retains the familiar routine of academic debate; the suffering requires a routine to survive, and that routine almost indirectly sparks independent thought. Pangloss's monologues, recited at times in tandem with Candide—regardless of the positions taken, true or false, changing or stagnant—have a soothing quality, like a duet sung in harmony. Yet very quickly Candide realizes some startling exceptions to Pangloss's optimistic interpretation of world events, not just in his travel, but, in retrospect, back home in Westphalia. It is of interest that there is no attempt to find a new internal logic to the suffering, if Leibniz's reasons for it are to be dismissed. The suffering is simply the given of life, and anything beyond the adversities was viewed as a bonus. Optimism could thus be viewed not as self-delusion but as tenacity and drive.

7 Synopsis

Candide is one of those few books that defines its intellectual age. Although the most popular interpretation of this work is that it is an attack on the optimism of Leibniz, it can be argued that much of the substance of Voltaire's thought (especially on free will, individual responsibility, and human freedom) was also drawn from Leibniz. This is a crucial point because Voltaire's views on the perfectibility of the human mind are often discussed in terms of his response to Leibniz. Likewise, the fairly simple, however preposterous and distressing, plot and characters in *Candide* are not simply allegorical devices, with each character representing one theme (as is done so well in Bunyan's *The Pilgrim's Progress*). Rather, in *Candide*, each character functions as a symbol with multiple possible interpretations. Just as the mid-eighteenth century is often described in terms from *Candide*, so too could more recent study of the history of ideas be analyzed in terms of this short book.

II UNIFORMS, MONKEYS, AND RAVENOUS WOMEN

1 Montesquieu and Voltaire

Sex is everywhere in this book.[40] Candide is kicked out of Thunder-ten-tronckh, his home in Westphalia, for kissing Cunégonde, even though it was Cunégonde's idea after watching Pangloss and Pacquette doing the same, and more. Topics such as sexually-transmitted diseases, prostitution, Europeans having a low sex drive, and the courtesans of Paris are repeatedly raised.

As in the earlier novel by Montesquieu, *Les Lettres persanes* (*The Persian Letters*, 1721), sex is used in *Candide* not just as diversion or titillation, but also as a metaphor for civic relations.[41] The themes of travel, suffering, love, and persecution, and the intellectual concepts of toleration, good government, and a flourishing economy in this work could all be examined in terms the dynamic of human relations at all levels. All of these topics appear in Candide. This list reminds the reader of topics now generally referred to simply as Freudian. The emphasis in *Candide* is on the struggle in human inner nature, not just the battle in the state of nature between peoples who have no developed form of language and indeed no motivation to communicate with each other. Thus, more directly, the emphasis is on innate factors such as sexuality, and on learned responses such as being able to suppress any indication that the sex drive is at work. It is useful in a book about abstract ideas and competing theories also to have the reminder of structural aspects of human nature, such as sexual instincts, that do not always respond well to coaching.

Readers of *Candide* in 1759 would have made direct and apt comparisons between this work and Montesquieu's *Persian Letters*, from 38 years earlier. Montesquieu's book presents a fuller range of political notions than even his renowned *L'Esprit des lois* (*The Spirit of the Laws*, 1748), which, along with Locke's *Second Treatise of Government* (1690), is recognized as a major source for the American Constitution.[42]

It is less well known that *The Spirit of the Laws* was written to clarify some of the many political and religious topics that put *Les Lettres persanes* (*The Persian Letters*, 1721), set in the court of Louis XIV, on the Catholic Index of forbidden books. Montesquieu's book is partially set in a Persian harem, which is far from a stable environment (perhaps not surprising for a closed society). Instead it is the setting for ever-shifting power relationships among a husband away in Europe, the eunuchs, and the wives. And it is the two most beloved and, predictably, the most beautiful of the wives who prove to be the most rebellious against their own circumstances. The book plays on both female and male sexual fantasies as a means of upturning the traditional understanding of power relationships. For in this story, it is almost never the declared leader, the husband, who has authority even when he is at home in Persia, and certainly not when he is in Paris. The tension is often between the husband, traveling in Western Europe with his younger male friend, and the eunuchs, minding the wives at home in Persia.

The Persian Letters is presented in epistolary form, written in the form of letters, in this case between the two Persian men traveling abroad and the older Persian man's family of back at home. The book offers political alternatives from the different perspectives of these two Persian travelers. It becomes clear to the reader relatively quickly that the real power in the harem is vested in the eunuchs—varying by color, with the blacker one, and thus the least western-European-looking one, having the most power—and in the wives, not in the husband. The arguments in *The Persian Letters* foreshadow Frantz Fanon's works: *Peau noire, masques blancs* (*Black Skins, White Masks*, 1952), which stresses the difficulty in substantiating the historical past of a black civilization, and also his *Les Damnés de la terre* (*The Wretched of the Earth*, 1961), which scrutinizes the limitations defining national culture without paying constructive attention to race. The dynamic in the harem in Montesquieu's *Persian Letters* indicates that it is not enough—in fiction or in life—to know who is in power (the name of the king, for example), but it is at least as critical to now who advises the one in power (and that could be, to give several textual examples from Montesquieu, an aristocratic friend, a paid servant, or even a wife).[43] Thus in *The Persian Letters*, even before his classic theoretical work, *The Spirit of the Laws*, there is a notion of a more balanced form of government. It might be worthwhile to consider *Candide*, published a year after Montesquieu's *The Spirit of the Laws*, as the means that eventually propels France to the much later, post-Revolutionary stage of political development sketched out in such detail, in fiction and then in theory, first by Montesquieu in fiction.

2 Orientalism

The Persian Letters forced Europeans to think, perhaps for the first time, about the role of women in their own society. In the exoticism of Montesquieu's Persian women, "Orientalism" cannot be denied. Edward Said defines Orientalism as "a style of thought based upon an ontological and epistemological distinction between 'the Orient' and (most of the time) 'the Occident.' "[44] In *The Persian Letters*, most of the women of the harem are gorgeous, demanding, and outspoken. The book, however, does present women of different types, physically, mentally, and temperamentally. And it gives a fuller range of types of women than was to be found in earlier European literature, even to the extent of giving the Persian women their own names.

Surprisingly, in a story about women incarcerated in a harem in Persia, and vapid society women in Paris, the book contains at least three constructive points about the treatment of women, and about power relations more generally. First, the women in this book are not caricatures; they vary in age, nationality, mental ability, and beauty. It is not news that some women are regarded as superior to others in a lifelong beauty contest, but note that in this book there is no single model for how women are to appear or to act. Second, the women, especially the Persian women, but also the Parisian women, are not just sexual objects, they are sexual creatures, with their own physical desires and the decision-making abilities of adults. Third, the influence of some of the wives over the eunuchs (the eunuchs are supposedly ruling the wives) is again a good reminder that the titular head of any state is not necessarily the one with the power by law—it could easily be a relative, a lover, or an unofficial adviser.

Voltaire's audience would have expected many of these same features to be present in his work, and *Candide* is certainly another study of Paris through the lens of very alien parts of the world. These two books, however, should not simply be given credit for adding to traditional political theory, and they cannot be dismissed for their stereotypical views on women. The multiple levels of women's experience in these works certainly challenge the traditional attitudes toward women, foreign and French, and thus begin to develop theories about the domestic sphere. *Candide*, as opposed to *The Persian Letters*, follows a more traditional story line of Europeans traveling around the world in search of adventure and enlightenment. Nevertheless, it presents the story of a young man who instead finds repeated suffering and only the growing realization that his idolized teacher is wholly wrong both about the world order and about the proper way to behave as philosophers and as men of the world.[45]

3 Now to the Uniforms

Perhaps Candide's greatest obsession is with uniforms, which helps to explain his fixation on soldiers and priests.[46] Candide is chivvied and harassed by uniformed men at all stages and in every country. He wants very much to best Cunégonde's brother, who becomes not only the new baron upon his father's death but also a colonel, as well as a Jesuit, thus rising to the top in society, the military, and the Church. Candide is not rebelling against the power structures embodied by uniforms, but more prosaically against his own inability to thrive in such systems. His fixation with these power figures is not that of a disgruntled academic, or a proto-revolutionary leader, but rather of a frustrated member of *la petite bourgeoisie* (a term often used pejoratively, for the small, petty class of workers). Candide could thus be viewed as an early role model for the *sans-culottes* of the French Revolution, rather than as a Lenin figure who would organize such people in the Russian Revolution. Candide would join a revolution only once it was already in progress and the revolutionaries seemed likely to win. This is surprisingly akin to Hobbes, at his most conservative, on revolution: it is acceptable to join a revolution only when the victory of the rebels seems inevitable, and then the imperative is to choose a new absolute monarch as soon as possible.

Candide's anger is that these uniformed men are the ones who make the decisions for all, notably decisions about marriage. Marriages in the eighteenth century were almost never the result of personal decisions by the two to be married, but were the subject of prolonged family negotiations, at times involved the transfer of substantial family property, and had to be sanctioned by the Church. Thus, from Candide's perspective, these uniformed men not only facilitate the continuation of established institutions, they also receive the pick of the desirable women whenever they please, in and out of wedlock. The division of power is not only gendered, but is also divided along status lines, especially class lines. At this time most men (and all women) would never have such authority and license as the uniformed male authority figures have.

The lessons learned from the Jesuit brother are altogether different from those acquired from the other characters; they offer a constructive, conservative interpretation of society. Cunégonde's Jesuit brother, a native of Westphalia, could not have been predicted to be either Protestant or Catholic (as neither religion was dominant, adding to the ambiguity of the setting). Cunégonde's brother's expedient behavior in the New World, his willingness to become both a Jesuit and a military officer, thus showing a penchant for uniforms, should not mask the recognition that he is the only one of the main characters who maintains loyalty to the *mores* of his aristocratic family of origin, albeit by refusing to allow Candide to marry his sister. Even though the text gives relatively few details about the cut or style of the uniforms, the reader is repeatedly told which uniform the latest authority figure is wearing. The success of Candide's assembly of an adopted family should not altogether diminish an appreciation of the Jesuit brother's desire to care for his sister in the way that he judges most appropriate. The book thus features both traditional and radical lifestyles as legitimate choices.

4 And the Monkeys

The rapid transition in this book from religious intolerance to killing monkeys is not difficult to follow, for the book constantly tests the limits of the readers' tolerance for those unlike themselves. It is Candide who shoots the monkeys (with a double-barreled Spanish revolver) he spots hanging onto two naked, young women in the jungle, over the border from Paraguay.[47] Cacambo then has to explain to Candide that he has not killed animals who were supposedly pestering the girls, he has killed the girls' lovers. The pairing here of two girls and two monkeys is very much part of the fabric of fantasy in the story. Nevertheless, the prime, perhaps only, example in the story of women sexually satisfied by their lovers is that of these two young women who choose to go not with the men of their village but with animals.[48]

Eighteenth-century French literature takes no prisoners on the theme of sexual proclivities; the combination of sexual satisfaction and love is presented as possible, if not probable, in both texts. Besides Voltaire's example of bestiality (the girls and the monkeys), in Montesquieu's *Persian Letters* the only example of true romantic and sexual love is between a brother and a sister.[49] Even though the one example is of sex with a creature too far removed, and the other of sex with someone too close, both examples emphasize the inflexible boundaries for appropriate human sexual behavior and the somewhat arbitrary nature of these choices—random in terms of the choice of boundaries set by society and also the choices made by the girls. It is of interest that the men of the girls' village defend the young women's choices, if not their dead monkey-boyfriends, at least against the intruders. For the Oreillon men defend the girls and their losses, irrespective of the type of lovers that have been lost. The implication here is perhaps that only in a place so far from civilization would young women be allowed to make their own sexual decisions and not be punished for it; the book shows surprising respect for such freedom.

Montesquieu and Voltaire both use the topic of bestiality to catch the readers' attention and also to force the reader to reassess established norms. Voltaire employs the theme of bestiality both to transgress normal social conventions and to demonstrate fairly straightforward human responses, such as deep grief when a loved one is lost, however unworthy others might view the love object. Candide and Cacambo leave the girls weeping over the bodies of the monkeys. After Candide's inability to show emotion at the sight of countless dead human beings, the dead monkeys, even ones he himself has killed, certainly have no power to move him. It is possible that Candide does recognize the monkeys as the girls' lovers, that his response is immediate and violent, and that perhaps his jealousy was even keener because the monkeys were so unlike himself. However, after he shoots the monkeys, the problem is not that animals have been killed, but that the girls' lovers have been killed, and Cacambo's concern is, appropriately, that they move on quickly from the scene of the slaughter.

Monkeys have been repeatedly used in European literature and popular culture to represent wild men. There is supposedly even a marvelous story, from as recently as the French Revolution, in which two monkeys, washed up on the shore of northern England, who were executed for being French spies. Thus, the monkeys in this Voltairean tale might represent Rousseauian men in the wild (or perhaps, for Voltaire, Rousseau in the wild), thus referencing Rousseau's theory of *le bon sauvage* (the noble savage) in the state of nature. Voltaire's view of Rousseau's state of nature was typically rude: "*On n'a jamais tant employé d'esprit à vouloir nous render Bêtes. Il prend envie de marcher à quatre pattes quand on lit votre ouvrage*"—that is, reading Rousseau made Voltaire want to get down on all fours like a wild beast.[50] In *Candide*, the monkeys caricature Rousseau's noble savages; they are not constrained by rules and social conventions, even of tribal society, and they are beloved by their girlfriends.

Perhaps Candide's strong response to the monkeys represents not only a fear of miscegenation, but also a fear of pregnancy—childbearing as a capability, a form of power, which women have, and men do not. He may even fear the result of such a union. Overall, the monkeys, alive or dead, symbolize the inability of couples outside of the accepted parameters to find a place where they will be left alone by others, couples who do not have a home of their own, who do not fit into each other's worlds, and who wander instead, separately, together, and then, alas, separately again. The dead monkeys might well also symbolize a generation slaughtered not even for a specific cause, just on a whim, and by a foreigner.

The animals thus represent not only foreigners, but also what is regarded as foreign in human nature, thus the oddities of human nature. The monkeys are literal targets for the insecurities of peoples who are not at all sure of their place in the world, whether they have settled homes or not. The monkeys serve as the icon for wandering peoples of all sorts, many of them at war with each other. Thus the book certainly acknowledges those whom Eric Wolf calls "the people without history," thus showing sympathy not only for those locked within arbitrary systems but also for those who are supposedly living outside of society.[51]

Although the monkeys could be viewed as Rousseauian noble savages (an interpretation perhaps intended by Voltaire), more directly, the book could be viewed as putting forward the monkeys as an overt means to target the practice of slavery.[52] There was an ongoing debate among the French *lumières* regarding the moral basis of slavery as an economic institution, including a consideration of the right to revolt. Their studies tend to center on the role of the colonial administrators, the relationship between colonialism and ideas of civilization, and the reception of the colonial power by the indigenous peoples.

The direct response of the Oreillon men to the killing of the young women's monkeys is to defend their women. They go after Candide and Cacambo, crying, "We will have a Jesuit for dinner. We will have a Jesuit for dinner." Candide and Cacambo are now identified with the Jesuits. This is not altogether surprising, given that Candide is wearing Jesuit robes throughout this scene. Cacambo had taken the Jesuit gown from the body of Cunégonde's brother, even the square *biretta* from his head (the brother is presumed dead at this point), and has put them on Candide. This is yet another shrewd move on Cacambo's part to gain them cover. However, symbolically, this garb could be interpreted as Candide's penance for yet another, earlier murder. And, even without necessarily recognizing the exact religious garb, the Oreillons know that the Jesuits were the most likely foreigners to be visiting this area.[53] Cacambo persuades the Oreillons that they are not Jesuits. (Despite their historical role in protecting the Paraguayan indigenes from Brazilian slave traders Jesuits are portrayed in this book as everyone's enemy, more generally the Jesuits serve as the symbol of arbitrary, self-serving church power in Europe and the New World. This had more to do with the role of the Jesuits in France and Europe than in the New World.) In any case, in *Candide*, once free of the Jesuitical taint, Candide and Cacambo are set free and offered girls, although presumably not the original two girls, even though they are now available. It is of interest to speculate on why the Oreillons were so easy to pacify. Perhaps they have limited concern for the monkeys, especially after establishing to their satisfaction that Candide and Cacambo were not Jesuits. For, at one stage of Ch. XIV, there is the suggestion from Cacambo that the dead monkeys are actually part human, Spanish speakers, just to complicate the story. In any case, the Oreillons are dealt with quickly in the story, and the focus shifts from the monkeys to Candide and Cacambo once again. Even though the emphasis changes rather quickly from the girls' loss to determining the identity of these enemies of the tribe, the Oreillons' defense of the women and implicitly of their choices is clear. The two young Oreillon women should perhaps be viewed as the only women in the story who are satisfied, however briefly.

5   Finally, to the Ravenous Women

The assumption throughout the book is that the women have active, sometimes voracious sexual appetites, thus bringing a touch of reality to an otherwise preposterous story, all the while shocking readers with its subject matter. Pacquette and Cunégonde both demonstrate this even as girls at Castle Thunder-ten-tronckh. Throughout the story, girls and women of all ages are not docile creatures, but rather sturdy, if somewhat disheveled ones, who wish to have a normal life in all respects, including a healthy sex life. This characterization is diametrically opposed to Rousseau's notion of girls as listless, dreary creatures, without good minds. It explodes the Rousseauian view of women in *Émile* as lacking both high intellect and high sexual energy. Certainly the numerous eighteenth-century cartoons of Voltaire himself hopping in and out of bed with a great number of different women indicate that he perhaps rejoiced in this combination of characteristics in himself. (In the Louvre today, the most prominent statue of Voltaire is of *Voltaire nu*; he is probably the only modern thinker to be found there not wearing clothes.) Voltaire did tend, like most thinkers, to view the abstract individual, even the abstract female, as very much like himself. Perhaps for him the abstract female was, if not in all ways like him, then very much like the blue-stocking (the eighteenth-century English term for intellectual women), academic, aristocratic, and rather impressive women with whom he chose to spend so much of his time, not all of it in bed.

Rather than being passive, repressed creatures, the major female characters in *Candide* of all ages, classes, and income brackets show a lively concern for sex, and for control of their own lives. The women's attitude can be explained in two respects. First, there is the stereotyped view (later termed Victorian) dictating the hiding of the body, the female body in particular, and toward suppressing even the discussion of sex, much less public displays of affection. Second, such repression, Foucault maintained, is based on the assumption that girls and women have both urges and powers that must be controlled, not that they are passive. The women in *Candide* are not so much in talking about sex, but specifically in getting it for themselves, with the partners they choose.

Voltaire was attacking not just his Parisian rival, but also one of the major thinkers about childhood education of their century. The contrast between Rousseau and Voltaire on the topics of both women's development and of sex is startling, especially remembering that Rousseau was regarded as one of the great writers of his century on education.[54] The Rousseauian attitude of deliberate sexual inhibition to be instilled in children, most especially in girls, indicates how wholly Rousseau was convinced that society had fallen from its golden age in the state of nature, the time of *"le bon sauvage."* Although an emphasis on the state of nature does not directly link a thinker to a particular attitude toward women, Rousseau maintains that the state of nature is a polite fiction, and he uses it to explain the transition to, and extreme problems of, modern society, many of which he believed were caused by women.[55] In contrast, Hobbes apparently believes in his historical version of the state of nature when human lives were "nasty, brutish, and short." Hobbes asserts that this odious situation could recur at any time, if there were no absolute monarchy. Hobbes stresses power, not gender, although the links between the two seem almost too obvious to mention, especially in the early-modern period, when women had no legal rights. In any case, according to Rousseau, the ennobled, abstract individual of the state of nature is no longer possible in modern society. Instead, a highly organized form of representative government, in which the few administers for the good of all, is the proper Rousseauian medicine—even if there is no cure—for modern society.

For Rousseau this democratic form of government, based on the social contract, was grounded on sexual inhibition of girls and women. This attitude is still best expressed by the advice, repeatedly attributed to Queen Victoria, that nineteenth-century English mothers supposedly gave their daughters about their wedding nights: "Close your eyes and think of England," (which is actually an Edwardian parody of Victorianism). In any case, to the contrary, the story of the girls and women in *Candide* demonstrates the Foucauldian view of Victorianism: only a society so obsessed by sex would have invented so many rules to try to suppress and supposedly to crush this instinct.[56] *Candide* is the story of women who have the capacity to think and plan with deliberation, knowingly following the pleasure principle, and their own choices. The intense concern for bodily pleasure, primarily for sex, could be linked throughout this work with constructive decision making by women in other spheres of life, even in the political realm.

The women in *Candide* tell their own stories, in their own voices. The book is unusual for its time in treating the female and male characters in similar, non-judgmental terms. Also, unlike the pattern outlined by

Carol Gilligan in *In Her Own Voice: Psychological Theory and Women's Development* (which focuses on girls in the late twentieth century), the girls and women in *Candide* are neither muzzled by adolescence nor paralyzed by their circumstances.[57] Somehow in the midst of their extremities, including forced prostitution, they are more vocal than they would have been at home. Pacquette, the maid from Castle Thunder-ten-tronckh, becomes a prostitute, and she demonstrates remarkable powers of survival, even in this tale of repeated, surprise resurrections and reunions. Her fall into prostitution was foreshadowed by her seduction by, or tryst with, Pangloss, before they were driven out of the Castle. It is the reader's first glimpse of these two characters, and it comes from Cunégonde's perspective: "Dr. Pangloss behind some bushes giving a lesson in experimental physics to her mother's waiting woman."[58] The book never lets the reader fall into the trap of accepting that it is only in foreign travel that we are likely to be taken advantage of by accident or by premeditation, or that only strangers perpetrate such attacks. Rather, this book asserts that this is at least as likely to happen to those with little power at home.[59] This incident could be viewed as the resident scholar at Castle Thunder-ten-tronckh casually raping, certainly exploiting, a servant girl. The alternative possibility is that Pacquette participates very happily in this experiment, and is not necessarily receiving any new instructions, but perhaps giving them to this unworldly scholar.

Whichever interpretation of Pacquette's time with Pangloss is accepted, she can nevertheless be read as an alternative model of the new world traveler: a modern woman, earning her own money (albeit by prostitution, still practically the only paid profession, certainly the most portable one, for a woman in the eighteenth century), and both embody the concept of hope. Pacquette is willing to do whatever it takes to survive; this resilience is demonstrated by her own resistance to the sexually transmitted disease that she first gets from Pangloss, and then passes on to many of her customers. The consequence of her sexual exploits seems not to be based on a hatred of men. She is not a wronged woman deliberately wreaking damage on everyone around her. She is nevertheless a carrier of the disease, and sometimes the ruination of the men who get very close to her. Unlike female characters from picaresque novels (for example, Courage in the Simplician Cycle), Pacquette must be so intent on surviving that she is never able to become wealthy or settled, although eventually she has the same improved fortune as the main characters in the conclusion.

In accord with most of Western literature and theory, the women in this story tend to be mentioned only in terms of male lust or, occasionally, as male love objects. However, these women get far more attention, even lines, than the women in the much longer *Don Quixote* and *Simplicissimus*, and certainly than those in *Gulliver's Travels*. The women in Candide's entourage have names that do not change, they have views of their own, and they are given entire chapters to tell their life stories and to debate their personal philosophies. The women in *Candide* seem not so much to be unsatisfied, sexually and otherwise, with their lives, but rather to be in pain. Yet at the same time, even in the midst of hideous suffering, the lead women are always self-contained. Their almost aristocratic sense of internal balance certainly does not come from privileged circumstances. This self-assured attitude is even shared by Pacquette, the maid turned prostitute, not just by the obviously upper-class Cunégonde and *la vieille*, the Old Woman, the proud daughter of a pope. Each has a vision of the past and present blending into the future that makes sense to her. Their adventures can be distinguished from those of the lead men as they cover less ground, and their situation throughout is linked directly to their physical appearance.

The Old Woman is not treated as a sex object anymore, although she recounts stories of remarkable sexual and physical abuse from the time when she was apparently strikingly attractive. She seemingly does not have a personal name at all, undoubtedly because she is old and supposedly no longer a desired, sought-after woman. Also, as she repeatedly announces, she has lost one buttock, making her both genuinely disabled and an object of ridicule. Meanwhile the younger and clearly named characters Cunégonde and Pacquette are used as sex toys. Both become prostitutes, although, because of class differences, their experiences vary markedly. Yet none of the three women has been worn down.

A feminist reading of this story would emphasize that a class analysis is not sufficient to distinguish the story of the female characters from that of the male characters. For all the women, regardless of class, the entire story is one of hope of regaining their original situation before they were forced out of their homes, even though their former lives were ones of genteel subservience at best. At no point in the story, except perhaps in the conclusion, is there even the risible proposal that there might be an equal, or even equitable, division of political and economic power between women and men.[60]

In terms of equity, there is not even a sense of the development of separate spheres for women and men as put forward by Christine de Pizan in *Le Livre de la cité des dames (The Book of the City of Ladies*, 1405). Christine was perhaps the first person to make her living by translation and writing, doing this at the French court in order to support her mother and children after the deaths of her father and husband. Christine reworks the Augustinian behemoth of a book, *The City of God*, and writes of a sphere, perhaps spiritual and personal, more than political but certainly intellectual, where women can be themselves, and thus not always on guard against the enemy, apparently often a male relative. Thus Christine serves as an early source for two arguments competing arguments: separate spheres for women and female independence, both of which are relevant to Virginia Woolf's 1929 *A Room of One's Own*.

Yet the female characters in *Candide* might be better linked to Christine's much more pragmatic work, *Le Trésor de la cité des dames (The Treasure of the City of Ladies)*, which gives women of every social class—from princesses to prostitutes—practical and cynical advice about how to survive in an unhelpful and inhospitable world.[61] (By implication, for example, young wives are urged to put up with the failings of their husbands by thinking of their husbands as slightly backward younger brothers.) Thus *Candide* can be compared with profit to some of the unconventional works of European thought and literature. This includes both the genre of the fool and survival manuals that masqueraded as books of etiquette, such as those from Christine de Pizan.

In a more eccentric interpretation, if Candide were taken to be female rather than male, the reading of the book seems sadly more positive. Her devotion to Pangloss might then seem explicitly sexual (and perhaps understandable, if Pangloss were not the object). Or, instead, Pangloss might be more overtly a father figure for this orphan who never knew either parent, whom she doted on, never mind his views or his state of mind. Her lack of education, in 1759, would be understandable for a girl, and some would see her slow development toward self-sufficiency as admirable for having occurred at all. Her desire to replicate her family of origin by marrying someone she knew in her childhood also would be deemed sensible. Her willingness first to try to kill her future brother-in-law and later to sell him off certainly seems callous, but she is staying true to her master plan of marrying Cunégonde (so now the interpretation is breaking down). Thus, she is logical like a machine, rather than intuitive about what would be best for her at any given stage. The life of a French courtesan, offered to Cunégonde herself as an option, might have been better than that of a peasant wife in the countryside. Her devotion to Cunégonde is impressive, as is her ability to filter out the nonsense of the intervening years when they were separated.

The question then presents itself of a female Candide's same-sex attraction to Cunégonde, which would then have to be addressed as part of a deliberate set of choices that would certainly not be rewarded by society at large. Thus, if Candide is read as female, she seems high functioning, whereas if read as male, he seems quite the reverse. This highlights the expectations for girls as not only different, but clearly much lower, if more constructive.

A less colorful distinction than a sex change for the main character has to do with education. This differentiation goes beyond the different social status of women and men; the key distinction for Candide, whether female or male, is how to be accepted by society. A female Candide is more explicable as a Topsy in the making. Topsy is, of course, the outrageous, high-spirited young female slave from St. Clare's plantation in *Uncle Tom's Cabin* (1852). If Candide is the worst possible student in Western literature, then Topsy is perhaps the best. She is difficult, strong willed, and does not give false respect to her supposed superiors. The vital missing ingredient in Candide, female or male, is spirit, which could be demonstrated either by fighting or debate. More charitably, this should not be seen as a lack of character in Candide, but as a difference in style and timing. Candide demonstrates the ability to move many times and to survive without changing who he is at the core. Thus he adapts and learns how to survive so that he can perhaps eventually thrive. Candide might, in this regard, be viewed as androgynous, a mixture of stereotypical female and male positive qualities. Education is clearly posited here as a means of overcoming deficiencies created by structural differences, including gender.

A distinction in personal style can be extended beyond personality types and varying life situations (even though both Candide and Topsy experienced forms of slavery) to embrace different ways of learning and producing one's own work. Candide could be compared to Beethoven, having to experience events over and over to make them his own, just as Beethoven wrote his music in multiple drafts. Topsy is like Mozart. She is able to form conclusions quickly and to make them clear to others rapidly, akin to Mozart's form of frenetic overnight composition.[62] In this interpretation, Candide, female or male, should be recognized as an individual who has managed, against literally impossible odds (just remember how many times he is killed and then resurrected) to achieve a personal and professional life that has some dignity, and has done so by means of a personal style that is always time-consuming and unrewarding.

Thus the remaining question is if Candide, if read as a woman, is satisfied. The political implications of recognizing different individual approaches could already be seen as part of the Enlightenment; this is in opposition to the view that the Enlightenment was producing supposedly better individuals with a cookie-cutter pattern of Modernist ideals. In this work, as in so many others later in the nineteenth century, the subjects of women, money, and independence are used as a *segue* to a larger debate concerning individual liberty for children, women, and men. Even if this book does not spell out more proactive alternatives for marginalized people in society, it does give damning criticism of their current situations and asserts the ability of human beings to survive despite determined efforts to crush them.

6 Link to François Rabelais's *Gargantua and Pantagruel* (1532–1546)

In addition to *Simplicissimus*, an earlier, French model for *Candide* can be found in Rabelais's salacious stories of father and son giants, Gargantua and Pantagruel.[63] They were both born in France and travel back and forth to Utopia (sometimes set in Asia, and sometimes near Paris) in the midst of the typically casual university education of the sixteenth century. Their lifelong pursuits are drinking, eating, whoring, and killing, in any order. All of this is portrayed by means of an atmosphere that Leo Spitzer has called "*le prétendu réalisme*" ("the pretend, so-called realism").[64] Rabelais employs the notion of a utopia, an idea very much in vogue at the time because of the relatively recent publication of Thomas More's *Utopia* in 1516. Rabelais makes use of the concept of a utopia not as a means of propagating a specific political theory, but as the opportunity to include yet another of his dazzling story-telling devices, and also as a means of exploring a range of practical political options for society. Erich Auerbach has rightly quibbled with the anti-Christian interpretation of this ribald book. Auerbach's own analysis, in his great chapter in *Mimesis*, "The World in Pantagruel's Mouth," is that Rabelais's writing should be read not as anti-Christian but as pre-Christian, indeed pagan.[65] This takes Rabelais's fiction beyond a criticism of the established Catholic hierarchy into the realm of preliterate mythology. In the midst of the Protestant Reformation and the Wars of Religion, Rabelais, like the later German writer, Grimmelshausen, concentrated virtually without exception on aspects of human nature that are generally viewed as unattractive. Generally, Rabelais scholars argue that Voltaire underestimated Rabelais, for there are many direct constructive connections between the two. Voltaire not only praised Rabelais as providing "*la peinture du monde la plus vive*" ("the most lively painting of the world") in a letter he wrote just months before writing *Candide*, and he also used many of the same literary devices as Rabelais.[66] Both writers employed preposterous means to teach their telling object lessons.

7 Link to Mario Vargas Llosa's *El Hablador* (*The Storyteller*, 1987)

Repeatedly, the suffering in this work leads not just to death but, often, to resurrections, numerous resurrections, of the same characters. There must be some purpose in Voltaire's killing off most of his characters, at least temporarily, and sometimes in countless numbers. Surely he was not writing only in jest, in order to remind us that our enemies will always be with us. (For example, Voltaire's hatred of critics can be found in *Candide* in his acid comments about publishers, and about the Jesuits and their publishers.) However, it is not Voltaire's enemies, or the enemies of the main characters, but the main characters themselves who suffer the most in *Candide*. These killings are of a different order than natural and man-made disasters. For this small band of individuals there will always be a rescue, although, incredibly, they never recognize that they will always survive, or indeed any other pattern. The reader wonders how the main characters might have lived their lives differently if they had known that they could not be permanently killed. Whereas bravery could be seen as deliberately proceeding despite the odds, it is not at all clear that the central characters deliberately chose to withstand the repeated assaults on them (their salvation always seems to happen by chance), nor is it clear which qualities were the ones that allowed the main characters to survive. Hope does not seem to be the correct answer. Their level of dissatisfaction is always so marked that happiness seems inconceivable. If good is to come from suffering, the question then is not would more general good accrue from even greater suffering, but rather what exactly is the good we are striving, suffering, to obtain?

The Voltairean theme of preposterous resurrections has been employed with style in modern literature as well. Mario Vargas Llosa in his novel, *El Hablador (The Storyteller*, 1987), writes of a Peruvian visitor to Florence who spots a photograph of a supposedly long-dead friend in an exhibit of recent photographs of the Machiguenga people from his own country.[67] Slowly this character begins to perceive his own culture as contributing to the removal of native Indians from their own land. A well-known producer of documentary films, albeit on a low budget, he nevertheless hopes for a substantial popular audience for what becomes his exotic and anti-modern subject. The affirmation of the process of intimately knowing peoples who either have never been exposed to civilization and/or who have resisted civilization goes beyond a straightforward desire to render intelligible the existing form of government in terms of the progress gained by that society.

The Peruvian novel advocates neither the assimilation of these native people nor the utopian preservation of them, but rather proposes new possibilities for those who still want to live such a pre-technological lifestyle. *El Hablador* shares many constructive characteristics of William Golding's *The Inheritors* (1955), a book explicitly influenced by Golding's reading of Vico, who argued for the distinctive qualities of early peoples, sometimes positive qualities that were lost in later stages of civilization. In addition, Vico, Voltaire, and Vargas Llosa apparently share the expectation that contact between different stages of the same culture will reveal ways of thinking that will both better explain modern patterns and possibly also lead to some direct and constructive suggestions for modern, as well as pre-modern, society.

8 Synopsis

Candide makes many of its intellectual points through the guise of sexuality, yet it does not diminish the attraction of sexuality, of physical pleasure, itself. Montesquieu and Voltaire employed the heightened sexual activity of their main characters as a means of showing both corruption and isolation in society, yet sex is always presented in tandem with the strong desire (even, indeed especially, from the Old Woman with one buttock, who declares that "I have wanted to kill myself a hundred times but I am somehow still in love with life") for a complete life in the present, not just in some abstract future.[68] The uniforms that appear throughout *Candide* reinforce established authority structures in the same way that they do more recently in theater (as in Bertolt Brecht) or in film (as in Rainer Werner Fassbinder). Likewise, the symbolism of animals—especially monkeys—is used to accentuate unresolved questions both about human sexuality and about the actual limits of the extension of political rights and human rights. The many ravenous women in this book are clear examples of individuals who manage not to be repressed and apathetic despite the most revolting circumstances. The fierce desire of these women to have a balanced, rich, contented life never goes away, supporting the Epicurean interpretation of this work of fiction that there is much more to life than suffering. Indeed, the shift in taste in French literature from the earthiness of Rabelais to the intellectual wit of Voltaire is not as stark as one might initially think. The emphasis on sexuality in *Candide* is perhaps the most powerful example of the book's strong Enlightenment argument that all people be given the freedom to pursue their own life choices.

NOTES

1 Thank you to Catherine Labio and Ellen (Puffin) D'Oench for their detailed comments on this chapter.

   The critical edition is Voltaire, *Candide* in *The Complete Works of Voltaire/ Les Oeuvres complètes de Voltaire*, René Pomeau, ed. (Oxford: The Voltaire Foundation at the Taylor Institution, 1980), vol. 48. For an English translation, I have chosen Voltaire, *Candide*, John Butt, tr. (London: Penguin, 1947). Quotations and citations are from the Pomeau French edition and the Butt English translation.

2 W. H. Barber, *Leibniz in France from Arnauld to Voltaire: A Study in French Reactions to Leibnizianism, 1670–1760*, p. 235.

3 See Laurence Brockliss, *French Higher Education in the Seventeenth and Eighteenth Centuries*. Also see Anne Goldgar, *Impolite Learning: Conduct and Community in the Republic of Letters, 1680–1750*, and Jonathan Israel, *Radical Enlightenment: Philosophy and the Making of Modernity, 1650–1750*.

4 In *Julie*, the main letter-writers—Julie, her lover Saint-Preux, and her eventual husband, the older Wolmar—are all presented as having admirable qualities (despite the husband's atheism). The backdrop is the story of the medieval lovers Abélard and Héloïse (both intellectual and strong willed, they are permanently separated; yet later, when they are both in the Church, they become passionate correspondents, writing each other intensely about personal and theoretical subjects).

5 Jean-Jacques Rousseau, *Julie, ou La Nouvelle Héloïse*. See also Judith Shklar, *Men and Citizens: A Study of Rousseau's Social Theory*.

6 Roger Pearson, *The Fables of Reason: A Study of Voltaire's 'Contes philosophiques.'*

7 Adam Smith, *Theory of Moral Sentiments*, III.2.11, p. 120.

8 See Michèle Duchet, *Anthropologie et Histoire au siècle des lumières*, esp. ch. 2, on Voltaire.

9 Cecilia Miller, "Defenders of the truth," Review of Darrin M. McMahon, *Enemies of the Enlightenment: The French Counter-Enlightenment and the Making of Modernity*, in *The Times Literary Supplement*.

10 The later works include, in particular, Thomas Carlyle's *Sartor Resartus* (1833–1844), which also targeted social injustice and the reform movements of the late eighteenth and nineteenth centuries. Not surprisingly, Carlyle was also much influenced by *Gulliver's Travels*. In turn, *Sartor Resartus* was a major influence on Romantic and early twentieth-century writers.

11 *Pace* Alan Kors. See Pearson, *Voltaire Almighty: A Life in Pursuit of Freedom*.

12 Darrin M. McMahon, *Enemies of the Enlightenment*.

13 On Cacambo, see Voltaire, *Candide*, Pomeau, ed., ch. XIV, #1–11, p. 168. Butt, tr., ch. XIV, p. 61.

14 Thank you to Amanda Thieroff.
15 Christopher Miller, *The French Atlantic Triangle: Literature and the Culture of the Slave Trade*, on Voltaire's own complicated views on the question of slavery.
16 See Pearson, *Voltaire Almighty: A Life in Pursuit of Freedom*.
17 On this atmosphere, see Daniel Gordon, *Citizens Without Sovereignty: Equality and Sociability in French Thought, 1670–1789*.
18 See Gottfried Wilhelm Leibniz, *Theodicy: Essays on the Goodness of God, the Freedom of Man, and the Origin of Evil*. For more on Leibniz, distinct from Voltaire's usage of him, see Matthew L. Jones, *The Good Life in Scientific Revolution: Descartes, Pascal, Leibniz, and the Cultivation of Virtue*. Also see Nicholas Jolley, ed., *The Cambridge Companion to Leibniz*. Thank you to Jeffrey Barnouw for his comments on Voltaire and Leibniz.
19 Voltaire, *Candide*. Pomeau, ed., ch. XIX, #52–55, p. 196; and Butt, tr., ch. XIX, p. 86.
20 Voltaire, *Candide*, Pomeau, ed., ch. III, #45–50, pp. 127–128. Butt, tr., ch. III, pp. 26–27.
21 Thank you to Jeffrey Barnouw.
22 See Leibniz, *Political Writings*, Patrick Riley, tr., ed. and Leibniz, *Philosophical Essays*, Roger Ariew and Daniel Garber, trs.
23 Richard A. Brooks, *Voltaire and Leibniz*, p. 14.
24 W. H. Barber, *Leibniz in France from Arnauld to Voltaire*, p. 212.
25 Barber, *Leibniz in France from Arnauld to Voltaire*, p. 215.
26 Barber, *Leibniz in France from Arnauld to Voltaire*, pp. 210–243.
27 Barber, *Leibniz in France from Arnauld to Voltaire*, p. 237.
28 Barber, *Leibniz in France from Arnauld to Voltaire*, p. 243.
29 Brooks, *Voltaire and Leibniz*, p. 25.
30 Most of this information comes from articles in Theodore E. D. Braun and John B. Radner, eds., *The Lisbon Earthquake of 1755: Representations and Reactions*. See especially the articles by Malcolm Jack, "Destruction and Regeneration, Lisbon, 1755" and Robert G. Ingram, "'The Trembling Earth is God's Herald': Earthquakes, Religion and Public Life in Britain during the 1750s."
31 Linda Colley, *Captives: Britain, Empire and the World, 1600–1850*.
32 Roger Pearson, *The Fables of Reason*, ch. 8, esp. pp. 112–115.
33 Some of this same debate about free will and the environment, indeed about chance, can be found in Hegel's *Phänomenologie des Geistes* (*Phenomenology of Spirit*, 1807).
34 W. H. Barber, *Leibniz in France from Arnauld to Voltaire*, pp. 107–122, esp. pp. 109–110.
35 Barber, *Leibniz in France from Arnauld to Voltaire*, pp. 113, 122.
36 Alexander Pope, *An Essay on Man: Moral Essays and Satires*, X, the last 4 lines. From Project Gutenburg.
37 Baldassare Castiglione, *The Book of the Courtier*. Voltaire was certainly not the first to lampoon Castiglione. See, for example, Pietro Aretino's sixteenth-century parody of Castiglione's *Il cortigiano* (*The Courtier*, written 1513–1518, published in 1528). Aretino's play was titled *La cortigiana* (*The Courtesan*, published 1534).
38 See Marina Warner, *Alone of All Her Sex: The Myth and Cult of the Virgin Mary*. A link could also be made to the earth-goddess of Egypt and Babylonia and the Greek goddess Artemis. According to Bertrand Russell, "Christianity transformed her into the Virgin Mary," and this could bring together Dante's earthly love for Beatrice with her translation into the Queen of Heaven. See Bertrand Russell, *A History of Western Philosophy*, pp. 16–17.
39 Arthur O. Lovejoy, *The Great Chain of Being: A Study of the History of an Idea*, p. 15. First published in 1936.

40 An earlier version of this section was given as a paper at the Columbia University Seminar in Eighteenth-Century Culture, November 16, 2006.

41 Montesquieu, *Persian Letters.*

42 Montesquieu (1689–1755) wrote *L'Esprit des lois* (*Spirit of the Laws*, 1748), one of the classics of political theory, which stresses that a government must adhere to the spirit, the customs, of its people, a relativist argument considered radical at the time. He argues for division of powers in government and for a common sense (not theoretical) approach to politics. This book is one of the major sources for the American founding documents.

43 For example, see Nancy Mitford, *Madame de Pompadour*, on Madame de Pompadour's intellectual and aesthetic influence on Louis XV.

44 Edward Said, *Orientalism*, p. 2.

45 Despite Said's often-literal readings of early-modern European literature, surely a disadvantage when studying fiction, the overall charges Said raises still retain their validity, and still need to be confronted. See Robert Irwin on Edward Said's legacy, "Lured in the East," *The Times Literary Supplement.* Also Peter Burke, *A Social History of Knowledge: From Gutenberg to Diderot*, "Acquiring Knowledge of Other Cultures," pp. 192–196.

46 Thank you to Alexander Bolland and Gordon DesBrisay for many entertaining conversations, several of them about uniforms.

47 *Candide*, ch. XVI, titled "*Ce qui advint aux deux voyageurs avec deux filles, duex singes et les sauvages nommés Oreillons,*" in Voltaire, *Candide*, Pomeau, ed., ch. XVI, p. 176.

48 See Rawson, *Gods, Gulliver, and Genocide*, ch. 2, "The Savage with Hanging Breasts: Gulliver, Female Yahoos, and 'Racism.' "

49 Montesquieu, *The Persian Letters*, Letter 67, pp. 135–143.

50 *Correspondance* in *The Complete Works of Voltaire/Les Oeuvres complètes de Voltaire*, vol. XVI (August 30, 1755), p. 259.

51 Eric R. Wolf, *Europe and the People without History.*

52 See Duchet, *Anthropologie et Histoire au siècle des lumières*, esp. ch. 3, "*L'idéologie coloniale,*" on the French Enlightenment debate regarding the practice of slavery.

53 Frederick J. Reiter, *They Built Utopia (The Jesuit Missions in Paraguay), 1610–1768.*

54 The other great eighteenth-century writer on education, Johann Heinrich Pestalozzi, was, like Rousseau, Swiss, he was Johann Heinrich Pestalozzi. See Fritz-Peter Hager, *Pestalozzi und Rousseau*. Thank you to Willi Goetschel for his comments on Pestalozzi.

55 Edward Abbey's *Desert Solitaire: A Season in the Wilderness*, first published in 1968, is remarkably Rousseauian in both its subject matter and its prejudices.

56 See Michel Foucault, *The History of Sexuality: An Introduction.* Also see Judith R. Walkowitz, *City of Dreadful Delight: Narratives of Sexual Danger in Late-Victorian London*, esp. the "Introduction," and ch. 7.

57 Carol Gilligan, *In Her Own Voice: Psychological Theory and Women's Development.*

58 Voltaire, *Candide. Pomeau*, ed., ch. I, #57–58, p. 120. Butt, tr., ch. I, pp. 20–21

59 On Pacquette, see Voltaire, *Candide*, chs. I, IV, XXIV, XXV, XXX.

60 This is one interpretation of the female Guardians and the generally positive treatment of women in Books V–VII of Plato's *Republic*. See Donald Kagan, *The Peloponnesian War*, p. 4.

61 Christine de Pizan, *A Medieval Woman's Mirror of Honor: The Treasury of the City of Ladies.*

62 Thank you to John Collins for this distinction regarding learning styles.

63 François Rabelais, *Gargantua and Pantagruel.*

64 Leo Spitzer, "Le prétendu Réalisme de Rabelais," *Modern Philology*, esp. 139 ff. Quoted in Ruth Cave Flowers, *Voltaire's Stylistic Transformations of Rabelaisian Satirical Devices*, p. 3.
65 Erich Auerbach, "The World in Pantagruel's Mouth," in *Mimesis: The Representation of Reality in Western Literature*, pp. 262–284.
66 *Correspondance* in Voltaire, *The Complete Works of Voltaire*/Oeuvres complètes de Voltaire 105, vol. XXI, 12 avril 1760, p. 233. Mikhail Bakhtin argues that Voltaire did not grasp the complexity of Rabelais's thought. Bakhtin, *Rabelais and His World*. Yet Flowers, in her textual study of the two writers, argues convincingly for a more sophisticated understanding of Rabelais by Voltaire, based on Voltaire's own letters. See Flowers, *Voltaire's Stylistic Transformations*, esp. ch. IV, pp. 91–126.
67 Mario Vargas Llosa, *El Hablador* and Vargas Llosa, *The Storyteller*, Helen Lane, tr.
68 Voltaire, *Candide*. Pomeau, ed., ch. 12, #91–92, p. 162. Butt, tr., ch. XII, p. 57.

REFERENCES

Abbey, Edward, *Desert Solitaire: A Season in the Wilderness* (New York: Touchstone/ Simon & Schuster, 1990).
Auerbach, Erich, *Mimesis: The Representation of Reality in Western Literature*, Willard R. Trask, tr. (Princeton: Princeton University Press, 2003).
Bakhtin, Mikhail, *Rabelais and His World*, Hélène Iswolsky, tr. (Cambridge, MA: The MIT Press, 1965.
Barber, W. H., *Leibniz in France from Arnauld to Voltaire* (Oxford: Clarendon Press, 1955).
Braun, Theodore E. D., and John B. Radner, eds., *The Lisbon Earthquake of 1755: Representations and Reactions* (Oxford: Voltaire Foundation, 2005).
Brockliss, Laurence, *French Higher Education in the Seventeenth and Eighteenth Centuries: A Cultural History* (Oxford: Clarendon Press, 1987).
Brooks, Richard A., *Voltaire and Leibniz* (Geneva: Librairie Droz, 1964).
Burke, Peter, *A Social History of Knowledge: From Gutenberg to Diderot* (Cambridge, U.K.: Polity, 2000).
Carlyle, Thomas, *Sartor Resartus*, Kerry McSweeney and Peter Sabor, eds. (Oxford: Oxford University Press, 1987).
Castiglione, Baldassare, *The Book of the Courtier*, Charles S. Singleton (Garden City, NY: Anchor, 1959).
Colley, Linda, *Captives: Britain, Empire and the World, 1600–1850* (New York: Pantheon, 2002).
Duchet, Michèle, *Anthropologie et Histoire au siècle des lumières* (Paris: François Maspero, 1971).
Flowers, Ruth Cave, *Voltaire's Stylistic Transformations of Rabelaisian Satirical Devices*(Washington, D.C.: The Catholic University Press, 1951).
Foucault, Michel, *The History of Sexuality: An Introduction*, Robert Hurley, tr. (New York: Vintage, 1990).
Gilligan, Carol, *In a Different Voice: Psychological Theory and Women's Development* (Cambridge: Harvard University Press, 1982).
Goldgar, Anne, *Impolite Learning: Conduct and Community in the Republic of Letters, 1680–1750* (New Haven: Yale University Press, 1995).
Gordon, Daniel, *Citizens without Sovereignty: Equality and Sociability in French Thought, 1670–1789* (Princeton: Princeton University Press, 1994).

Hager, Fritz-Peter, *Pestalozzi und Rousseau* (Berne: Paul Haupt, 1975).

Israel, Jonathan, *Radical Enlightenment: Philosophy and the Making of Modernity, 1650–1750* (New York: Oxford University Press, 2001).

Jolley, Nicholas, ed., *The Cambridge Companion to Leibniz* (Cambridge: Cambridge University Press, 2006).

Jones, Matthew L., *The Good Life in the Scientific Revolution: Descartes, Pascal, Leibniz, and the Cultivation of Virtue* (Chicago: University of Chicago Press, 2006).

Kagan, Donald, *The Peloponnesian War* (New York: Penguin, 2003).

Leibniz, Gottfried Wilhelm, *Philosophical Essays*, Roger Ariew and Daniel Garber, trs., eds. (Indianapolis, IN: Hackett, 1989).

———. *Political Writings*, Patrick Riley, tr., ed. (Cambridge: Cambridge University Press 1972).

———. *Theodicy: Essays on the Goodness of God, the Freedom of Man and the Origin of Evil*, E. M. Huggard, tr. (Chicago and LaSalle, IL: Open Court, 1990).

Lovejoy, Arthur O., *The Great Chain of Being: A Study of the History of an Idea* (Cambridge, MA: Harvard University Press, 1964).

McMahon, Darrin M., *Enemies of the Enlightenment: The French Counter-Enlightenment and the Making of Modernity* (Oxford: Oxford University Press, 2001).

———. Miller, Cecilia. "Defenders of the Truth," *The Times Literary Supplement*, no. 5205 (January 3, 2003): 29.

Miller, Christopher, *The French Atlantic Triangle: Literature and the Culture of the Slave Trade* (Durham: Duke University Press, 2008).

Mitford, Nancy, *Madame de Pompadour* (New York: Random House, 1954).

Montesquieu, *Persian Letters*, C. J. Betts, tr. (London: Penguin, 1973.)

Parker, Geoffrey and Lesley M. Smith, eds., *The General Crisis of the Seventeenth Century* (London: Routledge & Kegan Paul, 1978).

Pearson, Roger, *The Fables of Reason: A Study of Voltaire's Contes philosophiques* (Oxford: Clarendon Press, 1993).

———. *Voltaire Almighty: A Life in Pursuit of Freedom* (New York: Bloomsbury Publishing, 2005).

Pizan, Christine de., *A Medieval Woman's Mirror of Honor: The Treasury of the City of Ladies* Charity Cannon Willard, tr. (New York: Bard Hall Press/Persea Books, 1989).

Pope, Alexander, *An Essay on Man: Moral Essays and Satires* (London: Cassell and Co., 1891).

Project Gutenburg, http://www.gutenberg.org, provider of classic books in electronic format.

Rabelais, François, *Gargantua and Pantagruel*, Burton Raffel, tr. (New York: Norton, 1991).

Rawson, Claude, *God, Gulliver, and Genocide: Barbarism and the European Imagination, 1492–1945* (New York: Oxford University Press, 2001).

Reiter, Frederick J., *They Built Utopia (The Jesuit Missions in Paraguay), 1610–1768* (Potomac, MD: Scripta Humanistica, 1995).

Rousseau, Jean-Jacques, *Julie, ou La Nouvelle Héloïse* (Paris: Garnier-Flammarion, 1967).

Russell, Bertrand, *A History of Western Philosophy* (London: George Allen & Unwin, 1946).

Said, Edward W, *Orientalism* (Harmondsworth, U.K.: Penguin, 1985).

———. Robert Irwin on Edward Said's legacy, "Lured in the East," *The Times Literary Supplement*, no. 5484 (May 9, 2008): 3–5.

Shklar, Judith, *Men and Citizens: A Study of Rousseau's Social Theory* (Cambridge: Cambridge University Press, 1969).

Smith, Adam, *The Theory of Moral* Sentiments, D. D. Raphael and A. L. Macfie, eds. (Indianapolis, IN: Liberty Press, 1982).

Spitzer, Leo, "Le prétendu Réalisme de Rabelais," *Modern Philology* 37, no. 2 (1939–1940): 139–150.

Vargas Llosa, Mario, *El Hablador* (Barcelona: Seix Barral, 1987).

———. *The Storyteller*, Helen Lane, tr. (New York: Farrar, Straus, and Giroux, 1989).

Voltaire. *Candide; or, Optimism*, John Everett Butt, tr. (London: Penguin, 1947).

———. *The Complete Works of Voltaire/Les Oeuvres complètes de Voltaire*, 142 vols. Theodore Besterman, et al., eds. (Oxford: The Voltaire Foundation at the Taylor Institution, 1970).

———. *Candide*, René Pomeau, ed. (Oxford: The Voltaire Foundation at the Taylor Institution, 1980), vol. 48 of *The Complete Works of Voltaire/Les Oeuvres complètes de Voltaire*.

Walkowitz, Judith R., *City of Dreadful Delight: Narratives of Sexual Danger in Late-Victorian London* (Chicago: University of Chicago Press, 1992).

Warner, Marina, *Alone of All Her Sex: The Myth and Cult of the Virgin Mary* (London: George Weidenfeld & Nicolson, 1976).

Wolf, Eric R., *Europe and the People without History* (Berkeley, CA: University of California Press, 1982).

5 *The Betrothed* (1825–1827, 1840–1842), Revolution, and the Perfectibility of the Human Mind

I BACKGROUND

1 Italian Historical Fiction

Set in a time of multiple crises, the backdrop of this book is the end of feudalism, the decline of the aristocracy, and foreign invasions.[1] *I promessi sposi* (*The Betrothed*, published 1825–1827, and then revised by Manzoni and published in a second edition in 1840–1842) takes place in and around Milan, in Northern Italy, in the midst of the Thirty Years' War; the plot covers roughly two years, between 1628 and 1630. Quiet yet thoughtful Lucia Mondella and brash but articulate Lorenzo (Renzo) Tramaglino, the betrothed title couple, demonstrate two separate, relatively gender-specific ways of confronting established constraints on their choice to be together. On the very eve of their wedding day, at the outset of the story, the local landowner, Don Rodrigo, who wants to seduce Lucia, thwarts Renzo and Lucia's marriage plans. Don Rodrigo is not shy about his intentions—he has even placed a bet with a visiting cousin that he could bed Lucia by a particular date. Two tortuous years go by before Renzo and Lucia can marry. During these years, Renzo, Lucia, and her mother Agnese all flee from this local tyrant who is pursuing Lucia; Lucia is then kidnapped; and Renzo is pursued by the police. This personal drama occurs in the midst of a background in which thousands die in the unholy trinity of war, famine, and plague. Notably, this book does not feature an aristocratic couple. Renzo has some education—he can read, but not write—and he has an abiding resentment against the authority of Latin, which he was not taught.[2] Renzo and Lucia are solidly working-class (the nineteenth-century political ideology of this work is often at odds with its seventeenth-century setting) at the outset of the story. Renzo is at various points a silk spinner, a farmer, a mill worker, and then mill owner. The couple is raised into the aspiring middle class mainly through their own physical efforts by the end of the story, not due to an inheritance (although they do receive a tidy sum of money as a gift) or to newly discovered privileged parents. They are not perfect (Lucia plays a trick on a visiting Capuchin lay priest who is collecting walnuts early in the story, and Renzo gets drunk at a critical juncture). Instead, they are the everyman and every woman: they are even the every couple. Overall, while highlighting the complexity of social relations, it is never clear in the book whether more emphasis is placed on social groups and institutions; on individuals—children, women, and women; or even on families—a particularly Italian trope.

This is also a decidedly political novel. Just as Thomas Paine's political pamphlet *Common Sense* (1776) is often claimed to have started the American Revolution, and Harriet Beecher Stowe's novel *Uncle Tom's Cabin* (1852) is taken to have started the American Civil War, many claim *The Betrothed* as having started *il Risorgimento*.[3] Thus *The Betrothed* is given credit both for the fight for Italian nationalism and for the creation of the state of Italy in 1866 (or 1870, depending on which dating one wants to follow, the initial unification or the addition of Rome), the two definitions of *il Risorgimento*.

At the same time, the author regularly and deliberately incorporates nineteenth-century political concepts, especially the idea of the working class, and he treats the poor masses of Milan as such, even though the book is set long before the nineteenth-century Industrial Revolution. An early example of historical fiction, this book was written in the first half of the nineteenth century but was set in the early seventeenth century, in the midst of the Thirty Years' War. It is, however, necessary to know more about history and the author to comprehend this book than some other works of political fiction, partially because the plot of this book is set two centuries before the book was written. In theoretical terms, looking forward and backward, this book can be compared with profit to both Erasmus on the dire need for the reform of the Catholic Church at the time of the Protestant Reformation in the sixteenth century, and to Antonio Gramsci on possible revolution during the interwar years of the early twentieth century.

The early seventeenth century was not one of the more glorious periods of Italian history. In the early 1600s the Spaniards controlled Milan and the surrounding region of Lombardy, as well as all the other Italian states, except Venice, which was, in the early 1600s, under pressure from the Turks from the East, and the Spanish, French, and Germans from the West and North. The Germans had recently ravaged the Northern Italian states as part of a southern swipe in the midst of the Thirty Years' War. Milan, traditionally the center of one of the wealthiest parts of the Italian peninsula, was, in the early seventeenth century, in the midst of famine, bread riots, and plague. These catastrophes are component parts of the book.

For reasons not entirely clear, despite its overwhelming reception in the mid-nineteenth century, *The Betrothed* is now relatively unknown outside the Italian-speaking world, despite early and repeated translations. Certainly this is the case compared to other European national bestsellers, such as *Don Quixote*, *Gulliver's Travels*, and *Candide*, all of which remain familiar far outside the country, and language, in which they were written. Although the relative obscurity of the book outside Italy today might be attributed to its being the story of the concerns of a very provincial part of the Italian peninsula, at a desultory time in Italian history, it actually has more to do with the decline in the transmission of Italian books into more general European and world culture in the twentieth and twenty-first centuries.

Nevertheless, the novel explores topics that are not just Italian or even European, but universal: the antipathy between the countryside and the city; the shift to a capitalist, industrialist society; rebellion and revolution; corruption on every possible level; and the startling goodness of the most unexpected individuals of every social class. The novel presents corrupt thugs and self-serving clerics on all social levels. It encompasses a love story, a betrothal, a local history, and a first-rate exploration of political and economic notions of the early-modern period through the tale of a devoted, engaged couple kept away from each other by a preposterous number of obstacles.

The book is grounded in European history as well as literature, even though historical fiction was just becoming an established genre in Manzoni's time. More specifically, Manzoni took Scott's *Ivanhoe* (1819) as his inspiration for *The Betrothed*.[4] And it is Walter Scott's *Waverly* (1814) that is often viewed as the primary model for later historical fiction as diverse as James Fenimore Cooper's *The Last of the Mohicans* (1826), as well as *The Betrothed* itself (1825–1827, 1840–1842), Leo Tolstoy's *War and Peace* (1862–1869), and Margaret Mitchell's *Gone with the Wind* (1936). The Scott, Cooper, Manzoni, Tolstoy, and Mitchell novels all mix actual historical characters, subordinate to the fictional heroes, into their stories.[5]

Manzoni's work counts as historical fiction both for its particular setting in late-seventeenth-century Northern Italy, and for the insertion into the plot of actual historical characters, such as Cardinal Federigo Borromeo (and the body of his more famous uncle, Cardinal Carlo Borromeo, a leading figure in the Counter-Reformation, is brought out of the cathedral and carried at the front of a parade in the novel). Cooper and Manzoni both adhered to Scott's emphasis on working-class heroes, many from earlier centuries, who often led more virtuous lives than their superiors. This was yet another way that Manzoni layered both his concern and respect for the poor directly into story.[6]

Edgar Allan Poe's florid but surprisingly balanced 1835 review of *The Betrothed* (written in a time when reviews were generally wholly raves or denunciations) ends not only with praise, but also with some insight about the book trade for later readers and about the demand for fiction in the mid-nineteenth century:

> This work [*The Betrothed*] comes to us as the harbinger of glad tidings to the reading world. Here is a book, equal in matter to any two of Cooper's novels, and executed at least as well, which we receive at the moderate price of forty-two cents! It forms one number of the Washington Library, published monthly, at five dollars per annum. At this rate, a literary gourmand, however greedy, may hope to satisfy his

appetite for books, without starving his children. The author has our praise, and the translator and publisher have our thanks.[7]

The book's astounding initial popularity on both sides of the Atlantic—this review of the first edition of *The Betrothed* was published in Richmond, Virginia—was nonetheless grounded in its specific call for Italian unification. Yet the working-class themes in *The Betrothed* represented not only a desire by contemporary readers to find models of genuine Italian patriots, but also resonated with a more general shift away from courtly and aristocratic themes to stories of people from all social classes and from different parts of the world, grounded in a specific historical context. Such stories were in demand from a growing reading public that was itself not generally wealthy, and the affordable price noted in Poe's review allowed more readers of moderate means to buy them.

2 The Betrothed as an Enlightenment as Much as a Romantic Text

Despite being written in the midst of nineteenth-century Romanticism, this book could be argued to represent the exact point of intersection of the European Enlightenment and Romanticism. For Manzoni, trained in Enlightenment modes of thinking, Romanticism helped to make sense of non-rational elements, including both spirituality and organized religion. The strange concoction in *The Betrothed* of religious and political topics can be attributed not just to Manzoni but also to his intellectual group, *i cattolici liberali*. The Catholic Liberals might be understood as forwarding a nineteenth-century liberation theology. This group was made up of religious writers and Italian nationalists (notably Vincenzo Gioberti and Antonio Rosmini) and advocated an early-nineteenth-century intellectual blend of religion and radical French politics. Both elements are so strong in *The Betrothed* that it is almost impossible to decide if the book is best understood as radical and pro-Enlightenment, or traditional and Counter-Reformation, in the latter case seeking the reform, not the abolition, of the Catholic Church. Despite the anti-clericalism of Italian nationalism, this book has less in common with the anti-clerical spirit of much of the French Enlightenment (this text thus helps to establish a more constructive concern for religion than is generally attributed to the Enlightenment), and much more to do with the desire to reform the Catholic Church (which is also expressed in much earlier writings, especially, in the clever writings of Erasmus, who was himself a Catholic priest).

3 Working-Class Leading Characters and World-Historical Figures as Supporting Characters

Beyond religion and politics, there is some debate about the reasons for the early popularity of this book. An unfriendly critic could argue that this is an unsuccessful novel, in literary terms, as the main characters are so small in comparison to the extraordinary crises, natural and man-made, that overwhelm the leading couple at regular intervals, and thus the book matters more as political pamphleteering than as great fiction in its own right. Granted, this is a highly unusual novel for its time in that the main characters (Renzo, Lucia, and Lucia's mother Agnese) are fairly humble, ordinary, and never to be revealed as aristocratic, the common medieval and early-modern trope, and also not particularly gifted. However, this presentation was not an accident. It marks the shift in modern literature to vibrant stories about working people as central characters in their own lives.

Nevertheless, the book also features several larger-than-life minor historical characters, and they are often the ones remembered by readers decades after having read the book. These characters are "world-historical" in the sense used by Hegel—individuals who force themselves upon their historical situations, against existing historical trends. In Manzoni's novel, there are at least three such characters: Gertrude, the Nun of Monza, a less-than-spiritual Mother Superior; l'innominato, an unnamed character, called the Unnamed, a local, unusually successful tyrant; and Cardinal Federigo Borromeo, an actual historical personage. One could invoke a concept from Nietzsche here: "plastic power," the astonishing adaptability, of such natural leaders who even in their lifetimes achieve some larger-than-life status.[8] Local and national leaders in the novel have, on occasion, the power even to survive plague, not just to best all forms of rivalry and to survive civil unrest. Manzoni's book is distinctive both in its strong emphasis on historical forces that engulf specific groups and in its identification of a few individuals who seem able to mold their extraordinary circumstances to suit their own purposes. Yet the strongest force in the book is not any character, named or unnamed: the force of history is the major player throughout, and this is made clear in the Prologue.

However, as a rebuttal to any unfriendly quibbling about unfinished character development in this novel, it could be argued that the title characters are intentionally undeveloped, thus representing real, and thus predictably limited, people. One striking example might be Lucia's mere presence in the home of the Unnamed (at this stage, she has been kidnapped and is being held there), which, without any preaching or proselytizing by her, led the Unnamed to change overnight from being the local tyrant to being a devoted Christian, which is often viewed as unlikely. Perhaps the Unnamed, as a local warlord, is unused to being challenged, and thus succumbs more easily than would an ordinary person, or this was simply the incident that triggered his religious epistemological break. In any case, if the characters in this book are thin and one-dimensional, as is the case in *Candide*, the presentation of them in *The Betrothed* is as Weberian ideal types—thus denoting qualities that a certain group has in common (shared characteristics of a mother and of a priest, to give two classic examples), not perfect models. These ideal types are more than partially responsible for the rich theoretical and political debate in this book.

Various creative writers and literary critics have extended this view, notably writer Ford Madox Ford, who creates such vivid, fiercely complicated characters himself in *The Good Soldier* (1915).[9] Ford actually strongly disagrees with any dismissal of the personalities in *The Betrothed* as stock characters in an otherwise marvelous book.[10] He regards the characters to be part of the political tension in the book, not just pawns of it. Overall, it can be argued that the characters in *The Betrothed* are not only representatives of political and historical trends, but also exist as discrete, particular, often flawed individuals, thus allowing Manzoni to temper theoretical arguments about the self-perpetuating nature of tyranny.

Although similar to *Don Quixote* in its presentation of stories within stories, an episodic approach, this Italian work is unlike *Don Quixote*, *Simplicissimus*, and *Candide*, and possibly even unlike *Gulliver's Travels*, for its basic premise is not of a fool, and it is not part of the clown genre of this period.[11] Certainly, some read Renzo as a country bumpkin, if not a holy fool, yet he shows more range, more human qualities, and more character development than do most of the beloved fools of European literature. Even the local priest Don Abbondio, despite his contemptibly timid behavior at times of clear moral crisis, is more of an object of fun than a proper fool, who would be, consciously or not, performing for others. Yet if the book has a fool, it would probably be he (and Don Abbondio is usually selected as the fool in stage productions of the book). Yet the book spotlights the mixed nature of all the characters and social classes, and the reasons for these incongruities, instead of focusing on foolishness. Institutions—particularly the Church and the government, in that order—are selfish, misguided, and even corrupt; not like adults with stunted intellectual ability, but like regular people when drunk, they spout the truth as they know it. Often the main characters are the most depraved, and this is the case for Church, political, and local leaders. It is seemingly not necessary for others to expose them as inadequate, for they deliberately reveal their own deficiencies, sometimes even their depravity. This reading advances the possibility for redemption not only for vicious characters, but also for corrupt institutions. The book puts forward the notion that institutions work only as well as the individuals who are in them, confirming that a strong bureaucratic structure will function properly even with incompetents in power. In *The Betrothed*, redemption of society comes about only through redemption of specific crucial individuals, and of core institutions, who may be foolish at times, but who are not locked into the category of "fool."

4 Manzoni and the Move toward Italian Unification

It is hard for modern readers—whether Italian or not—to imagine the immense popularity of this book even in a century with limited literacy, and the celebrity status Manzoni held in the Italian states both during his lifetime and for many years after his death. Giuseppe Verdi's *Requiem* was composed to mark the one-year anniversary of Manzoni's death, which had occurred in 1873. Throughout his prime years, Manzoni had a remarkable ability to win admirers for his writing and for himself from across the political spectrum. Certain aspects of his own life seem to forecast his later popularity across generally antagonistic groups; these include his move toward Protestantism, at the time of his marriage to a Calvinist, and then his later reconnection to Catholicism.

Manzoni reflected the religious questioning of his time; he was, for example, profoundly influenced by Jansenism, a reform movement within the early-modern Catholic Church, through his reading of Blaise Pascal's *Lettres provinciales* (*The Provincial Letters*, 1656–1657, which was placed on the Catholic Index of Forbidden Books), and by his intense conversations with Jansenist friends and priests. The tenets of Jansenism will actually sound familiar to the reader of *The Betrothed*:

> Jansenism with its vigorous ethical principles, its struggle against worldly and material interests in the Church, its austere conviction, its contempt for State favour, its disinterested devotion to public affairs, its insistence on first principles, in fact its dignity of life, was bound to coincide with the aims of the [French] Revolution.[12]

By adopting a form of Jansenism, Manzoni was able to bring together his Protestant desire for reformation of the Church within the Church he was born into in Milan.[13] According to the well-known story, all this intensity was brought to a head one day when Manzoni apparently lost his wife in a crowd in Paris; in great agitation he rushed into the closest church, San Roch (Rocco), and there made a vow to reenter the Catholic Church if only his wife were found. She reappeared and together they became Catholic. This gave Manzoni the strength of a convert in the religion into which he was born.[14] To some degree Manzoni's conversion back to Catholicism was also a way for him to re-embrace his Italian roots while he was living in France and speaking French (although France was also overwhelmingly Catholic, the Papacy, however, was based in Rome). These shifts made him, even when not openly commented upon, more attractive to the Church, for Manzoni was born Catholic, then became a prodigal son, and later was appropriately restored as one of the most eminent members of the Italian Catholic Church in his lifetime and beyond.

In addition to these religious elements, *The Betrothed* was almost unimaginably popular for secular reasons. It was taken up as a major component of the *Risorgimento*, the move toward Italian unification. Two operas were composed about *The Betrothed* in the second half of the nineteenth century, and there have been numerous film versions of the book. It is still required reading today in all Italian schools, along with Dante's *Commedia*, not just in the *liceo classico* (the competitive, classical high schools in Italy). Love of this book has been repeatedly expressed in both high and popular Italian culture from the time it was first published until today.

There had been a call for a unified Italy for many centuries; to give the classic example, the final book of Machiavelli's *Prince* (written in 1513, published posthumously in 1532) is trenchant on this point. (Even earlier Marsilius of Padua, around the year 1320, had called for a World Leader, presumably the Italian Emperor, thus in effect, he advocated unlimited monarchical power.) The intellectual reasons for the move toward unification varied greatly by group and time. In the nineteenth century, there was a desire to find pre-Roman, pre-imperial roots for the Italian people.[15] Some early nineteenth-century calls for Italian unification included a republican model, others put forward a union of Italian states under the Pope. The Northern region of Lombardy, the setting of *The Betrothed*, is just to the east of Piedmont, which, along with the royal House of Savoy, became the focal points of revolutionary activity for the entire Italian peninsula. Camillo Cavour, an aristocrat who became prime minister of Piedmont, allowed war to break out with the Austrians as a means to unite the Italian states, by secret negotiations with Napoleon III in 1858. This occurred just 16 years after the final version of *The Betrothed* was published. In general, the Piedmontese contingent wanted the removal of Austrians from the Italian peninsula, and a unified Italy under a king drawn from the House of Savoy. In contrast, Giuseppe Mazzini, from Genoa, founder of *La giovine Italia* (Young Italy), favored popular uprisings, a republican government based in Rome, religious freedom, universal school education, and the end to the death penalty. Yet more radical than the break from the Austrians by Cavour, or the armed rebellion of Mazzini, the revolutionary leader in later stages was clearly Giuseppe Garibaldi (born in Nice, which had been taken by the French). Garibaldi returned from exile in Brazil and Uruguay and began to build up his band of *Camicie rosse* (Red Shirts). Garibaldi landed with his men in Sicily in 1860 and moved north up the Italian coast, thus provoking Cavour to move south with troops toward Rome. Garibaldi yielded to the leadership of Piedmont. On March 17, 1861, a new kingdom of Italy was proclaimed; Venetia finally joined this new kingdom in 1866.[16] In 1870, Rome became part of united Italy, and its capital. This all occurred in the generation that first read, and then celebrated, Manzoni.

A substantial part of the effort to create a unified Italy was the parallel move to create a single Italian language. Nineteenth-century Italian dialects (and even twentieth-century dialects, until the advent of television) were in many cases as diverse as different languages, so much so that people from the North and South literally could not understand each other. Manzoni is as well known in Italy for his linguistic achievements as for *The Betrothed*; indeed, the two topics cannot be separated. Between the first publication in 1827 and the final publication in 1840–1842, Manzoni rewrote the book entirely from Milanese dialect into the educated form of the Florentine dialect. This was an outgrowth of his firm belief that it was essential to have a standard version of Italian, and increasingly, that the choice should be the spoken Florentine dialect of his time rather than any other Italian, even any other version of Tuscan (the dialect of the greater region surrounding Florence). Florentine was the dialect of Florence, the setting of the Renaissance, and the self-acknowledged cultural center of the Italian states. Manzoni decided to rewrite his book for larger political and cultural reasons, even though neither Florentine nor Tuscan was appropriate in terms of the setting of *The Betrothed* in the North. Rewriting the book was particularly difficult for Manzoni, as he himself was from the North; his native languages were Milanese and French, and he was more familiar with educated Tuscan from the older Renaissance Cruscan model than the spoken Tuscan of his own time. (The Cruscan model, also from Florence, was named after the famous Renaissance academy and dictionary of the same name, and it was Manzoni's direct model; and, partially because of the success of *The Betrothed*, the Cruscan dictionary has maintained its dominance as the highest standard.) Manzoni's extraordinary effort to rewrite his book and its subsequent popularity are generally taken to be responsible for the acceptance of the Florentine dialect as standard Italian for the new Italian state. This should not be taken as a shift in political allegiance from Milan to Florence on Manzoni's part, but rather his desire to designate a single, set version of Italian for all Italians—Dante's Italian—regardless of whether they lived in the city of the countryside. His goal was that all Italians could communicate easily with one another thus preparing the way toward political unification. In order to achieve this, in 1827, in the midst of his revisions, Manzoni made a trip to Tuscany so that he could become more familiar with contemporary spoken Tuscan. Indeed, in *The Betrothed*, the narrator goes so far as to mock Milanese, Manzoni's own dialect, in favor of Florentine/Tuscan. Ironically, the freshness of Manzoni's own surprisingly colloquial Florentine became ossified soon after, for it was quickly copied by countless admirers who attempted to reproduce his style exactly. This closely paralleled Manzoni's own experience. Manzoni had railed against the Renaissance Cruscan model, blaming it for having deadened the language of later Italian writers, even as late as the eighteenth century. He rebelled by writing in colloquial, local Italian dialect. Two short phases later, many Italian authors rebelled against Manzoni's model, colloquial Italian, which was already resented as a straitjacket for new Italian authors. Even though *The Betrothed* does not overtly discuss the concept of unification, Manzoni used language as his great contribution, his weapon, in the battle for Italian unification, and he makes this explicit in his 1837 work, *Della lingua italiana* (English translation entitled *Treatise on Language*). The presentation of *The Betrothed* in what he hoped would become—and indeed what did become— standard Italian was a major part of Manzoni's concerted effort to promote Italian nationalism and the move toward a unified Italian state.

5 The Author: Alessandro Manzoni (1785–1873)

Manzoni was the product of two social extremes of the late eighteenth century: aristocratic traditionalism and Enlightenment radicalism. These conflicting instincts are clear even in his paternity. Although legally the son of the aristocratic Don Pietro Manzoni, his natural father was widely assumed to be the Milanese radical thinker Alessandro Verri.[17] Just as the aristocratic versus radical tensions in his novel are impossible to resolve fully, Manzoni also carried the names of his most likely fathers.

Much work remains to be done on his talented and strong-willed mother, the poetess Giulia Beccaria Manzoni, yet it is clear that she was crucial to her son's intellectual and religious development. Most of the attention to date has been on her own remarkable father (Cesare Beccaria, who will be discussed at length later), on her son, and on her own colorful personal life, in a time when divorce was not an option. At age 20, following some years in religious schools, Alessandro left Milan to join his mother in Paris. Thus following his attendance at a series of boarding schools, Giulia Beccaria Manzoni then provided her son with a cosmopolitan, literary European experience, which complemented his own voracious reading as a boy, and his growing reputation as a poet. Their household became a center for both radical and establishment figures. In certain respects, it is actually incorrect to view Manzoni as a foreigner in France. Bilingual in French and Italian (although it is not technically correct even to use the term "Italian" at this point), Manzoni embraced both French and Italian culture as his own. Indeed, many Europeans in the long eighteenth century, especially aristocrats, from St. Petersburg to Milan, spoke French as their mother tongue or were bilingual in French. Manzoni adopted French and Italian cultures in a way that was not just for status. He identified with the extreme difficulties and failings of both cultures, which is often a sign of belonging. However, at the same time, he shared the sense of superiority distinctive to each society. From age 20 to 25, Manzoni traveled with his mother, married, and lived in Paris; at age 25, he had his religious conversion.

As suggested above, this was the first of a series of profound religious transitions, which took him from Catholicism to Protestantism and then back to Catholicism. He converted from Catholicism to Protestantism, specifically to Calvinism, the religion of his wife, Enrichetta Blondel, the daughter of a Swiss banker. Then, a few years later, he converted back to Catholicism. This time his wife converted to Catholicism, and they remarried in the Catholic Church.[18] Each transition gave him an awareness of a different secular, specifically political, worldview, not just a different set of religious practices.

This was also a decade of profound academic as well as religious growth for Manzoni. Although the claim is made that many thinkers experienced a rapid intellectual conversion experience, Manzoni does indeed appear to have been one of the few intellectuals who did experience a fairly rapid (not gradual) and lasting (although jarring and painful, an ultimately highly constructive) epistemological break, which occurred when he was relatively young. The first break gave him an appreciation for the simplicity of individual faith and the emphasis on the individual that are both stereotypically Protestant. The second religious conversion, the return to

Catholicism, was accompanied by a period of intense study and concern for the subjects of politics, religion, and literature, and by a reaffirmation of concern for social groups and institutions.

In his 20's, Manzoni's first literary efforts were in poetry, and he continued to use a broad range of literary genres to make his case, be it political, religious, or both. Throughout his life he wrote plays, especially historical tragedies inspired by Shakespeare; hymns; essays on the Italian language; defenses of Catholicism; an historical work on the plague in Milan (written as an historical appendix to *The Betrothed*, similar in purpose to Harriet Beecher Stowe's *The Key to Uncle Tom's Cabin*, 1854, which was written to bolster the historical accuracy of *Uncle Tom's Cabin*, 1852); a work on the French Revolution; and patriotic essays. Thus even after his return to Milan as a young married man, Manzoni continued his interest in broader European and British themes. Manzoni's best-known, explicitly political piece was *Cinque Maggio* (*The Fifth of May*), an ode produced to mark the death of Napoleon; this poem was exceedingly popular throughout Europe in the nineteenth century. Johann Wolfgang von Goethe, the first to translate *Cinque Maggio* into German, regarded Manzoni's ode to be the greatest tribute to Napoleon written at the time of his death. Manzoni admired Napoleon for trying to unite Italy, although Manzoni disapproved of this having been done through warfare and violence.

In his personal life, Manzoni showed grace under pressure: he suffered from serious financial troubles throughout his life and from a series of personal tragedies, the deaths of both his wives—Enrichetta Blondel died in 1833; four years later he married Teresa Borri Stampi, who died in 1861— as well as the deaths of most of his children by late in his life. Yet at the same time he was well known throughout these years as a gracious public figure. At age 75, he was elected as a senator to the new Italian Senate in 1860; however, he never went to Rome to take up this position. He lived to be 88 and was given a state funeral when he died. Throughout his life, Manzoni deliberately presented his concerns for politics, religion, and literature in ways that were accessible to a wide audience, yet somehow without diluting his very particular ideological messages.

6 Seventeenth-Century and Nineteenth-Century Historical Settings

The reader must keep in mind that the setting of this novel in the seventeenth century was not a random choice; Manzoni consciously used this device in order to condemn the abuses of his own century, the nineteenth, in a supposedly indirect manner. However, there were strong parallels between the centuries. In the seventeenth century, the Northern Italian states, including the area in which the story was set, were often drawn into the Thirty Years' War. The Spanish ruled the Italian peninsula throughout the seventeenth century (again with the exception of Venice, which, although under foreign pressure from all sides, was nevertheless a republic, ruled by an elected Venetian official, the Doge). Thus not only were there military incursions into the Northern Italian regions during this period, but even more fundamentally Spain was draining the Italian states financially in order to fund its own major participation in the war. Unlike other Italian regions, Milan, along with Naples and Sicily, did have limited political representation in the Spanish capital of Madrid. Nevertheless (or, because of this, some scholars of revolution would argue) anti-Spanish sentiment was strong among Italians, and certainly in Milan, throughout this period.[19] Over the centuries, Italian commentators and scholars have not been reluctant to blame Spain for the economic backwardness of the Italian states during these decades, stressing the dependence of them on a larger Spanish empire, and an emphasis on form over substance, called *spagnolismo* (Spanish style, although this term was used only derisively). Modern scholarship is still needed on the benefits, if any, for seventeenth-century Italians of Spanish rule, they might include the opportunity for the early-modern Italian states to concentrate on the arts—culminating in the Baroque—as their economies were run by the Spanish, and the Spanish were the patrons of Italian artists. Overall, this period is brought to life most famously in Fernand Braudel's *La Méditerranée et le monde méditerranéen à l'époque de Philippe II.*[20] The region of Lombardy, the main setting of *The Betrothed*, was ruled by Spain in the seventeenth century, and the Catholic Church in Milan was given special privileges by the Spanish. An example is the case of Cardinal Borromeo— the older cousin of the Cardinal Borromeo who is a key player in Manzoni's novel, an actual historical character—who was influential in extending the scope of education and social welfare supported by the Church in late-sixteenth-century Milan. Milan's status as a colony of Spain deserves much more attention, and should include the study of influential Italians working under the rule of Spain.

Despite special privileges, the General Crisis of the seventeenth century, nevertheless, took a particularly hard toll on the Italian states, particularly as these were years not only of overpopulation and famine but also of little hope, as commerce and industry moved north and west, from the Mediterranean to the Atlantic Coast, especially to France, Britain, and the Dutch states.[21] War, plague, and declining agricultural products and economic markets were the principal reasons for the General Crisis. It was in the midst of this financial collapse that the seventeenth century saw the rise of the Baroque, the distinctive art form that featured decadence and excess. It is described as such even by its admirers. Perhaps the best examples are in Southern Italy, especially in the Kingdom of Naples. These are not casual references. Indeed, Southern Italy is invoked repeatedly in this Northern Italy novel, demonstrating the call for a better economic and political situation for the entire Italian peninsula.[22] This novel presents both the suffering and the surprising achievements of this age.

By the time Manzoni wrote *The Betrothed*, there had been efforts toward economic recovery during the more than 100 years since the time in which this novel was set, and many of these efforts had been explicitly proposed by Italian writers. The primary centers of intensive Enlightenment activity in the Italian peninsula in the eighteenth century were Milan and Naples. Indeed scholars are now recognizing that the Italian states were leading centers of the European Enlightenment. Pietro Verri (who was probably Manzoni's uncle) was the head of the literary circle in eighteenth-century Milan, *Il Caffé (The Café,* meaning "salon" as well as "café" and "coffee"), named after their literary journal of the same name. Cesare Beccaria (again, Manzoni's maternal grandfather) was the leading intellectual of the Italian Enlightenment in Milan, which focused on *la questione de la lingua* (the Question of Language, the controversy surrounding the proper form of Italian) as part of the even larger debate regarding politics. The calls by Italian Enlightenment thinkers for legal and political reform led to a more popular desire to throw off foreign oppression—in nineteenth-century Milan, now by the Austrians—and to a more general move toward Italian nationalism. The French Revolution was a symbol for nineteenth-century Italian intellectuals of what could be accomplished against tyranny, and the rise of Napoleon did not weaken this sentiment. Indeed, Napoleon was viewed by many Italian intellectuals, including Manzoni, as a natural part of this post-1789 change to a more modern state. The French government supported Italian Jacobins, albeit as part of its anti-papal policy. There was, however, little popular Italian support for the French, despite French support of the Italian Jacobins and the brief establishment of Italian republics at this time.

Manzoni's inspiration for *The Betrothed* would have come not only from the French Revolution but also from the Decembrist Revolt in Russia in 1825, and the crushed revolutions in Paris, Belgium, Poland, and elsewhere, from 1830 to 1832.[23] With the fall of Napoleonic rule across Europe, following the Congress of Vienna, and lasting until Italian unification in the late 1860s, the Italian states were divided among many foreign powers. This had been the case previously; however, now new powers intervened. Milan became the property of the Austrian Hapsburgs. There was yet another economic downturn in the Italian states in the first half of the nineteenth century. Political concessions, such as the end to censorship in Tuscany by Grand Duke Leopold II, only led to more open rebellion. The Revolutions of 1848 in Italian cities, especially in Milan and Naples, were motivated by nationalism and led to the triumph of Italian unification a couple of decades later. Much the same argument can be made for the Revolutions of 1848 in German cities, and the later national unification in that area, but this does not explain the reasons for the Revolutions of 1848 in Paris or in Eastern Europe, for example. Italian politics was always part of, as well as separate from, larger European concerns.

In 1861, at the time of the initial Unification, there were 26 million Italians, almost 80 percent of whom were illiterate and almost 70 percent were agricultural workers. There was as well a sharp division of wealth between the North and South. *Il Risorgimento* represented a desire both for individual liberties and for a government that would support these rights and provide protection against both foreign enemies and domestic tyrants. The first Italian governments followed the lead set by Manzoni; they were free trade, anti-violent (or at least anti-ongoing-violent) revolution, and pro-French.[24] Manzoni in *The Betrothed* stresses these stark economic and social disparities, and outlines possible means to use French and Enlightenment thinking on trade and political rights to reorient Italian social, political, and economic life, especially in terms of free trade.

7 Intellectual Influence of Cesare Beccaria (1738–1794)

The one aspect of Manzoni's family background that was never in doubt was that his maternal grandfather was the radical writer Cesare Beccaria.[25] Beccaria himself initially would have appeared to be an unlikely Enlightenment figure. He was the oldest son of an aristocratic Milanese family. Beccaria's close association with the Verri brothers, Pietro Verri and Alessandro Verri, leaders of *Il Caffé*, led to the writing of *Dei delitti e delle pene* (*On Crimes and Punishments*, 1764), taken to be the first piece written against torture and capital punishment.[26] Thus one of Manzoni's intellectual influences was his grandfather, even though his grandfather died when Alessandro was only nine years old. The intellectual connection between Beccaria and Manzoni (as between Mary Wollstonecraft and her daughter Mary Shelley, to give another such familial/literary example) was established after the death of the older, distinguished relative.

Yet the family connection was in some ways just a bonus, as Beccaria's ideas were known so broadly by this time. It was not necessary in the late eighteenth, early nineteenth century to have been a relative to have known of Beccaria's political contributions, now known as part of the fabric of classical liberalism. Voltaire and Denis Diderot, among others, accepted Cesare Beccaria's *On Crimes and Punishments* as the greatest force in the attack on the practices of torture and the death penalty. This work had tremendous influence throughout Europe at the time. Beccaria's writing, along with that of Montesquieu and Voltaire, was credited as being the major reason for the diminution and sometimes abolition of these practices throughout Europe. Although Sweden abolished torture in 1734, as did Friedrich II in Prussia in 1740 (this became law only in 1805), both these practices were otherwise all too common in Europe. In Beccaria's time torture was a regular part of the European legal system. Tuscany abolished torture in 1786, mainly due to the influence of Beccaria. His short work was fêted as a great success in free-thinking circles across the continent and on both sides of the Atlantic. It went through six editions in the first six months after it was published. Voltaire wrote the anonymous introduction to the French translation of this marvelous piece. Yet for all its well-known influence as a political pamphlet, little study has been done on the theoretical concepts it explores, especially regarding justice and law, and most particularly mob mentality and the question of how to prevent crime. Enlightenment scholars would be well advised to look to Beccaria for vibrant political and economic theory as well as for the call for radical changes in European law on a range of subjects including torture and the death penalty.

It was Pietro Verri's suggestion that Beccaria write an essay on this topic. Beccaria's *On Crimes and Punishments* is usually discussed as a European work and certainly the Verri brothers, as well as Beccaria, had a strong desire to connect with intellectuals throughout Europe. Beccaria's and later Manzoni's writings, however, must also be read as part of the specific, lively, and diverse literary life in the Italian peninsula, one that was marked by strong concerns for its own political parties, economic situation, and cultural history. Manzoni, although deeply religious and much more conservative than his aristocratic yet free-thinking grandfather, nevertheless carried on many of his grandfather's convictions. Like Beccaria before him, Manzoni was grounded in Italian culture and in radical, pan-European political ideology.

The intellectual connections between grandfather and grandson are evident in Manzoni's forceful political novel: both regarded wealth rather than privilege to be the determining factor in society (clearly an antithetical position for aristocrats, and one that acknowledged the growing power of the middle class; however, keep in mind that the middle class was not usually any more committed than the old aristocracy to helping the poor).[27] *The Betrothed* depicts the plague in graphic detail, condemns individuals who take advantage of such natural disasters, and attacks the corruption of both the Church and powerful individuals who, even in prosperous times, could terrorize entire regions into submission. Beccaria and Manzoni both wrote of the horrors of excess, especially of torture and of riots. They both recognized that the poorer classes were systematically oppressed by both the traditional aristocracy and by the rising middle class. Although neither writer discussed the mechanics of government in detail, they were both conscious of the evident flaws in the Italian system. Perhaps most strikingly, Beccaria's Utilitarian approach and Manzoni's own Enlightenment and Romantic approaches both demonstrate astonishing concern for people of all social classes. Manzoni, the best known of the Catholic Liberals of his generation, produced a work in which an authoritarian, generally religious bias remains in competition, perhaps in tandem, with commitments that are easily interpreted as post-Enlightenment, as well as post-French Revolution. The winner of the struggle between these two competing forces is left deliberately unclear in this book.

8 Link to Giambattista Vico (1668–1744)

Although Vico's work has attained a certain popularity in the past decades, it is still regularly presented on the assumption that he is merely a precursor to more celebrated and/or notorious intellectual figures who followed him.[28] Nevertheless, even given this bias, which generally ignores the range of

Vico's own writings, more work remains to be done on the direct influence of Vico on later Italian and European writers and schools of thought. One such fruitful linkage is that of Vico and Manzoni. Manzoni's sources were theoretical as well as pragmatic, as attested to by his interest in the theorist Vico.[29] By reflecting on the two thinkers together, it becomes apparent that Vico's thought, as well as Manzoni's, is embedded in both material culture and abstract ideas. According to Giuseppe Mazzotta, Manzoni read Vico in the manner that so many people read Marx until the fall of the Soviet Union: Manzoni found in Vico abstract ideas, an emphasis on material culture, patterns of historical change, and the possibility of lasting political change for the individual as much as for society.

The reader can easily find, even in Vico's best-known work, the 1744 edition of *La scienza nuova*, not just grand theories of the rise and decline of nations, but also of materiality; for example, dogs that tear apart orphan children. More pertinently, for Vico, the recognition of the patterns of the human mind is the only way to begin to comprehend the relationship between innately selfish human beings, their material circumstances (including class and economic differences), and how these individuals interact, for good or ill. Vico's overarching concern is for patterns of group behavior, especially concerning the major social institutions of marriage, burial, and religion. He also traces the development of spoken language (starting with inarticulate sounds) and of law (originating in common customs). Thus materiality for Vico has to do not just with living creatures or with physical property; fundamentally, it has to do with labor—how human beings in groups create routines that not only help a particular individual succeed but also allow that individual's group to succeed.

Clearly any grand speculative theory of culture can be faulted for not viewing the vast differences between the good of the individual and the good of society. Somewhat surprisingly, both Adam Smith and Marx, rightly considered in most respects to be antithetical in their commitments, are both primary examples of such grand speculative theorists of culture. All three thinkers—Vico, Adam Smith, and Marx—fall into both the fallacy of division (what is best for the whole is best for the part) and the fallacy of composition (what is best for the part is best for the whole). Yet, Vico, Adam Smith, and Marx, in three radically distinct modes, all asserted the foundational interconnectedness of the individual and society.

Vico brings our attention to the origins of human society and the primacy of the imagination. He asserts that social behavior and law are both cultural constructs. His work, following a set academic pattern, falls into at least three stages. Traditionally, Vico's early literary attempts and his writing on education have been viewed as distinctly and merely anti-Cartesian. Yet there is an argument for the critical place of Vico's early writings.[30] In his middle period, he moved toward development of law as a means of studying early history and as the key to comprehending the development of a specific culture. In his final, some would say his best, period, Vico produced

La scienza nuova, which manages to be both an analysis of the phases of intellectual and cultural development for social groups, especially the first phases, and a work that could itself be regarded as poetic. Dante (one of Vico's four *autori*, a term often used for an author's own favorite writers) and William Golding (a great admirer of Vico, Golding wrote *The Inheritors* as an homage to Vico) also mixed creative writing with philosophy. Vico's overarching concern for all aspects of the philosophy of history is reflected in Manzoni's work perhaps as well as by any other writer, although many others, including James Joyce, are better known as Vico's self-proclaimed disciples. Thus Vico is of tremendous help in understanding Manzoni, most particularly because of Vico's theories concerning the power of human creativity and imagination as a means of making sense of history.

For both Vico and Manzoni, radical change in social structures comes about when intolerable material circumstances converge with abstract ideas regarding change that, as they gain popularity, fundamentally shift people's outlook, including how they view and judge their social world on a daily basis. These notions not only predate Marx but also indicate that Vico and Manzoni developed theories of social change that led in an altogether different direction from that signposted later by Marx. The originality of their approach is that it takes the ideology of social reform away from one particular tradition (specifically that of socialism and Marxism) and demonstrates that the means of bringing about lasting political change is embedded in our own way of thinking, regardless of place and time, and whatever our political views. Thus, just as we can comprehend history because it is man-made, according to Vico we can also make our own future, as it will also be man-made.

If Manzoni's narrator in *The Betrothed* implies the twinning of the individual and society, the political message on revolution is, if less overt, nevertheless just as strong for he recognizes the time element and the determination necessary for successful revolutions, both in order to start a revolution and then to continue its ideals in later, perhaps less auspicious times.[31] Manzoni's narrator acknowledges the writings of revolutionaries, and this would by larger implication include the earlier Rousseau and Voltaire. However, the decisive point made here by Manzoni's narrator is that the actual ideas of these French *philosophes*, however proto-revolutionary, did not actually filter down at all to working French people in the several decades between the traditional French Enlightenment of the mid-eighteenth century and the French Revolution in the late eighteenth century. Instead, there is a confluence: in a country and century when thinkers wrote that "*L'homme est né libre, et partout il est dans le fers*" ("Man was born free, and everywhere is in chains"), nevertheless the genuine political muscle of the French Revolution came, according to Manzoni's narrator, from everyday people who used their judgment (for Vico, this would be "*senso commune*," "common sense") in order to work as a group, and thereby potentially bring about lasting political change.[32] This illustrates what

Vico called *"le modificazioni della nostra medesima mente umana,"* ("the modifications of our own human mind").[33] In more recent academic terms, this is an argument for the French Revolution as instigated from below—from the people, not from revolutionary leaders.

9 Synopsis

The Betrothed is a remarkable text in many respects, an early work of historical fiction and a story of a protracted courtship: it also embodies ideals drawn not just from the Enlightenment and Romanticism, but also from the Church, and from the aristocracy. Set in the early-modern period yet written in the modern age, the novel has fictional, working people as the major characters and, amusingly, a few powerful historical figures as supporting characters. The goal of its explicit political agenda was to push Italians toward both political and linguistic unification. Manzoni himself was a symbol of *il Risorgimento* in his own lifetime, mourned by the entire, young country when he died. Probably the greatest influence on his intellectual life was his maternal grandfather, Cesare Beccaria. Beccaria and Manzoni were not typical aristocrats, for they shared not only a commitment to abolishing torture and capital punishment but also the desire to reorganize Italian, and European, legal and political systems in ways that would benefit all people, regardless of birth. Vico's ideas on history and materiality help to make sense of the stress in *The Betrothed* on the role of abstract ideas in bringing about lasting political change.

II RENZO, THE FAILED REVOLUTIONARY, AND THE BETROTHED, THE MANIFESTO FOR ITALIAN NATIONALISM

1 The Reluctant or Failed Revolutionary?

Renzo can be considered a revolutionary; the question is whether he is a reluctant or failed revolutionary.[34] This subject could be approached in terms of Manzoni's grandfather, Cesare Beccaria, on legal reform; eighteenth-century Southern Italian economic thinkers on famine, bread crises, and agrarian society; and the more colorful characters as well as the major secular and religious institutions that dominate the work. Instead, however, the emphasis here will primarily be on only six chapters, Chapters 11 through 16, of *The Betrothed*, which concern Renzo's first visit to Milan. While accepting the book as leading directly to the creation of a democratic state based on a condemnation of all forms of violence—assuredly still the correct overall interpretation of the novel—one can also suggest an alternative reading of at least these six chapters of *The Betrothed* that places them firmly in the tradition of European revolutionary theory, and is of interest in terms of crowd theory as well.

2 Literary Style: Realism

It is striking that a story so universal, transcending both the seventeenth and nineteenth centuries, is nevertheless grounded in a very specific time and place. The book begins not in Milan or even in Renzo and Lucia's unnamed village, but rather with three full paragraphs of geographical description of the area surrounding their village. Their village is apparently a mile east of Lecco, which is near Milan. Lecco's textile industry, still in existence in the twenty-first century, was already functioning in the early seventeenth century. This book demonstrates that it is not necessary for works of literature to be even partially placed in a utopia (as in *Simplicissimus* and *Candide*), or with characters that function as classic types (as in *Pilgrim's Progress*) in order to put forward a universal political message.

The Betrothed propounds a realist interpretation of literature, a view of life that is not at all idealized or romanticized. Honoré de Balzac and Gustave Flaubert in France, and George Eliot and George Gissing in England, are often named as key exemplars of the nineteenth-century realist movement.[35] In sharp contrast to the Scholastic, medieval use of the term "realist" (that is, in a Platonic sense in which universals exist separately from the entities they represent, and also separately from the thinking about them), the term is now used in the opposing Kantian sense to denote anti-theoretical qualities. In accord with this new understanding of realism, the attention to geographical detail in *The Betrothed* sets the straightforward tone of the entire book.

The Betrothed (unlike *Gulliver's Travels*, for example) fulfills the proper definition of a novel: it is a fictional account, delivered without any recourse to fantasy. The account of group hysteria at the time of the plague in *The Betrothed* does not disqualify it at all as a novel in the strictest sense, as it is an extended description of an historical outbreak of group hysteria, grounded in popular belief in magic. The narrator uses every mention of magic as an opportunity to denounce the belief in it.[36] Thus *The Betrothed*, rightly categorized as historical fiction, fits into the new nineteenth-century approach in three other ways as well: it features working-class protagonists, it dismisses magic, and it is written in a realist style.

3 Agrarian Society

The initial placement of the main characters in a specific, if unnamed, village, before their troubles begin, is thus one of many references in the book to the superiority of agrarian society over urban life; this could be extended to a corollary claim that the book is concerned more with the betterment of the economic standard of living than with the political rights of individuals. This approach might be taken as a choice of liberalism before liberty (to reverse the title phrase of Quentin Skinner's book, *Liberty before Liberalism*).[37] In *The Betrothed*, calls for liberty are only made in the city, whereas calls for economic liberalism, occur in both the city and the countryside. Yet this claim might be thrown into question by the highly personal nature of Renzo and Lucia's marriage, which seems to be a love match, not a pairing determined by larger geographical or ideological forces. Nevertheless, for the most part, if somewhat counter-intuitively, in this story the constructive efforts to raise the standard of living for working people come from the countryside, whereas efforts to assert the rights of individuals occur only in the city (albeit the plague also spreads more quickly in the city), thus affirming the interdependence of a major city and its hinterland.

Renzo and Lucia's village, although flawed in many respects, functions much more effectively than the nearby major city, Milan. In a Dickensian manner, the village is described in more detail than perhaps some readers indeed actually want, but the relentless emphasis on place, geographical details, and the fabric of the houses themselves can be used to demonstrate that location is vitally critical in determining financial success and a higher standard of living for the group as a whole. The city is portrayed in this work as transient, whereas the countryside represents permanence and the people. The book suggests that economic theory can have no meaning without its application to a particular time and place; the novel does not denigrate theory, but expects it to serve a practical purpose.

The village might perhaps be best understood by its gossip, which is considered both a flaw and a demonstration of a rapid means of communication in a pre-technological society. During the plague and the consequent dislocation of countless people, the sense of the village's isolation is compounded. There is, for example, the constant need to put together the story of the current crisis by the many refugees.[38] In numerous instances, the book reiterates the advantages as well as the struggles of living in a small, rural community; this distinguishes *The Betrothed* sharply from other nineteenth-century Romantic works.

4 Theoretical and Literary Sources on a Preference for the Countryside or the City

The Betrothed breaks from the disdain for farm workers (always somewhat inexplicable, given their essential role in providing food for society) to be found in classical political and economic theory. In Plato's *Republic*, farmers have no "metallic" status whatsoever in Socrates's class system, thus putting them below the bottom level of his ideal society. Slightly later, Aristotle mentions farmers with repugnance: for him, these non-city dwellers could never be capable of taking their place in the type of good government based on his dictum of "ruling and being ruled in turn." The shared assumption in Greek thought was that rural working people were incapable of fully developed reason. Throughout Western thought, the urban working class has been viewed as more sophisticated than its rural counterparts: rural workers regularly tend to be the butt of stereotypical jokes about less fashionable, often the hottest parts of that society (thus still stressing national stereotypes based on geography and climate). However, this mockery of the countryside is in contrast to aristocratic ideals of living on a country estate and, to some extent, of participating in the running of that estate, all in addition to having a social and perhaps political life in the nearby capital city. This was the life of Manzoni's aristocratic grandfather Beccaria. (Beccaria had not been impressed by his one extended visit to Paris, arranged at the invitation of Voltaire, even though French intellectuals doted on him.) As is almost always the case, the stigma of living in the countryside tends to be only applied to the working people, not the upper class; this certainly was no different in the time of the shift to the modern economy.

In several respects *The Betrothed* breaks from all these stereotypes about the countryside. In a nineteenth-century manner, Manzoni presents the Italian working class of the seventeenth century as on the verge of forming a separate identity. At the same time, the book makes clear that in the late seventeenth century, there was virtually no middle class yet in Lombardy. Historically the middle class in Western Europe generally coalesced before the working class. The major storyline in *The Betrothed* of working people becoming middle class indicates a desire in the text to diminish class conflicts between these two groups, and instead to emphasize the stark divide between rich and poor.

The tension between the countryside and the city can be taken to represent starkly the seemingly forever-unbridgeable chasm between one group made up of the privileged—with its own subgroups of aristocrats, the super-rich, and in a different way, intellectuals—and a wholly distinct group composed of poor people who worked when they could find work. Manzoni's story of the tension between the countryside and its capital city of Milan, for example, was deliberately written (in the 1820s and 1840s) to resonate with the same financial tensions and grief that had helped to topple the Bourbon monarchy in France in the 1790s.

The main characters—Renzo, Lucia, and Lucia's mother Agnese—retain their allegiance to the countryside throughout the book. Passionate and opinionated, Renzo constantly, by actions if not by words, renounces urban life and calls for a return to agrarian society. He could even be argued to be calling for Christian communal farming—community living—as the ideal form of economic organization: some of the most attractive relationships show Renzo and his neighbors sharing with each other freely in times of need, not just during times of plenty.[39] This call for a shift to the countryside is not unlike nineteenth-century formulations of Manzoni's time, the utopian socialist communities of New Lanark in Scotland, and of New Harmony in Indiana, to give two examples. The work of Robert Owen, a Utopian Socialist, founder of both New Lanark and New Harmony, could be read as the outline of the utopian society longed for by Renzo and his companions.

The Betrothed thus breaks from both the classical and popular-culture stereotyping of rural peoples, instead glorifying them in ways that reflect the practical aspects of eighteenth- and nineteenth-century Utopians, such as Charles Fourier and Owen. Owen brought actual workers into a fully functioning town and factory in New Lanark (and later in New Harmony). He outlines his system in *A New View of Society; or, Essays on the Principle of the Formation of Human Character* (1813). The term "Owenism" is now taken in a broad sense to denote the possibility of awakening human potential by changing individuals' material circumstances. Owenism implies that people behave not according to innate human nature, but almost entirely according to environment.

A much later, post-Romantic example of the glorification of the land and the people who live on it comes from the turn-of-the-twentieth-century Norwegian writer Knut Hamsun, who, in his novel *Growth of the Soil* (1917), advocates a return to the countryside.[40] This is one of several post-Romantic segues back to very traditional manners and *mores*. Likewise, *The Betrothed* recognizes the difficulties of rural life, but does not regard it necessarily to be as a life of servitude. The substantial conflicts within, and trials of, country life are certainly recorded, sometimes in amusing detail, in this book. Yet the story poses rural life as perhaps the best model for early-modern Christians—which Manzoni wanted for all of society—and thus for all those hoping to make an honest yet profitable living for themselves and their families.

The novel's emphasis on the land does not have to be viewed as backward looking or even Romantic in its supposed rejection of science, industry, and commercialization. Its view of the countryside should instead be viewed as constructive in the sense of the radical William Morris in late nineteenth-century England. Morris wanted to empower people through not only up-to-date industrial practices but also by means of domestic furnishings predicated on a respect for the workers (to give the quintessential example, he specialized in making attractive, affordable wallpaper for the homes of the working poor). Morris's utopian novel, *News from Nowhere* (1890) is still worthy of attention as a manifesto for a higher quality of life for all people.[41] Morris was not a Utopian, but rather a progressive Socialist, determined to give all workers, not just a few of them, the benefits of a Utopian experiment, such as access to beauty in architecture, painting, and literature in particular. Morris's approach embraced an aesthetic goal for the new society. At the end of *The Betrothed*, the main characters are in a new city, which seems to have some of the benefits of both their original village and of Milan—especially protection from invasion, protection from want, and steady employment—thus affirming the advantages of both the city and the land.

Symbolically, the setting of Renzo and Lucia's home in a rural village calls up the notion of state of nature, but it also hints at the benefits of early-modern, proto-industrial society. The book thus does not have to be read as a rejection of modern society, but as a reformulation of it. Unlike the work of Rousseau, which extols the freedom of the noble savage in a theoretical sense, Manzoni's novel can be read as a call for a refurbished life in the countryside with the benefits of traditional and modern life. The description of agricultural life in the book could also be taken as a detailed social history of the time. Although much more is learned about agricultural workers than about urban workers, both groups feature prominently. Again, the emphasis on agriculture might suggest a form of Catholic, communal, or even communistic life. The emphasis on the land is a reminder as well that some of the peasants would have owned their property, thus stressing property rights even for the poorest of society. Farming is indeed at the core of many utopian societies, and references throughout the book, practical and theoretical, portray in repeated ways how life outside urban centers is often better, potentially much better, than in the city.

Yet to offer a brief counter-argument, far from idealizing agrarian society, this book not only shows the small-mindedness of the powerful and the middling in the countryside but also highlights the often neglected, if obvious, point that those without power are most fully at the mercy of their superiors in a sparsely populated region, where industrial action and work-to-rule efforts are difficult to organize. Yet life in Manzoni's Milan is no workers' paradise, filled as it is with bread shortages, riots, plague, fanatics, and the *lazaretto* (which was to become the communal place of death for the poor and the sick, a place almost no one left alive, even if they were not terribly sick when they entered). The city thus contained more social and physical problems than did a village in the countryside—more problems in total, as well as in terms of scale—but the city also possessed the possible solutions to these problems.

5 Economic Transitions

Renzo's forced flight to Milan should not be viewed as an embrace of modernization at all costs. He is fleeing his village because he tried to trick the local curate into performing his marriage to Lucia (the curate would not marry them because the local landlord, the one who lusts after Lucia, opposes the marriage). This is perhaps early evidence of Renzo's proto-revolutionary tendencies, even before he is exposed to the temptations of the city. Moreover, Renzo leaves his village because Don Rodrigo, the local landlord, is now in pursuit of him, presumably in order to kill him and to get Lucia for himself. Lucia and her mother Agnese also flee the village. As the story unfolds, Renzo's constant desire is to go back to rural life, albeit perhaps to another village, with the new family he wants to support. In capsule form, this demonstrates a return to rural values and a rejection of the early-modern mercantilist value of laying up treasures of gold and silver (which was associated with court life and high society). The book is Smithian in its repeated examples of small firms that rekindle the local economy and in its overwhelming stress on productivity. There is an emphasis on currency and the region's growing silk industry, which parallels Renzo's own transition from being a silk spinner in his village, to working as a miller, and finally, to becoming the owner of a mill, along with his cousin. Yet Renzo identifies himself, over and over, as a farmer as well as a textile worker and then a mill owner. The move back to the countryside expresses a rejection of the hideous living and working conditions in the city. This book could instead be taken as an assertion of the physiocratic value of the land as the prime source of wealth for the country. All of these economic interpretations reinforce the idea that the clash between the countryside and the city in early-modern Europe, between older and newer forms of making money, played out in practice, not just in competing economic theories. In sum, Manzoni is putting forward both a serious historical reconstruction of early-modern Europe and also a response to intellectual preoccupations of his own time.

6 Renzo as a Reluctant Revolutionary

Now to the story. Rural life has not given Renzo polish, but it has given him self-confidence. He is viewed both as a rube and as a young revolutionary in the autumn of 1628 on his first day in Milan, a city seemingly so starved for revolutionary leadership that, on one frenetic day, many view him, for good or evil, as a political force in the city. The city had suffered from multiple forms of economic hardship: the Thirty Years' War was still in full force; the ruling Spaniards, full participants in this war, raised taxes on the Milanese; the weather that autumn was dreadful and the harvest was poor; there was little bread, and what bread there was was too expensive. In this situation, Renzo appears for a few hours as a leader, at times of the crowd, and also briefly as an advocate of the Spanish, because he speaks out whenever he is upset. Renzo is hailed that day as a revolutionary, and he is accused of being a police spy. As a revolutionary, speaking to the mob, he is a direct authority and, briefly, an idol of the people, yet he takes on this role by accident. He is caught up in a mob and is moved to express his views about the bread crisis, and then about political oppression in general, in a loud and surprisingly articulate manner. At an inn, following the riot, he speaks his mind still more freely. He chats with a man, revealed to the reader to be a police spy, and together they speculate wildly, indeed drunkenly, that the bread shortage could be resolved simply by introducing a system of ration cards. This was not such a far stretch from the price-fixing, however inadequate, that the Spanish had already instituted.[42] The drunkenness could be viewed as the means of bringing the truth out of Renzo, yet it also mocks his sincerity as an agitator. Renzo arrives in a city in revolt. He finds bread thrown on the ground in the midst of a time of starvation. He, like most people in Milan and early-modern Europe, is convinced that the bakers were hoarding the bread; he views bread thrown on the streets as a sign of liberation. At times the novel presents Renzo as missing the political significance of signs because of his literal interpretation of them; in this case he is reading too much symbolism into the situation. In both cases Reno is shown as slowly, falteringly trying to adapt to a new world in which he realizes that he must read signs in order to make his way.

Renzo's revolutionary activities are confined primarily to just 6 of the 38 chapters, of this long book. Yet the overtly political aspects of these scenes are present in a muted, subtler form throughout. It is worth remembering that even the final version of *The Betrothed* was completed a few years before the Revolutions of 1848, the great upsurge from Paris to Milan to Frankfurt to Vienna, which were student led in many cities. As noted above, the model for *The Betrothed* was not only the French Revolution, but also the Decembrist Revolt in Russia in the 1820s, and the led revolutions across Europe in that era.[43] Further work on the later Revolutions of 1848 would perhaps show a strong relationship between the outbreak of revolutionary activity in the Italian states in 1848 and the political message of *The Betrothed*. It might be claimed, in more general terms, that the failed Revolutions of 1848 led to the unification of Italy and of Germany. The student revolutionaries of 1848, working together with workers in revolt, were, as grown men, the supporters of the unifications of Italy and of Germany. There is a textual parallel: one of the claims being made in these chapters is that Renzo's failure as a revolutionary makes this book a greater force for political change than if the character had succeeded, because he becomes a symbol of the need for a much more profound, widespread change in the future.

When Renzo enters the city for the first time, even he senses that the atmosphere is unnaturally quiet, and that it is odd to find flour and bread on the street. There is even a round loaf of the whitest bread, such as Renzo seldom ate except on feast days, thrown down on the ground.[44] The narrator tells us that in the second year of drought, extreme heat, and bad harvests, the people start to loot the bakeries, and this was not all—the city is in revolt.[45] This indicates crisis for all parts of society, not just the poor. The idea of free bread on the streets in a time of famine invokes the notion of manna from heaven. Bread also represents hope, not just a literal meal. This free food is not, however, provided by God but rather by rioting crowds, and Renzo, although he is pleased to see the *status quo* upset, at this stage just tries to stay away from the looters.[46]

In *Das Kapital* (*Capital*, 1867, 1885, 1894) Marx stresses a perhaps unsurprising common theme with Manzoni: in any modern economy, people of all social classes buy food from bakers. Marx wrote, for example, of the British diet in the nineteenth century:

> His report . . . together with the evidence given, moved the public not in its heart but in its stomach. Englishmen, with their good command of the Bible, knew well enough that man, unless by elective grace a

capitalist, or a landlord, or the holder of a sinecure, is destined to eat his bread in the sweat of his brow, but they did not know that he had to eat daily in his bread a certain quantity of human perspiration mixed with the discharge of abscesses, cobwebs, dead cockroaches and putrid German yeast, not to mention alum, sand and other agreeable mineral ingredients.[47]

Bread for all urban homes, regardless of rank, and since the early-modern period, tended to come from bakers. "Human perspiration" as an ingredient in bread is disgusting not just in terms of the quality of the food, but also as an indication of a society that has little regard for its workers. For Marx, that perspiration is embedded in the commodity itself.

In much the same way, American novelist Upton Sinclair, the author of the still disturbing novel, *The Jungle* (1906), an *exposé* of early twentieth-century Chicago slums and slaughterhouses, was angered that his book led only to the reform of food-production practices, specifically of the meat-packing industry, but did not extend to the reform of labor and housing practices and regulations, which had been his primary goal. Sinclair, following Marx, maintained, "I aimed at the public's heart and by accident I hit it in the stomach."[48] In *The Betrothed*, the rioters likewise first demand bread, and then a number of political rights; they fail on both counts.

This story of the mob in *The Betrothed* is based on the common belief that there was actually no bread shortage, but rather that the authorities and their henchmen, the bakers, were hoarding bread. The mob does not view the bakers as oppressed workers, but as cogs in the political and economic authority structure. People of all social classes have an irrational belief in the existence of hoarded bread; in turn, the bakers feel so oppressed that they threaten the Spanish authorities that they would emigrate.[49] The people are correct in believing that price-fixing set in place by the authorities in this time of scarcity did not in reality produce any more bread.[50] The Spanish authorities tried to set prices at a reasonable level for basic foodstuffs, yet this did not take into account the price to the grocers and bakers to obtain the raw materials needed to make the bread in a time of famine. The official price-fixing can be viewed either as proof of the insincerity of official reforms or as an effective measure to maintain order. The narrator tells us in Chapter 12:

> People hastened to the bakeries to demand bread at the official price; and they demanded it with that air of threatening resolution which comes from the combination of passionate conviction, physical strength, and legal rights.[51]

Although it was not possible to raise the output of local grain and no effort was made to import it, the official price of bread was less than half of what bakers could get for their product. The blame for the bread shortage was spread widely, landowners were targeted in particular.[52] People of all backgrounds blamed bakers for bread shortages, and they called for bakers to be punished. Even the Grand Commissioner of Milan could not get fresh bread.[53] There was even fear that the bread would be poisoned.[54] These were not just working-class preoccupations but were wide-spread fears in society. Bread is perhaps the major symbol of this story, transcending the countryside and the city, and all economic arguments about it. Bread becomes more critical in symbolic ways, secular as well as religious, as it becomes scarcer.[55] Increasingly, the people use the riots to express their communal desire not just for bread but also for control over their own lives.

Bread shortages were undoubtedly not just the fault of the Spanish authorities' mismanagement. The shortages indicate poor harvests and patchy communication between countryside and city. The novel offers hints at, but it does not develop the multiple causes of the famine, one of which was certainly the impact of the Thirty Years' War. In any case, apparently there are no hidden stores of grain to be opened in the midst of the riots in this novel, and alas, this was actually the case in historical Milan in 1628.

7 Back to the Story

The story crisply continues: "At this time of increasing tension, people lurk in the bakeries to watch the bakers work and to make sure that the bread did not disappear."[56] Bakers are not breaking even financially because of the high price of grain and the low official price of bread. Even delivery boys on their rounds were publicly attacked and robbed in the street. The day before Renzo arrives in Milan large crowds formed and there was a sense that something substantial needed to be done.[57] The next day, when Renzo arrives in Milan, the rioting took a Luddite turn; the crowds destroy the sifting machines and bread bins in the bakeries.[58] As the narrator comments wryly, this is "not really the best way of ensuring long life to a plenteous supply of bread."[59]

This type of behavior is not a fictional invention. Ned Ludd and his followers from many trades destroyed the machines that had taken their place in their agricultural and industrial jobs in West Riding, in England, in 1811 and 1812. The term "Luddite" was coined from this incident. At least apocryphally, this English scrum (as if it were a coordinated advance by a sports team) is taken to indicate the belief, beyond fear of modern technology, that destroying the physical machines will destroy the technology as well. However simplistic the views of Ned Ludd and his followers regarding technology might actually have been, at least five of the group were executed in York, England, in 1813. According to the judge when he condemned them to death, this was "one of the greatest outrages that ever was committed in a civilized country."[60] Similarly, this story of Renzo repeatedly emphasizes the benefits of free trade although it also acknowledges that strong support of private property is often a bane of poor people (as in Renzo and Lucia's encounter with a corrupt rural lawyer) and that this is the case regardless of the political system under which the poor live, whether feudal or capitalist.

Renzo is struck by the sense of purpose of the rioters. The crowd displays no sense of doubt about the righteousness of its actions, and Renzo at first believes in the moral superiority of their cause because of their confidence and determination. Also, initially, Renzo tremendously enjoys the excitement of the mob. He has never before experienced, much less participated in, such a colorful spectacle. Two young boys are killed in the rioting.[61] Renzo is revolted by the call for revenge, for more blood. He is the young man who, at the beginning of the story, was proud of never having committed a crime and who was horrified when he heard about a murder.[62] Renzo's sympathies seem always to be with the underdog; his views change as the crowd begins to demonstrate the aggressive qualities of an unchecked force. The mob is so intense at this slightly later stage that Renzo's sympathy quickly shifts toward the intended victim, even though he is a Spanish high commander in Milan. Renzo instinctively cries out against this.[63] For this humanitarian response, the tide turns against Renzo, the mob quickly now views him as a traitor to their cause. Those who had praised him moments before even more quickly condemn him as a spy.[64] The story notes not only the fluctuating emotions of the crowd, but also how the best and worst qualities of human beings are brought out in mobs.[65]

The attitude toward corruption is exemplified in this scene by the presence of the Spanish official, the Grand Chancellor Antonio Ferrar, second in command in Milan, but in charge at the time of this incident because his superior is away commanding troops in the Thirty Years' War. At this point, Ferrar, along with his coachman, unfortunately decides to reason with the crowd, and instead of conversation he finds himself in the middle of the mob that Renzo for a brief moment commands. From the beginning of the story, Ferrar is portrayed not as evil but as optimistic, even childish, in his efforts to contend with the bread shortage and rapidly rising prices. However, ineptitude, even without evil intent, is shown to result in ruin just as easily as the machinations of the overt villains of the story.

Language is used as a means of control in this incident. Buoyed by the excitement of the riot, Renzo begins talking excitedly with those around him. This is exactly when Ferrar and his coachman arrive in a coach in the midst of the mob:

> The coachman also smiled with graceful affection at the mob, as he had been a gentleman of rank. With indescribable elegance he swung the whip very slowly to left and right, to ask the bystanders who were in the way to move back a little and make way for the coach.[66]

Throughout this scene, Ferrar goes back and forth between Italian and Spanish, depending on whether he wants his thoughts to be known to the crowd, or just to his driver.

At this point, Renzo quickly transfers his loyalties, and this shift has less to do with language than with charisma. Renzo is charmed by Ferrar, the Spanish official, as well as by his servant, the coachman, marooned together in their coach in the midst of the mob. Ferrar feels compelled to address the crowd, presumably because of his guilty conscience regarding the bread shortage. Renzo is so captivated by Ferrar, this glimpse of authority, and especially by Ferrar's coachman's easy manner in the midst of the incensed rioters, that Renzo tells the crowd later that they should go the next day to Ferrar to appeal directly to him as he is, apparently, the highest authority in the city.

The mutability of Renzo's views can be read both as a sign of weakness and as an indication that individual reason, however intuitive, can transform a mob's call for blood into a legitimate call for progressive reform.[67] Some of the crowd realize for themselves that the goals of the riot are becoming muddled: " 'Every ragged fellow wants to say his piece,' muttered another, 'and with this asking for other things we shall end up without the cheap bread we set out to get in the first place.' "[68] This confusion regarding the exact motivation for the riot highlights the tension between individual rights and standard of living. Implicitly, the novel both condemns mob violence and suggests that only through revolution will lasting, significant, institutional change ever be achieved. In similar manner, Ferrar is presented as likeable, and yet the results of his actions, or generally his inaction, are ruinous for Milan, leaving the city without bread. Ferrar incorporates the rhetoric of the crowd, and when threatened, he himself declares ' "*pane e guistizia*" ' (' "Bread and justice!" '), for which he is then cheered by the crowd that had been about to attack him.[69]

Not only are the characters throughout these scenes viewed as changeable, but the constructive elements of collective actions are underlined, even though the mob is clearly composed of undesirable elements. The story details the fight for the emotions of this mass of people that is being waged by the two extremes in the crowd, as if it is the fight for the single soul of the crowd.

A similar struggle for one soul, carried out by the forces of good and evil, takes place in much older books, such as Augustine's *Confessions*. Indeed, even in the final, philosophical books of *Confessions* there is a reflective comment on Carthage, the site of much of Augustine's wild youth, as well on Rome and Milan, where he also lived before his dramatic conversion. Throughout *Confessions*, Augustine outlines in colorful detail, most of it from personal experience, the multiple temptations for a young man in a major city in the fourth and fifth centuries.

For Renzo, in the midst of the mob in Milan in 1628, there is relatively little temptation, but much danger. There are some nasty characters present, and they were disappointed that the day was turning out to be so "tame and incomplete."[70] Yet there are such "dregs" at all points of the social spectrum. In his speech to the crowd, Renzo rightly argued that

> 'It's clear enough that the King, and the people at the top, want the criminals punished; but nothing happens, because they're all in league with each other. What we've got to do is break the league.'[71]

Throughout the book the distinction is drawn between "a young lord who has to have cotton sheets on his bed" and Renzo, who later asks simply for "freshly washed sheets: for I'm a poor lad, but used to cleanliness"; the former are "men whose family names were high titles in themselves," and who are wholly removed from the problems of the rest of society.[72] The book makes clear that the working class has no monopoly on villainy. The themes of monarchy and aristocracy are not taken as new subjects in the story; invoking the ruling classes was taken as a shorthand means of contrasting the situation of the rich from that of the poor.

8 Mobs and the Concept of Individuality

The willingness of the people to revolt indicates a shift in the political climate overall in the city. The book repeatedly stresses that only when people sense some freedom will they acknowledge their outrage at how they have been treated.[73] To set this scene in historical context it must be remembered that riots in Europe before the French Revolution were generally an exercise in futility at best. Most revolts lacked organization and appropriate leadership. Often the leaders, at times the majority of the participants, were summarily and publicly executed once social control was re-imposed. After 1789 and the onset of the French Revolution, an intense fear of mobs, and of the overthrowing of monarchical government, gripped Europe. This led to a shift across Europe toward more conservative forms of government in order to guard against rioting in particular. By the nineteenth century, the potential power of the rioters gave labor agitators a power that derived not only from the Industrial Revolution, but also from the legacy of the rioters, particularly *les sans culottes,* the artisan leaders of the riots of the French Revolution.

That Renzo could become a leader of the bread riots on his first full day in Milan, beginning on the streets and later in dangerous talk in a tavern, is an indication of how this riot was the result of an emotional reaction to years of oppression, but by people who lacked leadership. No revolutionary cell had been at work to enact radical political change on its own timetable. According to the theory of crowd psychology from Gustave Le Bon, in his work, *La Psychologie des foules (The Crowd,* 1895), one of the first works of theory to contend with the violent force of a crowd: a mob must be understood as much more than the sum of its parts. This pre-Freudian work (indeed it is directly cited by Freud) nevertheless gestures toward a theory of the unconscious and a theory of leadership, both of which are distinct from Marxist reflections of Manzoni's time.[74] The desperate bread riots in *The Betrothed* are cited by scholars of crowd theory as evidence of early-nineteenth-century fears of crowds and packs.[75] Overall the stress on the crowd in *The Betrothed* highlights the unspoken desires and frustrations of people generally unable to express their own thoughts even to themselves, regardless of whether they are part of the crowd or whether they are frightened onlookers.

9 Theories of Revolution

Despite the full incorporation of religion into this story, Manzoni deliberately wrote *The Betrothed* as an homage to the French Revolution; however, it is less often discussed that the novel also foreshadows the work of the three major theorists of revolution: Marx, Lenin, and Trotsky. The novel suggests multiple perspectives on all three thinkers. Marx's views on the Machinery Question do not call for the destruction of machines, but rather their use for and by the workers themselves. Marx drew many of his ideas about historical materialism from Ludwig Feuerbach, a student of Hegel. Yet Marx separated himself from Feuerbach's idealist approach to bettering the situation of humankind. Marx and Friedrich Engels, most famously in *Das Manifest der Kommunistischen Partei* (*The Communist Manifesto*, 1848), declared: "The history of all hitherto existing society is the history of class struggle." *The Manifesto* ends with the challenge: "Working men, of all countries, unite!"[76] Marx and Engels's assumption about the possibility of change was grounded in a Hegelian notion of a dialectical view of history—that there would be a natural, spontaneous shift to this new social order, an idea Lenin was to question. Lenin argued that revolution would come about only through violence directed by revolutionary leaders. This question divided socialists in the early twentieth century: at issue was whether revolution would occur spontaneously, or whether it had to be induced, as Lenin claimed, through violence by revolutionary leaders who might themselves not even be working-class. This was just one of the many quarrels of socialist and communist thinkers from the early nineteenth to the early twentieth century. Even later, the debate centered on where the revolution should take place. For example, one contrast (in addition to the intellectual level of their thought) between the ideas of Stalin and Trotsky was that Trotsky argued for the need for world revolution, whereas Stalin was willing to accept revolution just in one country, given that it was his country. *The Betrothed* is just one of many works of nineteenth-century fiction that could be used to exemplify the back and forth of multiple revolutionary demands, but it surprises most readers that these revolutionary ideas appeared first in the fiction rather than in the theory of the time.

10 That Night at the Inn

In this story, soon after the riot, Renzo goes to an inn, but his arrival at this particular inn is not an accident. He is taken there by a man seemingly impressed by his speech-making to the crowd and who offers to introduce him to his friend, an innkeeper. This man is actually the police spy, who is searching throughout the riot for someone, a patsy, to be charged with inciting it. Upon his arrival at the inn, Renzo is greeted with enthusiasm because he has arrived with bread. He is indeed very welcome, even though everyone is convinced he stole the bread, not that he found it on the ground as he insists. Any mention of paying for bread is treated like a joke.[77] However, some legalities are enforced on that day. Renzo raises suspicions at the inn when he refuses to give his name and personal details to the innkeeper for the record. Renzo finds such prying offensive, as a country person he does not recognize this as part of normal procedure for a guest at an inn. However, in this situation, he is right to be wary.

Renzo soon loses his caution, however, and continues to speechify at the inn. He is aided by countless glasses of wine pressed on him by his supposed new friend, the police spy, who identifies himself as a sword-maker. Renzo, apparently only used moderate drinking at home, quickly becomes drunk. Exhaustion, exhilaration, and alcohol bring on his detailed criticism of the existing political rule and his discourse on the need for ration cards as a means of making sure that all people received some bread in a time of bread shortages. Renzo does not seem to notice that ration cards would require the type of collection of personal information that he had objected to when the landlord wanted his personal details earlier. Renzo's intense discussion of ration cards with the sword-maker at the inn strikes his listeners at the inn as just bizarre, not revolutionary. Nevertheless, price-fixing, however flawed, is already in place, and ration cards are a viable option of the time. Ferrar, who at one point is most concerned that he "cannot even take a siesta in beleaguered Milan," later does institute a system of rationing for bread.[78] The dividing line between outrageous demands and practical economic reforms is tested repeatedly in these six chapters in a staccato series of jarring and then amusing scenarios—riot scenes and political declarations, followed by the main character very, very drunk.

The innkeeper, who takes the money for the night's stay off Renzo's drunken body late that night rather than waiting to be paid the next morning, has a set of his own opinions worthy of analysis.[79] He despises Renzo both for being a revolutionary leader of sorts and also for coming in with a police spy, thus doubly threatening the innkeeper's livelihood. The innkeeper has no time for either the revolutionary or the spy.[80] The innkeeper represents the sector of society that would fight to resist improvements for their social group if there were any immediate personal costs. When the innkeeper escorts Renzo to the police the next day, he lectures him on the way, while reflecting to himself how naïve Renzo is to think he can change the political system.[81]

Renzo's speeches at the end of the riot and again that night at the inn make him the perfect example for the officials of "some individual agitator, and [they want to] make an example of him."[82] It was not just the amount he had to drink at the inn that is at issue. Drinking is certainly not frowned upon; instead, other people were mocked for not drinking. The concern is his political views. The police spy, named Ambrogio Fusella, deliberately searches the crowd for a dupe. He surmises that, even sober, Renzo would be the perfect person to blame for the riot."[83]

This makes Renzo a prototype for the character Barnaby Rudge, the half-wit hero and leader of a mob in the anti-Catholic Gordon Riots in London in

1780, in Dickens's eponymous novel, the most explicitly political of Dickens's novels.[84] Both novels could be read as putting forward a cynical view of mobs as directly guided by the lowest common denominator, mentally as much as morally, in the group. The innkeeper goes to the police that night to report that he was harboring a malcontent, but the police already know from the police spy about Renzo's stolen bread and his speeches at the inn, and the innkeeper is berated rather than praised by the authorities. Following the rules is not enough to gain the innkeeper any credit with them. However, the police spy and the innkeeper together conspire to keep tabs on Renzo until he can be delivered to the police the following day. They are an awkward pair, and they have very different reasons for helping the police.

The next morning, a notary and his two henchmen roughly wake Renzo, shouting his name (the drunken Renzo was tricked the night before into telling his name). By morning, it becomes clear even to Renzo that the men are there to deliver him to the police. However, when Renzo, now handcuffed, is escorted by the rough trio, he lets the passers-by know that he is being taken to prison for calling for bread and justice the day before. The people on the street press in around him until he is released. The notary himself is then in danger of being attacked by the growing mob. The crowd encourages Renzo, as he breaks free of his captors. Well-wishers point out nearby churches and monasteries where Renzo could find refuge. Instead, he decides to escape from Milan immediately, and he goes to his cousin who lives in the territory of Bergamo, thus outside of Spanish-controlled Milan and Lombardy and into the Venetian territory, where he would be safe.[85]

Renzo is already outside of Milan when he learns that he is now considered a dangerous felon, a hunted man, and so he takes a circuitous route to his cousin, as he fears that he is being followed by the police. On the way, he lies when asked where he is from, and he asks directions to places he is not going, in order to throw off his pursuers. Thus, after two days in Milan, Renzo, unable until then to lie, finds is now able to do so at will. However, he still continues to make speeches as he travels, most of them about the riots in Milan, an odd way to deflect attention. Indeed, he is visible in other ways as well. He is still wearing the clothes he had put on the day he had tried to trick the cowardly Don Abbondio into performing his marriage to Lucia back in their village. Renzo, after having left Milan, and then hunted by the authorities throughout the region, has become a notorious figure. He hears his speech to the mob in Milan quoted back to him later in a more violent version. He is remembered to have incited the crowd to murder the gentry.[86] The reports depict Renzo's actions as very dark. And, as Agnese, Lucia's mother, notes later, "It doesn't take much to make a poor man look like a criminal."[87] The people in the countryside carefully follow the revolts in the city through travelers' stories, as they know that there would be repercussions, probably of the worst sort, for them as well.

The political situation is not only tenser in all respects, but the extent of the economic devastation is becoming starker, even in a matter of days.

Many of those on the road were simply fleeing; they were not professional beggars.[88] Renzo gives his last coins to a family clearly in much worse straits than he, a family that is poor apparently for the first time.[89] He encounters beggars who do not even yet look destitute.[90] Later, on his second visit to Milan, when Renzo returns to try and find Lucia, the economic situation has worsened even more, as is once again made clear with reference to social class: professional beggars are now outnumbered by the new poor.[91]

When he arrives at his cousin's home, there is no work for him, but Renzo's story of his time in Milan makes the sudden arrival comprehensible; Renzo is found a job at the silk-spinning mill, part of the textile business that his cousin manages. The authorities continue to search for him, even in his hometown. Although they never locate him, Renzo continues to feel hunted until he is able to receive an official pardon for a crime he never meant to commit in the first place—the crime of being a revolutionary leader.

11 Exit of the Failed Revolutionary

Despite the overall preference for the countryside in this book, symbolically it is in the city that Renzo has the chance to claim, if not receive, his rights. There is no venue for claiming rights in a rural area with the likes of *il dottore* Azzecca-garbugli (which means "an adroit weaver of tangles," sometimes translated as Dr. Quibbler). He is the rural lawyer who accepts payment but refuses to help Renzo and Lucia in their quest to get married. *Il dottore* is a regular dinner guest at the castle of Don Rodrigo, the same local lord who wants to seduce Lucia.[92] At these dinner parties, "the words which rang out most sonorously and frequently were 'nectar' and 'hangings,'"[93] thus making explicit how the ruling classes take pleasure not only in subjugating the masses, but also in explicit violence, not just the threat of it. There are very few avenues for legal aid in the countryside, and seemingly, the local landowner controls any that do exist.

Renzo represents the agricultural worker forced by the poor decision making of the local landlord to leave his home in order to find work in the city so that he can support the new family he wishes so much to start. Thus Don Rodrigo, the local landlord, is a much more immediate threat than the often absent, but financially demanding landlords who dominated the countryside throughout Europe on both sides of the English Channel at this time. The Highland Clearances in Scotland in the late eighteenth century is only one of the most vivid examples of the dispossession of agricultural workers from their homes in Europe in the century when this book was written. The Irish fleeing from the potato famine of 1845–1849 and the mass emigration of Southern Italians, dating from about 1876, in both cases often to America, are two later examples blamed, at least partially, on wildly unsympathetic landlords. Renzo's flight from home would have resonated with early readers of this book who had heard of such forced migrations from the countryside to the city; increasingly, many readers would have experienced this in their own families, or, at least indirectly, by watching it happen to their former servants.

In addition to the view of Renzo as the emerging, urban, modern citizen, he could just as well be taken to be the symbol of early-modern, Italian, Catholic peasants or, somewhat amusingly, as representing Calvinist pre-determination, the Weberian Protestant work ethic. Renzo's combination of attributes is consistent with Manzoni's own Catholic Liberalism, which embraced both a reformed Catholicism and *laissez-faire* economics, which begins with Adam Smith in Protestant Scotland. Renzo, by his very nature and in the choices he makes, perhaps indicates to society and to his God that he is part of the elect by living a highly productive life on his own land in the countryside. In this oddly Weberian (and thus Protestant) interpretation, the shift is toward the new industrial state, not a rejection of it.[94]

Again, if Renzo's only wish is to survive in order to marry Lucia, and he is willing to move to another rural area in order to obtain the country lifestyle he desires, it is only because he is being prevented from staying in his own home village. Renzo is not, at the beginning of this story, searching for a new kind of work, urban and/or technological, even to the extent that it was available in early seventeenth-century Northern Italy. Rather, he wants to reproduce the life and work of his home village in some other rural setting, where he and his future family can settle permanently. This is a decision that he makes almost unconsciously for a mixture of political and economic, not just personal, reasons.

In the final pages of the book, Renzo finally marries Lucia, and at the same time he is forced to decide between his two careers, farming and industry.[95] The narrator tells us that Renzo does not know it, but these are exactly the subjects that would be discussed in the learned societies of the eighteenth century. Agriculture and industry were virtually the only two ways for an early seventeenth-century young man to make his living. Service industries, generally a less physically demanding choice for workers in transition since the nineteenth century, did not exist on the same scale in the seventeenth century.[96] There were fewer shops, restaurants, and public social spaces. Even the choice of working in industry was relatively new.

Despite Renzo's feeling that he could only go in one direction or the other, after repeated discussions, he and Lucia make a second move later, to become owners of a mill. Ownership of the mill indicates a slight upward shift in social class for both of them. In this sense they once again bridge a gap, continuing a profession that has existed since antiquity, but contributing as well to the technological advances not only in their own mill but also in their region. The passage quoted above praises the ordinary worker for thinking shrewdly about a choice that was not a false dichotomy, but is probably a final choice for life. It also indicates the time lag for intellectuals' investigations into the realities of working-class life, in this case, about one hundred years. Thus seventeenth-century rural workers could arguably have set the agenda for the arguments of eighteenth-century intellectuals, not just by their actions, but even in their casual debates.

12 Economic Theory about Famine from the Eighteenth Century to Amartya Sen

The concerns in this work are not all metaphysical, but also have to do with religious conversion, political rights, and economic need. Manzoni's deep commitment to the subject of bread shortages stemmed both from actual famines in Italy in the seventeenth century and into the eighteenth century—the last great famine in Italy occurred as late as 1764—and from the remarkably high level of debate about bread crises among Italian economic thinkers of the eighteenth century. Famine was an ongoing problem in the South, *il Mezzogiorno* (referring to the burning midday sun in the South of the Italian peninsula), in particular. The Kingdom of Naples, in the South, is crucial in this book, even though Florence is Manzoni's model for spoken Italian. The Kingdom of Naples became a center for economic studies—particularly the question of how to avoid famine—in the intervening century between the setting of this book and the writing of this book. Antonio Genovesi, at the university in Naples, became the first person ever to hold a Chair of Political Economy. Franco Venturi, the twentieth-century Italian scholar of the Enlightenment, notes that the school around Genovesi sought to bring about direct change in the economy, to revive local industries (oil and silk as well as grain), to establish connections to academies throughout Europe, and to directly reform the government.[97] Genovesi already held this position in 1764, the year of the great famine, when thousands died in Naples alone. Genovesi recognized that famine was caused not just by the degree of government intervention—and he favored more free trade and less control of grain stocks by the government—but also by the low level of education of the population. In a direct Enlightenment move, he worked for greater public education as a means to enact change, and he appealed to the emerging middle class to become the instruments of this change.[98] It is not by accident that Manzoni refers to Southern as well as Northern Italian thinkers and historians in *The Betrothed*; it is an indication that Naples and Milan were the two centers of the Italian Enlightenment.

In the generation after Genovesi, the economic approach to poverty and famine shifted, but Southern Italians were still generating the ideas. Ferdinando Galiani, a popular Neapolitan diplomat in Paris, was well known across Europe and in America for his work on corn prices, and also for his wit and excellent French. Galiani was at first pro-free trade, but later became anti-physiocrat (thus anti-free trade), especially because of the 1764 famine in Southern Italy and the wholesale inability of the Bourbon (French) government in the Kingdom of Naples to contend with the famine. Tuscany was able to function well in this period with free trade, and little government intervention, but the same was certainly not the case for the South of Italy, especially Naples, where thousands died of starvation. Galiani was one of the first public figures to challenge the physiocrats' approach to the emerging modern economy via free trade and a crucial stress on agriculture. In Paris, the French *encyclopédistes* were split on this question. Slowly, Galiani's views were accepted in France and elsewhere as more realistic than those of the free-trade physiocrats. Diderot himself was one of Galiani's champions on this issue.[99] This theoretical economic debate had practical implications for the Kingdom of Naples, ruled by the Bourbons, and had a theoretical base. The profound disappointment among Italian reformers at the failure of the French Revolution led some of them to become involved in the Neapolitan Revolution of 1799. When this Revolution was put down, the leaders fled Southern Italy, and subsequently spread their doctrines throughout Europe and beyond. Intriguingly, Manzoni could just as easily have learned about these Italian economic thinkers during his years in Paris as during his time in Milan.

Much more recent economic theory, that of Indian economist Amartya Sen, is also grounded in an Enlightenment tradition. Sen's 1981 work *Poverty and Famines: An Essay on Entitlement and Deprivation* puts forward a new theory of famine.[100] Sen rejects older theories of famine that emphasize food supply; he instead highlights capabilities, thus stressing "(1) well-being, and (2) the freedom to pursue well-being."[101] His entitlement approach goes further to emphasize ownership and exchange. Sen argues that

> A person starves *either* because he does not have the ability to command enough food, *or* because he does not use this ability to avoid starvation. . . .
> The entitlement approach concentrates on each person's entitlements to commodity bundles including food, and views starvation as resulting from a failure to be entitled to a bundle with enough food.[102]

This statement is remarkably similar to Renzo's declarations about the right of every person to have enough to eat, which he proclaims during the bread riot.

All these theories from Southern Italy, and now from Sen, are to some degree rejecting, or at least modifying, classical economic theory. Classical economic theory is exemplified, almost caricatured, in the early-eighteenth-century view of Bernard Mandeville, writing before Adam Smith. According to Mandeville, lavish spending of the rich and powerful should be encouraged as it would add to the strength of the national economy overall; the poor should not be coddled. This is an extreme version of mercantilism. *The Betrothed* indicates that there was no Smithian "invisible hand" that would work out the difficulties at play for this Italian region ruled by the Spanish, and invaded, seemingly at will, by the Germans, who were the invaders in the Italian Peninsula at this stage of the Thirty Years' War. The bread shortages lead the people to the immediate assumption that the government, even a foreign government, must take control and dole out the remaining available food supplies. In *The Betrothed*, there is no call—during the riot or at the inn where Renzo debates on the evening following the riot—to wait until the market goes up once again. Thus *The Betrothed* actually is putting forward a modified view of classical economic theory: free trade, with little government intervention in business, but nevertheless the establishment of government emergency services, such as an arrangement to fend off famine. This is an early example of neo-classicism with some of the benefits of a welfare state, a mixture generally attributed to John Maynard Keynes in the mid-twentieth century.

13 Theoretical Implications of Renzo as a Revolutionary

Renzo's time as a revolutionary, however reluctant, conflicted, and ultimately failed, can nevertheless be read as a Marxist moment. The class consciousness of this illiterate young man from the countryside has been awakened; he has shed his false consciousness and realizes who he is. In a Marxist sense, he understands himself as oppressed and as one of the working people. In a Freudian sense, he also understands himself as separate from his parents and his family background. Renzo recognizes and responds to his material circumstances in the urban setting. Even though many of the same problems had been present in the rural setting—lack of food, lack of appropriate work, and oppression by social betters—there were enough familiar and pleasant distractions, including his supposedly imminent marriage to Lucia, to distract Renzo from recognizing all this at home. His newly revealed but deep feelings of being oppressed by higher social and especially economic classes were apparently present earlier, but only become clear to him in the midst of the urban crisis. Renzo is aware—in the midst of his own rapid epistemological shift in the hours of the riot and just afterward in the tavern—that he is at the bottom of the economic structure of his society, and that only a rebellion would enable not only him and the people he loved, but all people, to survive. He also recognizes that there are a great many other oppressed peoples in similar circumstances. Some of these people he has just met, others he would never meet, but all were, in a visceral way, his siblings. Only revolution would enable them to enact major social change, which would allow them to achieve the type of material and personal satisfaction that they both desired and deserved.

Yet Renzo is reluctant at various points on the day of the riot. He hesitates to take the bread strewn on the ground; he immediately doubts his own violent instincts when those around him become very aggressive; he wants to turn to the foreign, Spanish ruler Ferrar for guidance; and he expects there to be a general recognition of the need for social change, not that such a new society must be imposed upon the old one. This last point would generally be associated with the ideas of conservative thinker Edmund Burke, not Marx.

Thus if Renzo is portrayed as the abstract individual in these scenes, he is one who finds leadership by accident, apparently not through predestination, and surely not through training. This raises the question of whether a Hegelian world-historical individual must have a sense of destiny, or whether he can be thrown into the role, thus leading to the possibility that many other individuals at the critical scene could have filled that predestined role in a Hegelian sense. Thus, in this interpretation, if Renzo had not spoken out at the critical moment in the riots, then someone else would have done so.

Class consciousness—the rising up of Marx's *Lumpenproletariat* against their supposed betters, those who are unable to make a living in a legal, regular manner, along with those who have fallen in status and financial rank—can be found throughout *The Betrothed*. (This is class consciousness as much from Manzoni's own experience of the nineteenth century as from his attempt to depict seventeenth-century Italians.) Marx calculates that this group, the "flotsam of society," includes:

> swindlers, mountebanks, *lazzaroni* [scoundrels], pickpockets, tricksters, gamblers, *maquereaus* [pimps], brothel keepers, porters, *literati*, organ grinders, ragpickers, knife grinders, tinkers, beggars—in short, the whole indefinite, disintegrated mass.[103]

Late in *The Betrothed*, during the plague, Manzoni puts forward a rather different, indeed touching version of Marx's *Lumpenproletariat*, these dispossessed people:

> And to all the indigent in these categories [former servants, in this instance, and their former masters who could no longer live as before] must be added many others who were normally more or less dependent on them and their earnings—women, children and old people, either huddling close to those who had formerly been their breadwinners, or scattering through the streets to beg separately.[104]

The mention of the masters evokes the fallen gentry, and their desire to present a front of calm, wealth, and power, even when the material possessions are no longer in place for this to be done with ease. This indicates as well the reluctance of institutions to admit their failings, indeed to carry on the pomp and circumstance of more lavish times as a means of reassuring both those in power and those not in power that the bulwarks of that economic structure have not changed despite the disasters. More directly, the "masters" represent a force of authority that is separate from wealth. This affirms (again in a way that would now be termed Foucauldian) that the attitude of power and control can be both learned and separated from the traditional means of asserting it. Thus, although this example is of traditional leaders, it also puts forward the early-modern stereotype of a Machiavellian prince, one who has the talents for charismatic leadership but is probably not part of a hereditary line of succession.[105] In more overarching terms, "the masters" stand for the selfishness and vanity of human nature, they are unable to admit humanity's most basic faults and thus they exacerbate problems until they explode so completely that not only people but other things the masters love—human, animal, architectural, and geographical—are destroyed.

The implications of Renzo's reluctance to take on the guise of a revolutionary, as he slips in and out of this role during his first visit to Milan, are mixed. This is the case whether he is read as the abstract individual, representing the most ordinary, bookish readers of this book, or he is read as a previously unrecognized political leader—or perhaps as both. It is worthwhile to think of Renzo, at times shown as a fool, semi-literate but with remarkable oratorical skills, as actually being the average individual. He seems to be both less savvy than most people in practical terms and yet better able to grasp overarching implications of current events. In any case, Renzo's revolutionary tendencies, and his reluctance, could be used both to confirm a Marxist reading (that revolutionary leaders will emerge naturally when needed) or a Leninist view (that only violence will bring about the new social order). Also to be found in this novel is an early version of Gramsci's theory of hegemony, of dominant groups that gain control of society out of all proportion to their legal status or even wealth. Renzo's failure as a leader also resonates with Gramsci's stress on the role of the intellectual in society. Gramsci considers all people to be intellectuals, but believes that not all would fulfill that role as their job or calling. This is reminiscent of earlier thinkers as well, including Kant in *What Is Enlightenment?* Perversely, in *The Betrothed*, there is also an echo of Alexis de Tocqueville's fear of mob rule, which is expressed most clearly in his work on democracy and America.

Thus *The Betrothed* is explicitly political on several fronts, including language. The Tuscan version of this book was finally published in 1842, only 28 years before the unification of Italy. The revolutionary aspect of the book was founded on the presentation of a standard Italian language that would unite Italians. Manzoni's willingness even to mock his own dialect, Milanese, in favor of the Florentine dialect, Tuscan, affirms conviction regarding the need for a single language for the Italian people.

The subversive element comes out most clearly in Renzo's entry into Milan, the most explicitly revolutionary part of the book. His character could be viewed as the leader needed to unite and rule the Italian peninsula. Again, the figure of a strong leader uniting Italy is invoked as early as the last chapter of Machiavelli's *Prince*, in 1513.

There are other political ways to read this book. The tyrannical dons (the Spanish term is used because the Spanish control Milan at this stage) can be seen as disturbing examples of the internal difficulties of uniting Italy, beyond ridding the peninsula of foreign oppressors, and of an existing system of control that would have to be broken or co-opted if Italy were to be ruled for the good of all. The symbolic significance of Don Rodrigo's death from the plague (he was the one who had been sexually harassing Lucia), and Renzo's survival from the plague, should be noted in this context. There are seemingly two reasons for this: Renzo is morally correct and he, and not

Don Rodrigo, has the vitality to do the work necessary to bring Italy into its next phase free of outside powers, notably Spain, France, and the Austro-Hungarian Empire. Don Rodrigo is not only corrupt, but also spent.

The bread shortage, followed by the plague, created the situation of want and despair that brought down people who ordinarily were employed and providing for others. In this proto-revolutionary setting, people were not just eager for employment or at least some small bit of money through begging or even theft, but also desired revenge on groups that had not suffered as much, even if those groups were not necessarily responsible for the disasters. The desire for change was often personal and vicious, not just proto-national and constructive.

Bertolt Brecht's theory of *Verfremdungseffekt* (popularly known as Alienation Effect, or A-Effect) is of use here, this theory proposes that in order to bring about political change the audience should leave the theater dissatisfied with the ending.[106] Brecht is himself a good example of the model of the intellectual set out by Gramsci. Brecht designed his theory in response to Lenin's question, "*Wie und was soll man lernen?*" ("How and what should one learn?"—as expressed, in German, by Brecht). Brecht was committed to using the performing arts as a political tool that was personal as well as overtly propagandistic. Using Brecht's A-Effect theory, *The Betrothed* is most successful as a call for a unified Italy not by showing Renzo as leading a successful revolution that day in Milan, or even a year or a decade later. To the contrary, the desired result would come about by leading readers themselves to the point of recognizing that only when Italians ruled a united Italy, when they "rule, and are ruled in turn," having thrown off all forms of foreign and domestic oppression, could the problems outlined with such ferocity in this book be overcome. This story of a reluctant, eventually failed revolutionary leader gestures toward all these political theories.

14 The Woman Question

Although the book features a number of strong women of different types (at least one of whom, the Nun of Monza, is deeply corrupt) and a positive view of family, the book does not appear at first to be particularly revolutionary in regard to what was called, in the nineteenth century, the Woman Question. The Woman Question was the debate regarding the role of girls and women in the family and in society, and it centered especially on the topic of education for girls. Lucia and Agnese, however, are more concerned about staying safe and finding Renzo so the marriage can take place than about changing the basic structure of their lives. Yet it is Agnese, not Lucia or Renzo, who represents the brains of the rural working class. Agnese has both traditional and revolutionary characteristics and easily moves between these two modes, depending on which will help her family the most at any given time. She is, for example, the one able to use gossip as a means of determining the best place for Renzo to go into hiding. She is presented as capable and attractive in a surprising number of respects. At many stages, the tension is between the more proactive characters, Renzo and Agnese, rather than between Renzo and Lucia. Lucia seems too young for a romantic relationship, or simply not particularly interested in Renzo (at least this was Renzo's perception at times), and this goes beyond age and maturity. Lucia's seeming unworldliness is at least partially the result of her spiritual instincts being more developed than those of her mother. Yet the difference between mother and daughter has to do not only with religion or even later with Lucia's vow of virginity made in a desperate pact with God in return for her freedom (although Lucia becomes more intrigued by Renzo after she takes her vow of virginity). Agnese has no mystical tendencies; her strength is that of a remarkably shrewd, proto-business woman. She retains financial independence and takes care of Renzo as well as her own daughter. It is Agnese who obtains and safeguards the money (one hundred gold *scudi*, a small fortune for them, given to them by *l'innominato*, the Unnamed, after he releases Lucia, but presented by Cardinal Borromeo) intended to serve as a dowry for Lucia, or for any other purpose that the mother and daughter choose.[107] Agnese hides the money until she can send half to Renzo to begin a new life for the three of them. (Toward the end of the book, this money is used to buy a mill, which then supports them all.) This payoff occurs toward the end of an epic series of almost mythical events culminating in the conversion of the most terrifying warlord of the region, the man to whom Don Rodrigo answered, someone so awe-inspiring that he was called only the Unnamed. The strong women in this novel generally confirm rather than subvert family values.

Beyond a stereotype about Italian culture, the notion of family is still very much part of this Italian story. Francis Fukuyama, in *Trust: The Social Virtues and the Production of Prosperity*, stresses the long-standing, traditional Italian emphasis on family as similar and yet distinct from that in Japan and as the basis of trust in business relationships for both of these economies still today.[108] The same close connections between family and career decision making can already be found in *The Betrothed*. In contrast, the commitment to family is muted in other famous works of national fiction such as *Don Quixote, Simplicissimus, Gulliver's Travels*, and *Candide*. In *The Betrothed*, all three of the lead characters are equally bound, long after they leave home, by promises made in their village. The betrothal of Renzo and Lucia is almost never doubted by anyone (with the exception of Renzo and Lucia themselves at times). Long absences and hardships intensify rather than diminish the devotion of the three main characters to one another. The three function as a family for the entire story, long before there is a wedding.

One of the surprising results here of the family, indeed extended family, as the basic social unit, rather than the individual or society, is that otherwise marginalized people, such as older, single women, are not viewed as abnormal. These older women are sometimes even powerful in a conventional sense, not just as outsiders and threats (for example, the supposed witches who are discussed in colorful detail in the plague section of *The Betrothed*). Agnese is never viewed as a hindrance, but rather as the means to allow Lucia and Renzo finally to marry. She is a full member of their new, emerging family. Agnese's ongoing role in their family, even after their multiple moves from their original village, is never doubted. This characterization of Agnese as shrewd, devoted, and attractive is a surprising change from the portrayal of older women in most of European literature (in Chaucer's *Canterbury Tales* and Erasmus's *Praise of Folly*, to give just two examples) which deliberately follows ancient texts in their disparagement of women, especially old women, as a major part of the satire. Thus, overall, many nuances in *The Betrothed* flesh out the discussion of the nineteenth-century Woman Question, which addressed public concerns for girls and woman, such as legal rights, access to education, and the availability of desirable jobs, more than on the question of how women are to find balance in their lives, most of which would probably be spent as wives and mothers, whether they work outside the home or not. At the time that this book was written, capitalism (which was now identified with Lucia) was as much a subject of debate as revolution (now represented by Renzo), with each main character designed to present a direct ideological challenge to the first readers of the book.

15 Romanticism Trumps Enlightenment

The Betrothed is generally argued to be a work of the Romantic Movement rather than of the late Enlightenment. Yet however much Manzoni was involved in the creation of Romanticism, he identified himself almost wholly (again, with reservations about its attitude toward religion) with the Enlightenment. This seeming paradox can be partly explained by a new understanding of the Enlightenment as not wholly anti-religious.

In any case, Manzoni's work, despite its Enlightenment roots, defined Romanticism for the Italian-speaking world and beyond. It is in his religious themes that most of his Romantic elements can be located. This is supported by recent work on the Counter-Enlightenment in France that sustains a belief in a multiplicity of views on religion even among those who support the Enlightenment. The insistence on genuine spirituality existing within corrupt Church institutions might be perceived not just as theological in orientation but as a more secular recognition of the force of spirit, even abstract ideas, over institutions. At all stages of this work, the instinctive pull of spirituality on individuals is grounded in a belief that even the most corrupt of individuals has a conscience that can never be wholly stamped out, however vile his or her actions. The conversion of the Unnamed could thus be argued to be only the most theatrical instance of this. There is a much more generous notion of forgiveness in this Catholic work than is to be found from Protestants (for example, Jonathan Edwards, an eighteenth-century, New England Calvinist, who believed in predestination and preached that there were certain "unpardonable sins" that were so heinous that such a sinner, even if later repentant, could never be saved). *The Betrothed*, written by an author who was born Catholic, converted to Protestantism as a young man, and then converted back to Catholicism along his Protestant wife, contains a struggle not only between rationality and emotion, but also between the inherent force of ideas over instinct in the actions of individuals and in the workings of human institutions over time. The strong emphasis on forgiveness in *The Betrothed* connects the rational and emotional aspects of this work.

16 Ending of the Book

At the end of the book, Lucia and Renzo's marriage seems, in some respects, to have been more exciting as a goal than it is in reality. Their eventual union could be conventionally interpreted as Renzo representing the free spirit and Lucia embodying the conventions that would tie him down to traditional marriage and family. Lucia finally symbolizes home and religion and Renzo finally represents emerging capitalism, indeed all work outside the home. This new pairing could support a Marxist interpretation: the couple could be taken to represent the two dominant ideologies of the seventeenth century, or more likely the nineteenth century, the thesis and the antithesis, and that in their life together they would quite literally form the synthesis from this clash of ideologies.

Somewhat oddly, in the final pages the villagers in the new place where Renzo has settled express disappointment that, after almost two years of hearing Renzo talking about his lost love, she turns out to be not beautiful, but fairly ordinary, and indeed some even say ugly. Renzo is deeply offended and becomes offensive in his manner. He has never been one to reflect before he speaks. Yet at the same time he knows that many of the family's problems have been caused by his impetuous nature, his willingness to talk out of turn. He later achieves calm only when they move to yet another area, one that had not heard the beautiful-lost Lucia story. Thus Renzo's sense of contentment at that later stage can also be attributed, at least partially, to no longer being told that his Lucia, whom he wanted so desperately, is not such a great catch, as much as to their improved economic status. Some people in the later village even think she is pretty, although perhaps that is because she is the wife of the new mill owner. The townspeople's criticisms, these bits of unattractive human nature—to be found in a grand love story that refuses to conform to all the classic features of such a story, questioning something as crucial as the beauty of the heroine, or more precisely the community's acknowledgement of the beauty of the heroine—indicate author's control, knowing full well that readers would be surprised by deviations from the set pattern. These squabbles are also another useful reminder that the book is not simply advocating life rural over urban life, for it was in a smaller town, where people tend to know each other's business, that Renzo is joshed for having expended so much energy on such an ordinary-looking girl. Clearly the novel puts forward the benefits of country life as a workable alternative, not in order to adhere to a medieval, chivalric model in a quixotic fashion, or as a modern utopia, but because rural life still has utility for modern society, for people in the countryside and not just for the goods produced there. Renzo's proposed revolution was designed not to bring down the superstructure of existing society but rather to expand the number of people who would benefit from it. This is of course closer to the transformation of society that Marx posed in his own writings than that of any later country later claiming to be Marxist. Finally, the question about Lucia's looks also suggests something about her inner beauty—perhaps Don Rodrigo was attracted to her in the first place because of her demeanor, not because of her striking beauty, and the Unnamed's conversion might have been triggered in the same way. Somehow Lucia's poise, not her beauty, triggers the entire plot.

17 Link to Nikolai Chernyshevsky's *What Is to Be Done?* (1863)

In a country that would later claim Marxism, Nikolai Chernyshevsky (1828–1889) wrote *What Is To Be Done?* while he was in prison in St. Petersburg; he was later sent into exile in Siberia.[109] This book was a direct inspiration for the Russian revolutionaries.[110] In this Russian novel, as in *The Betrothed*, violence and the desire for a better quality of life are inextricably linked. Lenin took the title of his famous tract, *What is to be Done?* (1902), the celebrated statement of the need for a cadre of revolutionary leaders, from Chernyshevsky's *The Vital Question,* much better known by its subtitle, *Or What Is To Be Done?* Chernyshevsky in turn was no doubt responding to the title of the Alexander Herzen novel, *Who Is To Blame?* (1841–1846), a morality tale, with three main characters, that uses marriage as the trope to understand and rework oneself and then society.[111]

Chernyshevsky presents the best of technological society in his novel; yet at the same time, it is a society in which women and men are equal, where factories are run for and by the workers, and appropriate working-class leaders must be located for the new working class. In Chernyshevsky's novel, the husband nobly leaves home, after contriving his own suicide, when he realizes that his wife and best friend are passionately in love with each other, but will not act on their impulses. Marriage here, as in Herzen's novel, is used to represent society, which must be revamped so that individuals can rework themselves and find authenticity within its structure. There is some tension in this work about whether the individual or the family is the core of society. For Aristotle and Machiavelli (remembering that they were both from the Mediterranean) the family was certainly the core; for most Enlightenment thinkers (arguably most of them from northern Europe) it was the individual. It is within the home, for Chernyshevsky (who was certainly not from southern Europe, and thus helps to explode the North/South division accepted throughout much of European thought) that the excesses of the public sphere can be sloughed off, relief can be found, and then new work accomplished. This almost utopian goal ignores any direct discussion of the state or of political organization, and was predicated on the necessity for major social and political reform based on class struggle. No doubt this was partially due to fear of censorship at the time, but more substantively because, as Chernyshevsky argued, the appropriate state apparatus would follow, or not be necessary, if there was the correct ideology and then the proper behavior. Chernyshevsky wished to use contemporary European thought to better Russia, and thus he was in contemporary Russian terms a Westerner, not a Slavophile. In terms of *The Betrothed*, Chernyshevsky's story deserves attention for portraying in fictional form the type of early socialist society only roughly sketched out by Marx himself. Likewise, *The Betrothed* contains, explicitly in a few chapters, visions of a new social order brought about by revolution from below.

18 Synopsis

This novel deliberately explores a variety of political themes. At its core, *The Betrothed* is focused on legal and economic rights for children, women, and men. This is clearest in Chapters 11–16. Renzo appears most vibrant in these six crucial chapters of the book, in which he plays a revolutionary, however reluctant and eventually unsuccessful he may be in this role. Grounded in the literary style of realism, this book praises the benefits of life in the countryside, yet notes the rights and privileges that are to be found only in the city. Most people go to the city in search of employment; Renzo, however, goes to escape a local tyrant who lusts after his *fiancée*. This very particular motivation serves to represent the variety of personal situations that often cause extreme distress, and which never seem to be forestalled by any particular law. In Milan, Renzo is caught up in a mob, and he behaves even more extremely than the regular city dwellers in the crowd. His flight from the city is a dash toward his relatives and to job security, not to stir up more insurrection. These chapters are fairly representative of the entire novel in that they do not contend directly with the Woman Question, the nineteenth-century debate regarding women's rights, yet the major points of contention about the Woman Question can nevertheless be found here. The main characters in Russian writer Chernyshevsky's *What Is To Be Done?* present a radical perspective on how to reshape not only their country but even their own already non-traditional personal relationships. The argument has been made here that *The Betrothed* is surprisingly sympathetic to overt rebellion (given its otherwise strong endorsement of liberal democratic government), but that the book also considers lasting change to be possible from revolutions of many different types. In this sense the book's political message is more modern than early modern, for it does not sketch out a required single means, or an essential route, to the best political system.

Overall, the political content of the book is of interest in terms of Marxist theories of revolution, the evolution of a liberal-democratic state, and crowd theory. The possibility of a better system of government is linked throughout the book to the belief in the perfectibility of the human mind.

NOTES

1 Thank you to Mary Ann Carolan for her detailed comments on this chapter. See Mary Ann McDonald Carolan, "*La monaca di Monza*: Manzoni's Bad Girl and the Repudiation of Imagination," *Rivista di Studi Italiani*.

> An early version of this section was given as "Vico, Beccaria, and the Italian Enlightenment" as a paper at a panel on "Literature and Science in Italian Literature from the Seventeenth to the Nineteenth Century," at the Modern Language Association (MLA) Convention, New Orleans, December 29, 2001.
>
> The critical edition is Alessandro Manzoni, *I promessi sposi* (Ezio Raimondi and Luciano Bottoni, eds. (Milan: Principato, 1988). For an excellent English translation, see Alessandro Manzoni, *The Betrothed*, Bruce Penman, tr. (Harmondsworth, U.K.: Penguin, 1972). Another useful translation, especially for its inclusion of a translation of a related work by Manzoni and for its scholarly apparatus, is Alessandro Manzoni, *The Betrothed: and History of the Column of Infamy*, David Forgacs and Matthew Reynolds, eds., Archibald Colquhoun and Kenelm Foster, trs. (London: J.M. Dent, 1997). Quotations and citations are from the Raimondi and Bottoni Italian edition and the Penman English translation unless noted otherwise.

2 See Manzoni, *I promessi sposi*. Raimondi and Bottoni, eds., ch. III, #120–121, p. 56, #120–121. Penman, tr., ch. III, p. 62 on "*i poverelli illetterati*," "the illiterate poor." On peasant illiteracy in the case of Renzo and Lucia, see Manzoni, *I promessi sposi*. Raimondi and Bottoni, eds., ch. XXVI, #96–222, pp. 602–607. Penman, tr., ch. XXVI, pp. 495–499.

3 Uncle Tom's Cabin was first published in serialized form 1851–1852; it was published as a book in 1852).

4 *Printing and the Mind of Man: A Descriptive Catalogue Illustrating the Impact of Print on the Evolution of Western Civilization during Five Centuries*, #273, pp. 165–166.

5 *Printing and the Mind of Man*, #273, pp. 165–166.

6 *Printing and the Mind of Man*, #273, pp. 165–166.

7 Edgar Allan Poe, review of Alessandro Manzoni, *The Betrothed* (May 1835) 520–522, also on the *European Intellectual History Database* Online. Authorship of this review has been generally attributed to Poe, who was a regular contributor to this journal.

8 Friedrich Nietzsche, *On the Advantage and Disadvantage of History for Life*, #1, p. 10.

9 Ford Madox Ford, *The Good Soldier*.

10 Ford, *The March of Literature*.

11 David Robb, ed., *Clowns, Fools and Picaros: Popular Forms in Theatre, Fiction and Film*.

12 Archibald Colquhoun, *Manzoni and His Times*, p. 90.

13 Francesco Ruffini, *La vita religiosa di Alessandro Manzoni*, vol. 1, "Introduzione," pp. 1–158.

14 Colquhoun, *Manzoni and His Times*, ch. 5. Francesco Ruffini, *La vita religiosa di Alessandro Manzoni*, ch. 1.1, "La conversione del Manzoni: Miracolo della Chiesa di San Rocco," pp. 159–183. Thank you to Antonio González, Ellen Nerenberg, and Michael Printy for their comments on this.

15 The work of Giambattista Vico on the desire to find pre-Roman sources for the Italians should be noted here.

16 Jackson J. Spielvogel, *Western Civilization, Vol. II, since 1550*, ch. 22, pp. 649–651.

17 Or perhaps it was the youngest Verri brother, Giovanni. See Natalia Ginzburg, *The Manzoni Family*, pp. 11–16, 357. Natalia Ginzburg was herself an excellent twentieth-century Italian author.

18 Ginzburg, *The Manzoni Family*.

19 See a similar argument for the French Revolution in Crane Brinton, *The Anatomy of a Revolution*. First published in 1938.

20 Fernand Braudel, *The Mediterranean and the Mediterranean World in the Age of Philip II*.

21 Ivo Schöffer, "Did Holland's Golden Age Coincide with a Period of Crisis?" in Geoffrey Parker and Lesley M. Smith, eds., *The General Crisis of the Seventeenth Century*, pp. 87, 97–98.

22 *The Encyclopaedia Britannica* (1911), vol. XVII, "Alessandro Francesco Tommaso Antonio Manzoni," pp. 626–627. See also *Encyclopaedia Britannica Online*, "Alessandro Manzoni.

23 R.R. Palmer and Joel Colton, *A History of the Modern World*, ch. XIII, "Reaction versus Progress, 1815–1848." More specifically, see Philip Pomper, *The Russian Revolutionary Intelligentsia*. Thank you to Philip Pomper.

24 Spielvogel, *Western Civilization, Vol. II, since 1550*, ch. 22, pp. 649–651.

25 Cesare Beccaria, *On Crimes and Punishments*.

26 Beccaria claimed Montesquieu's *Les Lettres persanes* (*The Persian Letters*, 1721) as his inspiration for his own work, *On Crimes and Punishments*.

27 See David Cannadine, *The Decline and Fall of the British Aristocracy*. Although a study of nineteenth- and early-twentieth-century British aristocrats, Cannadine's book nevertheless serves as well as a model for the study of aristocrats in other parts of Europe. In particular, it highlights the tardiness of aristocrats to grasp their loss of political and economic power in their own countries, and how, in many cases, all social classes suffered from the lack of appropriate shifts in investment by the aristocracy in the nineteenth century.

28 See Giuseppe Mazzotta, *The New Map of the World: The Poetic Philosophy of Giambattista Vico*. Review of this book by Cecilia Miller, "Ancient *and* modern," *The Times Literary Supplement*.

29 This subsection was given as part of a paper, "Vico and Manzoni: Abstract Ideas, Material Culture, and Political Change," at "*Tra Amici*: A Symposium in honor of Giuseppe Mazzotta," University of Mary Washington, Fredericksburg, Virigina, March 28, 2008.

30 Cecilia Miller, *Giambattista Vico: Imagination and Historical Knowledge*.

31 Manzoni, *I promessi sposi*. Raimondi and Bottoni, eds., ch. XXVIII, #81–91, p. 602. Penman tr., ch. 28, p. 512

32 Jean-Jacques Rousseau, *Du Contrat social et autres oeuvres politiques*, p. 236; and *The Social Contract*, p. 49. Vico, *The New Science*, Bergin and Fisch, trs., book I, section 2, #142, p. 63.

33 Vico, *La scienza nuova*, Nicolini, ed., vol. I, Sezione Terza, #331, p. 173; and Vico, *The New Science*, Bergin and Fisch, trs., book 1, section III, #331, p. 96.

34 This section was first given as a paper, "Renzo, the Failed Revolutionary, in Alessandro Manzoni's *I promessi sposi*," Department of Italian, Yale University,

October 12, 2006. A later version was given as "Reading Fiction for Political Theory: Alessandro Manzoni's *I promessi sposi (The Betrothed)*, the Manifesto for Italian Nationalism," Center for the Humanities, Wesleyan University, May 5, 2008.

35 Flaubert, however, did not accept the term of "realist" for his writing, even though the term "realism" became widespread following his trial in 1857, at which *Madame Bovary* was declared obscene. "Realism in Literature," in the *Dictionary of the History of Ideas*, IV, pp. 51b–56a.

36 "Realism in Literature," in the *Dictionary of the History of Ideas*, IV, pp. 51b–56a. This is in line with the attack on magic from thinkers as early as Lucretius, and in the eighteenth century, especially from Hume.

37 Quentin Skinner, *Liberty before Liberalism*.

38 Manzoni, *I promessi sposi*. Raimondi and Bottoni, eds., ch. 24, #461–462, p. 448. Penman, tr., ch. 24, p. 448.

39 Manzoni, *I promessi sposi*. Raimondi and Bottoni, eds., ch. XXXVIII, #360–370, p. 884. Penman. tr., ch. 38, the final chapter, p. 714.

40 Knut Hamsun, *Growth of the Soil*, Worster, tr. (New York: Vintage Books, 1972).

41 William Morris, *News from Nowhere*. Bellamy, *Looking Backward*.

42 Manzoni, *I promessi sposi*. Raimondi and Bottoni, eds., ch. 14, #351–361, p. 321. Penman, tr., ch. 14, p. 276.

43 Palmer and Colton, *A History of the Modern World*, ch. XI, "Reaction versus Progress, 1815–1848." See also Philip Pomper, *The Russian Revolutionary Intelligentsia*.

44 Manzoni, *I promessi sposi*. Raimondi and Bottoni, eds., ch. XI, #461–462, pp. 260–261. Penman, tr., ch. 11, pp. 226–227.

45 Manzoni, *I promessi sposi*. Raimondi and Bottoni, eds., ch. XI, #461–462, pp. 260–263, and ch. XII. Penman, tr., ch. 11, pp. 226–229, and ch. 12.

46 Manzoni, *I promessi sposi*. Raimondi and Bottoni, eds., ch. XI, #461–462, p. 263. Penman, tr., ch. 11, p. 229

47 Marx, *Capital*, vol. I, pt. 3, ch. 10, p. 359.

48 Upton Sinclair, *The Jungle*, "Foreword," by Eric Schlosser, p. xi.

49 Manzoni, *I promessi sposi*, ch. XII.

50 Manzoni, *I promessi sposi*, ch. XII.

51 Manzoni, *I promessi sposi*. Raimondi and Bottoni, eds., ch. XII, #68–71, p. 272. Penman, tr., ch. 12, p. 233.

52 Manzoni, *I promessi sposi*. Raimondi and Bottoni, eds., ch. XII, #31–36, p. 270. Penman, tr., ch. 12, p. 232.

53 Manzoni, *I promessi sposi*. Raimondi and Bottoni, eds., ch. XIII, #1–5, p. 288. Penman, tr., ch. 13, p. 247.

54 Manzoni, *I promessi sposi*. Raimondi and Bottoni, eds., ch. XII, #275–281, p. 279. Penman tr., ch. 12, p. 241

55 Thank you to Evans Anyanwu.

56 Manzoni, *I promessi sposi*. Raimondi and Bottoni, eds., ch. XII, #347–349, p. 282. Penman tr., ch. 12, pp. 243–244.

57 Manzoni, *I promessi sposi*. Raimondi and Bottoni, eds., ch. XII, #111–112, p. 273, & #122–123, p. 274. Penman, tr., ch. 12, p. 235.

58 Manzoni, *I promessi sposi*. Raimondi and Bottoni, eds., ch. XII, #347–349, p. 282. Penman, tr., ch. 12, pp. 243–244.

59 Manzoni, *I promessi sposi*. Raimondi and Bottoni, eds., ch. XII, #347–349, p. 282. Penman, tr., ch. 12, pp. 243–244.

60 "The Luddites," in *Contemporary Civilization in the West: A Source Book*, vol. 2, pp. 254–261. Manzoni, *The Betrothed*, ch. 12, pp. 243–244.

61 Manzoni, *I promessi sposi.* Raimondi and Bottoni, eds., ch. XII, #229, p. 278. Penman, tr., ch. 12, p. 239.

62 Manzoni, *I promessi sposi.* Raimondi and Bottoni, eds., ch. II, #335–337, pp. 44–45. Penman, tr., ch. 2, pp. 55–56.

63 Manzoni, *I promessi sposi.* Raimondi and Bottoni, eds., ch. XI, #88–90, p. 291. Penman, tr., ch. 13, p. 250.

64 Manzoni, *I promessi sposi.* Raimondi and Bottoni, eds., ch. XI, #88–90, p. 291. Penman, tr., ch. 13, p. 250.

65 Manzoni, *I promessi sposi.* Raimondi and Bottoni, eds., ch. XI, #141–151, p. 293. Penman, tr., ch. 13, p. 252.

66 Manzoni, *I promessi sposi.* Raimondi and Bottoni, eds., ch. XIII, #256–261, p. 297. Penman, tr., ch. 13, p. 256.

67 Thank you to James Steiner.

68 Manzoni, *I promessi sposi.* Raimondi and Bottoni, eds., ch. XIV, #110–112, p. 312. Penman, tr., ch. 14, p. 268.

69 Manzoni, *I promessi sposi.* Raimondi and Bottoni, eds., ch. XIII, #342–343, p. 300. Penman, tr., ch. 13, p. 259.

70 Manzoni, *I promessi sposi.* Raimondi and Bottoni, eds., ch. XIV, #8–14, p. 308. Penman, tr., ch. 14, p. 264.

71 Manzoni, *I promessi sposi.* Raimondi and Bottoni, eds., ch. XIV, #73–75, pp. 310–311. Penman, tr., ch. 14, p. 266.

72 Manzoni, *I promessi sposi.* Raimondi and Bottoni, eds., ch. XIV, #143–144, p. 313; ch. XIV, #28, p. 316; ch. XIX, #40–41, p. 413. Penman, tr., ch. 14, p. 269; ch. 14, p. 271; ch. 19, p. 351.

73 Manzoni, *I promessi sposi.* Raimondi and Bottoni, eds., ch. XXV, #9–12, p. 553. Penman, tr., ch. 25, p. 460. See also on individual character: Raimondi and Bottoni, eds. ch. I, #347–353, p. 21, & ch. VII, #439–446, p. 150. Penman, tr., and ch. 1, pp. 37–38, and ch. 7, p. 139.

74 Gustave Le Bon, *The Crowd: A Study of the Popular Mind.* Sigmund Freud, *Group Psychology and the Analysis of the Ego,* ch. II, esp. on Le Bon.

75 Andrea Mubi Brighenti (November 2010), "Tarde, Canetti, and Deleuze on crowds and packs," *Journal of Classical Sociology.* Thank you to Aaron Marcus.

76 Marx and Engels, "Manifesto of the Communist Party," in *The Marx-Engels Reader,* p. 473.

77 Manzoni, *I promessi sposi,* chs. XI–XIV.

78 On price fixing, see Manzoni, *I promessi sposi.* Raimondi and Bottoni, eds., ch. XII, #25–54, pp. 270–271. Penman ch. 12, p. 232. And again on Renzo's proposal of bread rationing, see Manzoni, ch. XIV, #351–361, p. 321. Penman tr., ch. 14, p. 276.

79 Manzoni, *I promessi sposi.* Raimondi and Bottoni, eds., ch. XV, #112–145, pp. 333–334. Penman tr., ch. 15, pp. 285–286, esp. p. 285

80 Manzoni, *I promessi sposi.* Raimondi and Bottoni, eds., ch. XV, #112–145, pp. 333–334. Penman tr., ch. 15, pp. 285–286, esp. p. 285.

81 Manzoni, *I promessi sposi.* Raimondi and Bottoni, eds., ch. XV, #112–145, pp. 333–334. Penman tr., ch. 15, pp. 285–286, esp. p. 285.

82 Manzoni, *I promessi sposi.* Raimondi and Bottoni, eds., ch. XV, #156–159, p. 334. Penman tr., ch. 15, p. 286.

83 Manzoni, *I promessi sposi.* Raimondi and Bottoni, eds., ch. XV, #169, p. 335. Penman tr., ch. 15, p. 287.

84 Manzoni, *I promessi sposi,* ch. XIV. Charles Dickens, *Barnaby Rudge.* Thank you to Steven Marcus for pointing me toward *Barnaby Rudge.*

85 Manzoni, *I promessi sposi,* ch. XVI. And see the useful Geographical Notes on p. 17 in Manzoni, *The Betrothed,* Penman, tr.

86   Manzoni, *I promessi sposi*, ch. XVI.
87   Manzoni, *I promessi sposi*. Raimondi and Bottoni, eds., ch. XXIV, #604–605, p. 541. Penman tr., ch. 24, p. 453
88   Manzoni, *I promessi sposi*. Raimondi and Bottoni, eds., ch. XVII, #306–308, p. 383. Penman tr., ch. 17, p. 327.
89   Manzoni, *I promessi sposi*, ch. XVII.
90   Manzoni, *I promessi sposi*, ch. XXVII.
91   Manzoni, *I promessi sposi*. Raimondi and Bottoni, eds., ch. XVIII, #123–125, p. 627. Penman tr., ch. 28, p. 513.
92   Manzoni, *I promessi sposi*, chs. III, V.
93   Manzoni, *I promessi sposi*. Raimondi and Bottoni, eds., ch. V, #446–447, p. 110. Penman, tr., ch. 5, p. 107
94   Phyllis Deane, *The First Industrial Revolution*.
95   Manzoni, *I promessi sposi*. Raimondi and Bottoni, eds., ch. XXXVIII, #361–368, p. 884. Penman, tr., ch. 38, p. 714.
96   Bonnie Smith, *Changing Lives: Women in European History since 1700*, chs. 1–8.
97   Franco Venturi, *Italy and the Enlightenment: Studies in a Cosmopolitan Century*, p. 202. For a specific case, see Patrick Chorley, *Oil, Silk and the Enlightenment: Economic Problems in XVIII Century Naples*.
98   Venturi, *Italy and the Enlightenment: Studies in a Cosmopolitan Century*, ch. 9, "The Enlightenment in Southern Italy."
99   Venturi, *Italy and the Enlightenment: Studies in a Cosmopolitan Century*, ch. 8, "The Position of Galiani between the *Encyclopaedists* and the Physiocrats."
100 Amartya Sen, *Poverty and Famines: An Essay on Entitlement and Deprivation*. See also Robert William Fogel, *The Escape from Hunger and Premature Death, 1700–2100*.
101 Sen, *Inequality Reexamined*, p. 39.
102 Sen, *Poverty and Famines*, p. 45.
103 Karl Marx, *The Eighteenth Brumaire of Louis Bonaparte*, V, p. 75; and Marx, *The Eighteenth Brumaire of Louis Bonaparte*, V, p. 73. Original date 1852. "Flotsam of society" is an alternative translation for the final phrase of this quotation.
104 Manzoni, *I promessi sposi*. Raimondi and Bottoni, eds., ch. XXVIII, #137–144, p. 628. Penman, tr., ch. 28, p. 514.
105 "Machiavellianism," in *The Dictionary of the History of Ideas*, III, pp. 116a–126a.
106 Bertolt Brecht, *Brecht on Theatre*.
107 Manzoni, *I promessi sposi*, ch. XXVI. And see Adrian Room, *Dictionary of Coin Names*. Thank you to Alan Nathanson.
108 See Francis Fukuyama, *Trust: The Social Virtues and the Production of Prosperity*, on the Italian family as a distinct unit of production, and by extension as a political institution in its own right. Instead of discussing the state and the people, Fukuyama recognizes family as a sphere of influence that does not disappear even as the state develops; thus for Fukuyama in the case of modern Italy—and it could be argued more broadly—study of the individual and the state, or of the public and private, without the inclusion of family, is thus insufficient.
109 Nikolai Chernyshevsky, *What Is To Be Done?*
110 See Pomper, *The Russian Revolutionary Intelligentsia*.
111 Svetlana Grenier, "Herzen's *Who Is To Blame?*: The Rhetoric of the New Morality," *The Slavic and East European Journal*. George Sand and Ivan Turgenev were other direct literary influences on Chernyshevsky, Rousseau and Ludwig Feuerbach being his theoretical sources.

REFERENCES

Beccaria, Cesare, *On Crimes and Punishments,* David Young, tr. (Indianapolis, IN: Hackett, 1986).

Braudel, Fernand, *The Mediterranean and the Mediterranean World in the Age of Phillip II* Siân Reynolds, tr., 2 vols. (New York: Harper & Row, 1974).

Brecht, Bertolt, *Brecht on Theatre: The Development of an Aesthetic,* John Willett, tr., ed. (New York: Hill and Wang, 1964).

Brighenti, Andrea Mubi, "Tarde, Canetti, and Deleuze on crowds and packs," *Journal of Classical Sociology* 10, no. 4 (November 2010): 291–314.

Brinton, Crane, *The Anatomy of a Revolution* (New York: Random House, 1965).

Cannadine, David, *The Decline and Fall of the British Aristocracy* (New Haven: Yale University Press, 1990).

Carolan, Mary Ann McDonald, "*La monaca di Monza*: Manzoni's Bad Girl and the Repudiation of Imagination," *Rivista di Studi Italiani* 19, no. 2 (2001): 65–85.

Chernyshevsky, Nikolai. *What Is To Be Done?* Michael R. Katz, tr. (Ithaca and London: Cornell University Press, 1989).

Chorley, Patrick, *Oil, Silk and the Enlightenment: Economic Problems in XVIII Century Naples* (Naples: Istituto italiano per gli studi storici, 1965).

Colquhoun, Archibald, *Manzoni and His Times* (London: J.M. Dent & Sons, 1954).

Contemporary Civilization in the West: A Source Book (New York, Columbia University Press, 1961.

Deane, Phyllis, *The First Industrial Revolution* (New York: Cambridge University Press, 1979).

Dickens, Charles, *Barnaby Rudge* (London: Penguin, 2003).

Dictionary of the History of Ideas: Studies of Selected Pivotal Ideas, 1st ed. (New York: Charles Scribner's Sons, 1974).

Encyclopaedia Britannica, The. 11th ed. (New York: The Encyclopaedia Britannica Company, 1911).

Encyclopedia Britannica Online: http://www.britannica.com.

Fogel, Robert William, *The Escape from Hunger and Premature Death, 1700–2100: Europe, America and the Third World* (Cambridge: Cambridge University Press, 2004).

Ford, Ford Madox, *The Good Soldier* (Toronto: Dover, 2002).

Freud, Sigmund, *Group Psychology and the Analysis of the Ego,* James Strachey, tr. (New York: Bantam, 1965).

Fukuyama, Francis. *Trust: The Social Virtues and the Creation of Prosperity* (New York: Free Press, 1995).

Ginzburg, Natalia, *The Manzoni Family,* Marie Evans, tr. (New York: Seaver Books, 1983).

Grenier, Svetlana, "Herzen's *Who Is To Blame?*: The Rhetoric of the New Morality," *The Slavic and East European Journal* 39, no. 1 (spring 1995): 14–28.

Hamsun, Knut. *Growth of the Soil,* W.W. Worster, tr. (New York: Vintage Books, 1972).

Le Bon, Gustave, *The Crowd: A Study of the Popular Mind,* translator not given (Mineola, NY: Dover, 2002.

Manzoni, Alessandro, *I promessi sposi,* Ezio Raimondi and Luciano Bottoni, eds. (Milan: Principato, 1988).

————. Edgar Allan Poe, in *The Southern Literary Messenger* 1, no. 9 (May 1835): 520–522.

————. *The* Betrothed, Bruce Penman, tr. (Harmondsworth, U.K.: Penguin, 1972).

————. *The Betrothed; and, History of the Column of Infamy*, David Forgacs and Matthew Reynolds, eds., Archibald Colquhoun and Kenelm Foster, trs. (London: J. M. Dent, 1997).

March, James, and Steven Schecter, "Passion and Discipline: Don Quixote's Lessons for Leadership," Stanford University Business School DVD, 2003.

Marx, Karl, and Friedrich Engels, Capital, Ben Fowkes, tr., Ernest Mandel, ed. (New York: Vintage Books, 1976).

————. *Eighteenth Brumaire of Louis Bonaparte*, translator not given, 2nd ed. (New York: International Publishing Company, 1972.

————. *Eighteenth Brumaire of Louis Bonaparte*, translator not given (Peking: Foreign Languages Press, 1978).

————.*The Marx-Engels Reader*, Robert C. Tucker, tr., ed., 2nd ed. (New York: W. W. Norton and Company, 1972).

Mazzotta, Giuseppe, *The New Map of the World: The Poetic Philosophy of Giambattista Vico* (Princeton: Princeton University Press, 1999).

Miller, Cecilia, "Ancient *and Modern, The Times Literary Supplement*, no. 5045 (December 10, 1999): 30.

————. *Giambattista Vico: Imagination and Historical Knowledge* (London: Macmillan, 1993).

Montesquieu, *Persian Letters*, C. J. Betts, tr. (London: Penguin, 1973).

Morris, William, *News from Nowhere; Or, An Epoch of Rest; Being Some Chapters from a Utopian Romance* (Boston: Roberts Brothers, 1890).

Nietzsche, Friedrich, *On the Advantage and Disadvantage of History for Life*, Peter Preuss, tr. (Indianapolis, IN: Hackett, 1980).

Palmer, R. R., and Joel Colton, *A History of the Modern World*, 7th ed. (New York: Alfred Knopf, 1992).

Parker, Geoffrey, and Lesley M. Smith, eds., *The General Crisis of the Seventeenth Century* (London: Routledge & Kegan Paul, 1978).

Pomper, Philip, *The Russian Revolutionary Intelligentsia* (New York: Crowell, 1970).

Printing and the Mind of Man: A Descriptive Catalogue Illustrating the Impact of Print on the Evolution of Western Civilization during Five Centuries, John Carter and Percy H. Muir, eds. (Munich: Karl Pressler, 1983).

Robb, David, ed., *Clowns, Fools and Picaros: Popular Forms in Theatre, Fiction and Film* (Amsterdam: Rodopi, 2007).

Room, Adrian, *Dictionary of Coin Names* (London: Routledge & Kegan Paul, 1987).

Rousseau, Jean-Jacques, *Du Contrat social et autres oeuvres politiques* (Paris: Éditions Garnier Frères, 1975).

————. *The Social Contract*, Maurice Cranston, tr. (Harmondsworth, U.K.: Penguin, 1986).

Ruffini, Francesco, *La vita religiosa di Alessandro Manzoni*, 2 vols. (Bari, Italy: Gius. Laterza & Figli, 1931).

Sen, Amartya, *Inequality Reexamined* (Cambridge, MA; Russell Sage Foundation/ Harvard University Press, 1992).

————. *Poverty and Famines: An Essay on Entitlement and Deprivation* (Oxford: Clarendon Press, 1981).

Sinclair, Upton, *The Jungle* (New York: Penguin, 2006).

Skinner, Quentin, *Liberty before Liberalism* (Cambridge: Cambridge University Press, 1998).

Smith, Bonnie, *Changing Lives: Women in European History since 1700* (New York: Houghton Mifflin, 1988).

Spielvogel, Jackson, J., *Western Civiliztion, Vol. II since 1550* (Belmont, CA: Wadsworth, 2000).

Venturi, Franco, *Italy and the Enlightenment: Studies in a Cosmopolitan Century*, Susan Corsi, tr., Stuart Woolf, ed. (London: Longman, 1972).

Vico, Giambattista, *La scienza nuova*, Fausto Nicolini, ed., 3 vols. (Bari: Laterza, 1911).

————. *The New Science of Giambattista Vico*, Thomas Bergin and Max Fisch, trs., eds., (Ithaca, NY: Cornell University Press, 1948).

Conclusion

> But apart from the contemporary mood, the ideas of economists and political philosophers, both when they are right and when they are wrong, are more powerful than is commonly understood. Indeed, the world is ruled by little else. Practical men, who believe themselves to be exempt from any intellectual influences, are usually the slaves of some economist. Madmen in authority, who hear voices in the air, are distilling their frenzy from some academic scribbler of a few years back.
>
> —John Maynard Keynes, *The General Theory*[1]

1 READING FICTION FOR POLITICAL AND ECONOMIC THEORY

This book is in full agreement with economist John Maynard Keynes's assertion above about the power of ideas as transmitted by intellectuals, and also that the impact of such ideas is generally only felt by later generations. However, in this book, I have taken a step backward and have attempted to identify the sources of Enlightenment thinking that were present even before they were codified by the marvelous theorists of that age. The five works of fiction considered in this book transcend national lines, bypassing arguments about particular forms of government and the economic strengths and weaknesses of certain nations. The mental puzzles put forward in these works are not about either the specificities of how to create a particular nation-state or how to better an existing country. Despite the manifest cultural specificities of each of these works, they are much more than national classics. Indeed, if not universalist, they are at least European, and certainly are cosmopolitan. These books take readers out of their particular corners of Europe—or of the world—to ponder questions of power politics as well as morality. And, if not these five works of fiction themselves, certainly the ideas expressed in them were to inspire the great theorists of their age.

The Enlightenment directly incorporated concepts from Greek and Roman antiquity, as well as from modern science, and emphasized the abstract individual—whether a child, woman, or man. It recognized that the individual is driven by emotion as much as by rationality, and that this is positive as well as negative. Nevertheless, post-Enlightenment social sciences have, almost without exception, separated the study of emotion from that of rationality. Classic exceptions are Gustave Le Bon's *The Crowd* (1895), and certainly Sigmund Freud's *Group Psychology and the Analysis of the Ego* (1922). There were also a few earlier theoretical texts, notably Robert Burton's *Anatomy of Melancholy* (1621), and also Adam Smith's *Theory of Moral Sentiments* (1759), which also explore emotions, even some constructive aspects of emotion. Yet it is primarily from seventeenth-, eighteenth-, and nineteenth-century works of fiction that the reader begins to gain a rich picture of human potential: emotion and rationality are presented as two sides of the same coin.

This suggests a synthesis of the traditional view of the Enlightenment, as rational and scientific, and of the Counter-Enlightenment, as proto-Romantic.[2] Recognition of Enlightenment contributions outside of the sciences does not downgrade the role of modern science in the Enlightenment but rather underlines that science was just one of the intellectual commitments of the long eighteenth century. The bringing together of the rational and emotional elements, both in scientific and creative writing, created an awareness that both are manifestly present in the abstract individual, and also in the each real individual; further, it is a recognition that both qualities are necessary for a full life, and yet that both are dangerous in excess.

Building on a growing literature in Enlightenment Studies from the past 20 years, this book has not sought to eliminate the use of the term "Enlightenment," as some, understandably, might now wish to do. Instead, the emphasis here has been to identify essential themes of the Enlightenment, almost all to do with the abstract individual. The *Don Quixote* chapter addressed rationality and forms of government, in terms of economic systems. The *Simplicissimus* chapter reflected on religious toleration and friendship. The *Gulliver's Travels* chapter examined science and social class. The *Candide* chapter focused on sexuality and the modern individual. Finally, the chapter on *The Betrothed* stressed revolution and the perfectibility of the human mind. Overall, the term "Enlightenment" has been used as a fluid, non-rigid category that can sometimes be applied over time and place, instead of accepting a restricted geographical range and a narrow historical period.

There is strong concern throughout this book for intellectual categories that were being used in time periods that might at first even seem too early or too late. A much broader ideological range has been proposed here for the Enlightenment, thus including both conservative as well as radical thinking of this time, as well as stressing the evolving relationship of the individual and society. It is hoped that the term "Enlightenment" might be accepted as designating not only a time and place but also as identifying a particular category of thought, a certain set of thematic concerns, to be found in other times and places.

This is not unlike the usage of many older concepts. Three specific examples—Platonic Forms, the Renaissance identification of the centrality of the individual, and the split between Church and state in Reformation writings—are concepts regularly discussed in later centuries, often apart from the thinkers and texts that originally propounded them. Certainly the concept of the individual was not new in the Enlightenment. It had been raised in late antiquity in terms of religion (the individual's personal relationship with God by Augustine in *Confessions*, for example), and in the Renaissance in terms of philosophy (especially by Florentine writer Pico della Mirandola, on free will in his *De hominis dignitate, Oration on the Dignity of Man*).[3] In the long eighteenth century, the shift was to discussing the abstract individual in political and economic terms. It could be argued that other modern intellectual movements, even those since the Enlightenment, have contributed theories that are intuitively used as well in more general, non-scholarly discussion. Another example is Romanticism, following shortly after the traditional Enlightenment, which could be rethought along similar lines. Even a cursory reading makes clear that Romanticism is bursting out of its chronological confinement to the early nineteenth century, as well as out of its usual limitation to literature and the arts. Certainly, much more attention must be paid, for example, to commonalities between Romanticism and the nineteenth-century sciences, thus going beyond the traditionally ascribed, conflictual relationship of Romanticism and modern science. Many such older concepts and categories are regularly used outside of their historical contexts, but there is a reluctance to do this for more recently formulated intellectual movements, such as the Enlightenment and Romanticism.[4] The problem here is not that these new categories and theories were formulated so recently, but that they are periodized too strictly.

Enlightenment ideas were grounded not just in hopes for a much better future, but also in a high regard for the past. Enlightenment texts stress a small number of authors—in particular Thucydides, Plato, Aristotle, and Marcus Aurelius—from ancient Greece and Rome.[5] However, although the Enlightenment was grounded in ancient ways of thinking, it was not antiquarian or nostalgic. Indeed, much the same is the case for modern thought, the intellectual landscape of our own time. Throughout the development of European thought, one theoretical system was built on the last, with older theoretical models rarely being jettisoned altogether. Not only do Enlightenment ways of thinking still persist, ancient thought and medieval thought persist today as well. Sometimes a way of thinking is, perversely, kept alive by its most ardent foes. Certainly, by constantly attacking Scholasticism, Enlightenment writers—certainly Swift—ironically helped keep Scholastic, medieval reasoning alive well into the eighteenth century. Nevertheless, the necessary layering of ideas over time was not treated as quicksand in the long eighteenth century; it was not based on an assumption that a later generation could never escape the intellectual mistakes of the past. Instead, the Enlightenment approach to the past was grounded in a belief in individual autonomy, a belief that individuals in later generations would be free to make deliberate choices regarding which ideas from the past they would champion.

Indeed, it could be argued with profit that much of Enlightenment thought was drawn not just from the fiction of that time, but from the ideas from antiquity that grounded these works of fiction. An overarching term for these ancient conceptions, elaborated in long-eighteenth-century fiction, and then adopted by the Enlightenment is the philosophy of history.

Long-eighteenth-century enquiries into justice, morality, and human nature are strikingly distinct from those of previous centuries. It can be argued that the intellectual shift was not simply from religious to secular concerns (and this argument itself can be countered with strong textual evidence from three disparate thinkers—Giambattista Vico, Edmund Burke, and Thomas Paine). The shift was, fundamentally, a change not so much in terms of categories or subject matter—justice, morality, and human nature—but rather (1) a change in the test group: a shift from the examination of a social group to the individual; and (2) a shift in intention: this examination was in many case deliberately crafted in order to benefit the abstract individual—actually real individuals—in society.

Thus Enlightenment thinkers did not abandon these established categories. They invoked the traditional concepts of justice, morality, and human nature, not to further a theoretical study of these topics but as evidence in support of their own political concerns. This was certainly not the first emphasis on the individual in works of European theory, but the stress was now no longer the individual's relationship with God (as in Augustine's *Confessions*; or following the Protestant Reformation, with the doing away of a priest to interpret the text—the Bible; and then, in a much different manner, during the Catholic Counter-Reformation), but rather on the relationship among the state, society, and the individual.[6] Even such a distinctive thinker as William Godwin (1756–1836), heralded and often derided for being the father of philosophical anarchism, looked upon justice as the means of bringing about equality in all social transactions, for the betterment of the life of the individual.[7] Thinkers of the eighteenth century were less concerned with abstract aspects of justice and equity for their own sake (which generally indicates a strong concern for society as a whole and a sense of corporate responsibility) and were very much more concerned with asserting individual rights and equality by means of invoking these abstract concepts (for example, justice). It could be argued that this shift somehow renders fiction a more powerful and immediate political as well as philosophical tool. However, this strong emphasis on the individual generally lacked a parallel debate concerning an individual's responsibility to others. Therefore, the criticism that eighteenth-century thought is self-centered and universalist, forcing a particular, uniform outlook and behavior, could, alas, be supported from a variety of perspectives, with abundant textual evidence from Jean-Jacques Rousseau, Voltaire, and Condorcet. This is, however, a very narrow interpretation of the richness and range of these writings, especially of the creative writers of the time. In sum, the long-eighteenth-century writers often employed ancient and medieval concepts of justice, morality, and human nature for their own immediate purposes, and regularly did this in terms of a reflection on history, and it was not universalist but cosmopolitan values—widely promoting humanist, urbane values, not homogeneity or parochiality—that infused their project.[8]

Two centuries before Karl Marx, creative writers as well as theorists were already focused on ideas as a force for change within society (which is now taken as a Marxist trope). There are two aspects to be identified here, only one of which is constructive. First, there was recognition in the eighteenth century that ideas could bring about positive social change, that they could have popular appeal, and that they could change the patterns of history. Some writers (for example, Condorcet) regarded such ideas to have a natural, intrinsic (as well as rational) appeal to the people. On a different level, the ideas of Bernard Mandeville and Adam Smith concerning how to increase the national wealth could also be placed in this same category of ideas that might change (for worse or for better) the history of a particular nation. The economic analyses of Bernard Mandeville, Adam Smith, even Thomas Robert Malthus, certainly Ferdinando Galiani, and Antonio Genovesi, were—despite marked distinctions in their views on the economy—inspired in remarkably similar ways by their shared belief that they must acknowledge forces at work in history in order to identify patterns within economic systems. In other words, these thinkers, whom we now call economists, were using previous forms of analysis from speculative philosophy of history (which stresses patterns in history—cycles, for example) and then employing these historical methodologies in order to discern patterns of behavior of present economic activity.

The second aspect of the force of ideas in history is not so attractive. During the long-eighteenth century, there was a parallel acknowledgment that powerful ideas existed that did not benefit most people in society: ideas of violence, cruelty, and rabid intolerance. There was a recognition that these ideas, and ideologies, have a force to move people, and thus they must not be ignored. Along with Enlightenment thinkers' belief in the perfectibility of the human mind and their emphasis on real, as well as abstract, individuals, they held a parallel, not wholly contradictory fear of the great appeal of the basest ideas and qualities (as expressed by Montesquieu, Vico, and Burke). Although the recognition that ideas have a force of their own in history was not altogether new, it is a distinctive recognition of this time that secular (not those from another religion), often hateful ideas, separate from specific material circumstances, have the power to rouse people and to change the course of human history. Surprisingly, considering his major status, one work on this theme that still needs more attention is Voltaire's *Essai sur les moeurs* (*Essay on Customs*, 1756). To give another example from the late eighteenth and early nineteenth centuries, Jeremy Bentham and James Mill crafted their Utilitarian approach on the assumption that when an idea such as the pleasure–pain principle was understood, it would capture the imagination of the people, and in time it would be grafted into its consciousness. However, according to Bentham and James Mill, there was no guarantee that such a process would necessarily be good for the society as a whole, much less for the good of each individual in that society.[9] Ample evidence throughout the writings of this period suggests that the study of past civilizations and the concepts of liberty and the individual were regularly rolled together, and that the result was often presented as the means to change both the future and the present.

It is possible now to make the claim that long-eighteenth-century thought included both theoretical and practical components that cannot properly be understood in isolation from each other, thus realigning our view of the Enlightenment.[10] The ideological outlook of this age could be viewed as an early form of Idealist Dualism. (This philosophical system was supposedly wholly theoretical yet with a particular political commitment that was not necessarily consistent with its theories; it is generally associated with early twentieth-century Italian and German thought, especially that of Benedetto Croce and Martin Heidegger.) The dualism, or one might call it contradiction, in the Enlightenment was as follows. In the eighteenth century, a great many concerns were viewed in rational, intellectual terms. However, one of the most powerful ideas of this century and from the same writers—the notion of personal liberty—cannot be explained in this logical manner alone. One way of expressing this concept at the time was to appeal to natural, God-given, innate rights that were somehow discernible through history. The emphasis in the twenty-first century is now on legal, not natural rights, as there has been, at least since John Stuart Mill, an awareness that certainly not all cultures at all times have recognized such rights. The eighteenth-century Age of Reason is perhaps best understood not as an Age of Cartesian Doubt, but as an Age of Assertion, despite the lack of historical or tangible evidence for some of the grandest claims of this Age. Few writers have attempted to link eighteenth-century notions of innate rights to modern legal rights. Lynn Hunt is one who does do this; she puts weight on the power of eighteenth-century sentimental fiction to move people to care about the lives of others in a visceral manner that led, Hunt argues, to demands for human rights, eventually claimed as legal rights.[11] It could thus be argued that the self-assurance of Enlightenment thought is based less on its rationalist premise than on the non-rational, clear, and distinct idea of the autonomy of the abstract individual.

This book, *Enlightenment and Political Fiction*, has argued that a scrutiny of long-eighteenth-century fiction in terms of the theory leads to a different understanding of the Enlightenment itself. There are three points here. (1) A consideration of literature and theory together indicates the new intellectual trends of this time were pan-European and not just French. These pan-European trends were of course part of larger trends internationally and in Europe's colonial relations with other cultures. After all, this was a time of massive colonial expansion and development of modern international relations. (2) A critical point about the pan-European nature of enlightened thought can be made by recognizing the significance of the timing of the German Enlightenment in the 1790s, some decades after the Enlightenment in France, for example. German thinkers and the many foreign scholars working in the German states at this time used an analytic and historical approach not only in their own subjects but also in their evaluation of the recent French Enlightenment, in order, deliberately, to structure their own Enlightenment experience a few decades later. The supposed German character—Candide, for example—seems well suited to stress this point, given his pan-European, anti-Grand Tour. (3) This emphasis on the historical interests in the long eighteenth century is not out of line with the traditional view that this was also the time of the rising middle and business classes. It must be noted that this historical approach was not the preserve of any particular privileged academic circle. Only in the German states and in Scotland were the major Enlightenment figures also university professors. The notion of the individual throughout history, and in present society, is to be found in the works of writers of this time from all social classes. In addition, these long-eighteenth-century thinkers were not necessarily writing only for target audiences made up of their own social and economic backgrounds. Perhaps the most startling aspect of these findings is the recognition that people across political lines were working on very similar topics, although sometimes from diametrically opposed positions, with Burke and Paine as a classic pairing. Attention to how long-eighteenth-century texts contended with ideas from the past is a necessary first step toward understanding the translation of those much older concepts into modern social theory by *librepensadors*, *Aufklärer*, Philosophical Radicals, *philosophes*, and *illuminati*—thus the major figures of enlightened thinking working in Spanish, German, English, French, and Italian.

2 WHAT IS THE ENLIGHTENMENT?

Overall, this study has changed my own views about the order of the development and influence of abstract political and economic ideas, whether revolutionary or conservative, during the European Enlightenment. As a theorist, I had previously assumed, unquestioningly, that the order was theory first, sometimes followed by literature, and then revolution. And I had tended to ignore conservative responses altogether. I have slowly, even reluctantly, been persuaded that the procession in the long eighteenth century in Europe starts with ideas rumbling within society that were translated into fiction first (although perhaps poetry and pamphlets were the actual starting point); then, sometimes much later, these fictional concepts mutated into theory; and finally the theory changed into action, both in the form of revolution and of reaction. Fiction played a marked role in the both the creation and transmission of Enlightenment ideas. The order of the shift from ideas to action is still very much in question. Even the actual need for each of these factors and stages is not clear. I now view even the progression of revolution followed by conservative counter-claims not always to be correct. Very often proponents of these points of view were responding directly to each other. This pattern deserves much more study.[12]

Whatever the order of social change, it becomes manifestly clear that thinkers of the long eighteenth century, however well versed in ancient philosophy and political theory, are best understood as responding to the vocal demands for change in their times, rather than as setting an altogether original agenda. Popular-culture and high-culture acceptance both seem to have been required for lasting transformation of the political culture. What is new for me is that it appears, for this time period, to be the ideas from below, first expressed in fiction (not those in more formal theory) that were the necessary, although not sufficient, cause for such revolution, and for lasting political change. Fiction thus prefigures Enlightenment-era theory. What is left is a series of core Enlightenment notions that can be found far beyond the traditional Enlightenment. Most of them were not new to the Enlightenment, and most are still with us today. There is a need for a new approach to these ideas that will enable us to recognize how much we have been shaped by this concoction of Enlightenment notions as first expressed in fiction.[13]

Sadly, largely missing from this textual study of abstract ideas embedded in popular fiction is an examination of the contemporary reading public and the development of modern European political institutions. Although this might be argued to be too large a project for a single author, much less a single book, there is, however, a non-European model that actually does accomplish this task. Doris Sommer does this well, in her work, *Foundational Fictions: The National Romances of Latin America*.[14] Following Sommer, it could be argued that a study of these five, at least initially, astonishingly popular national works of European fiction is also the beginning of an analysis of the deliberate development of modern European political culture.

Enlightenment and Political Fiction is inspired by the contextual approach to texts, thus collapsing the distinction between major and minor texts, in an attempt to identify more texts to be considered major. However, alas, in addition to the many other constructive approaches not put forward by this book (particularly that of ideas in context, as articulated by Quentin Skinner), it could also be argued that the demarcation of Enlightenment thought here into just five categories, one major theme for each work of fiction, is nevertheless both too narrow and too broad.[15]

For example, the useful corrective to the emphasis in this book on the crucial and constructive role of emotion in the Enlightenment might be the argument that the examination of excess emotion—for example, from

Cervantes or Hume—could rightly be viewed to be itself simply part of a rationalist approach (although Hume was much less rationalist, especially on this topic, than Kant was later to be), not part of an Enlightenment commitment to emotion as much as to rationality. Hume's position is particularly problematic: he certainly does take account of emotions, but ultimately rates human as slaves to passion. It could be argued that in the fiction of this time, there is a more balanced view of the positive and negative aspects of emotions than even from the most balanced works of theory of this same time on emotions. These debates need to continue.

In future, I hope that there will be more books that not only play with the category of Enlightenment in these ways but that also blend the study of literature and theory in a sophisticated and natural manner.[16] This *modus operandi* is in line with the range of intellectual commitments in the three centuries in which these five books—*Don Quixote, Simplicissimus, Gulliver's Travels, Candide,* and *The Betrothed*—were themselves written. This is a call for a multidisciplinary approach to the writings of the past, one that is deeply literary as well as theoretical.

Enlightenment and Political Fiction has argued not only that much of the development of abstract ideas in the long eighteenth century took place in fiction but also that this shifts our understanding of theorizing. Abstract ideas—from philosophy, such as the philosophy of history; from political theory, such as limited government; and from economics, such as the development of the market economy—have been developed as means of studying theory as it is created in fiction. One of the contentions of this book, for example, is that it is much more useful to take the notion of the abstract individual rather than rationality to be the core emphasis of the Enlightenment. There is a concern for emotion—in both its constructive and destructive aspects—that can be found throughout seventeenth- and eighteenth-century fiction and theory. It is not necessary to wait until nineteenth-century Romantic writings to find this particular preoccupation with emotion. Thus the approach taken in this book does not seek to downgrade the writings of the major French Enlightenment thinkers (certainly not Voltaire, but also not Montesquieu, Rousseau, Denis Diderot, and Jean le Rond d'Alembert), rather it recognizes that an emphasis on logic and science, along with the attack on the hegemony of the church, were complemented by a concern for the daily life of the individual, who was not always an abstract individual. Indeed, Voltaire's *Candide* is a study of emotion, a marvelous rendition of flattened affect—particularly evident in Candide's inability to express grief, not to mention less powerful emotions—as the result of perpetual trauma. In the works of fiction presented here, the fate of the minor, or supporting, characters sometimes represents the fate of the abstract individual, and the possible fate of the very real reader: the false Don Quixotes in *Don Quixote*; the female warrior, Courage, in the *Simplicissimus* cycle; the all-but immortal Struldbruggs in *Gulliver's Travels*; the two monkeys slaughtered in front of their young women lovers, as well as the red sheep briefly bearing a fortune from Eldorado, in *Candide*; and the evil Nun of Monza, and the unlikely convert, a local tyrant, the Unnamed, in *The Betrothed*. These fictional characters put forward new views of the individual in society that were not yet to be found in theoretical works, and were grounded in a firm understanding of theory from antiquity in particular. In these works, the coupling of the individual and society was often done by means of a reflection of liberty. These marginalized yet determined characters demand, in Isaiah Berlin's terms, both negative liberty ("absence of constraints") and positive liberty ("self-mastery"), an approach that demands both rights and responsibilities for all.[17]

It is not a coincidence that, with greater emphasis on the individual in society, emotion becomes a major component of the Enlightenment debate. In other words, almost all of the writers of the Enlightenment were concerned about the individual, but only some of them pursued this subject in terms of rationality, because, notably, ideas of liberty are very often discussed in terms of emotion. The emphasis on emotion is a clear gesture toward the good life as a practical goal, of a life far beyond subsistence, for each person. If modern readers do not read the fiction as well as the theory, they will miss major theoretical contributions that are often to be found first embedded in the glorious literature of the long eighteenth century.

NOTES

1 John Maynard Keynes, *The General Theory of Employment, Interest, and Money*, concluding notes, p. 383. First published in 1936.
2 Peter Gay, *The Enlightenment: The Rise of Modern Paganism* and *the Enlightenment: The Science of Freedom*. Isaiah Berlin, *Against the Current: Essays in the History of Ideas*, pp. 1–24.
3 Pico della Mirandola, *On the Dignity of Man*. Written in Latin, as *De Homine Dignitate*, in the year 1486, when he was 23 years old.
4 For a useful discussion of an intellectual category appearing outside of its supposed time period, see Savannah Lee Jahrling, "The Persistence of the Romantic Paradigm in Popular Art in the Late Twentieth Century," unpublished Ph.D. thesis in Art History, University of Wisconsin-Madison. Thank you John Basinger.
5 To give an example from the American Enlightenment, James Madison's greatest intellectual influence was Aristotle's *Politics*. On this, see Colleen A. Sheehan, *James Madison and the Spirit of Republican Self-Government*, ch. 7.
6 Another argument to be made at least in passing is that the emphasis on the philosophy of history ordinarily diminishes the role of the ruler in history. Two exceptions to this are, of course, Machiavelli on the prince and Hegel on world-historical individuals.
7 William Godwin was the father of Mary Shelley, author of *Frankenstein*.
8 On cosmopolitanism, see Franco Venturi, *Italy and the Enlightenment: Studies in a Cosmopolitan Century*.
9 Jeremy Bentham and James Mill's pleasure–pain principle states that the avoidance of pain and desire for pleasure explain almost all human actions— this is the basis of Utilitarianism, which is wholly consequentialist, implying that actions are to be judged by their results.

10 This is in line with Brian Fay's understanding of a critical social science (although Fay is using this categorization for present social science, not for Enlightenment thought). See Brian Fay, *Critical Social Science: Liberation and Its Limits*.

11 See the Preface of this volume on Lynn Hunt's argument in *Inventing Human Rights: A History*.

12 A classic example of a surprising *rapprochement* of classical liberal and conservative thought is Alexis de Tocqueville's *L'ancien Régime et la révolution française* (1856); Tocqueville argues that the success of the French Revolution was attributable primarily to the use of the bureaucracy and traditions of the Old Regime by the revolutionaries for their own antithetical purposes. See Tocqueville, *The Old Régime and the French Revolution*.

13 This is similar in scope to the Enlightenment shift away from speculative philosophy of history toward analytic philosophy of history; now the two approaches are generally fused.

14 Dorris Sommer, *Foundational Fictions: The National Romances of Latin America*. Thank you to Ann Wightman. And see Michael Valdez Moses, *The Novel and the Globalization of Culture*.

15 Quentin Skinner, *The Foundations of Modern Political Thought*, is still the classic example of this approach.

16 To give several examples, Giuseppe Mazzotta, *Cosmopoiesis: The Renaissance Experiment*; Rawson, *Gods, Gulliver, and Genocide: Barbarism and the European Imagination, 1492–1945*, and Catherine Labio, *Origins and the Enlightenment: Aesthetic Epistemology from Descartes to Kant*.

17 Berlin, *Four Essays on Liberty*, "Two Concepts of Liberty," pp. 118–172, esp. 127 and 134.

REFERENCES

Berlin, Isaiah, *Against the Current: Essays in the History of Ideas* (London: The Hogarth Press, 1979.

———. *Four Essays on Liberty* (Oxford: Oxford University Press, 1979).

Fay, Brian, *Critical Social Science: Liberation and Its Limits* (Oxford: Polity Press, 1987).

Gay, Peter, *The Enlightenment: The Rise of Modern Paganism* and *The Enlightenment: The Science of Freedom*, 2 vols. (New York: Knopf, 1966–1969).

Hunt, Lynn, *Inventing Human Rights: A History* (New York: W. W. Norton, 2007).

Jahrling, Savannah Lee, "The Persistence of the Romantic Paradigm in Popular Art in the Late Twentieth Century" (Unpublished Ph.D. thesis in Art History, University of Wisconsin-Madison, 1998).

Keynes, John Maynard, *The General Theory of Employment, Interest, and Money* (Amherst, NY: Prometheus Books, 1997).

Labio, Catherine, *Origins and The Enlightenment: Aesthetic Epistemology from Descartes to Kant* (Ithaca, NY: Cornell University Press, 2004).

Mazzotta, Giuseppe, *Cosmopoiesis: The Renaissance Experiment* (Toronto: University of Toronto Press, 2001).

Pico della Mirandola, *On the Dignity of Man*, Charles Glenn Wallis, Paul J. W. Miller, and Douglas Carmichael, trs. (Indianapolis, IN: Hackett, 1998).

Rawson, Claude, *God, Gulliver, and Genocide: Barbarism and the European Imagination, 1492–1945* (New York: Oxford University Press, 2001).

Sheehan, Colleen A., *James Madison and the Spirit of Republican Self-Government* (Cambridge: Cambridge University Press, 2009).

Skinner, Quentin, *The Foundations of Modern Political Thought*, 2 vols. (Cambridge: Cambridge University Press, 1978).

Sommer, Doris, *Foundational Fictions: The National Romances of Latin America* (Berkeley, CA: University of California Press, 1991).

Tocqueville, Alexis de, *The Old Régime and the French Revolution*. Stuart Gilbert, tr. (New York: Random House, 1955).

Valdez Moses, Michael, *The Novel and the Globalization of Culture* (Oxford: Oxford University Press, 1995).

Venturi, Franco, *Italy and the Enlightenment: Studies in a Cosmopolitan Century*, Susan Corsi, Stuart Woolf, ed. (London: Longman, 1972).

Name Index

Nov 15   Fri.

Special Collections

→ Candide

→ 3 ~~thesis~~ thesis
   a test cases
          ↳ 3 diff. types

→ no short p.

→ quiz ↳ → review

→ article

↳ December 6th

→ Betrothed

→ theses, test cases

→ article → quiz

~~~~